NEW CENTURY BIBLE COMMENTARY

General Editors

RONALD E. CLEMENTS   MATTHEW BLACK
(Old Testament)   (New Testament)

Exodus

THE NEW CENTURY BIBLE COMMENTARIES

EXODUS (J. P. Hyatt)
LEVITICUS AND NUMBERS (N. H. Snaith)
DEUTERONOMY (A. D. H. Mayes)
JOSHUA, JUDGES AND RUTH (John Gray)
EZRA, NEHEMIAH AND ESTHER (L. H. Brockington)
JOB (H. H. Rowley)
PSALMS Volumes 1 and 2 (A. A. Anderson)
ISAIAH 1–39 (R. E. Clements)
ISAIAH 40–66 (R. N. Whybray)
EZEKIEL (John W. Wevers)
THE GOSPEL OF MATTHEW (David Hill)
THE GOSPEL OF MARK (Hugh Anderson)
THE GOSPEL OF LUKE (E. Earle Ellis)
THE GOSPEL OF JOHN (Barnabas Lindars)
THE ACTS OF THE APOSTLES (William Neil)
ROMANS (Matthew Black)
1 and 2 CORINTHIANS (F. F. Bruce)
GALATIANS (Donald Guthrie)
EPHESIANS (C. Leslie Mitton)
PHILIPPIANS (Ralph P. Martin)
COLOSSIANS AND PHILEMON (Ralph P. Martin)
1 PETER (Ernest Best)
THE BOOK OF REVELATION (G. R. Beasley-Murray)

Other titles in preparation

NEW CENTURY BIBLE COMMENTARY

Based on the Revised Standard Version

EXODUS

J. PHILIP HYATT

WM. B. EERDMANS PUBL. CO., GRAND RAPIDS

MARSHALL, MORGAN & SCOTT PUBL. LTD., LONDON

© 1971 Marshall, Morgan & Scott Ltd.
First published 1971 by Marshall, Morgan & Scott, England
Revised softback edition published 1980

All rights reserved
Printed in the United States of America
for
Wm. B. Eerdmans Publishing Company
255 Jefferson Ave. S.E., Grand Rapids, Mich. 49503
and
Marshall, Morgan & Scott
A Pentos company
1 Bath Street, London ECIV 9LB
ISBN 0 551 00843 1

Library of Congress Cataloging in Publication Data
Hyatt, James Philip, 1909-1972.
Exodus.

(New century Bible commentaries)
Reprint of the ed. published by Oliphants, London under title:
Commentary on Exodus, which was issued in series:
New century Bible.
Bibliography: p. 9
Includes index.
1. Bible. O. T. Exodus — Commentaries.
I. Title.   II. Series: New century Bible commentary.   III. Series:
New century Bible.
BS1245.3.H9   1980   222′.1207   80-21785
ISBN 0-8028-1844-7

CONTENTS

ABBREVIATIONS 7

SELECT BIBLIOGRAPHY 9

INTRODUCTION

1 Title and Place in the Canon 14

2 Arrangements and Contents 14

3 Sources: Literary Analysis 18

4 Oral Tradition, Tradition-History, and Form Criticism 28

5 The History of the Exodus Period 37

6 Table of Literary Analysis 47

7 Outline of the Book of Exodus 50

COMMENTARY

FIRST SECTION (1:1–22): The Bondage of the Hebrews in Egypt 56

SECOND SECTION (2:1—6:30): Preparations for Deliverance 61
(*Excursus: The Origin of* Yahweh *and of Mosaic Yahwism*) 78

THIRD SECTION (7:1—13:16): The Ten Plagues in Egypt 96
(*Excursus: The Historicity of 11:1—13:16, and the Origin of Passover and Unleavened Bread* 144

FOURTH SECTION (13:17—15:21): The Exodus from Egypt and Crossing of the Sea 147
(*Excursus: The Site and Manner of the Israelites' Crossing of the Sea*) 156

FIFTH SECTION (15:22—18:27): The Journey from the Sea to Mount Sinai 170

SIXTH SECTION (19:1—40:38): Events and Laws of Mount Sinai 195
(*Excursus: The Location of Mount Sinai*) 203

5

MAP 334

APPENDIX: On the 'Natural' Explanation of the
Plagues 336

INDEX 347

ABBREVIATIONS

Am. Tr.	*The Complete Bible: an American Translation*, 1939
ANEP	*The Ancient Near East in Pictures Relating to the Old Testament*, ed. J. B. Pritchard, 3rd edn., 1969
ANET	*Ancient Near Eastern Texts Relating to the Old Testament*, ed. J. B. Pritchard, 3rd edn., 1969
AV	Authorised Version (King James version)
BA	The Biblical Archaeologist
BASOR	*Bulletin of the American Schools of Oriental Research*
BZAW	*Beihefte zur Zeitschrift für die alttestamentliche Wissenschaft*
CBQ	*Catholic Biblical Quarterly*
E	(see Introduction, section 3)
HDB	*Dictionary of the Bible*, ed. J. Hastings, 5 vols., 1898–1904
HTR	*Harvard Theological Review*
HUCA	*Hebrew Union College Annual*
IB	*Interpreter's Bible, 12 vols.*, 1953
IDB	*Interpreter's Dictionary of the Bible*, 4 vols., 1962
J	(see Introduction, section 3)
JAOS	*Journal of the American Oriental Society*
JB	*Jerusalem Bible*
JBL	*Journal of Biblical Literature*
JNES	*Journal of Near Eastern Studies*
JTC	*Journal for Theology and the Church*
LXX	The Septuagint
M.T.	Masoretic Text
NEB	*New English Bible*
P	(see Introduction, section 3)
RB	*Revue Biblique*
(RD)	(see Introduction, section 3)
RV	*Revised Version*
RSV	*Revised Standard Version*
VT	*Vetus Testamentum*
ZAW	*Zeitschrift für die alttestamentliche Wissenschaft*

SELECT BIBLIOGRAPHY

(*Note*: This bibliography has been revised for the second edition by the Old Testament editor of the New Century Bible Commentaries.)

LITERARY INTRODUCTION

Otto Eissfeldt, *The Old Testament: an Introduction*. Oxford, 1965 (3rd German ed., 1964).
O. Kaiser, *Introduction to the Old Testament. A Presentation of its Results and Problems*. Oxford, 1975 (2nd German ed., 1970).
R. H. Pfeiffer, *Introduction to the Old Testament*. New York and London, 2nd ed., 1952.
Introduction to the Old Testament, initiated by Ernst Sellin; completely revised and rewritten by Georg Fohrer. Nashville and New York, 1968 (10th German ed., 1965).
J. A. Soggin, *Introduction to the Old Testament*. London, 1976 (2nd Italian ed., 1974).
Artur Weiser, *The Old Testament: its Formation and Development*. New York, 1968 (4th German ed., 1957).

HISTORY

W. Beyerlin (ed.), *Near Eastern Religious Texts Relating to the Old Testament*. London, 1978 (German ed., 1975).
John Bright, *A History of Israel*. Philadelphia, 1959; London, 1960.
J. H. Hayes and J. Maxwell Miller (eds.), *Israelite and Judean History*. London, 1977.
S. Herrmann, *A History of Israel in Old Testament Times*. London, 1975 (German ed., 1973).
Martin Noth, *The History of Israel*. 2nd ed., London, 1960.
John A. Wilson, *The Culture of Ancient Egypt*. Chicago, 1951.

COMMENTARIES

Georg Beer, *Exodus*, mit einem Beitrag von Kurt Galling (*Handbuch zum AT*, ed. Otto Eissfeldt, 1/3). Tübingen, 1939.
Brevard S. Childs, *Exodus. A Commentary*. London, 1974.
R. E. Clements, *Exodus* (Cambridge Commentaries on the New English Bible). Cambridge, 1972.
Abraham Cohen, *The Soncino Chumash (Soncino Books of the Bible)*. London, 1947.
G. H. Davies, *Exodus: Introduction and Commentary (Torch Bible Commentaries)*. London, 1967.
S. R. Driver, *The Book of Exodus (Cambridge Bible for Schools and Colleges)*. Cambridge, 1911.
A. H. McNeile, *The Book of Exodus (Westminster Commentaries)*. London, 1908.

Martin Noth, *Exodus: A Commentary*. London and Philadelphia, 1962 (German ed., 1959).
J. C. Rylaarsdam, 'Introduction and Exegesis to the Book of Exodus', *IB*, I, pp. 833–1099.

SPECIAL STUDIES

Moses Aberbach and Leivy Smolar, 'Aaron, Jeroboam, and the Golden Calves', *JBL*, LXXXVI (1967), pp. 129–40.
W. F. Albright, *Yahweh and the Gods of Canaan*. New York and London, 1968. (References are to the American edition.)
——'Baal-Zephon', *Festschrift Alfred Bertholet*, ed. W. Baumgartner *et al.* Tübingen, 1950, pp. 1–14.
Albrecht Alt, *Essays on Old Testament History and Religion*, trans. R. A. Wilson. Oxford, 1966.
D. M. Beegle, *Moses, The Servant of Yahweh*. Grand Rapids, 1972.
Walter Beyerlin, *Origins and History of the Oldest Sinaitic Traditions*. Oxford, 1965 (German ed., 1961).
'Die Paränese im Bundesbuch und ihre Herkunft', *Gottes Wort und Gottes Land*, ed. H. Reventlow. Göttingen, 1965, pp. 9–29.
F. S. Bodenheimer, 'The Manna of Sinai', *BA*, x (1947), pp. 2–6.
Jean Bottéro, *Le Problème des Habiru à la 4e rencontre assyriologique internationale*. Paris, 1954.
C. H. W. Brekelmans, 'Exodus XVIII and the Origins of Yahwism in Israel', *Oudtestamentische Studiën*, Leiden, x (1954), pp. 215–24.
Martin Buber, *Moses*. London, 1946.
H. Cazelles, 'Les Localisations de l'Exode et la critique littéraire', *RB*, LXII (1955), pp. 321–64.
——'Les Origines du Decalogue', *Eretz-Israel*, IX (1969), pp. 14–19.
B. S. Childs, 'The Birth of Moses', *JBL*, LXXXIV (1965), pp. 109–22.
R. E. Clements, 'Exodus, Book of', *The Interpreter's Dictionary of the Bible*, Supplementary Volume. Nashville, 1976, pp. 310–12.
G. W. Coats, *From Canaan to Egypt* (*CBQ* Monograph Series 4), Washington, 1976.
——*Rebellion in the Wilderness*. Nashville and New York, 1968.
——'The Song of the Sea', *CBQ*, XXXI (1969), 1–17.
——'The Wilderness Itinerary', *CBQ*, XXXIV (1972), pp. 135–52.
F. M. Cross, *Canaanite Myth and Hebrew Epic*. Cambridge, Mass., 1973.
——'The Song of the Sea and Canaanite Myth', *JTC*, v (1968), pp. 1–25.
G. I. Davies, *The Way of the Wilderness. A Geographical Study of the Wilderness Itineraries in the Old Testament* (SOTS Monograph Series 5), Cambridge, 1979.
G. R. Driver and J. C. Miles, eds., *The Babylonian Laws*, 2 v. Oxford, 1955–56.
Otto Eissfeldt, *Hexateuch-Synopse*. Leipzig, 1922.
——*Baal Zaphon, Zeus Kasios und der Durchzug der Israeliten durchs Meer*. Halle (Saale), 1932.
Ivan Engnell, *A Rigid Scrutiny: Critical Essays on the Old Testament*, trans.

and ed. by J. T. Willis with the collaboration of H. Ringgren (Nashville, 1969).

F. C. Fensham, 'New Light on Exodus 21:6 and 22:7 from the Laws of Eshnunna', *JBL*, LXXVIII (1959), pp. 160f.

Georg Fohrer, *Überlieferung und Geschichte des Exodus: eine Analyse von Ex. 1—15 (BZAW*, 91). Berlin, 1964.

V. Fritz, *Israel in der Wüste*. Marburg, 1970.

W. Fuss, *Die Deuteronomische Pentateuchredaktion in Exodus 3–17 (BZAW* 126), Berlin–New York, 1972.

D. W. Gooding, *The Account of the Tabernacle: Translation and Textual Problems of the Greek Exodus*. Cambridge, 1959.

John Gray, 'The Desert Sojourn of the Hebrews and the Sinai-Horeb Tradition', *VT*, IV (1954), pp. 148–54.

J. G. Griffiths, 'The Egyptian Derivation of the Name Moses', *JNES*, XII (1953), pp. 225–31.

M. Haran, 'The Exodus', *The Interpreter's Dictionary of the Bible*, Supplementary Volume. Nashville, 1976, pp. 304–310.

L. S. Hay, 'What Really Happened at the Sea of Reeds?' *JBL*, LXXXIII (1964), pp. 297–403.

S. Herrmann, *Israel in Egypt* (Studies in Biblical Theology: Second Series 27). London, 1973 (German ed., 1970).

Greta Hort, 'The Plagues of Egypt', *ZAW*, 69 (1957), 84–103; 70 (1958), 48–59.

J. P. Hyatt, 'The Origin of Mosaic Yahwism', *The Teacher's Yoke*, ed. E. J. Vardaman and J. L. Garrett, jr. Waco, 1964, pp. 85–93.

——'Was Yahweh Originally a Creator Deity?' *JBL*, LXXXVI (1967), pp. 369–77.

——'Were There an Ancient Historical Credo in Israel and an Independent Sinai Tradition?' *Translating and Understanding the Old Testament*, ed. H. T. Frank and W. L. Reed. Nashville, 1970, pp. 152–70.

Alfred Jepsen, *Untersuchungen zum Bundesbuch*. Stuttgart, 1927.

A. R. S. Kennedy, art. 'Tabernacle', *HDB*, IV, pp. 653–68.

Rolf Knierim, 'Exodus 18 und die Neuordnung der Mosaischen Gerichtsbarkeit', ZAW, LXXIII (1961), pp. 146–71.

Hans Kosmala, 'The So-called Ritual Decalogue', *Annual of the Swedish Theological Institute*, I (1962), pp. 31–61.

T. O. Lambdin, 'Egyptian Loan Words in the Old Testament', *JAOS*, LXXIII (1953), pp. 145–55.

Sigo Lehming, 'Versuch zu Ex. XXXII', *VT*, X (1960), pp. 16–50.

D. J. McCarthy, *Old Testament Covenant. A Survey of Current Opinions*. Oxford, 1972.

——*Treaty and Covenant* (Analecta Biblica 21A), Rome, 1963, revised edition, Rome, 1978.

——'Moses' Dealings with Pharaoh: Exod. 7:8—10:27', *CBQ*, XXVII (1965), pp. 336–47.

I. Mendelsohn, 'The Conditional Sale into Slavery of Free-born Daughters in Nuzi and the Law of Exod. 21:7—11', *JAOS*, LV (1935), pp. 190–5.

G. E. Mendenhall, *The Tenth Generation*, Baltimore, 1973.
Julian Morgenstern, 'The Oldest Document of the Hexateuch', *HUCA*, IV (1927), pp. 1–138.
Sigmund Mowinckel, *Le Décalogue*. Paris, 1927.
James Muilenburg, 'The Form and Structure of Covenantal Formulations', *VT*, IX (1959), pp. 347–65.
——'A Liturgy on the Triumphs of Yahweh', *Studia Biblica et Semitica Theodoro Christiano Vriezen Dedicata*. Wegeningen, 1966, pp. 233–51.
M. L. Newman, jr., *The People of the Covenant*. New York and Nashville, 1962.
E. W. Nicholson, *Exodus and Sinai in History and Tradition*, Oxford, 1973.
Eduard Nielsen, *The Ten Commandments in New Perspective*. London, 1968.
Robert North, 'Date and Unicity of the Exodus', *American Ecclesiastical Review*, CXXXIV (1956), pp. 161–82.
Martin Noth, *Überlieferungsgeschichte des Pentateuch*. Stuttgart, 1948.
——'Der Schauplatz des Meereswunders', *Festschrift Otto Eissfeldt*. Halle, 1947, pp. 181–90.
G. H. Parke-Taylor, *Yahweh: The Divine Name in the Bible*. Waterloo, Ontario, 1975.
S. M. Paul, *The Book of the Covenant: Its Literary Setting and Extra-Biblical Background*. Ann Arbor (Mich.), 1966.
Johannes Pedersen, 'Passahfest und Passahlegende', *ZAW*, LII (1934), pp. 161–75.
Gerhard von Rad, *The Problem of the Hexateuch and Other Essays*. Edinburgh and London, 1966.
——*Die Priesterschrift im Hexateuch*. Stuttgart-Berlin, 1934.
H. H. Rowley, *From Joseph to Joshua*. London, 1950.
——'Moses and the Decalogue', *Men of God*. London, 1963, pp. 1–36.
——'Moses and Monotheism', *From Moses to Qumran*. London, 1963, pp. 35–63.
Wilhelm Rudolph, *Der 'Elohist' von Exodus bis Josua (BZAW)*, LXVIII Berlin, 1938.
E. Schild, 'On Exodus III, 14—"I am that I am"', *VT*, IV (1954), pp. 296–302.
Hartmut Schmökel, 'Jahwe und die Keniter', *JBL*, LII (1939), pp. 212–29.
C. A. Simpson, *The Early Traditions of Israel*. Oxford, 1948.
J. J. Stamm and M. E. Andrew, *The Ten Commandments in Recent Research*. London, 1967.
Roland de Vaux, *Ancient Israel: Its Life and Institutions*. New York, 1961. (French ed.: *Les Institutions de l'Ancien Testament*, 1958–60.)
——'Sur l'Origine Kenite ou Madianite du Yahvisme', *Eretz-Israel*, IX (1969), 28–32.
Paul Volz, *Mose und sein Werk*, 2nd ed. Tübingen, 1932.
T. C. Vriezen, *"'Ehje "ᵃšer 'ehje'*, *Festschrift Alfred Bertholet*, ed. W. Baumgartner *et al.* Tübingen, 1950, pp. 498–512.
F. V. Winnett, *The Mosaic Tradition*. Toronto, 1949.
E. Zenger, *Die Sinaitheophanie. Untersuchungen zum jahwistischen und elohistischen Geschichtswerk* (Forschung zur Bibel 3), Würzburg, 1971.

INTRODUCTION
to
Exodus

1. TITLE AND PLACE IN THE CANON

In the Hebrew Bible this book is known from its first two words, *Weēlleh šemôt* ('These are the names'), which are usually abbreviated to *Šemôt* ('Names'). The title in the *RV* and *RSV* is 'The Second Book of Moses Commonly Called Exodus'. The name 'Exodus' is derived from the Vulgate, which has taken it over from the LXX *Exodos*, meaning 'the going out'. The name is not wholly descriptive of the contents, as we shall see below. While the story of the exodus of the Israelites from Egypt occupies a central place in the book (chapters 13–15), it also tells of events which led up to the exodus and of the journey of the Israelites to Mount Sinai, and the events which occurred there.

As a constituent part of the first division of the Hebrew Bible, known as The Torah ('The Law'), the book of Exodus was canonized at the time when that division became a part of the Hebrew canon. Very little is known about the earliest history of the canon, but it is probable that the Torah was accepted as canonical in the fourth century B.C. It may have been canonized in the time of Ezra, but nothing definite is known concerning the process by which it came to be accepted as authoritative. It must have been canonized before the translation of the LXX in the third century B.C., and before the Samaritan schism, the date of which is disputed. However, parts of the book of Exodus were probably considered authoritative for a long period before the canonization of the book as a whole—particularly the decalogue in 20:2–17 (which is repeated with some changes in Deut. 5:6–21); the 'Book of the Covenant' (20:22—23:33), parts of which probably constituted law as early as the pre-monarchial period; and some of the regulations in chapters 25–31, though they were not put into written form by the Priestly writer until shortly before the completion of the Pentateuch.

2. ARRANGEMENTS AND CONTENTS

FIRST SECTION (1:1–22): THE BONDAGE OF THE HEBREWS IN EGYPT

The Hebrews, who went down to Egypt in the time of Joseph, multiply greatly and are oppressed by the Egyptians, who put them to hard labour (1:1–14). The king of Egypt commands that the midwives kill the male children of the Hebrews when they are born (1:15–22).

SECOND SECTION (2:1—6:30): PREPARATIONS FOR DELIVERANCE

a. *The Birth of Moses*, 2:1–10. A son is born to Levite parents, and exposed in a basket on the Nile; he is rescued by Pharaoh's daughter.

b. *Flight of Moses to Midian*, 2:11–25. After killing an Egyptian for beating a fellow-Hebrew, Moses flees to the land of Midian, where he marries Zipporah, daughter of the priest of Midian.

c. *The JE Account of the Call of Moses*, 3:1—4:17. The deity Yahweh appears to Moses in a burning bush on Horeb, commissions Moses to return to Egypt to rescue the Hebrews, and reveals the divine name to him (3:1–15). Yahweh gives Moses detailed instructions and teaches him three signs (3:16—4:9). When Moses pleads that he is not eloquent, Yahweh appoints Aaron as his spokesman (4:10–17).

d. *The Return of Moses to Midian*, 4:18–31. Moses departs from the mountain to go to Midian; on the way Yahweh seeks to kill him, and Zipporah circumcises her son (4:18–26). Moses meets Aaron at the mountain of God, assembles the elders, and shows them the signs in the sight of the people (4:27–31).

e. *The First Unsuccessful Appeal to Pharaoh*, 5:1—6:1. Moses and Aaron demand that Pharaoh let the Israelites go, but he refuses, and increases their hardships by withholding straw for brick-making (5:1–14). The Israelite foremen appeal directly to Pharaoh for relief, but are denied (5:15–21). Moses complains to Yahweh that he has been doing only evil to Israel, and Yahweh promises to act with a strong hand against Pharaoh (5:22—6:1).

f. *The Priestly Account of the Call of Moses*, 6:2–30. This parallels roughly the JE account in 3:1—4:17. Yahweh tells Moses of his plans for the Israelite people, but Moses objects that he is a man of uncircumcised lips (6:2–13). A genealogy of Moses and Aaron, and some of Aaron's descendants (6:14–25), and a recapitulation (6:26–30).

THIRD SECTION (7:1—13:16): THE TEN PLAGUES IN EGYPT

Aaron is appointed as a spokesman of Moses, and Yahweh recounts in advance what he will do to Pharaoh (7:1–7). Aaron performs before Pharaoh the miracle of transforming a rod into a serpent, and the miracle is repeated by the magicians of Egypt (7:8–13). Then follow in succession the ten plagues: i. fouling of the waters of Egypt (7:14–24); ii. frogs (7:25—8:15); iii. gnats (8:16–19); iv. swarms of flies (8:20–32); v. plague on cattle (9:1–7); vi. boils on man and beast (9:8–12); vii. hailstorm (9:13–35); viii. locusts (10:1–20); ix. darkness (10:21–29); x. death of the first-born of men and cattle in Egypt (11:1—13:16). The account of the tenth plague is extensive, including the following: announcement of the plague (11:1–10); instructions for observing Passover and unleavened bread (12:1–28,43–51); the tenth plague and release of the Israelites (12:29–36); the journey from Rameses to Succoth (12:37–42); and regulations concerning firstlings and unleavened bread (13:1–16).

FOURTH SECTION (13:17—15:21): THE EXODUS FROM EGYPT
AND CROSSING OF THE SEA

a. *Journey from Succoth to the Sea*, 13:17—14:4. God leads the Israelites by way of the wilderness toward the Red Sea. They are led by a pillar of cloud by day and a pillar of fire by night.

b. *Pursuit by the Egyptians*, 14:5–20. When the Egyptians pursue them, the Israelites cry in complaint to Yahweh; Moses promises that Yahweh will fight for them.

c. *Crossing of the Sea*, 14:21–31. Two accounts (J,P) are here interwoven. In J, Yahweh drives the sea back by a strong east wind, the sea is dried up and the Israelites cross; after they have crossed, the sea returns to its usual flow, and the pursuing Egyptians are routed in the midst of the sea, their chariot wheels being clogged in the mud. In P, Moses stretches out his hand over the sea, the waters are divided, and the Israelites pass over between two walls of water. When Moses stretches out his hand again, the waters flow back together and overwhelm the Egyptians.

d. *Two Victory Hymns Praising Yahweh*, 15:1–21. Here are two hymns praising Yahweh for leading the Israelites safely through the Sea overthrowing the Egyptians: the 'Song of the Sea' (15:1–18), and the 'Song of Miriam' (15:21).

FIFTH SECTION (15:22—18:27): THE JOURNEY FROM THE SEA
TO MOUNT SINAI

a. *Healing of the Water at Marah*, 15:22–26.
b. *Encampment at Elim*, 15:27.
c. *The Gift of Manna and Quails in the Wilderness of Sin*, 16:1–36.
d. *Water from the Rock at Massah and Meribah*, 17:1–7. A combination of two accounts, one concerned with an event at Massah, the other at Meribah.
e. *Victory over Amalek*, 17:8–16.
f. *Visit of Jethro with Moses*, 18:1–27. This takes place at the mountain of God, presumably Sinai-Horeb, and hence appears to be out of place. Jethro and the elders of Israel partake together of a sacrificial meal (18:1–12), Jethro gives advice on judicial administration (18:13–26), and Jethro departs to his own land (18:27).

SIXTH SECTION (19:1—40:38): EVENTS AND LAWS
OF MOUNT SINAI

a. *Formation of the Covenant*, 19:1—24:18. This consists of five subdivisions:
1 Theophany on Mount Sinai, 19:1–25;
2 Giving of the Ten Commandments, 20:1–17;
3 The people request that Moses act as mediator, 20:18–21;
4 The Book of the Covenant, 20:22—23:33, containing: (i) an introduction (20:22) and a title (23:1), (ii) a body of heterogeneous laws and admonitions, civil, cultic and humanitarian, 20:23–26; 21:2—23:19, and (iii) closing promises and exhortations, 23:20–33.
b. *The Priestly Ordinances of the Cult*, 25:1—31:18. These are very detailed ordinances concerning the following:
1 The making of the Tabernacle and its furnishings, 25:1—27:21; 30:1–10, 17—31:11;
2 The garments of the priesthood, chapter 28;
3 Consecration of the priests, chapter 29;
4 The half shekel offering, 30:11–16;
5 Observance of the Sabbath, 31:12–17.
At the conclusion, Yahweh gives to Moses the two tables of the testimony, written by the divine finger (31:18).
c. *The Golden Calf*, 32:1–35. At the request of the Israelites, Aaron makes for them a golden calf, to which they sacrifice

(32:1–6). When Moses comes down from the mountain and sees what they are doing, he breaks the tables of stone and destroys the calf (32:15–20). He rebukes Aaron (32:21–24), and twice makes intercession for the people (32:7–14,30–34). The Levites rally around Moses and kill three thousand men, thus ordaining themselves for the service of Yahweh (32:25–29). Yahweh sends a plague upon the people for making the golden calf (32:35).

d. *God's Presence with his People and Moses*, chapter 33. The Israelites set out from Sinai to go to Canaan; Yahweh refuses to go; but promises to send his angel with them (33:1–6). Description of the way in which Moses would seek Yahweh in the tent of meeting (33:7–11). Yahweh promises Moses that his presence will go with him (33:12–17), and promises a revelation of his goodness to Moses (33:18–23).

e. *Renewal of the Covenant*, 34:1–35. Yahweh reveals himself to Moses (34:1–9). He then renews the covenant with Moses and Israel, and gives them a group of ordinances in which many scholars find a 'cultic decalogue' (34:10–28). As Moses descends from the mountain, the skin of his face shines; Moses covers his face with a veil as he speaks with the Israelites, but removes it when he goes to speak with Yahweh (34:29–35).

f. *Execution of the P Ordinances for the Cult*, 35:1—40:38. The ordinances given in chapters 25–31 are carried out: the Tabernacle and its furnishings are built, and the garments of the priesthood are made. The wording of chapters 25–31 is often repeated verbatim, with the tenses changed from future to past. There are abridgments and minor omissions, and a different order is followed in making the Tabernacle and its furnishings from the order in the instructions; there are some expansions, especially in 35:4—36:6 and chapter 40. The consecration of the priests, commanded in chapter 29, is not recorded here but in Lev. 8. When the people finish making the various parts of the Tabernacle, they bring it to Moses and he blesses the people (39:32–43). Then the Tabernacle is erected and the glory of Yahweh fills it (chapter 40).

3. SOURCES: LITERARY ANALYSIS

Both Jewish and Christian tradition consider Moses to be the author of the book of Exodus, as of the other books in the Pentateuch. This has been the traditional view probably since the time of the canonization of the Pentateuch. Exodus relates the circumstances of Moses' birth and incidents occurring before he was born, and he is the principal figure throughout the book, but there is nothing in it which indicates that he is the author of the entire work. In 17:14 he is commanded to write in a book the curse on Amalek; in 24:4 he is reported to have written 'all the words of the Lord', presumably the preceding 'Book of the Covenant' (20:22—23:33); and in 34:27 Moses is reported to have written, at the command of Yahweh, the 'ten words' on the basis of which Yahweh made a covenant with him and Israel. Moses is said to have spoken the words of the 'Book of the Covenant' (20:22), and the instructions in 25:2—31:17 concerning the Tabernacle and other matters, and of course various other verses and passages.

For a variety of reasons critical OT scholars, since the latter part of the nineteenth century, have believed that Exodus is not the work of Moses, but that it is made up of three 'sources' or 'documents', or strands of tradition, to which are given the symbols J, E and P. The same 'sources' are to be found in the books of Genesis and Numbers, and possibly Judges. For detailed reasons for this critical view, one may consult any introduction to the *OT* (such as those of Eissfeldt, Fohrer, Pfeiffer, or Weiser), and compare the introductions to the various books of the Pentateuch and to Joshua and Judges in the present series.

J is used as a symbol for the Jahvistic or Judaean source. It uses the divine name *Jahveh* (usually pronounced and written 'Yahweh') even in the book of Genesis and the early chapters of Exodus; according to it, men 'began to call upon the name of Yahweh' in the time of Seth (Gen. 4:26). It is usually considered as originating in the south, and thus is called a Judaean source. The date of J has often been given as approximately 850 B.C., but in recent years scholars have pushed the date backward, usually to the time of Solomon, at a time when the Israelite tribes were united. This is probably correct.

E is used as a symbol for the Elohistic or Ephraimite source, because it employs the divine name *Elohim* ('God') before the revelation of the name Jahveh in Exodus 3:15, and frequently thereafter. It is generally considered to be of northern origin, and thus is called 'Ephraimitic'. Its date is in the eighth century B.C. Exodus 32:34, which declares that in the day when Yahweh visits

Israel he will 'visit their sin upon them', may have a bearing on the date of E. If that verse refers to the fall of Samaria in 721 B.C., and is true prophecy, it is before that date; if it is a *vaticinium ex eventu*, it is after 721 B.C. We shall see that E in Exodus is not a unified 'document'; thus it is impossible to give a single date for it; generally the eighth century B.C. is a satisfactory date.

P stands for the Priestly source, which dates from approximately the fifth century B.C. Its date cannot be fixed precisely, and it too is not a unity; but it is the latest source. However, it contains some ancient traditions.

Some scholars have sought to subdivide one or more of these sources, and attempts have been made to eliminate E entirely.

Several reasons have led to the subdivision of J: internal inconsistences or contradictions in the material attributed to J, such as the variant attitudes toward agricultural civilization as contrasted to nomadism; triplicate narratives (e.g. the three stories with a similar theme in Gen. 12:10–20; 20; and 26; and the three commands to Moses to leave Egypt, Exod. 3:10,16; 4:19); the observation that some of the portions assigned to J are much more primitive theologically than others (e.g. Gen. 18–19 and Exod. 4:24–26); and possible vocabulary differences, such as the various designations for Moses' father-in-law (see on 2:18). In 1912 Rudolph Smend proposed to subdivide this document into J¹ and J² which he considered to be independent and parallel documents that were subsequently woven together. His analysis was followed, with some modifications, by Otto Eissfeldt (*Introduction*, pp. 194–99) and Georg Fohrer (*Introduction*, pp. 159–65). Eissfeldt uses the symbol L (for 'Lay Source') instead of J¹. He thinks it is the oldest document, dating from some time between the end of David's reign and the appearance of Amos and Hosea. He calls it a 'lay' source, because it is the source 'least dominated by clerical and cultic tendencies'. It gives expression to the nomadic ideal.

Fohrer uses the symbol N for his 'Nomadic Source Stratum', generally equivalent to J¹ and L. But he thinks it is later than J, about 800 B.C., and yet represents older traditions than J.

C. A. Simpson makes his own analysis of J¹ and J², somewhat independent of the above (*The Early Traditions of Israel*, 1948). They are not parallel documents, but J² is an elaboration and transformation of J¹. J¹ records traditions of the southern tribes, written about 1000 B.C. J² is a century later, and adds traditions of the Joseph tribes; one of the important goals of this document was to preserve the spiritual unity of Israel.

Following a different procedure, Julian Morgenstern has sought to prove that there was a Kenite document (abbreviated K) in Exodus and Numbers which was the oldest document of the Hexateuch (*HUCA*, IV [1927], 1–138). He thinks it was written in the reign of King Asa, in 899 B.C., by leaders of the prophetic party in association with Rechabites, and formed the basis of that king's religious reforms. It began with Moses' birth and early life and continued through the account of the entrance of the Israelites and some Kenites into Canaan from the south. He finds portions of this document in Exodus 4:24–26; the original form of chapter 18; parts of chapters 33 and 34, including a Kenite law code; and Num. 10:29–33. This attempt we do not consider successful, because the passages attributed to K are not a literary unity, and it makes assumptions about the relationship between Yahweh and the Kenites which we do not consider valid.

These attempts to find documents older than J are efforts to deal with significant problems, but we have not followed any of them in our literary analysis. It is possible to account for the phenomena that have given rise to them by viewing J, or the Yahwist, as one who collected heterogeneous traditions from various quarters—some much older than others, some at variance with others, some written and some oral—and transmitted them without always trying to iron out their inconsistencies (cf. Weiser, *The Old Testament: its Formation and Development*, pp. 102f.).

There have been significant attempts to eliminate E as a distinct source. Of special significance for Exodus is the work of W. Rudolph, *Der 'Elohist' von Exodus bis Josua* (1938). He recognized two independent sources, J and P, but not E. The material which other critics attribute to E he either attributed to J or considered to be miscellaneous additions to the great work of J, made by several hands over a long period of time. The most extensive addition is the story of the golden calf in Exodus 32, with its introduction in 24:12–15, 18*b* and sequel in 33:3*b*–11. The purpose of the various additions was to explain, improve, and theologically enrich the J document.

Finally, we may note that there have been scholars who have subdivided P. The document designated by that symbol has considerable uniformity in style, vocabulary and theology, but many scholars have recognized inconsistencies and other evidences of its composite nature, even beginning with Wellhausen. For example, Gerhard von Rad, writing in 1934 (*Die Priesterschrift im Hexateuch*), advanced the view that P consists of two parallel strands, PᴬA and Pᴮ, and a 'Book of Generations'. He thought that Pᴮ had a more pronounced cultic and priestly character than Pᴬ. Von Rad's division was carried farther by K. Galling in his contribution to Beer's commentary which dealt with chapters 25–31, 35–40. We should note, however, that in his *Old Testament Theology* (1, p. 233) von Rad speaks only of 'the original P' and Pˢ, consisting of varied cultic material secondarily inserted into P.

It seems very probable that P is a composite work, but we should consider it as consisting of a basic document which was supplemented in various ways; we cannot expect a consensus of critics in identifying the supplements, because of the dominant impression of unity given by P, particularly in comparison with the other parts of the Pentateuch.

In the table on pp. 48–49 below, we give our analysis of Exodus into the principal sources, J, E and P. Here it is sufficient to make a brief statement regarding each of the sources that will indicate our point of view concerning its origin, date and general characteristics.

J is undoubtedly the earliest source, and the one which shows more markedly than the others the stamp of a single mind. Viewed as one of the major strands within the Hexateuch, J is a truly magnificent and monumental work in its vision and its execution. It begins with creation of the world, and continues through the initial conquest of Canaan. In Exodus, it is the basic narrative, furnishing virtually the whole story of the oppression of the Israelites in Egypt, the birth and preparation of Moses for his task, the exodus from bondage in Egypt, the journey to Sinai, and the making of a covenant there between Yahweh and Israel. Only minor passages, such as 19:20–4 and possibly part of 33:13–23, can be assigned to a secondary J tradition; most of the narrative seems to come from the hand of the magnificent genius whom we call 'the Yahwist'. He was a creative writer, but at the same time a collector and transmitter of traditions who did not always go to the trouble of integrating all of the traditions he recorded (e.g. 4:24–26).

The Yahwist probably lived in the time of Solomon; his work cannot be earlier, and there is nothing in it that must be dated later. He is usually considered to be a Judaean who transmitted

Judaean traditions, but we should not consider him as a narrow partisan. He wrote at a time when the Israelite tribes were united, and he was concerned with the history and fate of all Israel, not with a limited number of tribes.

J does not record the revelation of the name 'Yahweh' to Moses, as E does in 3:14–15, because he had been using the name throughout most of Genesis. Yet in the theophany of 34:5–7 he records a solemn proclamation of the name 'Yahweh' and of the nature of Yahweh as a God of steadfast love and faithfulness; this is somewhat parallel to the theophany of E in 3:14–15. J conceives of Yahweh as a deity who worked directly in dealing with Israel: Yahweh brings on the plagues without intervention by Moses or Aaron (7:17,25; 8:13,21; 9:6,18; 10:13), sends a strong east wind all night to dry up the sea so that the Israelites may cross it (14:21b), and directly sends the manna to feed them in the wilderness (16:15).

Moses is a more credible and human figure in J than in the other sources. He is a representative of Yahweh in speaking to Israel, but his role is to announce and interpret what Yahweh does, and with Israel to watch Yahweh work on behalf of his people. He fills the rôle of a prophet, or, as von Rad says of him, 'an inspired shepherd whom Jahweh used to make his will known to men' (*Old Testament Theology*, I, p. 292).

In his account of the story of the Hebrews in Egypt, J thinks of them as dwelling apart in the land of Goshen (8:22; 9:26), whereas E apparently has them living throughout the whole of Egypt. In the theophany on Sinai J depicts Yahweh as descending from Heaven upon the mountain (19:11,18; 34:5), and describes the theophany with features of a volcano in eruption (19:18); E on the other hand depicts God as dwelling on the mountain (19:3) and describes the theophany with features of a violent storm (19:16; 20:18). J does not hesitate to depict the Israelites as gladly leaving Sinai, accompanied by Yahweh, to go to Canaan, 'a land flowing with milk and honey' (3:8; 33:3a). J accepts and affirms the history and life of Israel more fully than in E; and it has no account of the apostasy of Israel in making the golden calf.

Some of the material in J has been displaced from its original position. The account of the making of the covenant in chapter 34 originally stood before chapter 24. Also we believe that an early form of the ethical decalogue, now found in chapter 20, originally stood in chapter 34 in the place now occupied by verses 17–27 (or 10–26). The ethical decalogue was subsequently transferred to chapter 20, probably after the combination of J and E, before the Deuteronomic Redactor. For details, see the commentary below on chapters 24 and 32.

E is not as fully preserved as J, and does not show the influence of a single mind. We would probably be correct if we called E a group of traditions, rather than the work of a single writer or 'collector'. Chapter 32, for example, contains several strands of E tradition, not all consistent. It is probable that there was a 'primary' E to which supplements were made, but that is difficult to identify. In some parts of Exodus E is preserved in only fragmentary form—e.g., in the Plague narratives. It is not possible to reconstruct E's account of the plagues as a whole; only the ninth plague may be preserved intact in its E form, and that is not certain (10:21–23,27). Since E is not a unity, we cannot ascribe a fixed date to it, but only give the eighth century B.C. as a general date. Though later than J, it may preserve some traditions older than J's. Its origin is generally considered to be in the northern part of Israel. While it does show some distinctively northern traits, such as the interest in Aaron, in its present form it could be from Judah. The story of the golden calf in its original form probably told of the founding of the bull-cult at Bethel in a manner that was favourable to Aaron, but it was transformed into a story that was unfavourable to him. Thus in its present form it may come from Judah, or at least from dissident circles in the north who opposed the cultic reforms of Jeroboam and favoured the Levitical priesthood (see commentary). In any event, E like J was concerned with the history and fate of all Israel and was not narrowly partisan (cf. Eissfeldt, *Introduction*, pp. 203–4).

In E the revelation of the name of Yahweh is recorded in 3:14–15, because E, like P, does not employ that divine name in Genesis and the early chapters of Exodus. E conceives of Yahweh as being somewhat more removed from man than does J. E makes Moses a wonder-worker who with his 'rod of God' brings about the plagues (4:17,20; 7:20; 9:23; 10:13,21f,; cf. 17:9). He thus makes Moses into the instrument by which Yahweh brings about the deliverance of Israel.

E also pictures Moses as an intercessor for Israel (18:19; 32:30–34), and even as priest in the ceremony by which the covenant on Sinai is sealed (24:6), and probably as a kind of oracle-priest for the tent of meeting. Von Rad rightly says that in E Moses represents prophecy of a special type—'the prophet of action, taking an active hand in the events, and doing so not only through the directions which he gives, but also, and supremely, by means of dramatic miracles' (op. cit. p. 293).

Aaron assumes an important rôle in E (he may not have appeared at all in J in its original form, although he has been secondarily introduced into that source in passages such as 4:29,30; 5:20; 8:8,12,25; 9:27; 10:3,8,16; 12:31; see commentary). He is appointed as the 'mouth', or spokesman, of Moses (4:15f.), and is represented as frequently being at his side. Yet his rôle in E is an ambiguous one, for he is represented as standing over against Moses and as the leader of the people in making the golden calf, or at least as their willing servant.

E is more religious and more theological than J, and has a more critical attitude toward Israel. The making of the golden calf was an act of apostasy whereby Israel broke its covenant with Yahweh, a covenant that had to be renewed. At the end of that story he represents Yahweh as reluctantly allowing Israel to go 'to the place of which I have spoken to you', but promises punishment at the time of his visitation (32:34; cf. 33:3, which may be originally from E, re-worked by R_D).

P, the Priestly source, occurs in the book of Exodus mostly in continuous sections: 6:2—7:13, which parallels the JE account of the call and commissioning of Moses, with the beginning of the plague narratives; 12:1-20,28,40-51; 13:1-2, mainly P's account of, and instructions for, the observance of Passover and Unleavened Bread; 25:1—31:18a, the instructions to Israel for the Tabernacle, the vestments and ordination of the priesthood, and the like; chapters 35-40, the execution of most of those instructions. Yet P is at times interwoven with other sources to produce composite narratives. This indicates that P is not just a supplement to JE, as some scholars have thought, but a separate narrative that once existed independently. P had a great interest in history; that interest was mainly, however, in fixing the origin in history of the great cultic institutions of Israel. P does not record a covenant on Sinai, for to him the covenant between Yahweh and Israel was that which had been made with Abraham, Isaac, and Jacob; it was because Yahweh remembered that covenant that he rescued Israel from Egypt (2:24). P's interest in Sinai was to set forth at that site the instructions of chapters 25–31. According to P, the Israelite cult began at Sinai.

The date of P is the fifth century B.C., or possibly the sixth century. It is clearly the latest source stratum of the Pentateuch, and is a programme for the post-exilic Jewish community. It may have been the 'law of God' which was introduced by Ezra, as described in Neh. 8–9, if that book was not the completed Pentateuch. Yet P is not a new creation of the fifth century; it often records earlier, even very ancient, practice. For example, in making the Passover a home ceremony rather than one performed in the Temple, and in prescribing that the meat be roasted rather than boiled, it reverts to ancient practice, older than Deuteronomy (Exod. 12:3,8; cf. Dt. 16:1–8).

P's conception of Yahweh is of a deity who is absolutely transcendent and sovereign. He manifests himself through his 'glory' (kāḇôḏ). The glory of Yahweh settles on Mount Sinai when the cloud covers it, and Moses alone is allowed to enter into the cloud (24:15b–18a). The glory is described as 'like a devouring fire on the top of the mountain' (24:17). Later, the glory of the Lord fills the Tabernacle (40:34–35), and Yahweh manifests himself in that manner among his people. The glory of Yahweh is also active in the history of Israel, for when Yahweh defeats the armies of the Egyptian king at the crossing of the Sea, Yahweh 'gets glory' for himself over Pharaoh and his host (14:4,17f.). Also, the Israelites see the glory of Yahweh when he provides them with manna in the wilderness (16:7,10).

Moses occupies a very special place in P. He is no longer the prophet, but the one who alone is allowed to have direct access to Yahweh in the cloud on the mountain (24:18a). When he descended from Sinai 'the skin of his face shone because he had been talking with God', and, because of the fear of the people, he had put a veil upon his face to protect them from the brilliance of Yahweh's glory reflected in his face (34:29–35). Moses is the one who gives Yahweh's ordinances to Israel. Aaron becomes in P more important than he has been in the earlier sources. The wonder-working rod is now in his hand (7:10,19; 8:5f., 16f.). However, Moses with his hand brings on the sixth plague (9:8–12), and causes the waters of the sea to be divided so that the Israelites may cross over, and later causes them to return (14:21,27).

P is not unified, as we have seen above. In the commentary on chapters 25–31 and 35–40, we have given the analysis of Galling in some instances where it seems to be illuminating; we cannot be certain, however, that his P^A and P^B are really different strands of P. The division may rather show the variant traditions upon which P has drawn.

The following sections of P seem to be secondary to the original P document: the genealogy in 6:14–30; 9:14–16; the additional instructions for keeping the Passover in 12:43–49; the law for the eternal lamp (27:20f.); probably all of 30:1—31:11, for 29:43–46 seems to be a natural conclusion to the original P instructions (see commentary); and all or most of chapters 35–40, which show acquaintance with chapters 25–31 in their present form.

In addition to the materials from the source strata or traditions designated by J, E and P, Exodus contains passages from the hand of a Deuteronomic redactor, whom we designate by the symbol R$_D$, living in the middle of the sixth century B.C., prior to P. The portions from R$_D$ are the following: 10:1*b*–2; 12:24–27*a*; 13:3–16; 15:25*b*–26; 17:14; 19:3*b*–8; 20:2*c*,4*b*–6,7*b*,9–11,12*b*,17*b*, 22; 23:20–33; 24:4*a*,7; 32:7–14; 33:1–6; 34:11–16,24. Most of these are recognized as Deuteronomic additions by such commentators as Noth, Beer, and Rylaarsdam. This redactor placed the Covenant code in its present position, supplying it with an introduction (20:22, and perhaps 21:1), and a conclusion (23:20–33). He then wrote 24:4*a*,7, thus giving to the set of laws the name, 'the Book of the Covenant'.

These R$_D$ passages exhibit some of the interests found in Deuteronomy and the work of the Deuteronomic historians, such as the following: the instruction of future generations, so that they may remember what Yahweh has done for Israel (10:2; 12:26–27*b*; 17:14; 19:4); the giving of ordinances to Israel, with injunctions to obey them and with promises of reward (12:24f.; 13:3–16; 15:25*b*–26; 19:5f.; 20:12b); promises concerning the settlement in Canaan, with instructions to overthrow the Canaanite idols and cult objects and to avoid making covenants with the Canaanites (23:20–33; 33:1–3; 34:11–16,24); and the rôle of Moses as intercessor before Yahweh on behalf of Israel (32:7–14).

Finally, we must note that Exodus contains independent units that have each a separate history. We list these on the table below (pp. 48–49) in square brackets, and assign them to the various sources or to R$_D$. However, in each case the material is not original, but has been inserted by an author or redactor. These independent units are: i. the Song of the Sea (15:1b–18); ii. the Song of Miriam (15:21); iii. the ethical decalogue or 'Ten Commandments' (20:2–17); and iv. the Book of the Covenant (20:23—23:19). See further commentary *in loc.*

4. ORAL TRADITION, TRADITION-HISTORY, AND FORM CRITICISM

In addition to the 'classical' literary analysis which we have just discussed in presenting the composition of Exodus, we must discuss briefly the contributions of those scholars who have emphasized oral tradition in the transmission of the materials of the Pentateuch, the tracing out of tradition-history, or the employment of the method of form criticism. Sometimes, but not invariably, all three of these, or two of them, have been used together.

All modern critics recognize that some of the materials of the Pentateuch must have been transmitted orally, or even composed orally, for some period of time. Even if J was written in the time of Solomon, it was separated by about three centuries from the events of the book of Exodus, and by a longer period from those in Genesis. E was still farther removed from those events. Oral composition and transmission were necessary in the early centuries because few people could write and read (perhaps only the priests or other religious functionaries and professional scribes). Very naturally, then, individual stories, poems, and the like were composed and transmitted orally until they were written down. Some critics of modern times have, however, maintained that this period of oral transmission was very long, involving not simply individual units but also complexes or collections or even whole *OT* books. This has been true particularly of certain Scandinavian scholars, amongst whom Ivan Engnell represents perhaps the most extreme position.

As for history of tradition, or tradition-history (*Traditionsgeschichte* or *Überlieferungsgeschichte*), we note that the analysis of the materials into the successive documents or sources J, E, D and P, represents in itself an attempt to trace the history of the traditions of Israel. But some scholars have sought to get behind written documents or sources to the earlier stages of the traditions, whether they are to be considered as oral, written, or both. In

Scandinavia there is a school of critics using the 'tradition-historical method' who attempt to replace the usual documentary hypothesis of the classical literary critics, putting great emphasis upon oral tradition and even 'oral literature' as they try to trace the history of Israelite traditions. Other scholars seek to maintain the usual documentary hypothesis, but to go behind those documents to earlier stages of the tradition, sometimes oral and sometimes written. Most representative of these are the Germans, Gerhard von Rad and Martin Noth. The scholars who practise the tradition-history approach differ among themselves as to the reliability of the traditions whose historical development they are able to trace.

Form criticism (or, more properly, 'form history', *Formgeschichte*) has been widely used in both the Old and New Testaments. Form critics seek initially to classify the literary materials with which they deal into broad or narrow classifications. Sometimes they are concerned mainly with broad classifications, e.g., narrative materials and legal materials, or prose and poetry. Usually, however, they deal with more detailed classification of the types (*Gattungen*) into which the broader divisions may be subdivided. Then they seek to set up forms or patterns for the various types, and to work out the laws by which the forms develop, the stability of the patterns, and so on. Form critics usually concern themselves also with establishing the 'life-situation' (*Sitz im Leben*) of the individual literary types, and that life-situation is often to be found in the cult. While form criticism has made spectacular contributions in some parts of the *OT* (e.g., the Psalms and Genesis), the contributions in respect of Exodus have not been spectacular, although profitable; perhaps the most fruitful use of the method has been that of Albrecht Alt in his study of the laws found in Exodus and some other parts of the *OT*, to which we shall call attention.

Many modern critics combine all three of these methods, as we have already noted, and as we shall see in detail in our discussion. They also are inclined to put great emphasis upon the cult for its rôle in the preservation and transmission, if not also the creation, of materials in the Pentateuch. Likewise they place great importance upon the comparison of Israelite literature and culture with the literature and culture of other ancient Near Eastern nations, sometimes to point out parallels or instances of borrowing, and sometimes to insist upon the uniqueness of Israel's life. Here we can only give a brief sketch of some of the more important theories and views of leading scholars, particularly as they relate to our understanding of Exodus. Then we may point out some of the areas in which these studies modify or enrich the understanding of the composition of Exodus as outlined in the last section.

Johannes Pedersen of Copenhagen was one of the earlier scholars to set himself against the usual documentary hypothesis, and to emphasize the rôle of oral tradition and the Israelite cult in the formation of the Pentateuch. Of special importance for us is his view of the origin of Exod. 1–15 ('Passahfest und Passahlegende', *ZAW*, LII [1934], 161–175; *Israel*, III–IV, pp. 384–415; 726–37). He considered Exod. 1–15 as the cult legend of the Passover which was developed over a long period of time, reaching its present written form after the exile. The Passover developed from two originally independent festivals, a pre-Canaanite pastoral feast which sanctified the firstborn, and a Canaanite peasant feast which sanctified the barley crops. These were connected with the exodus from Egypt, and the feast came to commemorate the deliverance of the Israelites from the bondage of Egypt. The legend was told with strong mythological features, in which Yahweh was depicted as doing battle with his enemies—a repetition of the Creation-Chaos motif found at the beginning of Genesis. Pedersen thought that this cult drama was recited and acted out annually at the time of the observance of Passover. It was the central nucleus around which the Pentateuch developed. Its purpose was not, however, to give a report of the events that led up to and included the exodus, but to glorify the God who had created Israel. It is not possible, he thought, to rediscover precisely the actual events, nor all the steps by which the cult legend reached its present form.

Many of the views of Pedersen were adopted and elaborated by Ivan Engnell of Uppsala, who is an extreme representative of the 'Uppsala School'. He stressed the great importance of oral tradition and employed form criticism, but he called his method of approach to the *OT* the 'traditio-historical method'. His major work (in Swedish) is entitled *The Old Testament: a Traditio-Historical Introduction*. Several of his essays dealing with the *OT* which appeared in *Svenskt Bibliskt Uppslagsverk* [Swedish Biblical Dictionary] (2nd ed., 1963) have been translated by J. T. Willis and H. Ringgren in *A Rigid Scrutiny: Critical Essays on the Old*

Testament (1969). Engnell believed that *OT* criticism must emancipate itself from a modern anachronistic 'book-view' which understands the *OT* as literature which was 'authored' and written throughout. To a large extent the *OT* is, in his view, an oral literature which was first written down at a relatively late period (in the post-Exilic age). Even in the oral stage individual units of tradition were elaborated and combined, so that one can speak of whole complexes or collections, or even 'tradition works' in the oral stage.

Yet he thought that the oral and written methods of transmission of traditional materials should not be considered as mutually exclusive, but rather as parallel methods which complement each other. Some texts were in fact written down early—for example, legal transactions, law codes, annals, and religio-sacral texts such as the Psalms. Such compilations were written in order to aid memory, to facilitate control over them, and to give them canonical authority. On the other hand, narrative stories and even genealogies were handed on orally for a long period of time. The characteristics of the *OT* books which have often led to their analysis into documents may usually be explained by what Engnell calls 'the epic law of iteration' and the basic principle of association (of words and ideas). While he considered the oral stage as a stage in which materials might undergo living transformation, he had great confidence in the reliability of materials which were transmitted orally. 'Although it is clear that oral tradition implies a certain living transformation of the inherited traditional material', Engnell said, 'still, in all essentials, the tradition remained fixed and reliable, especially because of the unique position of the Old Testament as cultic-religious literature' (Willis, op. cit., p. 9).

As for his specific views that bear upon the composition of Exodus, Engnell posited the existence of two independent 'tradition-works': one was a 'P-work' which comprised the books of Genesis-Numbers, containing mostly southern traditions, written down at Jerusalem in the time of Ezra-Nehemiah; and the other, 'the Deuteronomic history', extending from Deuteronomy through 2 Kings, containing many north Israelite traditions, although also written in Jerusalem in the time of Ezra-Nehemiah by a 'D-circle'. Since Exodus is a part of the P-work, we need not concern ourselves here with the second work, except to note that in Engnell's view the two works were subsequently put together (possibly even by the Deuteronomist); but no revision of the P-work took place.

The P-work, or Tetrateuch, was the product of a P traditionist circle in Jerusalem. This circle was responsible for producing the material called 'P' by literary critics, but the extent of this cannot be determined in every detail. To this the P-circle added older traditional material, much of it in oral form. Engnell does not consider J and E important as sources for tradition, because the traditions represented by those symbols were fused together in the stage of oral transmission. The P-work has a very pronounced antiquarian interest, and often preserves very ancient materials —narrative, cultic and legal. At the very centre of all the material stands the Feast of Passover; Engnell followed Pedersen in considering Exod. 1–15 as a cult legend for that festival. At the centre also stands Moses, who is described throughout by royal categories.

Two German scholars who have been especially interested in tradition-history are Gerhard von Rad of Heidelberg and Martin Noth of Bonn. They disagree with Engnell in that they basically accept the documentary analysis of the Pentateuch; their concern is to get behind the written sources and show how the traditions were formed that entered into those sources. Von Rad's views can be seen especially in his essay *Das formgeschichtliche Problem des Hexateuch* (1938) (English trans. as *The Problem of the Hexateuch and Other Essays*, pp. 1–78) and in his *Old Testament Theology*, I. Noth's views are set forth particularly in his *Überlieferungsgeschichte des Pentateuch* (1948). They are in general agreement on topics relating to the Pentateuch, but differ in some details.

Von Rad begins by affirming that Dt. 26:5b–9 is a very old summary of the saving facts in the history of Israel—a 'short historical creed' originating before the monarchy. Similar creeds are to be found in Dt. 6:20–24 and Joshua's address to the assembly at Shechem in Jos. 24:2b–13, which is 'a Hexateuch in miniature'. The Hexateuch was a long elaboration of Israel's basic creed. Free adaptations of this early creed may be seen in the cult-lyrics of 1 Sam. 12:8; the 'Song of the Sea' in Exod. 15; and within Psalms 78, 105, 106, 135 and 136. Von Rad is impressed by the fact that all of these passages, except Ps. 106 (which he says is post-Exilic in origin), have no reference to the revelation of Yahweh on Sinai. The earliest example of the interpolation of the Sinai episode into the canonical story of the redemption of Israel is to be found in the prayer of Neh. 9:6ff. Von Rad considers the Sinai pericope, Exod. 19—24, as being originally the festival legend used at Shechem in a ceremony of covenant renewal in the autumn, at the time of the festival of Booths. (Mowinckel before him had connected this pericope with the New Year's festival in the autumn, which he suggested was a ceremony of covenant renewal; see his *Le décalogue*, pp. 121ff.)

Noth works out in great detail the history of the traditions prior to J and E in his *Überlieferungsgeschichte*. The main themes of those traditions were five in number: (a) the leading out of Egypt, (b) the leading into Canaan, (c) the promise to the patriarchs, (d) the leading in the wilderness, and (e) the revelation at Sinai. These main themes were filled out and linked together by various traditional materials, such as (in Exodus) the plagues and the observance of Passover, the encounter with the Midianites, and the apostasy on Sinai in making the golden calf. The order in which these themes are listed is the chronological order in which they appeared. The tradition concerning the exodus from Egypt is the earliest, and the kernel about which the Pentateuchal narratives were formed; it is basic to nearly all categories of *OT* literature. The revelation at Sinai is the latest; it existed as an independent tradition before it was worked into the whole story. According to von Rad, the Yahwist was not only a collector of traditions but a great creative author with a definite theological point of view; it was he who worked in the Sinai tradition, elaborated the patriarchal history, and prefixed the primeval history of Gen. 1–11. Noth, on the other hand, posits the existence of a *Grundlage* (G) before the time of J and E. It contained those traditions common to J and E, but Noth does not decide whether it was in oral or written form. That *Grundlage* had the essentials of the Sinai story.

In the view of Noth and von Rad, the traditions contained in the Pentateuch are of great value in revealing to us the ancient faith of Israel, but they are of limited value for historical reconstruction. The Pentateuch did not originate as a historical work, but resulted from the coalescence of sacred traditions which were often based on historic events, many of which were originally separate traditions. Noth says concerning Moses, for example, that the most concrete fact we have about him is the tradition that his tomb was located in a very definite spot; therefore he should be thought of as belonging to the preparations for the

B

occupation of Canaan by the tribes of central Palestine, not as an organizer or legislator of Israel, and not as the founder of a religion (*History of Israel*, p. 135). This is in contrast to the view of Engnell, who believes firmly in the reliability of oral tradition, and says that Mosaic religion cannot be explained without assuming the existence of a person of Moses' stature.

The views of von Rad and Noth concerning the history of tradition are of importance for any study of the composition of Exodus and evaluation of the book as history. Many scholars have accepted von Rad's theory that Dt. 26:5b–9 and related passages constituted early historical creeds or lyrical adaptations of the basic Israelite creed, and the view that the Sinai tradition was originally an independent tradition that was only later worked into the larger historical account. Yet these views have been subjected to searching examination and criticism and should not be considered as proved; we refer especially to the criticisms by A. Weiser, *The Old Testament: its Formation and Development*, pp. 83–90; C. H. W. Brekelmans, 'Het "historische Credo" van Israël', *Tijdschrift voor Theologie*, III (1963), pp. 1–11; L. Rost, *Das kleine Credo und andere Studien zum Alten Testament*, pp. 11–25; and G. Fohrer in Sellin-Fohrer, *Introduction to the Old Testament*, pp. 118f. Cf. J. P. Hyatt, 'Were There an Ancient Historical Credo in Israel and an Independent Sinai Tradition?' in *Translating and Understanding the Old Testament*, ed. H. T. Frank and W. L. Reed (1970), pp. 152–70.

Criticism must be directed first to von Rad's theory that Dt. 26:5b–9 is a type of historical creed of which Dt. 6:20–24 and Jos. 24b–13 are further examples. He asserts that this Credo was very ancient, originating in the time of the settlement of the Israelites in Canaan before the monarchy—the period of the amphictyony or sacral federation, as conceived by Noth and others. Yet von Rad offers little proof of the antiquity of this creed; he only asserts in a footnote that 'the rhythmical and alliterative character of the opening phrases in particular reveals its antiquity' (*Problem of the Hexateuch*, p. 4., n. 3). He notes the Deuteronomic retouching (*Übermalung*) of the latter half of Dt. 26:5–9, but does not attempt to reconstruct the original form.

There is no sound evidence for the antiquity of this creed and the other passages related to it, and the Deuteronomic phraseology is much more pervasive than the words of von Rad suggest. Rost in particular has shown that the clearest vocabulary parallels

to Dt. 26:5-9 are found in the framework sections of Deuteronomy
and the 'Baruch biography' of Jeremiah. He points to Gen.
15:13-16 as a precursor of the so-called creed, containing virtually
all the elements of the latter. Rost thinks that Dt. 26:5-11 is based
upon a very old brief formula which contrasted the nomadic life
of the ancestor of the Hebrews with the agricultural life of Canaan,
but that in its present form it originated in the time of Josiah.

Von Rad speaks of the historical creed as if it were an independent literary genre used in the cult. He applies the name especially
to Dt. 26:5b-9 and in his original study also to Dt. 6:20-24 and
Jos. 24:2b-13, the latter admittedly in expanded form. Brekelmans
subjects these passages to a searching form-critical study, and
shows that von Rad can so classify them only by taking each out
of its context. When seen in the light of its context, Dt. 6:20-24
must be considered as a catechetical instruction, like Exod. 12:
26f.; 13:14f.; Jos. 4:6f.,21f. Jos. 24:2-13 is a long speech in which
Yahweh speaks to Israel in the first person; it is to be viewed as the
historical prologue of a covenant ceremony, analogous to the
historical prologue usually found in Near Eastern vassal treaties.
As for Dt. 26:5b-9, it must be interpreted in the light of verses
1-11; the beginning of verse 10, 'And behold now I bring . . .'
clearly connects that verse with verses 5-9. The whole is a ceremony used in the offering of first-fruits. Incidentally, there is no
mention here of a festival, and the situation presupposes the
bringing of first-fruits by individuals at various times. Thus, it is
misleading to speak of these various passages as historical creeds,
as von Rad does.

If these passages are late, coming from the seventh or sixth
century B.C., they cannot be taken as indications that the Sinai
narratives originally formed an independent tradition which was
worked into the whole at a time before J wrote them down. The
absence of the Sinai narratives from these passages must be
explained on other grounds, particularly since our view suggests
that they were written at a time when the Sinai tradition was
well-known as a part of the early stories. The explanation must be
sought along the lines of that offered by Weiser: the subject
matter of the Sinai tradition was not considered as a historical
event in the same sense as the other events, such as the exodus
from Egypt and the entry into Canaan; those events told of the
mighty acts of God in behalf of Israel, whereas the Sinai tradition
concerned an encounter with God—which led up to the people's

acceptance of the will of God proclaimed in the Commandments. Both 'history' and 'law' were from early times the fundamental pillars of the tradition of Israel. The law itself is presupposed in most of those passages which are called creeds or that are lyrical expansions of it, particularly Jos. 24, but also Dt. 6:20–25 and 26:1–11.

From the standpoint of the book of Exodus itself, we cannot easily isolate the Sinai tradition. There are indeed difficulties in the literary analysis of the JE material of chapters 19–24, 32–34, and problems are raised by the occurrence of wilderness narratives both before and after the Sinai narratives, but we must point out that the early chapters in Exodus look forward to Israel's being at Sinai—see 3:12,18; 5:3; 7:16; 8:27. Furthermore, the rôle of Moses is so important in the traditions of Sinai, and he is so well integrated into them, that we cannot consider Moses to be only a secondary insertion into those narratives.

We have discussed the work of von Rad and Noth as representative of scholars who use the tradition-history method. It is obvious from what we have said, however, that they also use the method of form criticism; this has been clearest in the case of von Rad. As a further example of the method of form criticism, we refer to the outstanding work of Albrecht Alt on the laws of the *OT* to be found in his essay, *Die Ursprünge des israelitischen Rechts* (1934), of which an English translation is included in his *Essays on Old Testament History and Religion*. On the basis of their form, he divides the early Israelite laws into two categories; *casuistic*, or conditional law, and *apodictic*, or unconditional law. The former is introduced by 'if' or 'when', and states the law for specific situations which are described in some detail; see, as examples, the laws in Exod. 21:1–11,18–36. Apodictic law is unconditional; examples of absolute prohibitions can be seen in most of the Ten Commandments (which may have all been originally in the negative). Alt also includes in the latter category the laws expressed by a Hebrew participle, such as 'Whoever strikes a man so that he dies shall be put to death', Exod. 21:12; and the list of crimes laid under a curse in Dt. 27:15–26. Alt maintained that the casuistic laws were borrowed from the Near Eastern neighbours of the Israelites, most probably the Canaanites, because they resemble the ancient law codes so closely, and that the apodictic laws represent native Israelite law. It has since been shown that apodictic law occurs rather frequently outside Israel, and Alt's historical conclusions have been brought into question. His form-critical work, however, remains of fundamental importance, and it is probable that his historical conclusions are generally valid, although they have exceptions.

This brief survey should demonstrate the importance of those methods of *OT* research which seek to study the 'pre-history' of the sources uncovered by classical literary criticism. These methods afford us a supplement to literary criticism, sometimes a corrective for it, particularly of its excesses. They also show some of the relationships which existed between Israel's literature and that of the surrounding nations. Furthermore, they make us conscious of the function which that literature may have served in the life of the ancient Israelite community. Special stress is laid upon the function it served in the Israelite cult—that is, in the worship of ancient Israel.

Yet our survey must also demonstrate that we can point to but a few 'assured results' reached by these methods, for their proponents often reach widely divergent conclusions. This is doubtless unavoidable, for such methods of research necessarily involve a high degree of subjectivity. Objective criteria for studying the pre-history of the sources are meagre. Some scholars have tended to exaggerate the importance of oral tradition, or of the Israelite cult, in the formation and transmission of literature. Nevertheless, such studies must continue, for they can enrich and deepen our understanding of Israel's literature. These methods reach their soundest results when they are viewed as supplements to literary criticism, not as substitutes for it.

5. THE HISTORY OF THE EXODUS PERIOD

The book of Exodus should not be read as if it were primarily a historical record. Our preceding discussion has shown that it is the deposit of Israelite traditions which were developed and transmitted over a long period of time, beginning before the Yahwist lived (tenth century B.C.) and going down to the date of P, perhaps in the fifth century. The latest material comes from nearly a millennium after the events of the exodus itself. The book of Exodus is, then, a record of the faith of Israel concerning the period of the exodus from Egypt, a period that was very crucial for their faith, for it was the time when Yahweh brought them out of the house of bondage and made a covenant with them at Sinai.

Nevertheless, the book of Exodus professes to be history, and its narrative undoubtedly rests upon a solid core of historical happening. It is possible that Hebrew interest in history *per se* was stronger, and arose earlier, than is generally supposed. Several nations of the ancient Near East had a historical consciousness and believed in the divine control of historical events. It was among the Hittites especially that genuine historical narrative developed at an early time; it is found not only in their annals but also in some of their prayers and other cultic texts (cf. Bertil Albrektson, *History and the Gods*, 1967).

It is not possible, however, for us now to disentangle all the historical and legendary elements in this book. We do not know enough to write a satisfactory narrative history of the period. Yet we can see that the biblical narrative is to some degree authenticated from extra-biblical sources, although frequently the significance of the extra-biblical materials is assessed in various ways by different scholars.

Here we shall only attempt to set down some of the more important extra-biblical materials that bear upon the study of this period, and give a summary of the history as we see it.

From about 1900 B.C. on, especially under the XIIth Dynasty, Asiatics from the general area of Palestine and Syria settled in Egypt, sometimes as slaves, but sometimes as freemen of importance and official standing. Egyptian objects of the period are found in Syria-Palestine (cf. *ANET*, pp. 228-29). There is a famous wall-painting on a tomb of Beni Hasan, from about 1890 B.C., which shows Ibsha, 'the ruler of a foreign country', leading a caravan of Asiatics who bring stibium into Egypt (*ANEP*, no. 3). Many of these Asiatics were Semitic, as seems to be the case with the Beni Hasan group.

By the end of the eighteenth century the Hyksos gained control over Egypt, and were not deposed until about 1550 B.C. The term 'Hyksos' does not signify an ethnic group; it means 'rulers of foreign countries' and should be applied only to the rulers themselves. Although Josephus, quoting Manetho, refers to the Hyksos rule as resulting from 'a blast of God' and speaks of them as 'invaders of obscure race' (*Against Apion* i. 14), recent studies have suggested that they were not really invaders but foreigners who had settled in Egypt, and by a *coup d'état* seized control with the co-operation of some of the native Egyptians (cf. John van Seters, *The Hyksos: a New Investigation* [1966]). It is certain that they included north-west Semitic elements, and van Seters has sought to prove that they were Amorite—that is, of the same race as the people who dominated the culture of Syria-Palestine and had rulers in Babylon and Mari. In any event, many of the names of the Hyksos are north-west Semitic. They were defeated and driven out by Ahmose I, founder of the XVIIIth Dynasty (1570–1545).

In the period from the fifteenth to the twelfth centuries B.C., Egyptian records contain several references to a people known as ʿapiru (see M. Greenberg, *The Ḫab/piru*, pp. 55–8; J. Bottéro, *Le Problème des Ḫabiru*, pp. 165–75). These ʿapiru are always in a socially inferior status as slaves or unskilled workmen, and often, if not always, they are of foreign origin. For example, in the time of Thutmose III, they are engaged in the making of wine, probably in the north-eastern delta; Amenhotep II lists 36,000 ʿapiru among captives taken in Syria-Palestine; and in the reigns of Rameses II and IV ʿapiru are being used in quarrying and building operations. Two Egyptian texts indicate the presence of ʿapiru in Palestine in the vicinity of Beth-shean and Joppa. There is undoubtedly a close relationship between the ʿapiru of these texts and the ḫabirū of cuneiform texts (the pronunciation of the name is uncertain; the Ugaritic name ʿprm suggests that the proper translation may be ḫapirū.) These are not ethnic designations; the ḫabirū/ʿapiru were members of a certain social class, usually dependent upon others for their livelihood, although the significance is not uniform. They are found as slaves, unskilled workmen, brigands, mercenary soldiers, and the like, but also at times as caravaners (cf. W. F. Albright, *Yahweh and the Gods of Canaan*, pp. 73–91).

The only Egyptian text which mentions Israel is the famous 'Hymn of Victory' of Merneptah (1224–1214), often called 'the Israel stela', to be dated in the fifth year of Merneptah's reign, about 1220 B.C. The hymn was produced to commemorate that Pharaoh's victory over the Libyans, but it is turned into a eulogy for a Pharaoh conceived as universally victorious. Near the end, the following line occurs: 'Israel is laid waste, his seed is not'. In the immediate context among the places named are Hatti (land of the Hittites), Canaan (Phoenicia and Southern Syria), Ashkelon, Gezer and Yanoam (in Palestine), and Hurru (the land of the Hurrians, perhaps a designation for Palestine as a whole). The word 'Israel' is written with the Egyptian determinative indicating a people rather than a land. This may indicate that Israel at this time was a nomadic rather than a settled people, but Egyptologists have pointed out that this stela is carelessly written, and that in it determinatives are not always precisely used. It is not certain whether Israel is in Palestine or the Sinai desert.

In addition to the above extra-biblical materials that come from Egypt, we must note that Palestinian archaeology has a bearing upon the history of this period. The most important evidence for the chronology of the exodus itself is that which relates to the Israelite conquest of Palestine. This subject is now fraught with much difficulty, partly because the dating of the destruction of some sites has been changed as excavation procedures have become more precise (e.g., the date of the 'fall' of Jericho), and partly because we cannot always be certain that a given city which was destroyed at a particular time was taken by the invading Israelites, or by the Sea Peoples, or possibly some other group. Nevertheless, we can say that there is valid evidence for the destruction of some of the cities of Palestine in the latter part of the thirteenth century—specifically Bethel, Hazor, Debir (Tell Beit Mirsim), Lachish (Tell ed-Duweir), Ashdod, and possibly others. The situation is complicated, however, by the absence (total or almost total) of evidence for occupation at Jericho, Ai, and Gibeon in the Late Bronze Age, at the very time when the Israelites may have been invading the land.

Another archaeological fact of significance is that surface exploration in Transjordan, especially that carried on by Nelson Glueck, has shown that there was a lacuna in settled occupation in that region between c. 1900 and c. 1300 B.C. Thus the nations of Edom, Moab and Ammon with which the Israelites had to deal could not have been formed as sedentary peoples before c. 1300 B.C.

THE SOJOURN AND OPPRESSION OF THE HEBREWS IN EGYPT.

It is easy to believe that a group of Semites such as the Hebrews entered into Egypt, dwelt there for a time, were oppressed, and eventually left. The problem is to determine the chronology of those events, and to relate them to Egyptian history as sketched above. There is wide divergence of opinion among OT scholars on these problems, and the Biblical sources are of such a nature

that a definitive solution is not possible; for a full discussion, see
H. H. Rowley, *From Joseph to Joshua* (1952).

The chronological data within the *OT* are in conflict. On the
one hand, the P chronology represents the sojourn in Egypt as
lasting 430 years (Exod. 12:40), and dates the exodus 480 years
before the founding of the Temple of Solomon (1 Kg. 6:1).
Gen. 15:13 (redactor of E?) says that the descendants of Abram
are to be oppressed in Egypt for 400 years, but Gen. 15:16 (E)
says that the Hebrews will return to Palestine in the fourth
generation after Abram. Genesis represents Joseph as the great-
grandson of Abram, but there is no indication as to the length of
time that elapsed before the rise of the Egyptian king 'who did
not know Joseph' (Exod. 1:8). If one takes the P chronology
literally, the sojourn in Egypt began *c.* 1880 B.C., and the exodus
was *c.* 1450, since the Temple was founded *c.* 970. There is little
reason, however, to accept the P chronology as literally correct,
since it is so late.

Some scholars consider the period of the Middle Bronze Age,
c. 1900–1500 B.C , as the 'patriarchal age', and associate Joseph
with the Hyksos in Egypt. While this is possible, it leaves a long
period before the most probable time of Moses (thirteenth
century), and the story of Joseph does not sound like the story of a
Hebrew at the court of a friendly Semitic Pharaoh but rather of
one of native Egyptian origin.

The next period which some scholars consider as the most
likely time for the Hebrews to have entered Egypt is the Amarna
age, roughly the first half of the fourteenth century B.C., particularly the reign of Amenhotep IV (Akhenaton) (1367–50 B.C.).
Rowley thinks that Joseph was associated with that Pharaoh; his
personality suggests that no pharaoh would have been more ready
to welcome ministers from unusual sources than Akhenaton.

Some consideration must be given to the possible connection
between the ʿ*apiru* of Egyptian sources, the *ḫabirū* who appear in
various parts of the Near East in the second millennium and
especially in the Amarna letters, and the 'Hebrews', for which the
word in the Hebrew language is ʿ*ibrîm*. In the Amarna letters the
ḫabirū are represented as making incursions into Syria-Palestine,
some by invasion and some by making arrangements with the
local rulers. It is possible to see a linguistic relationship between
the three words, but it is not certain that ʿ*ibrîm* is the exact
equivalent of ʿ*apiru*/*ḫabirū*. However, the ʿ*ibrîm* in the period of

their oppression are represented as having a social status similar to that of the ʿapiru, particularly under Rameses II and IV. We should note, however, that Rameses IV lived in the twelfth century, after the most probable date for the exodus of the Hebrews, as we shall see below. In Exodus, the word 'Hebrew' is not frequently used. It is employed most often to distinguish Hebrews from Egyptians (1:15-19,22; 2:6,7,11,13), and to identify Yahweh as the 'God of the Hebrews' (3:18; 5:3; 7:16; 9:1,13; 10:3). It is not clear that the term is derogatory, as some scholars have claimed.

Martin Noth thinks that no historical conclusions can be drawn from the Joseph story, which is a late element in the tradition, nor from the P chronology. He puts the sojourn and exodus in the thirteenth century, saying that the sojourn lasted only a short time (*History of Israel*, pp. 117-21).

All of the evidence which we have from Egypt indicates that at various times in the second millennium 'Asiatics' from Syria-Palestine or from the Sinai desert found their way into Egypt. The Genesis narratives reflect several such occurrences. Because of the very nature of the Genesis materials, which must be considered for the most part as legends rather than as history, it is difficult for us to associate specific figures of those narratives with specific figures or periods in the history of Egypt. The present writer is doubtful, in any event, of the suggested association of Joseph with the Hyksos. If we can consider him to be historical and associate him with any specific Pharaoh, it is more likely to be one in the XVIIIth Dynasty, and Akhenaton is a possibility.

We are on much firmer ground in seeking to date the oppression of the Hebrews and identify the Pharaoh of the oppression. The most likely candidate is Rameses II (1290-1224 B.C.), although it is possible that the oppression was begun under his immediate predecessor, Seti I (1303-1290). Several facts point to Rameses as the appropriate king. His capital was in the eastern delta, not far from the biblical Goshen, which is called 'the land of Rameses' in Gen. 47:11 (P). He carried on building operations all over Egypt, including Pithom and Raamses, the latter being his delta capital (Exod. 1:11; see commentary *in loc.*). Rameses was quite capable of oppressing a people such as the Hebrews; we have seen that he made use of ʿapiru in his quarrying operations. He had a long reign, and was boastful and given to self-advertisement; but he was not a strong personality in international affairs.

THE EXODUS FROM EGYPT.
Since the date of the exodus of the Hebrews is closely tied to the
date of the oppression, we may first deal with that problem.
Various times have been suggested, in accordance with the various
dates suggested for the sojourn and oppression.
    (a) About 1550 B.C., the expulsion of the Hyksos. But this event
seems little like the biblical exodus, and there is nothing in the
history of the Hyksos that resembles the Egyptian oppression of
the Hebrews.
    (b) The Amarna Age, the incursion of the *ḫabirū* into Palestine.
The *ḫabirū* may be one of the groups which eventually united to comprise 'Israel', but there is no indication that they came from Egypt.
    (c) The thirteenth century. If the evidence for the oppression of
the Hebrews under Rameses II is valid, then we must date the
exodus in the same century.
    It is difficult to decide on a precise date, partly because of the
problems involved in the interpretation of the Victory Hymn of
Merneptah which mentions 'Israel', and partly because of
differing assessments of the statement in Exod. 2:23 that the
pharaoh who oppressed the Hebrews died, and a new pharaoh
came to the throne who was to let them depart. Rowley thinks
that the oppression occurred under Rameses II, and the exodus
soon after Merneptah came to the throne; then after only *two*
years' wandering, Joshua led the Hebrews across the Jordan into
central Palestine. Subsequently, Merneptah carried out a raiding
expedition into Palestine which involved him with 'Israel'.
Some scholars interpret the Hymn of Merneptah as referring to
Merneptah's attempt to keep the Hebrews from making their
exodus, an attempt which the Egyptian hymn-writer proclaimed
as successful but the Hebrew writers proclaimed as unsuccessful.
W. F. Albright has recently placed the exodus in the eighth
year of Rameses II (about 1282 according to the chronology used
here), because in that year a revolt against the Pharaoh in Syria-
Palestine was at its height. Merneptah later made a raid against
Israel in Palestine (*Yahweh and the Gods of Canaan*, pp. 159–64).
Whatever precise date we adopt, we are safe in adopting a date
within the thirteenth century for the exodus from Egypt and the
beginning of the entrance into Canaan of those Hebrews who had
been in Egypt. Either Rameses II or Merneptah was the Pharaoh
involved in the exodus. If we choose Rameses II, we must ignore

Exod. 2:23 or assume that the oppression began under Seti I; if Merneptah, we must follow Rowley in supposing that the wilderness wandering was very short, or interpret Merneptah's 'destruction' of Israel as taking place as the Israelites were making their escape from Egypt, or soon thereafter in the Sinai desert, not in Palestine.

We cannot reconstruct all the details of the exodus from Egypt, but the general outline in the book of Exodus is credible. We deal below in some detail with the problems of the plagues (pp. 336–45, the historicity of 11:1—13:16 (pp. 144–46), and the site and manner of the Israelites' crossing of the sea (pp. 156–61). Here we give only a brief summary of what we consider the probable course of events.

The plagues, about which the contest between Moses and the Pharaoh was centred, may be considered as phenomena natural for Egypt, though presented here in exaggerated form and in close sequence. The topographic and climatic features of Egypt made it subject to diseases, insects, dust-storms and the like, dependent in part upon abnormal inundation of the Nile River. A series of natural calamities, totalling perhaps six or seven, occurred in such a manner as to bring fear upon the pharaonic court when the climactic misfortune occurred, a severe epidemic which struck even the Crown Prince. The Hebrews took advantage of the situation, which they believed was brought about by their God Yahweh, and secured their release from bondage. They had sought permission to go out into the desert to worship Yahweh, but now they left Egypt to return to the land of Canaan from which some of their ancestors had originally come. Their departure took place in the spring near the time of their celebration of the Passover, a pre-Mosaic nomadic family festival at which animals from the flocks were offered up, with great emphasis placed upon a blood rite that was designed to ward off evil from their homes and flocks. In later years this Passover was combined with the Canaanite festival of Unleavened Bread and made a memorial observance of the exodus from Egypt.

Some scholars have professed to see in the Exodus account traces of a two-fold exodus (or two exodi). In several places the Hebrews are said to be driven out of the land, or at least are permitted by the Egyptian king to leave (J: 6:1; 12:29–32,39; E: 11:1), whereas in one verse they are said to have fled from Egypt in secret, without the king's permission (14:5 J?). Some

scholars associate the first exodus, in which the people are driven
out, with the expulsion of the Hyksos, and the second with the
hurried escape of the Hebrews in the thirteenth century. This does
not seem probable; see above the reasons against associating the
Hebrews with the Hyksos. There is basically nothing incredible in
the biblical account that the Pharaoh suddenly gave his permission,
the Hebrews fled as soon as they could, and the Pharaoh changed
his mind when he realized what a labour force he was losing.
The two differing representations do not correspond to different
sources.

The site at which the Hebrews crossed from Egypt into the
Sinai desert is most likely to have been at the southern end of
Lake Menzaleh, the so-called 'northern crossing'. The earliest
tradition probably told only of the crossing of a *yām*, a Hebrew
term which could apply to various bodies of water, even a
shallow lake or marsh. The *yām sûp* of the present account is not
the Red Sea; a better translation of the Hebrew term is 'Reed
Sea' or 'Papyrus Marsh'. The crossing of the sea was made
possible by a combination of natural occurrences and some fighting
between the fleeing Hebrews and the Egyptians. A strong east
wind, probably lasting for several days, dried the marsh sufficiently
for the lightly armed Hebrews to cross; a sudden violent storm
brought aid to the Hebrews so that they were able to defeat the
Egyptians, who were more heavily armed, but whose chariots
became bogged down in the mud. Doubtless some of the Hebrews
lost their lives, but many of them made good their escape into the
desert. The number who escaped was probably not more than a
few thousand, not the 'six hundred thousand men on foot,
besides women and children' of the late P tradition (12:37).
The early tradition indicates that they were accompanied by a
'mixed multitude' (including some Egyptian slaves?) and by
flocks and herds (12:38).

Which of the Israelites were oppressed in Egypt and subsequently made their exodus from that land? The late tradition
says that all of the descendants of Jacob were there, and all
participated in the exodus (1:1-4; 12:50f.). But that is improbable.
Scholars today usually say that it was the tribe of Levi, or the
Josephites, or the Rachel tribes; sometimes it is said that all
except the so-called concubine tribes were in Egypt. The presence
of several names of Egyptian origin among the Levites argues for
their having been in Egypt (Moses, Hophni, Phinehas, Merari,

Putiel). However, the organization of the twelve tribes is a product of a later time in the land of Canaan; it is impossible to trace in detail the earliest history of the tribes before their confederation in Canaan. A number of originally separate groups came to make up the people of Israel, and those who had been in Egypt probably had descendants in several of the tribes (cf. Noth, *History of Israel,* pp. 117–19).

SOJOURN IN THE WILDERNESS AND AT SINAI.

After making their escape from Egypt and crossing the *yām sûp,* the Hebrews found themselves in the desert of the Sinai peninsula. According to tradition they were in the desert for forty years (a round number for a generation) before proceeding to invade Palestine from the east. The book of Exodus is concerned with only a part of this period of their history, most of the events with which it deals being placed at Sinai. In the Exodus narrative the Israelites reach Sinai in chapter 19 and remain there through the rest of the book. Some of the events recorded in 15:22—18:27 probably took place *after* the sojourn at Sinai (see introductory remarks on that section, pp. 170–71).

The oldest tradition seems to have taken the Israelites directly from the *yām sûp* to Kadesh or its vicinity. Many of the places mentioned in their desert itinerary cannot be satisfactorily located, and the location of Mount Sinai itself is a vexed question. We suggest below in an excursus on the location of Mount Sinai (pp. 203–07) that many of the difficulties can be resolved by locating that mountain in the vicinity of Kadesh rather than in the southern part of the peninsula of Sinai. The latter location has little to commend it, and a location in some northern part of the peninsula is far more probable. It is very likely that, in any event, the Hebrews spent much of the period of 'wilderness wandering' at Kadesh (Kadesh-barnea), because there were three good springs in the vicinity, the largest being ᶜAin el-Qudeirat, though the name survives as ᶜAin Qedeis. Some scholars place at Kadesh events which the biblical record places at Sinai. For example, Walter Beyerlin thinks it was at Kadesh that the Israelites made the covenant with Yahweh and received the Ten Commandments, while Mount Sinai was a place where they had received a revelation of Yahweh and to which they made pilgrimage (*Origins and History of the Oldest Sinaitic Traditions,* pp. 145f.). We do not think the reasons for changing the location are valid.

In the desert the Israelites faced problems caused by scarcity of water and food, and the hostility of other tribes. They defeated the Amalekites (17:8–16), and made a treaty of friendship with the Midianites (18:1–12). Many complained against Moses, and longed for the fleshpots of Egypt. At Sinai they experienced a theophany, and made a covenant with Yahweh. Many laws and regulations in Exodus and later books of the *OT* are attributed to Moses on Sinai, but the only set of regulations which we would assign to the historical Moses is the ethical decalogue, in its original short form. The ethical decalogue was not in fact a code of law; it was rather a statement of the obligations which the Israelites took upon themselves when they made a covenant with Yahweh.

The story of the making of the golden calf (chapter 32) has little or no historical value for the desert period. In its earliest form it was probably the cult legend of the bull-sanctuary at Bethel. Of course it is not impossible that in the wilderness period the Israelites committed some great act of apostasy by worshipping a god other than Yahweh, or by worshipping Yahweh by means of an idol, but it is hardly possible to recover a historical kernel from the passage. As it now stands that chapter forms the transition to the account of the renewal of the covenant in chapter 34; originally the latter was an account of the making of the covenant on Sinai, containing an early form of the ethical decalogue.

The only cultic institution which can with confidence be assigned to the desert period is the simple 'tent of meeting' described in 33:7–11. This was a relatively large desert tent to which Moses would go on certain occasions to meet with Yahweh. The existence of this tent of meeting was one of the sources for the description of the elaborate Tabernacle of chapters 35–40.

6. TABLE OF LITERARY ANALYSIS

The following table gives the literary analysis of the book of Exodus which is employed in the present volume. This table does not seek to take into account the possibly 'secondary' additions to the sources or documents, since we are really dealing with what we have termed 'strands of tradition'. See section 3 above, pp. 18–28, for details concerning the various strands and for the meaning of the symbols used.

Literary Analysis of Exodus

Chapters 1–3

J	8–12		1–23a		1ab	2–4a	5 7–8
E	**1**	15–22 **2**		**3**	1c	4b	6
P	1–7 13–14		23b–25				

Chapter 4

J	16–18	1–12	19–20a	22–26	29–31
E	9–15 19–22 **4**	13–18	20b–21	27–28	
P					

Chapters 5–7

J	3 5–23	1		14–15a	16–17ab
E	**5** 1–2 4	**6**	**7**	15b	17cd
P		2–12,13–30	1–13		

Chapter 8

J	18	21a	24–25	1–4	8–15a 20–32
E		20b	23 **8**		
P	19–20a	21b–22		5–7	15b–19

Chapters 9–10

J	1–7	13	17–21	23b	24b	25b–34	1a
E	**9**		22–23a	24a	25a	35 **10**	
P	8–12	14–16					

Chapter 11

J	3–11	13b	14b–15a	15c–19	24–26	28–29
E		12–13a	14a	15b	20–23	27 **11** 1–3
R_D	1b–2					
P						

Chapter 12

J	4–8	21–23	27b	29–34	37–39
E	**12**			35–36	
R_D		24–27a			
P	9–10 1–20		28		40–51

Chapters 13–14

J		20–22	5–6	10–14		19b–20
E		17–19 **14**	7		16a	19a
R_D	**13** 3–16					
P	1–2		1–4	8–9	15	16b–18

J   21b   24-25   27b   30-31   20 [21]
E
R_D   **15**
P 21a,c 22-23   26-27a 28-29   1a [1b-18] 19

J   22b-25a   4-5   13b-15a   21   27-30
E
R_D   25b-26 **16**
P 22a   27   1-3   6-13a   15b-20   22-26   31-36

J   2b-3 7a 7c
E **17** 1b-2a 4-6 7b 8-13 15 **18** 1-27 **19** 2b-3a / 3b-8
R_D   14
P   1a   1-2a

J 9-16a   18   20-24
E   16b-17   19   25 **20** 1 [2-17] 18-21 **23**
R_D   22 [23-   19] 20-33
P

J   1-2   9-11
E **24** 3 4b-6 8   12-14   18b **25**   **31**   18b
R_D   4a   7
P   15-18a   1-   -18a

J   1-2   9-11   12-23   1-10 17-23
E **32** 1-6 15-35 **33** 1-6 7-11 **34** 11-16   24
R_D   7-14
P

J 25-28
E   **35**   **40**
R_D
P 29-35   1-   -38

7. OUTLINE OF THE BOOK OF EXODUS

THE BONDAGE OF THE HEBREWS IN EGYPT — 1:1-22
  MULTIPLICATION OF THE HEBREWS — 1:1-7
  OPPRESSION OF THE HEBREWS — 1:8-14
  COMMAND TO KILL THE HEBREW MALE INFANTS — 1:15-22
PREPARATIONS FOR DELIVERANCE — 2:1—6:30
  THE BIRTH OF MOSES — 2:1-10
  FLIGHT OF MOSES TO MIDIAN — 2:11-25
  THE JE ACCOUNT OF THE CALL OF MOSES — 3:1—4:17
    Appearance of God in the Burning Bush — 3:1-6
    The Commission of Moses — 3:7-12
    Revelation of the Divine Name — 3:13-15
    Instructions to Moses — 3:16-22
    Moses Taught Three Signs — 4:1-9
    Aaron Appointed as Spokesman — 4:10-17
  THE RETURN OF MOSES FROM MIDIAN — 4:18-31
    Departure of Moses from Midian — 4:18-23
    Incident at a Lodging Place — 4:24-26
    Meeting of Aaron and Moses — 4:27-31
  THE FIRST UNSUCCESSFUL APPEAL TO PHARAOH — 5:1—6:1
    Pharaoh Scorns Yahweh — 5:1-5
    The Oppression Increased — 5:6-14
    Appeal of the Foremen to Pharaoh — 5:15-21
    Appeal of Moses to Yahweh — 5:22—6:1
  THE P ACCOUNT OF THE CALL OF MOSES — 6:2-30
    Yahweh's Plan for Israel — 6:2-9
    Moses' Objection — 6:10-13
    The Genealogy of Moses and Aaron — 6:14-25
    Recapitulation — 6:26-30
THE TEN PLAGUES IN EGYPT — 7:1—13:16
  AARON APPOINTED AS PROPHET OF MOSES — 7:1-7
  THE MIRACLE OF TRANSFORMING RODS INTO SERPENTS — 7:8-13
  THE FIRST PLAGUE: Fouling of the Waters of Egypt — 7:14-24
  THE SECOND PLAGUE: Frogs — 7:25—8:15
  THE THIRD PLAGUE: Gnats — 8:16-19
  THE FOURTH PLAGUE: Swarms of Flies — 8:20-32
  THE FIFTH PLAGUE: Plague on Cattle — 9:1-7
  THE SIXTH PLAGUE: Boils on Man and Beast — 9:8-12
  THE SEVENTH PLAGUE: Hailstorm — 9:13-35

THE EIGHTH PLAGUE: Locusts   10:1–20
THE NINTH PLAGUE: Darkness   10:21–29
THE TENTH PLAGUE: Death of the First-Born   11:1—13:16
    Announcement of the Tenth Plague   11:1–10
    Instructions for Observing Passover and Unleavened
      Bread   12:1–28
    The Tenth Plague, and Release of the Israelites   12:29–36
    The Journey from Rameses to Succoth   12:37–42
    Further Regulations for Passover   12:43–51
    Regulations concerning Firstlings and Unleavened
      Bread   13:1–16
THE EXODUS FROM EGYPT AND CROSSING OF THE SEA
                                                               13:17—15:21
  JOURNEY FROM SUCCOTH TO THE SEA   13:17—14:4
  PURSUIT BY THE EGYPTIANS   14:5–20
  CROSSING OF THE SEA   14:21–31
  TWO VICTORY HYMNS PRAISING YAHWEH   15:1–21
    The Song of the Sea   15:1–19
    The Song of Miriam   15:20–21
THE JOURNEY FROM THE SEA TO MOUNT SINAI   15:22—18:27
  HEALING OF THE WATER AT MARAH   15:22–26
  ENCAMPMENT AT ELIM   15:27
  THE GIFT OF MANNA AND QUAILS IN THE WILDERNESS OF SIN
                                                               16:1–36
  WATER FROM THE ROCK AT MASSAH-MERIBAH   17:1–7
  VICTORY OVER AMALEK   17:8–16
  VISIT OF JETHRO WITH MOSES   18:1–27
    The Sacrificial Meal on the Mountain of God   18:1–12
    Advice on Judicial Administration   18:13–26
    Departure of Jethro to his own Land   18:27
EVENTS AND LAWS OF MOUNT SINAI   19:1—40:38
  FORMATION OF THE COVENANT   19:1—24:18
    Theophany on Mount Sinai   19:1–25
    The Ten Commandments   20:1–17
    The People Request a Mediator   20:18–21
    The Book of the Covenant   20:22—23:33
      Introduction   20:22
      Cultic regulations   20:23–26
      A title   23:1
      Laws on slavery   21:2–11
      A list of capital offences   21:12–17

Laws concerning injury   21:18–32
Laws concerning damage to property   21:33—22:17
Three capital offences   22:18–20
Various humanitarian and religious duties   22:21–32
Admonitions concerning conduct in cases at law   23:1–9
The sabbatical year and the sabbath day   23:10–12
A general admonition   23:13
A calendar of annual feasts and other cultic regulations   23:14–19
Closing promises and exhortations   23:20–33
The Covenant Ratified   24:1–18
THE P ORDINANCES FOR THE CULT   25:1—31:18
The Offering by the People   25:1–9
The Ark   25:10–22
The Table of the Bread of the Presence   25:23–30
The Lampstand   25:31–40
The Tabernacle   26:1–37
The Altar of Acacia Wood   27:1–8
The Court of the Tabernacle   27:9–19
Oil for the Lampstand   27:20–21
The Garments of the Priesthood   28:1–43
The Consecration of the Priests   29:1–46
The Altar of Incense   30:1–10
The Half Shekel Offering   30:11–16
The Laver of Bronze   30:17–21
The Holy Anointing Oil   30:22–33
The Holy Incense   30:34–38
Appointment of Bezalel and Oholiab   31:1–11
Commandment to Observe the Sabbath   31:12–17
Conclusion   31:18
THE GOLDEN CALF   32:1–25
Making of the Golden Calf   32:1–6
Moses' First Intercession for Israel   32:7–14
Breaking of the Tablets by Moses   32:15–20
Rebuke of Aaron and his Self-defence   32:21–24
Ordination of the Levites   32:25–29
Moses' Second Intercession   32:30–34
The Plague Sent by Yahweh   32:35
GOD'S PRESENCE WITH HIS PEOPLE AND MOSES   33:12–17
The Departure of Israel from Sinai   33:1–6
The Tent of Meeting   33:7–11

Promise of Yahweh's Presence with Moses   33:12–17
Promise of a Theophany to Moses   33:18–23
RENEWAL OF THE COVENANT   34:1–35
Revelation of Yahweh to Moses   34:1–9
Making of the Covenant   34:10–28
Transfiguration of Moses   34:29–35
EXECUTION OF THE P ORDINANCES FOR THE CULT   35:1—40:38
Sabbath Observance   35:1–3
The Offerings and Work of the People   35:4—36:7
The Tabernacle   36:8–38
The Ark   37:1–9
The Table of Acacia Wood   37:10–16
The Lampstand   37:17–24
The Altar of Incense   37:25–28
The Holy Anointing Oil and Incense   37:29
The Altar of Burnt Offering   38:1–7
The Laver of Bronze   38:8
The Court of the Tabernacle   38:9–20
Summary of Metals Contributed   38:21–31
The Garments of the Priesthood   39:1–31
Completion and Presentation of the Tabernacle   39:32–43
Erection of the Tabernacle and its Equipment   40:1–33
The Glory of the Lord fills the Tabernacle   40:34–38

THE BOOK OF
Exodus

THE BONDAGE OF THE HEBREWS IN EGYPT

1:1–22

1–7(P). *The names of the sons of Jacob, and the number of his off-spring, seventy in all. Joseph and all his brothers, and their generation, die. Jacob's descendants in Egypt become very numerous and strong, filling the land.*

8–12(J). *A new Pharaoh arises, 'who did not know Joseph'. He is alarmed at the increase of the Israelites, and subjects them to forced labour, in order to keep them in check and prevent them from joining the enemies of Egypt in case of war. They build the store-cities of Pithom and Raamses, and continue to increase. The Egyptians consequently become more and more alarmed.*

13–14(P). *The Egyptians oppress the Israelites, compelling them to work at building operations and in agriculture.*

15–22(E). *Pharaoh calls the two midwives who attend the Hebrew women, and commands them to kill all the male children that are born, leaving alive only the female children. The midwives disobey, explaining that the Hebrew women are so vigorous that they bear their children before the midwives can arrive; God rewards the midwives with prosperity and families. Finally, the Pharaoh charges all his people to cast into the Nile all male children born to the Hebrews.*

The literary analysis of this chapter is not difficult. It contains repetitions and some inconsistencies which indicate multiplicity of sources. For example, the imposition of forced labour is related in verse 11 and again in verses 13–14; the two midwives of verse 15 would hardly suffice for the great number of Hebrews implied by verse 7. The analysis is as follows: J—1:8–12; E—1:15–22; P—1:1–7,13–14. Some critics assign 1:6,20*b*,22 to J.

The 'new king over Egypt' who oppressed the Hebrews was probably Rameses II (1290–24 B.C.), though it is possible that the oppression began under Seti I (1303–1290). Rameses II engaged in many building operations, and made his delta capital at Raamses (1:11), the *Per-Ramessu* of Egyptian inscriptions. We can hardly dissociate the Hebrews (*'ibrîm* in the Hebrew language) from the *'apiru* known from Egyptian texts. The *'apiru* were people of inferior social status, in some cases (perhaps all) foreign captives from Syria-Palestine. A letter of the time of Rameses II gives instructions to issue grain to the men of the army and the *'apiru* who were

drawing stone for the great pylon of the house of the Pharaoh
(M. Greenberg, *The Ḥab/piru*, p. 56). Yet we cannot completely
identify the ʿibrîm and the ʿapiru, because the latter were still
present in Egypt in the next century under Rameses III and IV.
The Hebrews may have been a branch of the ʿapiru, or they may
have been related in some other way. See further above, pp. 39, 43,
and for full discussion, cf. K. Koch, 'Die Hebräer vom Auszug aus
Agypten bis zum Grossreich Davids', *VT*, xix (1969), pp. 37–81.

MULTIPLICATION OF THE HEBREWS I:I-7

These verses provide the connection between the events of the
patriarchal age in Genesis and the account of the oppression in
Egypt and subsequent exodus of the Israelites. According to
Martin Noth and Gerhard von Rad, the two themes of the
patriarchal narratives and the exodus from Egypt were originally
separate, and circulated separately before being joined in the
Pentateuch (see above, p. 33).

1–4. The order of **the names of the sons of Israel**, i.e. the
patriarch Jacob, is the same as in Gen. 35:23–26 (P), where the
sons are listed according to their mothers, in the order Leah,
Rachel, Bilhah and Zilpah, the last two being concubines.

5. seventy persons: this number is the same as in the Hebrew
text of Gen. 46:27 (P). In both passages LXX has the number
seventy-five, which it obviously arrives at by including the three
grandsons and two great-grandsons of Joseph (cf. Num. 26:28–37).
Ac. 7:14 also has the number seventy-five. The numbers are
symbolical, designed to indicate that all of the sons of Jacob, and
their households, went down to Egypt, and it was they who were
the ancestors of the Israelites—**the descendants of Israel** (lit.
'sons of Israel') of verse 7.

6 is frequently assigned to J, but we may (with Noth) consider
it as P. The death of Joseph is earlier recorded in Gen. 50:26,
usually assigned to E.

7. the land is probably not the whole land of Egypt, but 'the
land of Rameses' of Gen. 47:11 (P), which is described as 'the
best of the land'. The designation is not known in Egyptian, but it
obviously applies to the region in the eastern part of the delta,
which J calls 'Goshen' (Gen. 46:28 and elsewhere). The northern
capital of Egypt in the XIXth Dynasty, which had several kings
named Rameses, was situated in this region (see below on verse 11).

OPPRESSION OF THE HEBREWS 1:8-14

8. a new king over Egypt: the writer apparently does not
know his name; neither here nor elsewhere in Exodus are the
names of Egyptian kings given. This king, the 'Pharaoh of the
oppression', probably was Seti I (1303-1290 B.C.) or Rameses II
(1290-24 B.C.). See pp. 42-43.

did not know Joseph does not necessarily mean that he had
never heard of Joseph, but rather that he had no appreciation of
his character and achievements, and thus took no special interest
in his descendants. The new king must have belonged to a
different dynasty from the king who elevated Joseph to a high
position.

10. let us deal shrewdly with them: the Israelites were
settled in the eastern delta of Egypt, in a frontier district near the
desert, from which enemies often invaded Egypt (Syrians, Hittites,
Mesopotamians, among others). The Egyptians fear that the
Israelites may make common cause with such enemies. They plan
to **deal shrewdly** with the Israelites in such a manner that the
Egyptians will retain their labour, but check their increase in
population, so that they may not become a menace to the Egyptian
overlords.

**11. set taskmasters over them to afflict them with
heavy burdens:** Hebrew for **taskmasters** is lit. 'overseers of
labour gangs' (*śārê missîm*). *Mas* is the technical term for forced
labour, the *corvée*. This institution was widely employed in the
ancient Near East. Solomon introduced it into Israel, forcing even
the native Israelites to work at *corvée* (1 Kg. 5:13-18; 9:15-22;
12:4). In Egypt, with its despotic government, even native
Egyptians were subject to forced labour. Thus, it was not unusual
for a foreign people such as the Hebrews to be compelled to
work for the State. The present text indicates that the Hebrews
were heavily oppressed; it may imply that they were actually
made slaves, lower than the native Egyptians.

Pharaoh is not a personal name, but the equivalent of 'king of
Egypt' (vv. 8,15,17). The Egyptian word (*pr-ᶜo*) means 'great
house'. In the third millennium B.C. it designated the royal
palace, but by 1800 B.C. it had become an epithet for the king.
In the XVIIIth and XIXth dynasties it was a royal title, and by
the ninth century it was prefixed to the royal name (e.g. Pharaoh
Shishak).

store cities, Pithom and Raamses. Pithom is the Egyptian *pr-ᶜItm*, 'house of (the god) Atum'. It is usually identified with one of two sites, Tell el-Maskhuta in the Wadi Tumilat, or Tell er-Retabeh, about 9 miles W. of the latter.

Tell el-Maskhuta was excavated in 1883 by Edouard Naville, who identified it with Pithom on the basis of the following arguments: (i) All the place names found on the monuments there correspond with place names in the eighth nome of Lower Egypt—particularly *čkw(t)* (Succoth), which he thinks was the civil name of the capital, and *pr-ᶜItm*, its religious name. (ii) A Latin inscription found there mentions Ero, which he interprets as Heroonpolis, the Greek name of Pithom. (iii) He believed that the architectural remains found there indicated it was a fortress and store-city. Unfortunately Naville's results were published in only sketchy form. Other Egyptologists think that the remains indicate only normal building operations, not necessarily store-chambers.

Identification of Pithom with Tell er-Retabeh has been advocated by Sir Alan Gardiner and others. He holds that *čkw(t)* and *pr-ᶜItm* were distinct terms, the former sometimes being a wider term than the latter, designating a region rather than a town. Further, he reads the Latin milestone so as to indicate that Tell el-Mashkuta was 9 miles from Ero. Tell er-Retabeh was excavated in 1906 by Sir Flinders Petrie, who identified it as the 'Raamses' of this verse. His excavations showed that the site was occupied as early as the Middle Kingdom, and that building operations were conducted there under Rameses II and III.

Raamses (or Rameses) is the Egyptian *(pr)-rᶜ-ms-sw* (usually vocalized Per-Ramessu), the meaning of which is '(house of) Rameses'. According to Exod. 12:37; Num. 33:3,5, it was the starting-point of the exodus of the Hebrews from Egypt. Egyptian texts show that Per-Ramessu was the northern and principal residence of the pharaohs of the XIXth and XXth dynasties (Thebes remaining the southern, seasonal capital). Rameses II established his capital there, and it was named in his honour. In the opinion of most scholars this was a re-building of the town of Avaris, the Hyksos capital; after the time of the Ramessides it was known as Tanis. Biblical Zoan was the same site (Isa. 19:11,13; 30:4; Ezek. 30:14).

Egyptian records indicate that Per-Ramessu was on the eastern frontier close to the desert, but had harbours, and was

noted for its vineyards and olive groves. It is usually identified
with modern San el-Hajar, believed to be the site of Tanis.
Some scholars, however, identify it with Qantir, 15 miles S. of
Tanis, where there was a palace and military post in Ramesside
times, and where many inscriptions were found praising Rameses
II as a god. One text found there appears to indicate that Tanis
and Per-Ramessu were separate places. Since San el-Hajar and
Qantir are close, the choice between these two places is not very
important, but the Egyptian descriptions seem to fit San el-Hajar
better than Qantir.

The above discussion shows that precise identification of
Pithom and Raamses is not possible with our present knowledge,
but it seems preferable to identify Pithom with Tell er-Retabeh
and Raamses with San el-Hajar, and to place Succoth, the first
stopping-place on the exodus after Raamses (Exod. 12:37;
Num. 33:5,6) at Tell el-Maskhuta.

This note regarding Pithom and Raamses is considered by
most scholars to be from J, and to be a highly valuable piece of
information for dating the oppression of the Israelites. However,
D. B. Redford, 'Exodus i:11', VT, xiii (1963), pp. 401–18 argues
that verse 11b is from P, and that the tradition it incorporates is
not older than the seventh century B.C. He says that Pithom was
the name of a *town* only from the Saite period onward, being
earlier the name of temple estates; and he raises questions concerning the name 'Raamses' here.

13–14 are P's account of the oppression of the Hebrews,
which is related by J in verse 11. P specifies that they worked in
building projects **in mortar and brick,** and also did agricultural
work **in the field**, probably tasks such as sowing of seed and
irrigation of fields referred to in Dt. 11:10.

COMMAND TO KILL THE HEBREW MALE INFANTS 1:15–22

15. If the number of midwives required by the Hebrew women
at this time was only two, as indicated here, the total number of
Hebrews in Egypt could not have been as great as is implied by
Exod. 12:37 and some other passages.

Shiphrah means in Hebrew 'beauty' or 'fair one'. The name
Sp-ra has been preserved in a list of Egyptian slaves of the eighteenth century B.C.

Puah has no obvious etymology in Hebrew, but it is usually

taken to mean 'splendour' or 'splendid one'. It may, however, be
related to the Ugaritic *pǵt*, 'girl', used as a personal name and a
common noun. For the names cf. W. F. Albright, *JAOS*, LXXIV
(1954), p. 229.

16. the birthstool: lit. 'two stones', a dual form. The same
word is used in Jer. 18:3 of the two stone discs of a potter's
wheel. The custom is attested from ancient nations, including
Egypt, of women kneeling or sitting on stones or bricks at the time
of their delivery. The killing of all sons would in time wipe out the
Hebrew people; the daughters could become slave-wives of
Egyptian men.

19. The excuse offered by the midwives belongs in the realm of
folklore, and is designed to show the superiority of the Hebrew
women. In point of fact the Hebrew women may have been
stronger and healthier than the Egyptian women of the upper
classes, but they were hardly more so than all the Egyptian women.
There is a touch of humour here.

21. he gave them families: lit. 'he made for them houses'.
It is possible that barren women were regularly used as midwives;
if so, their reward is that they become fertile and have families.
In any event the narrator represents God as rewarding the
midwives for refusing to obey the Egyptian king and turn against
their own people.

22. The Pharaoh gives a command to **all his people** that they
put to death all the Hebrew male children by throwing them into
the Nile. This is the third stratagem of the Egyptian king, the
first being forced labour, the second a command to the midwives
to kill the males. This implies a more rigorous campaign to
exterminate the Hebrews. Some scholars assign this verse to J and
consider it as a variant to E's account of the killing of the male
children, but it is better to view it as the continuation of E's
narrative.

PREPARATIONS FOR DELIVERANCE 2:1—6:30

THE BIRTH OF MOSES 2:1–10 (J)

A child is born to parents of the tribe of Levi. After hiding him
for three months, his mother places him in a basket ('ark', *AV*,
RV) of bulrushes, and puts the basket on the brink of the river.
There he is found by an Egyptian princess. First he is nursed by

his own mother, and then is adopted by the princess and brought up by her.

This narrative is a legend and should be read as such, not as history. Similar stories were widespread in the ancient world, with the principals sometimes being gods, sometimes human beings, and sometimes both. The motif has been studied in detail by D. B. Redford, 'The Literary Motif of the Exposed Child', *Numen*, xiv (1967), pp. 209–28. He lists thirty-two myths and legends with the motif from the ancient world, including stories about Hercules, Perseus, Romulus and Remus, Semiramis, Cyrus, and Ptolemy Soter. He thinks the motif was not used in ancient Egypt before Graeco-Roman times, and that it originated in Mesopotamia and the highlands to the north and east of Mesopotamia. He finds three reasons for the exposure of the child in the various stories: a feeling of shame at the circumstances of the birth; a ruler seeks to kill the child who is destined to supplant him; or a general massacre endangers the life of the child. The present story obviously belongs to the third category, but a version of it which was preserved in later Jewish legend has elements of the second category. The story here involves belief that a special providence watches over the child from his birth, although the Deity is not mentioned in it.

The closest parallel to the biblical legend is the story about Sargon, a Mesopotamian king of the middle of the third millennium b.c. (translated in *ANET*, p. 119). The legend is told in the first person by Sargon himself. He says that his mother gave birth to him in secret and placed him in a basket of rushes, the lid of which she sealed with bitumen. She then cast him into the river, which bore him up and carried him to Akki, the drawer of water. Akki lifted him out of the water, took him as his own son, and reared him. He became Akki's gardener, and the goddess Ishtar granted him her love. He eventually became king of Agade. Surviving texts are fragmentary, and we do not have the whole of the legend, but similarities to the Moses legend are striking. We need not assume that the Sargon story as such was known to the Israelites, for the motif was widespread.

The biblical story has unique features. It has no mythological elements but is told as if it were history. Moses is nursed by his own mother, and is rescued and brought up by the daughter of the tyrant who had sought to destroy him. The legend is told, however, without specifically religious features; the Deity appears

nowhere in the account. The relatively simple biblical narrative
was greatly expanded by later imagination. For example, Josephus
says his father had a vision foretelling how Moses would deliver
his people (*Ant.* II.ix.3), and Philo gives details of his elaborate
education (*De vit. Mos.* I.v).

This narrative is assigned to E by most scholars, but it is more
likely that it originated with J (so Noth, Rudolph). Decisive
indications of E are lacking (it is not clear, for example, that the
Hebrews are here represented as living outside of Goshen).
The straightforward, almost secular, narrative lacking in names is
likely to come from the basic J source, who would hardly have
passed over the birth of Moses. Some inconsistencies in the
narrative—such as the suggestion in verse 1 that Moses was the
first-born of his parents, whereas later he is shown to have an
older sister—should not be considered as indicating separate
written sources. They derive from successive stages in the formation
of the legend in oral tradition; folklore that developed over a
period of time cannot be expected to have the consistency of
history. For form-critical analysis of the legend, see B. S. Childs,
'The Birth of Moses', *JBL*, 84 (1965), pp. 109–122. He sees a close
relationship to the Joseph cycle, and argues that it is a historicized
wisdom tale that originated in the older wisdom movement in
Israel that saw the providence of God working through human
actions but made few statements about the activity of God.
It belongs to one of the latest strata of tradition in Exodus.

1. The parents of Moses are anonymous here. Their names are
given in 6:18–20 (P): his father was Amram son of Kohath, and
his mother Jochebed, paternal aunt of Amram.

3. The child was placed in **a basket made of bulrushes.**
The word for basket is Hebrew *tēḇāh*, elsewhere used only of
Noah's ark (Gen. 6:14ff.). The traditional rendering here is 'ark';
the reference is to a basket or chest with a cover. A different
word is used for the Ark of the covenant.

bulrushes were stalks of the papyrus plant, *Cyperus papyrus*, very
abundant in ancient times along the banks of the lower Nile, but
no longer found there.

the reeds at the river's brink were the tall grasses growing along
the river's edge, probably consisting of several species. The Hebrew
word *sûp* appears in the name of the 'Red Sea', *yām sûp*, properly
'sea of reeds'.

4. It is surprising to read here that Moses has a **sister,** for verses 1–2 seem to imply that he was the first-born of his parents. Many scholars consider this an indication of the presence of another source; however, we should not expect complete consistency in a legend such as this, especially one which is told with great brevity. The sister is unnamed, but presumably is Miriam, named later in Exod. 15:20; Num. 12; 20:1.

5. the daughter of Pharaoh likewise is unnamed. In tradition of a much later time she was given several names: Thermuthis (Josephus, *Ant.* ii.ix.5), Tharmuth (Jubilees 47:5), Merris (Eusebius, *Praep. Ev.* ix.27), and Bithiah (Talmud, B.Meg. 74,91; B.Ber. 41). We cannot identify her with any known Egyptian princess.

She **came down to bathe at the river:** this could mean to bathe in or alongside the river, but we have no historical verification for the custom of bathing either in or alongside the Nile at this time. It does not seem probable that this would be customary for an Egyptian princess.

8. The sister is here designated as a **girl,** Hebrew *ʿalmāh*, which was used of a young woman of marriageable age. It is the same word that is employed in Isa. 7:14.

9. The child is nursed by his own mother, who is paid wages for the task by the princess. Little is known about procedures in Egypt with regard to the treatment of foundlings and adoption, but the procedures here followed conform generally to practices known from Mesopotamian documents. The mother becomes wet nurse for the child; she presumably takes him to her own home; she is paid wages for the task; she delivers the child to the princess, presumably after the child has been weaned; and finally the child is adopted by the person who found him. (For details, see B. S. Childs, *JBL*, LXXXIV [1965], pp. 110–15). It is likely that procedures were the same in Egypt as in other parts of the Near East.

10. he became her son: the legend intended to say that the Egyptian princess actually adopted Moses, not simply that she treated him as a son. Cf. Ac. 7:21. It is she who gives him his name.

Moses: Hebrew, *mōšeh*. The explanation that is given here must be considered as folk etymology, depending upon similarity in sound, and not scientific etymology. Hebrew *mōšeh* is an active participle of the verb which means 'to draw out'. The meaning strictly is 'one who draws out'. Here it is interpreted as if it were a passive form of the verb, and it is similar in sound to the Hebrew of **I drew him out,** which is *meš̄iṭihú*. The legend represents the Egyptian princess as knowing Hebrew!

There has been much discussion of the original meaning of the name *mōšeh*. Josephus explained the Greek form of it, *Mōusēs*, as meaning 'saved from water', from two Egyptian words, *mou* meaning 'water' and *eses* meaning 'saved' (*Ant.* ii.ix.6; cf. Philo, *De vit. Mos.* i.iv.17). This explanation is rejected by most modern scholars as unscientific, and in any event does not explain the Hebrew form of the name. Most scholars now favour the view that the name *mōšeh* is to be associated with the Egyptian verb *ms*, which means 'to bear, give birth', probably in the form *mose*. This form occurs in theophorous names such as Thut-mose, the name of several Pharaohs, which means 'The god Thut is born' (with reference to the birthday of the god) or 'Born of the god Thut'. The former meaning is more probable. Names of this type were common in the New Kingdom, including Ptah-mose, Ah-mose, and Amen-mose. *Mōšeh* is thus to be explained as the shortened form of a name which contained as the first element the name of a deity. There are several known Egyptian names in the shortened form *mose*, one or two apparently being used as nicknames for reigning Pharaohs.

FLIGHT OF MOSES TO MIDIAN 2:11-25

11-25*a*(J). *Moses, seeking to identify himself with his fellow-Hebrews, kills an Egyptian who was beating a Hebrew. When the next day Moses tries to intervene between two Hebrews, he is rebuked by one of them, who reveals that the murder of the Egyptian is known. Pharaoh seeks to kill Moses.*

15*b***-23***a*(J). *Moses flees to Midian, where he marries Zipporah, daughter of a Midianite priest. A son Gershom is born to them.*

23*b***-25**(P). *The Israelites cry out for help. God remembers his covenant with the patriarchs and recognizes their need.*

This section is almost completely from J, continuing the story of the birth and adoption of Moses. Only verses 23*b*-25 are from another source, P. The tradition connecting Moses with the land of Midian is a very ancient one; see comment on verse 15. According to this tradition Moses married into the family of a Midianite priest. In the opinion of many scholars, the religion of Moses was

c

deeply influenced by that of his father-in-law: see the excursus (pp. 78–81) on the name 'Yahweh' and the origin of Mosaic Yahwism.

This account says nothing of the education of Moses. The tradition recorded in Ac. 7:22 affirmed that 'Moses was instructed in all the wisdom of the Egyptians'. Josephus says he was 'educated with the utmost care' (*Ant.* II.ix.7), and Philo describes in detail his education not only by Egyptians, but by Greeks and others (*de vit. Mos.* I.v). Philo says he was so precocious that he soon surpassed his instructors, and propounded problems they could not easily solve.

The present story reveals much of the character of Moses: his readiness to take the initiative in identifying himself with his people, his passionate sense of justice, his capacity for flaming anger, and his tendency on occasion to impetuous action.

11. when Moses had grown up: according to a later tradition, this was at the age of forty-two years (Jubilees 48:1) or forty years (Ac. 7:23). According to Heb. 11:24–25, 'Moses, when he was grown up, refused to be called the son of Pharaoh's daughter, choosing rather to share ill-treatment with the people of God than to enjoy the fleeting pleasures of sin.'

12. he killed the Egyptian: Hebrew says literally, 'he struck the Egyptian', but the context indicates that he killed him.

14. The motive of Moses is misunderstood, and the Hebrew who had done wrong refuses to recognize his authority and is afraid for his own life. Ac. 7:25 says, 'He supposed that his brethren understood that God was giving them deliverance by his hand, but they did not understand.'

15. the land of Midian is usually located on the east shore of the Gulf of Aqabah, to the south of Palestine. This is where Ptolemy, geographer of the second century A.D., and later Arab geographers located Madiana or Madyan. However, the *OT* represents the Midianites as nomads who ranged over a wide territory to the south and east of Palestine; therefore we should not seek to locate them precisely to a specific territory. According to Gen. 25:2, Midian was a son of Keturah, wife of Abraham; verse 6 says that Abraham sent her sons away 'eastward to the east country'. The Hebrews thus claimed some kinship with the Midianites. Midianite traders are reported to have sold Joseph into Egypt in Gen. 37:28. Later, elders of Midian sought to expel Israel from Moab (Num. 22:4,7), and the marriage of an

Israelite man to a Midianite woman brought a plague on
Israel (Num. 25:6–7). Subsequently the Israelites were at war
with the Midianites (Num. 31:1–12). In the time of Gideon,
camel-riding Midianites invaded Canaan from the east (Jg. 6–8).
Because the Midianites and Hebrews are so often represented as
being at war, we should consider the tradition of the peaceful
association of Moses with a group of them as a very ancient tradition. The term 'Midianite' may, however, be a rather general
term; we cannot be certain of the identity of the various people
designated by it.

16. the priest of Midian is here nameless, as is characteristic
of J. See below on verse 18 for the name Reuel. The priest may
have been the chieftain of his tribe, or may have occupied some
position of authority other than that of priest. This is not, however,
clearly stated in the record.

17. These Midianites are represented as shepherds, living a
pastoral nomadic existence. In 3:1 Moses serves as a shepherd.

18. Reuel: there is confusion in the biblical narratives regarding
the name of the priest of Midian who became Moses' father-in-
law. In 3:1 and chapter 18 he is called 'Jethro the priest of
Midian', and in 4:18 'Jether' (some Hebrew MSS. have Jethro).
In Num. 10:29 he is 'Hobab the son of Reuel the Midianite.'
In Jg. 4:11 he is 'Hobab', one of the Kenites; and in Jg. 1:16 he is
called simply 'the Kenite', with some MSS. of the LXX inserting
the name 'Hobab'.

These variations are often explained as due to the fact that the
traditions concerning Moses' father-in-law gave him different
names, sometimes identifying him as a Midianite, sometimes as a
Kenite. It is usually assumed that the Kenites were a subdivision
of the Midianites, or a clan (probably of metal-workers) associated
in some manner with the Midianites. The name 'Reuel' in the
present verse is often explained as a gloss, erroneously taken from
the name of Hobab's father in Num. 10:29.

An ingenious solution of the problems involved here has been
proposed by W. F. Albright, 'Jethro, Hobab and Reuel in Early
Hebrew Tradition', *CBQ*, xxv (1963), pp. 1–11. He conjectures
that 'Reuel' in Num. 10:29 is the name of the clan to which
Hobab belonged; in the names of nomads in early times the name
of the 'father' is often really a clan name. He points out that
Reuel is the name of a clan affiliated with Midian in the LXX of
Gen. 25:3, and of a clan of Edom in Gen. 36:4,13; 1 Chr. 1:35,37.

Thus he suggests that the original reading in the present verse
was 'they came to Jethro, son of Reuel their father.' The name
Jethro was accidentally dropped in the transmission of the text.
Then Albright suggests that Jethro and Hobab were different
persons. Jethro in chapter 2 is an old man with seven daughters
(2:16; cf. Exod. 18), whereas Hobab in Num. 10:29–32 is a
vigorous younger man whom Moses wants as guide in the wilderness. Albright proposes to change the vocalization of *ḥōṯēn*,
'father-in-law' in Num. 10:29 to *ḥāṯān*, 'son-in-law'. We should
not be surprised that both Hobab and Jethro belonged to the same
clan, since west Semitic nomads were often endogamous. Albright
notes that a number of scholars have adopted this change in
vocalization, but think that *ḥāṯān* should mean 'brother-in-law'.
Such a meaning is possible for the cognate word in other languages,
but Albright's meaning is in keeping with Hebrew usage. Finally
Albright conjectures that in Jg. 1:16; 4:11 the word *ḳênî*, usually
rendered 'Kenite', should be translated as 'smith'. Thus, Hobab
was Moses' son-in-law, a Midianite of the clan of Reuel, but a
smith by profession. Albright's theory may be correct, but some
of the crucial elements in it lack textual support. He is probably
correct concerning Reuel as a clan-name, but the relationship of
Hobab to Moses was as likely to have been brother-in-law as
son-in-law.

19. The women probably thought Moses was **an Egyptian**
from his clothing; in any event they had not had enough experience
to identify him as a Hebrew, which at this time was hardly an
ethnic term, but a term signifying a social status, like the Egyptian
ʿApiru.

21. Zipporah is the feminine form of the noun meaning 'bird'.
Some scholars have taken this name as indicative of totemism
among the Midianites. This is not necessarily true. We know
very little of Midianite religion. Names of birds and animals are
fairly frequent among the Hebrews and other ancient Semitic
peoples. A nomadic people living in the open air much of the
time naturally gave such names, when the parents hoped the
child would have the qualities associated with a particular
animal.

22. The name **Gershom** is here explained as if it were *gēr-šām*,
meaning 'a sojourner there', a popular etymology. The name
occurs also as that of a son of Levi (1 Chr. 6:1), and of a descendant of Phinehas, who was the head of a father's house that re-

turned from exile with Ezra (Ezra 8:2). In Jg. 18:30 Jonathan the
son of Gershom, son of Moses, is listed as a priest of the tribe of
Danites, and it is said that his sons were priests of that tribe until
the captivity. The Levitical clan of the 'sons of Gershon' (Num.
3:21-26 and elsewhere) may be the same, with confusion of the
final consonant.

23-25 is frequently considered as the introduction or pre-
face to the account of the call of Moses which follows in 3:1—
4:17. Note that the account of God's hearing the cry of the
Hebrews and responding to it is told also by J (3:7-8) and by
E (3:9-10).

23. In the course of those many days: the word **many**
appears to be a gloss. J represents Moses as marrying Zipporah
soon after he arrives in the land of Midian, and Gershom is very
young when they leave Egypt (4:20,25). The period of Moses'
stay in Midian was thus not long, according to J. P, on the other
hand, seems to represent Moses as remaining there for about
forty years (see 2:11; 7:7; cf. Jubilees 48:1). The gloss was made
in the light of P's chronology.

the king of Egypt died: this would have been the 'Pharaoh of
the oppression', Seti I or Rameses II (see 1:8).

23b-25 is P's continuation of 1:13-14. When the people cried
out to God, **God remembered his covenant with Abraham,
with Isaac, and with Jacob.** P emphasizes the covenant which
had been made with Abraham and Isaac (Gen. 17:7,19) and
implicitly renewed with Jacob (Gen. 35:11-12). In P's subsequent
account of the appearance of Yahweh to Moses, appeal is made to
the covenant with the patriarchs (6:4).

God knew their condition: this is interpretation of the Hebrew
text, which has *wayyēda^cɔelōhîm*, 'God knew'. LXX here reads,
'he was known to them'—i.e., he made himself known to them
(Hebrew *wayyiwwāda^c ɔalêhem*). This may be the original reading.
The continuation of P is in 6:2ff., where God is represented as
revealing himself to Moses for the first time by the name Yahweh
and saying, 'By my name the LORD I did not make myself known
to them (the patriarchs).'

THE JE ACCOUNT OF THE CALL OF MOSES 3:1—4:17

1-10(J,E). *While Moses is keeping the flock of his father-in-law on
Horeb, God speaks to him from a bush that burns without being consumed.*

God tells Moses that he has heard the cry of the Hebrews, and is now about to deliver Israel from Egypt and bring them into the land of the Canaanites. Moses is to be their leader.

11–12(E). *Moses protests that he is not equal to the task, but God promises his presence. After their deliverance, the Israelites will worship God on Horeb.*

13–15(E). *Moses asks what is the name of the God who is sending him. God reveals his name as Yahweh, with the explanation, 'I am who I am'.*

16–22(J,E). *Moses is instructed to announce his mission to the elders of Israel, who are to go with him to the king of Egypt for permission to make a three days' journey into the wilderness to sacrifice to Yahweh. The king will refuse, and Yahweh will perform wonders to make him release them. As they leave, the Hebrews are to borrow jewels and clothing from the Egyptians.*

4:1–9(J). *When Moses objects that the people will not believe him, Yahweh gives him three signs by which he is to convince them: the sign of the rod that becomes a serpent, the sign of the hand that becomes leprous, and the sign of the Nile water becoming blood.*

10–12(J). *Moses protests that he is not eloquent. Yahweh declares that he has made man's mouth, and that he will teach Moses what to say.*

13–17(E). *Moses still demurs and asks Yahweh to send someone else. In anger Yahweh replies that Aaron his brother will be his spokesman. God gives Moses a rod with which to do signs.*

Chapter 3 is one of the most significant chapters in all of Exodus, for here Moses receives his commission to lead the Israelites out of Egypt, and God reveals his name 'Yahweh' for the first time. This account of the call of Moses has many similarities to accounts of the call of several later *OT* prophets, and may have provided the model for them.

The literary analysis is generally not difficult, and there is little disagreement among scholars. For the first time we have a lengthy section from E, verses 9–15, in which the Elohist introduces the word 'Yahweh' for the first time. In the preceding verses the variation in use of the divine names and the occurrence of doublets point to the presence of both J and E. Verse 1 is from J, except the gloss 'Jethro' and the final clause. 2–4*a*,5, and 7–8 are also from J, as indicated by the use of 'Yahweh'. E is preserved here in only fragmentary form; to that source we must attribute in 1 **and came to Horeb, the mountain of God,** and then 4*b*, 6 and the long section 9–15. J resumes in 16–18, and E in 19–22; Eissfeldt

attributes 21–22 to L, and Fohrer to N. Thus the sources are:
J—3:1*ab*, 2–4*a*, 5, 7–8, 16–18; E—3:1*c*, 4*b*, 6, 9–15, 19–22.

The analysis of chapter 4 presents some difficulties. It is
mostly from J, but 4:17 is clearly from E (see comment below).
13–16, which speak of Aaron, are widely believed to be a secondary insertion in either J or E. Aaron probably does not appear in
the oldest stratum of J; his rôle here is similar to the one he usually
plays in E. It is best to consider it as E, but without certainty.

There are elements of awkwardness in 4:1–9 that indicate
secondary additions, probably.both 5 and 9.

APPEARANCE OF GOD IN A BURNING BUSH 3:1–6

1. Jethro is an E gloss to harmonize the personal name with
that given to Moses' father-in-law in chapter 18; see comment on
2:18. J calls him simply **the priest of Midian. the west side of
the wilderness** is in Hebrew, 'to the back of the wilderness'.
It cannot be located precisely, since the Midianites were wide-
ranging nomads (see comment on 2:15). It could have been in the
southern part of the peninsula of Sinai, where the sacred mountain
is traditionally located, or in any region where the Midianites
pastured their flocks. Moses was apparently taking the sheep to a
higher elevation where grass could be found when the lower
elevations had dried up. The last clause, **and came to Horeb,
the mountain of God** is from E. 'Horeb' is the name used by
E and D for the sacred mountain, for which J and P use 'Sinai'.
They are to be taken as different names for the same mountain; on
the location of this mountain, see discussion below, following
comments on chapter 19, pp. 203–207.

2. the angel of the LORD is a self-manifestation of Yahweh.
Here the angel is not to be thought of as a supernatural messenger
of the Deity; the term is simply interchangeable with 'Yahweh',
which is used alone in verse 4, when the Deity is represented as
speaking. For this practice, cf. especially the experience of Gideon
in Jg. 6:11ff.
a bush: Hebrew, *sᵉneh*, which is similar in sound to 'Sinai'.
It occurs elsewhere only in Dt. 33:16, where Yahweh is called
'he who dwelt in the bush', referring to the present account.
However, this name has nothing to do with the origin of the name
of the mountain (which is probably to be associated with the
Deity Sin), and there is no obvious play on words here. The bush
is usually identified as a thorn bush, but we do not have enough

information to identify it with any particular bush that grows in the region south of Palestine. The monks at St Catherine's monastery on Jebel Musa cultivate a bush known as *rubus collinus* which they point out as the burning bush. However, it has not been shown that this bush grows wild in the region, and in any case the location of Sinai is uncertain.

the bush was burning, yet it was not consumed: various explanations of this phenomenon have been attempted: the bush had leaves of a brilliant hue, or leaves that reflected the bright sunlight; or the phenomenon known as 'St Elmo's fire' occurred. All such naturalistic explanations of this narrative are vain; the Hebrews lived in a world in which they expected supernatural appearances, and they were accustomed to explain many events and occurrences as manifestations of the divine.

4. The first half of this verse, which uses the name 'Yahweh', is assigned to J, and the second half, using *Elohim*, is assigned to E.

5. put off your shoes from your feet: this practice, still observed by Moslems, indicates the presence of a sanctuary. **the place on which you are standing is holy ground** is frequently taken to indicate that this was already a sacred place when Moses came upon it; some scholars believe that Sinai had been a sanctuary of the Midianite deity Yahweh. Another interpretation is that this place came to be considered as holy as a result of Moses' experience here; legend which developed after the appearance to Moses told of it as if it were an ancient holy place.

6. I am the God of your father: the text of the Samaritan Pentateuch here reads, 'God of your fathers'. Because the phrase which has the plural form of the noun is more frequent, this is considered by some scholars as the original reading here. However, because the Hebrew text has the unexpected reading with a singular noun, it is better to consider this as the original. It may be very significant that here the Deity speaks of himself as 'the God of your father' thus indicating that Yahweh was originally a patron deity of Moses' own father, or of a more remote ancestor. See discussion of the origin of Mosaic Yahwism in the Excursus, pp. 78–81. The phrase with a singular form of 'father' occurs in Gen. 26:24; 31:5,42,53; 43:23; 46:1,3; 49:25; 50:17: Exod. 15:2; 18:4. In the theology of E, this deity is also **the God of Abraham, the God of Isaac, and the God of Jacob.**

THE COMMISSION OF MOSES 3:7–12

8. I have come down to deliver them out of the hand of the Egyptians; a characteristic expression of J, who spoke of Yahweh as coming virtually in bodily form to deliver Israel; cf. Gen. 3:8, where Yahweh walks in the garden of Eden in the cool of the day, and Gen. 11:5, where Yahweh comes down to see the city and tower that men built, and in later passages, Exod. 19:11, 18,20; 34:5.

a land flowing with milk and honey: a phrase frequently used to describe Canaan in J, Deuteronomy, and elsewhere. To a nomadic people of the desert, or to slaves in Egypt, this describes a land with abundant food.

the place of the Canaanites ... and the Jebusites: lists of the peoples occupying the land which the Israelites invaded, such as this, are frequent in Exodus and Joshua, and occur in other books. The number and order vary, but these six are the most frequently named. Some of them are used in restricted senses that we cannot now fully understand.

the Canaanites were in general the Semitic inhabitants of Palestine west of the Jordan. Sometimes the term is used specifically for dwellers in the coastal plain and the valleys, especially the Jordan valley (Num. 13:29; 14:25; Jos. 11:3). This is probably the meaning here.

the Hittites were an Indo-European people who had a large empire in Anatolia and northern Syria in the latter part of the second millennium B.C. It came to an end around 1200 B.C. and thereafter the Hittites had several small kingdoms or city-states in Syria and Anatolia. Hittites are frequently referred to in the *OT*, and some are known by name, such as Ephron, from whom Abraham purchased a field (Gen. 23:10ff.) and Uriah, husband of Bathsheba (2 Sam. 11–12). Specific references seem to locate them in the southern part of the territory of Judah, in the area particularly of Hebron and Beersheba (Gen. 23; 26:34; Num. 13:29).

the Amorites were properly the inhabitants of Amurru, which at one time comprised Syria and perhaps part of northern Palestine. They furnished several important dynasties in Mesopotamia and Syria in the early part of the second millennium B.C., among them the First Dynasty of Babylon. In the *OT* the word is sometimes a general equivalent to Canaanites (e.g. Gen. 15:16).

More specifically it refers to inhabitants of the hill country of Palestine (Num. 13:29; Dt. 1:19ff.; Jos. 10:5ff.; 11:3) and to the two kingdoms of Heshbon and Bashan in Transjordan (Jos. 2:10; 9:10 etc.). Here it probably means inhabitants of the hill country, with **Canaanites** referring to dwellers in the plains (see especially Num. 13:29).

the Perizzites are known only in lists such as the present one, occurring twenty-three times. If they are an ethnic group, we cannot identify or locate them. Some scholars believe that Hebrew *perizzî* 'Perizzite', has the same meaning as *perāzî*, a term applying to unwalled villages or dwellers in such places (Est. 9:19; cf. Dt. 3:5; 1 Sam. 6:18). The term thus may refer to peasants living in unwalled villages, and designate a class rather than an ethnic group.

the Hivites occur mostly in lists, but are specifically found at Shechem (Gen. 34:2), Gibeon (Jos. 9:7; 11:19), between Sidon and Beersheba (2 Sam. 24:7), on Mount Lebanon (Jg. 3:3), and at the foot of Mount Hermon (Jos 11:3). They are completely unknown outside the Bible. It is quite possible that the name 'Hivite' is everywhere a corruption for an original 'Horite'. The Horites (properly Hurrians) were an important ethnic group who were widespread in the Near East in the second millennium B.C. Support for this view is found in the fact that LXX has 'Horites' twice where Hebrew has 'Hivites' (Gen. 34:2; Jos. 9:7); and in the fact that Hebrew speaks of 'Zibeon the Hivite' in Gen. 36:2, but calls his father a 'Horite' in 36:20. Confusion between *ḥry* and *ḥwy* in Hebrew would not have been difficult (see further E. A. Speiser in *IDB*, *s.v.* 'Hivite', 'Hurrians').

the Jebusites were the inhabitants of Jerusalem before its capture by David (Jos. 18:28; Jg. 19:10–11; 2 Sam. 5:6–8; 1 Chr. 11:4–6; cf. Gen. 10:16).

11. This is the first of Moses' four protests against accepting the commission to lead Israel out of Egypt. He expresses his feeling of being inadequate for the task. The three others are in 4:1, 10, 13.

12. this shall be the sign for you, that I have sent you: a 'sign' is often a natural occurrence or a supernatural phenomenon that confirms the truth of what is said by God or by a prophet (cf. 1 Sam. 10:7,9; 2 Kg. 19:29; 20:8–9; Isa. 7:11,14; Jer. 44:29). As the text stands, the sign is that when Moses succeeds in bringing the Israelites out of Egypt, they will serve God on this same mountain. Subsequently Moses does demand of Pharaoh that the Israelites be allowed to go three days' journey into the wilderness to sacrifice to their God (3:18; 5:1,3 etc.). Some interpreters feel that this is an unnatural sign; what Moses desires is some present assurance that God has truly sent him. Thus some hold that 'this' refers back to the burning bush, which is the sign. Others believe there is a lacuna in the text after **I have sent you,** and that **when you have brought forth . . .** is a new sentence. In the lacuna was a reference to a more normal type of sign, such as one or more of those in 4:1–9. In reality the word 'sign' covers a great variety of events and phenomena, and we should not restrict its reference too narrowly.

REVELATION OF THE DIVINE NAME TO MOSES 3:13–15

13. Moses wants to know the name of the God who is sending him back to Egypt. He asks the name primarily for identification, but more than that is implied. Among the Hebrews, as among ancient Semites generally, possession of a name was important, for nothing existed without a name. To 'call a name' is sometimes equivalent to 'create'. Gods as well as men had names, and their names had meaning. A name indicated the nature and character of its bearer. To pronounce the name of a deity meant to call upon his power.

14–15 are of central importance in this chapter. They are E's account of the first revelation and use of the divine name 'Yahweh'. According to J, 'men began to call upon the name of Yahweh' long before, in the time of Enosh (Gen. 4:26), and J frequently uses the name in Genesis.

14. I am who I am: Hebrew, *'ehyeh 'aser 'ehyeh,* which can have several different meanings, as indicated in *RSV* mg. 'I am because I am' is another possibility. *'ehyeh* may mean 'I am', 'I will be', or 'I will become'. The particle *'aser* has a variety of meanings, such as 'who', 'what', 'that', 'he who', 'that which', 'one who', 'because'. The more important interpretations that have been given to this sentence may be summarized as follows:

(i) The reply is intentionally evasive. God refuses to give a direct answer to the question, (a) because he does not wish to reveal his name and his nature to man—he is *deus absconditus;* or (b) because man should not know God's name and acquire power over him, for God is not to be man's slave;or (c) because the nature of God cannot be fully expressed in a name, and man cannot really comprehend the nature of God, which must remain a mystery.

(ii) God is the eternally existent one.

(iii) 'I am because I am'. There is no cause for God's existence outside himself. He is the ultimate fact, not to be explained by reference to anything or anyone other than himself.

(iv) 'I will be what I will be', or 'I will be that which I intend to be'. God will in the future reveal himself to man as he himself wills; he is the master of his own destiny. He will disclose his name and nature to Moses and Israel as he is active in their life and history.

(v) 'I am he who is', or 'I am the one who is'. This deity is the only one who has real existence. He is the only one who truly is; there is no other beside him.

The first of these explanations overlooks the fact that God does in fact reveal his name to Moses in verse 15. We should not, then, say that the sentence is intentionally a refusal to answer, although it is in accord with Israelite theology to say that man cannot fully comprehend the nature of God, which remains in part a mystery.

Most critics who comment upon this sentence agree that in Hebrew thought the emphasis is not upon pure or abstract being, but rather upon active being and positive manifestation of the Deity in activity. Specifically, the stress is upon God's presence with Moses and Israel; his 'being' is a 'being with', a divine presence. Hence, the fourth explanation above is more in harmony with Israelite thinking than the second and third.

If the correct rendering of the phrase is 'I am what I am' or 'I will be what I will be', it is an example of the Hebrew syntactical construction known as *idem per idem*. Other examples in Exodus are: 4:13, 'send, I pray, by the hand of whom thou wilt send'; 16:23, 'bake what you will bake, and boil what you will boil'; and 33:19, 'I will be gracious to whom I will be gracious, and will show mercy on whom I will show mercy'. See also 1 Sam. 23:13; 2 Sam. 15:20; 2 Kg. 8:1; Ezek. 12:25; etc. In this construction the speaker (or writer) is intentionally indefinite, because he is either unwilling or unable to be definite and precise. We must see in the phrase here, as Noth says (p. 45), that kind of indefiniteness 'which leaves open a large number of possibilities', in which the deity implies, 'I am whatever I mean to be'. For full discussion, with many examples and with emphasis upon the word-play involved, see T. C. Vriezen in *Festschrift Alfred Bertholet*, ed. W. Baumgartner *et al.* (1950), pp. 498–512.

The fifth possibility listed above involves a different interpretation of the syntax of the Hebrew here. For defence of the translation and the resulting meaning, see E. Schild, in *VT*, IV (1954), pp. 296–302, and J. Lindblom, in *Annual of the Swedish Theological Institute*, III (1964), pp. 4–15. The principle of Hebrew syntax involved is that in a relative clause such as *ᵃšer ʾehyeh*, the verb must be in the first person in order to agree with the subject of the main verb. Specifically, Hebrew says, translated very literally, 'I am the one who *am*', whereas the same statement is made in English with the sentence, 'I am the one who *is*'. An attempt has been made to show that this view of the syntax is not valid by B. Albrektson, in *Words and Meanings*, ed. P. R. Ackroyd and B. Lindars (1968), pp. 15–28, but the view must remain a possibility. This translation makes the assertion that Yahweh is the only deity who has real existence, other gods being unreal or non-existent. If this is the correct interpretation, the phrase is not likely to come from an early time, but rather from the seventh or sixth century B.C., when the problem of monotheism was considered in a sophisticated manner.

Verses 14–15 are over-crowded in their present form. In verse 13 Moses asks to be told the name of God. In 14a God replies, *ʾehyeh ᵃšer ʾehyeh*. In 14b the name is given as 'I am' which in Hebrew is *ʾehyeh*. Finally, in the third reply, the whole of verse 15, the name is given as 'Yahweh, the God of your fathers . . .' It is not likely that all three of these were in the original account given by E.

Some scholars hold that the original reply was in 14b in the form, 'Say this to the people of Israel, "Yahweh has sent me to you".' Subsequently 14a was prefixed, and the original 'Yahweh' was changed to *ʾehyeh*, 'I am', to conform with 14a. Verse 15 was then an even later addition. It is, however, much more natural to suppose that the original reply to verse 13 was verse 15, which gives the name of Yahweh in a straightforward way, identifying him with the God of the patriarchs (so Noth, Beer, and others). If this is true, verse 14 is a secondary addition, made at one time, or—as is more likely—at two different times. Verse 14a was first added, and subsequently verse 14b. The latter was an attempt to make a little better sense of a difficult text; it is an infelicitous

addition, fitting awkwardly into the context and obscuring the
original answer given in verse 15.

The sentence in 14*a* is the only attempt made anywhere in the
OT to explain the divine name. Nowhere in the *OT* is this
explanation alluded or referred to, except possibly in Hos. 1:9.

15. As *RSV* mg. explains, the divine name YHWH is printed in
small capital letters. This appears as 'Jehovah' in *RV* and some
other English versions. Although we cannot be absolutely certain,
it is probable that the ancient Israelites pronounced the divine
name as 'Yahweh' or something very similar. This pronunciation
was preserved by some early church fathers. 'Jehovah' is a
hybrid name that should never have existed, being made up of the
consonants of the divine name and the vowels of the Hebrew
ʾadōnāy, 'Lord'.

EXCURSUS: *The Origin of 'Yahweh' and of Mosaic Yahwism*
Much has been written on the origin of the name 'Yahweh' and
of Mosaic Yahwism. This is not the place to enter into a full
discussion of the topic, but a few words may be said, especially in
order to set forth briefly the point of view of this commentary.

It is often held that Moses derived his knowledge of Yahweh
and his worship from Jethro, his father-in-law, while he was in
the land of Midian. Jethro is known to have been a priest, and in
Exod. 18 he participates in a sacrificial ceremony which is interpreted as the occasion of the induction of the Israelites into the
formal cult of Yahweh. In the same chapter Jethro gives advice to
Moses regarding the administration of justice, which was a
religious function. Mount Sinai is held to be a Midianite sanctuary
of Yahweh, and it was there that Moses had an experience of
Yahweh which persuaded him to return to Egypt with the belief
that this deity could lead the Israelites out of their bondage.
Further, it is pointed out that Cain is the eponymous ancestor of
the Kenites, and he is reported in Gen. 4:15 to have had the
mark of Yahweh upon him. For a modern exposition of the
Midianite-Kenite theory of the origin of Yahwism, see H. H.
Rowley, *From Joseph to Joshua*, pp. 149–60.

Doubts have been raised concerning this view of the origin of
Mosaic Yahwism, in spite of the logic of some elements in the
theory. It has been pointed out that Jethro is called 'priest of
Midian', but never 'priest of Yahweh', and that in fact the *OT*
never directly says that Yahweh was the deity of the Midianites

or Kenites. It has been questioned whether the Hebrews in Egypt would have had faith in Moses if he had come to them in the name of a completely new deity, derived from a foreign source. Difficulties have been discovered in interpreting Exod. 18 as a ceremony in which the Israelites were inducted into the worship of Yahweh (see below, *in loc.*). Because of these and other questions that have been raised concerning the Midianite-Kenite theory, scholars have sought for the origin of 'Yahweh' and of Mosaic Yahwism in other places.

It is difficult to avoid associating the origin of the name 'Yahweh' with the element *Yahwi* (written *yaḥwi* or *yawi*) which occurs in Amorite personal names, such as 'Yahwi-Ila', 'Yahwi-Addu', and 'Yahwi-Dagan'. The element *Yahwi* is a verbal form that means 'he [the god Ila, Addu, or Dagan] causes to be, or live', or, less likely, 'he is (present)'. Further, there is a place name 'Yahwe' that occurs in Egyptian texts of the latter part of the second millennium; one is 'Yahwe of the land of the Shasu [a semi-nomadic people living in south Palestine or Edom]' (see R. Giveon, *VT*, XIV [1964], pp. 239–55).

These names take us back to the time before Moses lived into the patriarchal age. The patriarchs had close relationships with the people known as Amorites, proto-Arameans, or the like. It is even possible that we should call the patriarchal figures Amorite or proto-Aramean. One of the significant forms of religion known to the patriarchs was the worship of patron gods, deities who revealed themselves to individuals and who then became the patrons of those individuals and of their descendants. Specifically, we hear in the patriarchal narratives of the worship of the 'Fear of Isaac' (Gen. 31:42,53), the 'Mighty One of Jacob' (Gen. 49:24), and perhaps the 'Shield of Abraham' (Gen. 15:1). Each of the principal patriarchs had a patron deity who was worshipped by himself and then in turn by his son, to whom the patron deity became known as 'the god of my father'. For further details of this type of cult, see A. Alt, 'The God of the Fathers', in his *Essays on Old Testament History and Religion* (1966), pp. 1–66. The phrase 'god of my father' appears in a cuneiform letter from Mari (*ANET*, pp. 628f.).

Now, there are three passages in which Yahweh is spoken of as 'the god of my (your) father' in relationship to Moses—Exod. 3:6; 15:2; 18:4. It seems quite possible, then, that Yahweh was the god of one of the ancestors of Moses, especially in view of the

fact that his mother, Jochebed, bears a name compounded with
Yo-, which is a shortened form of 'Yahweh' (6:20). The present
writer believes, therefore, that Yahweh (whose name is of Amorite
origin) was in the first instance the patron deity of one of the
ancestors of Moses; then he became the deity of the clan or tribe of
Moses; and finally, through the mediation of Moses himself, the
deity of the Hebrew people whom Moses led out of Egypt to the
border of the land of Canaan. He was at first the god of an individual, and his cult was especially suited to the needs of a nomadic
or semi-nomadic people. Following the analogy of the patriarchal
deities mentioned above, and using the Amorite meaning of the
verbal form, we may conjecture that the name of the patron
deity of Moses' unknown ancestor (whom we symbolize by the
letter N) was 'Yahweh-N', meaning 'He causes N to live', or
simply, 'the Sustainer of N'. When this deity ceased to be the
patron deity of an individual and became the deity of a clan and
then a people, the name of the ancestor was dropped and he was
known as 'Yahweh'. For further details of this view, see: J. P.
Hyatt, 'Yahweh as "the God of my Father",' *VT*, v (1955),
pp. 130–36; 'The Origin of Mosaic Yahwism', *The Teacher's
Yoke: Studies in Memory of Henry Trantham*, ed. E. J. Vardaman and
J. L. Garrett, jr., 1964, pp. 85–93; and 'Was Yahweh Originally a
Creator Deity?' *JBL*, LXXXVI (1967), pp. 369–77.

A somewhat different suggestion for the origin of the name
Yahweh along the lines of the present writer's theory has been
made by H. B. Huffmon (in a private communication). He points
to the existence of the name of the god of Tarqa, *ᵈyakrub-ʾel*,
meaning 'El has blessed' (sometimes written *ikrub-ʾel*); for details
see his *Amorite Personal Names in the Mari Texts*, 1965, p. 76.
In form and meaning this is like many names of persons, but it is
marked as a divine name by the use of the deity determinative
(*dingir*), and it appears to be Amorite rather than Akkadian.
Huffmon suggests that there may have been a god by the name of
ᵈyahwi-ʾel, who was designated as *ilu ʾabiya*, 'god of my father'.
This name was shortened to 'Yahweh, god of my father', perhaps
to indicate rejection of the god (in this instance El) in the second
element of the divine name.

An alternative theory of the origin of the name Yahweh has
been proposed by F. M. Cross, jr., 'Yahweh and the God of the
Patriarchs', *HTR*, LV (1962), pp. 225–58. He suggests that the
divine name developed from a form that was originally an

epithet (or cultic name) of El, perhaps ʾel *ḏū yahwī* (*ṣabaʾōt*), 'El who creates (the hosts of heaven)'. In the course of time, as he says, 'the god Yahweh split off from ʾEl in the radical differentiation of his cultus, ultimately ousting ʾEl from his place in the divine council'.

Further discoveries of texts and studies of the subject may bring a definitive answer to the problem of the origin of the name Yahweh and of Mosaic Yahwism.

INSTRUCTIONS TO MOSES **3:16–22**

16. Moses is instructed to speak to **the elders of Israel,** and they will accompany him when he goes to the king of Egypt (verse 18). These were the older, leading men of the Hebrew families in Egypt, who represented the people in a number of instances. Note that J says nothing about Aaron accompanying Moses; contrast 4:29.

17. On the list of people here, cf. on 3:8 above.

18. Yahweh is here called **the God of the Hebrews,** a designation frequently used by Moses and other Israelites in speaking to the Pharaoh (5:3; 7:16; 9:1,13; 10:3).

has met with us: J seems to imply that the experience related above was shared by the elders of Israel. Since the preserved account is largely from E, it is possible that J's account did differ in this detail, although it is difficult to see how the elders of Israel could have been included in the theophany on Sinai-Horeb. The request which they were instructed to make is not that they may go to the land of Canaan, but rather, **let us go a three days' journey into the wilderness, that we may sacrifice to the LORD our God.** This is implied in verse 12, and is the demand made later in 5:1,3 etc. Whether there was conscious deceit in their request we cannot now determine; the whole story is told from the viewpoint of a later time. But note that in 3:8,17 (both J), the promise to Israel is that God will bring them into the land of the Canaanites.

21–22. This instruction is repeated to Moses in 11:2, where both men and women are to ask of their neighbours, but only jewelry is mentioned; the spoliation of the Egyptians is later carried out, according to 12:35f. See comment on 12:35f.

MOSES TAUGHT THREE SIGNS **4:1–9**

When Moses protests that they will not believe Yahweh has appeared to him, he is taught three miracles which are to be 'signs' giving assurance of his divine commission. Moses is thus taught magic by the Lord of all wonders. The three he learns are transformation-miracles, in which one substance is changed into another. Moses himself performs two of the miracles immediately, perhaps to gain confidence, but the third can be carried out only in Egypt with the Nile water. We should note that Moses is repeatedly represented in the traditions as a wonder-worker, but the later classical prophets are seldom represented in this rôle.

There is some confusion in this narrative that can be partly resolved by source analysis. What is the audience before whom Moses is expected to perform his signs? The most natural assumption is that it is the Hebrew people, or their representatives the elders of Israel; we are told in verses 29–31 (J) that Moses and Aaron gathered the elders of Israel; then Aaron spoke the words of Yahweh and did the signs before all the people, who believed. Yet, in verse 21 (E) Moses is told to do the miracles before Pharaoh, and in 7:8–13 (P) the miracle of the rod becoming a serpent is performed by Aaron before the Pharaoh.

It is certain that Aaron played little, if any, rôle in the earliest tradition, and that his importance was greatly magnified by P. It is likely that J in its original form told how Moses gathered the elders of Israel and spoke to them about the appearance of Yahweh to him, as he is instructed to do in 3:16–17, and then went on to relate the performing of the signs when they expressed belief. Aaron has been secondarily introduced even in the J narrative of 4:29–31.

2. The rod in Moses' hand here was his shepherd's staff. E speaks later of a 'rod of God' which is given by Yahweh to Moses (verses 17,20b), and in P the rod wielded by Aaron plays a very prominent rôle (7:9,19; 8:5,16).

3–4. The magical trick here performed is probably based on knowledge of an Egyptian snake-charmer's trick. The sign appears to be the reverse of the trick in which the charmer makes the snake straight and rigid by some form of mesmerism, and then breaks the spell when he grasps the snake by the tail. Snakes were common in Egypt and in the wilderness; in Num. 21:9 Moses erects a bronze serpent to heal persons bitten by snakes.

5 is very loosely connected with the preceding and is doubtless an addition; it virtually repeats the words of 3:16.

6–8. Leprosy was generally considered by the Israelites as an affliction sent directly by God, and its healing was an act of

divine grace. Here the instantaneous affliction and the equally
instantaneous healing constitute a supernatural wonder that may
serve as a 'sign'. Nowhere are we told later that this wonder was
performed.

9. This is not specifically called a 'sign', but is no doubt intended
as such. Moses does not carry this out, but in 7:17–24 Aaron
strikes the Nile water with his rod and it becomes blood; the
Egyptian magicians are able to do the same. There it is the first of
the ten plagues related in Exodus.

AARON APPOINTED AS MOSES' SPOKESMAN 4:10–17

10–12. Moses enters his third protest: he is not eloquent, but
slow of speech; even the appearance of Yahweh to him has not
given him the ability to speak eloquently. The Hebrew literally
translated is picturesque: 'Not a man of words am I . . . for heavy
of mouth and heavy of tongue am I'. In a similar circumstance,
Jeremiah says, 'Ah, Lord God! Behold, I do not know how to
speak, for I am only a youth' (Jer. 1:6). The reply to Moses is
that Yahweh is his Creator who has made his mouth and is able to
make him speak well. He will accompany Moses, and make it
possible to speak what he is required to speak.

13–17. Moses makes his fourth and final protest, as he says
brusquely, in the Hebrew literally rendered, 'Oh, my Lord, send
I pray by the hand of whom thou wilt send!' It is not surprising
that on this occasion **the anger of the LORD was kindled
against Moses,** but Yahweh is still patient with him and meets
this final protest by appointing Aaron as his spokesman. We assign
this section to E, who makes Aaron a person of considerable
importance, though not as much as P. Some critics consider it to
be a secondary addition to J.

14. Is there not Aaron, your brother, the Levite? Aaron is
here apparently considered the blood brother of Moses. We
should note, however, that Aaron is represented as calling Moses
'my lord' in 32:22; Num. 12:11; and that in Num. 12 Aaron is
pictured as an antagonist of Moses, along with Miriam. In Exod.
33:11 (E) Joshua is named as Moses' assistant in the tent of
meeting, not Aaron. Possibly the word 'brother' is here intended
in a general sense as 'kinsman'. In any event, it is only in the less
ancient tradition that Aaron is so closely associated with Moses.
In the P account of 6:30—7:5, he is Moses' brother and is appointed
to be Moses' spokesman.

Aaron is a **Levite**. The term may mean only 'priest', and not necessarily a member of the tribe of Levi. In P, Aaron is the first high priest and the ancestor of all legitimate priests.

15–16. A prophet was one who spoke for God; God placed his words in the mouth of the prophet, who thus became the mouth or the spokesman of God. This is set forth in passages such as Dt. 18:18; Jer. 1:7; 15:19; Ezek. 3:1–3. Moses is here to be **as God**, in that he is to be the one for whom Aaron is the speaker; this is more clearly stated by P in 7:1, 'I make you as God to Pharaoh; and Aaron your brother shall be your prophet'.

We should observe, however, that Aaron serves only seldom as the spokesman or representative for Moses. Moses usually acts and speaks himself as a representative of Yahweh. Cf. comment on 7:1.

17. Here the **rod** is the same as the **rod of God** given to Moses in 20*b* (also E), a wand by which Moses performs miracles. In 4:2 the rod is the shepherd's staff; with it Moses does a 'sign', turning the rod itself into a serpent.

THE RETURN OF MOSES TO EGYPT 4:18–31

18–23(J,E). *Yahweh commands Moses to return to Egypt, and he obtains permission from Jethro for the journey. Taking his wife and son(s), he sets out for Egypt. Yahweh tells him to perform before Pharaoh the miracles he has put in his power, and to declare that Yahweh will kill Pharaoh's first-born son if he does not release Israel, Yahweh's first-born.*

24–26(J). *At a lodging place on the way, Yahweh attempts to kill him (Moses?). Zipporah circumcises her son and touches his (Moses'?) feet, saying 'You are a bridegroom of blood to me'. So Yahweh lets him alone.*

27–31(J,E). *Yahweh sends Aaron to meet Moses. They gather the elders of Israel, speak to them the words of Yahweh, and do the signs in their presence. The people believe and bow down in worship.*

The sources are principally J and E. The inconsistency between 18 and 19 indicates clearly the presence of two sources. 24–26 is assigned to J as one of the most 'primitive' passages in the whole of the Pentateuch, and 29–31 relate the carrying out of instructions given in 3:16ff., with the name of Aaron as a secondary insertion. E is recognizable in 20*b* by the 'rod of God', and in 27–28 by the 'mountain of God' and other evidence.

21–23 present problems in source analysis as well as interpretation. Most critics assign verse 21 to E and verses 22–23 to J.

However, verse 21 has some marks of P: the Hebrew word for 'miracles' (*mōpᵉṭîm*) is used elsewhere in Exodus only by P (7:3,9; 11:9–10); the word describing the hardening of heart of Pharaoh is used by both P and E (see comment on 7:3). Yet, there is apparently no P material in 3:1—6:2. The words in verse 23 by which Moses demands the release of Israel are similar to those employed by J in the plague narratives (7:16; 8:1,20; 9:1,13; 10:3), but it is only in this section within the entire *OT* that Israel is called the first-born of Yahweh (used of Ephraim in Jer. 31:9). It is quite possible, as some scholars have suggested, that verses 22–23 originally stood before 10:28 or 11:4 as J's introduction to the tenth plague; the natural place for them would be between the first nine plagues and the tenth plague (the tenses in verse 22 are more accurately rendered: 'and I *said*' and 'you *have refused*'). These two verses may have been removed to their present place by a redactor in order to indicate what he took to be the purpose of the series of ten plagues, for they attach easily to verse 21.

The source analysis here is as follows: J—4:19–20*a*,22–26, 29–31; E—4:18,20*b*,21,27–28.

DEPARTURE OF MOSES FROM MIDIAN 4:18–23

18. Moses receives permission from his father-in-law to return to Egypt to see if his kinsmen are still alive. Most Hebrew MSS. have 'Jether' instead of **Jethro** as the name of the father-in-law; see the comment on 2:18. The **kinsmen** (Hebrew, 'my brothers') would be his own physical kin, perhaps just his own brothers, and not all of the Israelites. Note that he is not represented as telling Jethro of the theophany on Sinai. This speaks somewhat against the theory that Yahweh was originally a Midianite deity.

19. It is very strange that here Moses is commanded by God to return to Egypt, when verse 18 has just said that he had determined to do so and obtained permission from Jethro. This must be from a different source, J. LXX has at the beginning of 19 the sentence, 'After those many days, the king of Egypt died', as in 2:23*a*. Some critics think that 4:19f. originally followed 2:23*a*, and thus that in J's original account the experience of Moses at the burning bush took place as Moses was on his way to Egypt. This could be correct only if 3:1 is from a source other than J.

20. Moses is here said to have taken **his wife and his sons** back to Egypt in the Hebrew text. However, the birth of only one son has been mentioned previously (2:22), and the presence of only one son seems to be implied in the incident of 4:24-26. In 18:2-4 the names of two sons are given, and it is said that Moses had sent his wife back to Midian from Egypt, and Jethro subsequently brought her and the children to meet Moses at the mountain of God. In the present verse we should possibly read 'his son'. The last clause **and in his hand Moses took the rod of God** is from E; see comment on verse 17.

21. Moses is to **do before Pharaoh all the miracles which I have put in your power:** these are not all the 'signs' of 4:1-9, but the rod wonder and the plagues that follow (7:8—11:10). The word here translated **miracles** is *mōpᵉtîm*, used elsewhere in Exodus only by P at 7:3; 11:9f., where *RSV* renders 'wonders'; in 7:9 the singular is rendered 'miracle'. The Hebrew word does not mean 'miracle' in the commonly accepted modern use of that word, an event or phenomenon that deviates from natural law or transcends our knowledge of it. The Israelites did not have a concept of natural law, but believed that God could act directly among men and in nature. The rendering 'wonders' would here be less open to misunderstanding.

I will harden his heart: it is repeatedly said in connection with the plagues that Yahweh hardens the heart of Pharaoh. God is in complete control, even to the point of making the Egyptian king stubborn and unwilling to release the Hebrews. See comment on 7:3.

22-23. This reference to Israel as **my first-born son,** and the threat to slay Pharaoh's first-born, are never repeated during the first nine plagues. This is the only passage in the *OT* in which Israel is referred to as the first-born, but Ephraim is called God's 'first-born' in Jer. 31:9.

INCIDENT AT A LODGING PLACE **4:24-26**

This is the most obscure passage in the book of Exodus. It has given rise to a number of different interpretations, none of which is wholly satisfactory. The obscurity arises in part from the extreme brevity of the account, and the indefiniteness of reference of several of the personal pronouns. In verse 25 the Hebrew does not say **Moses' feet,** as *RSV* renders, but only 'his feet', leaving open several possibilities as to the reference of the pronoun. The ancient versions differ at some points, but offer little help. They too sought to interpret a difficult text.

This section is assigned to the earliest strand of tradition by those who subdivide J (J[1], Eissfeldt's L, Fohrer's N). It is a very ancient, primitive story that pictures a 'demonic' Yahweh. It is very probable that it has been borrowed by the Israelites from a pagan source, possibly Midianite, and imperfectly assimilated to Israelite theology. The closest parallel is the story of Jacob's wrestling at night with a 'man' in Gen. 32:24-32. The original story may have concerned a demon or deity of the boundary between Midianite territory and Egypt whom Moses failed properly to appease. Some scholars have suggested it was a night demon contesting with Moses for the *ius primae noctis*.

The most common interpretation is as follows: As Moses and his family were journeying to Egypt, Yahweh sought to kill him, being angry because Moses had not been circumcised. Zipporah rose to the occasion and immediately circumcised her son; she touched the bloody foreskin of the son to the genitals of Moses (for which the euphemism 'his feet' is used). This served as a substitute for the circumcision of Moses, to whom Zipporah now said, 'Surely you are a bridegroom of blood to me!' Then Yahweh left Moses alone.

As an alternative interpretation which has recently been offered, we may refer to that of Hans Kosmala, 'The "Bloody Husband",' *VT*, xii (1962), pp. 14-28. He thinks the story was told here because the preceding verses speak of the death of a first-born son. The anger of the deity, who is a god of the Midianite desert, is directed against the child because he has not been circumcised. Zipporah cuts off his foreskin, and touches with the foreskin the legs of her son, as a blood rite to ward off evil by proving the circumcision has been performed. She then says a ritual formula to the child, 'A blood-circumcised one are you with regard to me'. The deity, seeing the blood and hearing Zipporah's words, disappears.

24. a lodging place: a place for spending the night; the same word is used in Gen. 42:27; 43:21 of the place where Joseph's brothers first stopped after leaving Egypt. It may have been a *khan*, with a rough enclosed court, or simply an open camping-ground.

sought to kill him: according to the Jewish commentator Rashi, Yahweh sought to kill Moses because he had not circumcised his son. See above for other interpretations. Cf. Gen. 38:10.

25. Zipporah took a flint: this indicates that circumcision originated in the age before iron implements began to be made (eleventh century B.C.); flint knives are prescribed for circumcision in Jos. 5:2.

touched Moses' feet: this is *RSV* interpretation; the Hebrew has only 'touched his feet'. In the usual interpretation, 'feet' is considered a euphemism for the genitals (cf. Isa. 6:2). Some interpretations take it literally.

a bridegroom of blood: this phrase is obviously an important part of the story, for it is repeated in verse 26. It is strange that Moses should be called a bridegroom long after his marriage, when one or more sons had been born to him and Zipporah. See above for an alternative rendering making it applicable to the child as one who had just been circumcised.

26 indicates that the story may have had an aetiological purpose, to explain the origin of the phrase used by Zipporah here. Some scholars think the story may have had some other aetiological purpose, such as to show when circumcision ceased to be a rite performed at marriage (or puberty) and was transferred to infancy. In any event, the narrator of this story (J) did not know the narrative in Gen. 17 which tells of the institution of circumcision in the time of Abraham; that narrative is by P, and was written much later.

MEETING OF AARON AND MOSES 4:27–31

27–28 is from E, relating how Yahweh sent Aaron to meet Moses, who told him of the words of Yahweh and the signs given to him. The mention of the **mountain of God** indicates that the incident is here out of place. The mountain of God was Horeb-Sinai (3:1; 18:5), which Moses had already left, according to 4:18. The correct place would be just after 4:17.

29–31 relates how the instructions given to Moses previously were carried out. It is most likely that Aaron is an insertion into the J narrative here. It was Moses who was charged to gather together the elders of Israel in 3:16, and he who was given the power to perform the signs and miracles, 4:1–9,17,21. Aaron was charged only with being Moses' spokesman (4:14–16), not a doer of signs. The name of Aaron has been inserted in other passages later, but not consistently and uniformly.

THE FIRST UNSUCCESSFUL APPEAL TO PHARAOH 5:1—6:1

5:1-5(J,E). *The Hebrews appeal to Pharaoh to let them go into the wilderness to sacrifice to Yahweh; he refuses, accusing Moses of wanting to make the people rest.*

6-14(J). *Pharaoh gives orders to the Egyptian taskmasters and Hebrew foremen to withhold straw from the Hebrews, but compel them to gather straw for the making of bricks and continue to produce the same daily quota of bricks. The foremen are beaten when it proves impossible to keep up the daily quotas.*

15-19(J). *The Hebrew foremen appeal to Pharaoh for straw, but he refuses, accusing them of idleness.*

20-6:1(J). *The foremen meet Moses and Aaron as they leave the Pharaoh's court, and blame them for putting them in danger of being killed. Moses turns to Yahweh and asks why Yahweh has done such evil to this people, and why Yahweh sent him to them. Yahweh replies that he will act in such a way that ultimately Pharaoh will with power drive the Hebrews out of Egypt.*

The source here is almost entirely J. However, verse 3 is a duplicate of verses 1–2, and verse 5 is a duplicate of verse 4. We assign verses 1–2 and 4 to E, partly because of their having Aaron as a partner of Moses. The rest, 5:3,5—6:1, is from J. Aaron has been secondarily introduced in verse 20.

It is remarkable that in this section Moses plays a rôle that is subsidiary to that of the Hebrew foremen, who deal directly with the king of Egypt. It appears that J has drawn upon a very ancient tradition in which foremen of the Hebrews who were working at the *corveé* in Egypt appealed to the Pharaoh as a result of their oppression. Noth has conjectured that underlying 5:3–19 was a special and probably very old narrative which began the account of the exodus from Egypt with the God of Israel meeting with his people *in Egypt* and summoning them to a feast in the wilderness. This seems improbable. There are close connections between chapter 5 and the two preceding chapters (especially with 3:18), and it seems hardly likely that a deity would appear to the Hebrews in Egypt and summon them to a feast elsewhere, in the desert. Nevertheless, the rôle which Moses is represented as playing in this chapter may be more historical than the rôle he is depicted as playing in later traditions, which magnified his power and importance.

PHARAOH SCORNS YAHWEH **5:1-5**

1. hold a feast to me in the wilderness: the Hebrew *ḥag*
was a pilgrimage to a sanctuary for the purpose of sacrifice; cf.
Arabic *haj*, the name for the pilgrimage to Mecca.

2. Who is the LORD? is here contemptuous, not a real
question. The Pharaoh was himself considered by the Egyptians
to be a deity, and he professes to know nothing of the God of the
Hebrews.

3. The words used here are almost exactly the same as those of
3:18. The appeal to Pharaoh was considered by J as being spoken
by Moses and the elders, according to the instructions given in
3:18. J's account of their going to the court of Pharaoh has not
been preserved.

5. the people of the land are now many: a better reading is
that of the Samaritan text, 'now they are more numerous than the
people of the land', the latter phrase meaning the natives of the
land of Egypt. *NEB* renders, 'Your people already outnumber the
native Egyptians'. Cf. 1:7,12 on the great numbers of the Hebrews
in Egypt.

THE OPPRESSION INCREASED **5:6-14**

7. let them go and gather straw for themselves: there is a
popular belief that the Israelites were ordered to 'make bricks
without straw', and that has given rise to a proverbial saying.
The biblical account says clearly that the Israelites were ordered
to secure their own straw, and yet not diminish their daily quotas.

Sun-dried mud bricks have been used in great numbers as
building materials in Egypt, from prehistoric times to the present.
The English word 'adobe' for such bricks is derived ultimately
from the Egyptian word for brick (*db-t*) by way of Arabic and
Spanish.

The mud of which these bricks were made was usually mixed
with some vegetable matter, ordinarily grass or straw. In the
bricks of the XIXth and XXth Dynasties this was most often
finely chopped straw. The vegetable matter served to make the
mud cohere, and thus strengthened the bricks. Some bricks were
made without such mixture. In the nineteenth century some
persons seriously claimed that the presence of bricks made without
straw—particularly at Tell el-Maskhuta (see comment on 1:11)—
proved the biblical account was authentic!

The details of ancient and modern brick-making in Egypt are well discussed in C. F. Nims, 'Bricks Without Straw', *BA*, XIII (1950), pp. 22–28. The process used in antiquity is represented in servant models and tomb paintings; see ANEP, no. 115. The context shows that **the taskmasters of the people** (verse 6) were Egyptian, and the **foremen** were the Hebrew overseers of labour gangs. The Egyptians dealt directly with the foremen, who supervised the Hebrew labourers. In verse 14, it is presumably the Egyptian taskmasters who beat the foremen, although this is not directly stated.

8. The Pharaoh thinks the Hebrews **are idle,** not having enough work to do (see also verse 17). He therefore takes measures to make their work harder, so that they will not have time to think about going into the wilderness for a sacred feast.

14. See comment on verse 7.

APPEAL OF THE FOREMEN TO YAHWEH **5:15–21**
The foremen of the people of Israel here make an appeal directly to the Pharaoh. The account represents them as having an audience with the King himself, while Moses and Aaron are waiting in an outer room to hear the results of their interview.

In the period of the XIXth Dynasty, slaves sometimes were permitted to make their complaints before the king, by-passing the complicated system of superintendents of State labour gangs. Sometimes their complaints were successful, as Egyptian records show. Here the Hebrew foremen appeal over the heads of the Egyptian taskmasters, perhaps thinking that the order may have been made by a subordinate. But the Pharaoh gives them no relief. He repeats the charge of idleness, and confirms the order that straw be withheld but the same quotas be maintained.

16. but the fault is in your own people: this rendering is based on a literal translation of the Hebrew as 'and your people have sinned'. It is doubtful, however, that the Hebrew can bear this translation, and such a rendering is very difficult to fit into the context. In what sense can the foremen be saying the Pharaoh's own people, the Egyptians, are at fault? LXX and Syriac appear to have a better text, which can be rendered, 'and you do wrong to your people'. This can mean either (a) you do wrong to the Egyptians by depriving them of a full quota of bricks, or (b) you do wrong to the Hebrews, who they here deferentially call, in speaking to the Pharaoh, 'your people'. The latter fits with their calling themselves three times **your servants.**

20–21. Aaron is a secondary addition here, as several other times in J (see comment on 4:29–30). In the succeeding verses Moses himself speaks to Yahweh (verse 22), and Yahweh replies to him (6:1). The foremen come out of the audience with Pharaoh to a point where Moses has been waiting for them. They blame him for their plight, and call upon Yahweh to punish him; they believe that Moses has put them in actual danger of death. They probably think the Pharaoh will kill them if they cannot continue to meet their daily quotas of bricks.

APPEAL OF MOSES TO YAHWEH **5:22—6:1**

22–23. Moses in his turn calls upon Yahweh, putting the blame upon him for the evil done to the Israelites by the Pharaoh. Moses had been reluctant to go at Yahweh's command, and now cries out, **Why didst thou ever send me?**

6:1. Yahweh promises Moses that he will act in such a manner that the Pharaoh will not simply wish to get rid of the Israelites, but will even want to **drive them out of his land.**
with a strong hand: with great power. This phrase sometimes refers to the power exerted by Yahweh (cf. 3:19), but here it may refer to the power with which Pharaoh will send the Hebrews away and drive them out. LXX and Syriac read in the last clause 'with outstretched arm'; this may be correct. The repetition of **with a strong hand** is somewhat awkward.

The continuation of J's narrative is in 7:14ff., the beginning of the plagues that impress the king of Egypt with Yahweh's power.

THE P ACCOUNT OF THE CALL OF MOSES **6:2–30**

2–9. *God reveals himself to Moses as 'Yahweh'. He recalls the covenant he had made, under the name of El Shaddai, with the patriarchs. Because of that covenant he is now about to redeem the Hebrews from Egyptian slavery, and bring them into the land he promised to the patriarchs. He sends Moses to the Israelites to announce their release, but they refuse to listen to him.*

10–13. *Yahweh then orders Moses to go to Pharaoh to demand the release of the Israelites. Moses objects that he is a man of uncircumcised lips to whom Pharaoh will not listen.*

14–25. *A genealogy that begins with three sons of Jacob and traces the*

ancestry of Aaron and Moses through Levi, and then of Phinehas, who was
five generations from Levi.
26–30. *A recapitulation of verses 10–12.*

This section is from P, the latest of the sources of Exodus. It is the
first long section in the book from that source. It is roughly parallel
to 3:1—4:31, which is JE's account of virtually the same events.
P has a somewhat different order, and differs in a few details.
When we come to 7:14, we are back at the point at which JE had
arrived at 6:1, when the plagues are to begin. 7:1–13 is somewhat
parallel to 5:1—6:1, but we have taken 7:1–13 as the introduction
to the long account of the ten plagues and the exodus of Israel.

Verses 13–27 break into the narrative, and verses 28–30 re-
capitulate what had been said in verses 10–12. These verses
(13–30) are thus secondary to the basic Priestly narrative, and have
as their primary purpose to give the lineage of Aaron and Moses,
especially the former.

Several of P's characteristics appear in this section. He depicts
the call of Moses as having taken place in Egypt, not Midian.
Aaron plays a prominent rôle. Yahweh is completely sovereign,
and is concerned to demonstrate his power.

YAHWEH'S PLAN FOR ISRAEL **6:2–9**

2. I am the Lord: that is, 'I am Yahweh'. This is P's parallel
to 3:15. He follows E in believing that God did not reveal himself
by that name until the time of Moses. God had used the name
Elohim before the time of Abraham, and then revealed himself to
Abraham and his descendants as *El Shaddai*. The phrase 'I am
Yahweh' appears several times as a refrain in this narrative:
6:2,6,7,8,29. For P it is an assertion not only that this is the name
of God, but that Yahweh is the only God who exists and exerts his
sovereign power in the affairs of men. It appears elsewhere in P,
and is especially frequent in the Holiness Code (Lev. 17—26).

**3. I appeared to Abraham, to Isaac, and to Jacob as God
Almighty:** see Gen. 17:1; 28:3; 35:11; 48:3. The Hebrew
rendered **God Almighty** is *ʾēl šaddai* (see *RSV* mg.). P considers
this as the principal name used by God in the patriarchal age, but
the precise meaning of *šaddai* is not known. It occurs in this form, or
as *šaddai* alone, in P, 31 times in Job, and a few times in other books.
The translation 'Almighty' is based upon the translation given in
some places by LXX, *pantokrátōr* and the Vulgate, *omnipotens*.

This is plausible if the word is derived from the Hebrew root *šdd*, meaning 'deal violently', 'devastate', and thus 'show great power'. Some scholars associate *šaddai* with the Assyro-Babylonian word *šadû*, 'mountain'. *Šaddai* would thus indicate a mountain deity, or a deity who is like a mountain—firm, solid, high etc.

4. P lays emphasis on the covenant made with Abraham. This covenant included the promise of the land of Canaan (Gen. 17:8). The Abrahamic covenant is now made the basis of the exodus from Egypt and the entrance into the land of promise.

5 is almost the same as 2:24. Here Yahweh says in the first person what was related there in the third person.

6. I will redeem you: it is unusual to employ the verb *gāʾal* 'redeem' for the exodus from Egypt, thus using figuratively the legal practice of redemption which is described in Lev. 25. It is used of the exodus also in Exod. 15:13. Second Isaiah uses the word frequently for the new exodus from the exile, Yahweh being the 'redeemer' (Isa. 41:14; 43:1,14; 44:22; 47:4 etc.).

with great acts of judgment: the Hebrew word *šépeṭ* (used in the pl. *šepāṭîm*) here has a meaning close to the meaning that the related word *ṣédeḳ* (or *ṣedāḳāh*) sometimes has—'deliverance', 'saving act', and the like (see RSV rendering in passages such as Mic. 6:5; Isa. 46:13; 51:5,6,8). God's acts will be punishment for the enemies of Israel, but salvation and deliverance for Israel; they will in the end create a condition of justice. The word is used by P in 7:4; 12:12; Num. 33:4. It is frequent in Ezekiel (5:10,15; 11:9; 16:41 etc.), where it usually means punishments.

7. The fundamental idea of the covenant relationship is expressed here: Israel is to be the people of Yahweh, and Yahweh is to be the God of Israel; cf. Lev. 26:12; Dt. 26:17f.; 29:13; Jer. 7:23; Ezek. 11:20 etc.

you shall know that I am the LORD your God: Israel will know Yahweh as her God through the acts that he performs on her behalf in their history.

9. The people refuse to listen to Moses or to believe his promises of deliverance from bondage, because they have become dispirited and brokenhearted under the cruel hardships of slavery. This is in direct contrast to 4:31 (J) where we are told that the people believed the words of Moses, and bowed their heads and worshipped. For P the refusal of the people to believe Moses is made the reason for his hesitating to go to speak to Pharaoh.

MOSES' OBJECTION **6:10–13**

12. Moses complains that he is **a man of uncircumcised lips:**
his lips are closed, and thus he is slow of speech and not eloquent;
cf. 4:10 (J). Elsewhere the figure is used of the uncircumcised
heart (Jer. 9:26) and of the uncircumcised ear (Jer. 6:10). Note
that the answer to Moses' complaint made here does not come
until 7:1.

THE GENEALOGY OF MOSES AND AARON **6:14–25**

Verses 14–30 are an interruption of the narrative, made by a
second Priestly hand. The main purpose of the insertion is to
give the lineage of Moses and Aaron, especially of Aaron. Aaron
occupies a very important rôle in P as the chief priest and as the
ancestor of the legitimate priesthood of the time when P wrote
(see especially Exod. 29:7–9; Lev. 8:1–9). P wishes to show that
Aaron the priest had an important part to play in the founding
of the nation, alongside Moses the prophet.

This is not a complete genealogical list. Of the sons of Jacob, it
lists only the first three, giving largely the information of Gen.
46:8–11. For Reuben and Simeon only one generation of descendants is given; the interest centres on the descendants of Levi,
traced out in part to the fifth generation. The descent goes through
Kohath, Levi's son, and then through Amram, Aaron, and Eleazar
to Phinehas. See the similar lists in Num. 3:17ff.; 26:57ff.

14. fathers' houses: this is a vague term. Theoretically it
should indicate a house or family descended from a single ancestor.
Sometimes it designates a tribe, but more often what we would
term a clan or a family. It has various meanings in this section.

20. Jochebed is the name of the mother of Moses and Aaron;
the name occurs elsewhere only in Num. 26:59 (P). The name
apparently means 'Yahweh is glory', the name of Yahweh appearing in a shortened form, Yo, as frequently in personal names.
If this is correct, it is evidence for knowledge of Yahweh in the
family of Moses before his own time. Because this name occurs
only in P, some scholars have no confidence in its authenticity.
Jochebed is here said to be Amram's **father's sister.** Amram
thus marries his aunt. Such a marriage is forbidden in Lev. 18:12,
a part of the Priestly code. P may therefore preserve an old tradition, but it is not necessarily historically accurate.
she bore him Aaron and Moses: at least one Hebrew MS., the

Samaritan text, and LXX add, 'and Miriam their sister'. She is
mentioned as sister of Aaron in 15:20. If she was the sister mentioned in Exodus 2, she must have been older than Moses.

21. Korah participated in a rebellion against Moses, and most
of those who took part were put to death (Num. 16), but the sons
of Korah did not perish with their father (Num. 16:32).

23. Eleazar succeeded Aaron as chief priest, according to
Dt. 10:6 and Num. 20:26 (P).

25. Putiel is not mentioned elsewhere, but the name is believed
to be Egyptian, meaning 'He whom El gave'. (Cf. Potiphar or
Potiphera, meaning 'He whom Re gave'). **Phinehas** is likewise
an Egyptian name, meaning 'The Nubian'. Phinehas is referred
to as a priest in Jg. 20:28, a successor to Eleazar and Aaron.

The interest of P is shown here in the fact that no descendants
of Moses are named, but Aaron's descendants are named for two
generations. It is somewhat strange that the genealogy is taken
beyond Aaron, and it is not obvious why it is given only through
Phinehas.

RECAPITULATION **6:26–30**
After this interruption the second P editor resumes the narrative, repeating in verses 26–30 the information of verses 10–12
above.

26. by their hosts: this might be rendered 'in battle order',
as by JB. The word 'hosts' (meaning armies) is used only
by P of the Israelites in their exodus from Egypt (Exod. 7:4;
12:17,41,51; Num. 1:3; 2:4,6 etc.). He seems to have thought of
the Israelites as marching out of Egypt and through the desert in
battle array.

30. I am of uncircumcised lips: see comment on verse 12
above.

THE TEN PLAGUES IN EGYPT 7:1—13:16

These six chapters constitute a well constructed unit, and should
be considered one of the major divisions of the book of Exodus.
There is first a general introduction, in which Yahweh declares in
advance what will happen (7:1–5). Then comes the 'miracle' of
changing a rod into a serpent, intended to authenticate Moses and
Aaron (in the Priestly narrative this may have been counted as the

first plague). Next follow nine plagues, after each of which
Pharaoh's heart is hard so that he refuses to release the Israelites
(7:14—10:29). Finally, the last plague occurs, the death of the
Egyptian first-born; the Hebrews are given permission to leave
Egypt after celebrating the Passover (11:1—13:16). The account
up to the tenth plague is artfully and skilfully constructed; the
final plague does not fit well into the literary pattern of the
others, but stands apart from all the others in that it is the last
and climactic plague, after which the Hebrews make their
exodus.

The literary analysis of these chapters is relatively easy. The
opening verses, 7:1–13, are from P. The account of the ten plagues
is a combination of at least two sources, J and P, and possibly of
the three sources J, E and P.

The J source constitutes the basic and oldest narrative of these
chapters. J usually follows a regular pattern in recounting the
story of the plagues. Moses is instructed to go before Pharaoh and
speak to him, demanding that he let the Israelites go in order that
they may worship Yahweh. The interview is described in some
detail, and Moses announces the plague that will come. Yahweh
brings the plague, without intervention by Moses or Aaron.
Then there are usually negotiations between Moses and the
Pharaoh, and the Egyptian king asks Moses to intercede for him.
Yahweh removes the plague, but the heart of Pharaoh is still hard,
and he refuses to allow the Hebrews to leave. J's pattern is not,
however, followed rigidly. J represents Israel as living in Goshen
apart from the Egyptians (8:22; 9:26). The style of these sections
is lively and vivid, like J in the preceding narratives. It has
certain peculiarities of vocabulary. For example, only J uses the
title 'God of the Hebrews' for Yahweh (7:16; 9:1,13; 10:3), and
in describing the hardness of Pharaoh's heart, J uses the Hebrew
word *kābēd* in *qal* or *hifil*, whereas the rest of the narrative uses
ḥāzak, except in one place, where *ḳāṣāh* is employed (7:3).

The P narrative differs from the above both in its literary
features and in its conception of the manner in which the plagues
are brought about. The main distinction is that Aaron is represented as co-operating with Moses; Aaron usually stretches out
his rod like a wand to bring on the plagues. There is no interview
with Pharaoh, and the descriptions are brief. In general the
plagues in P tend to be more spectacular and more 'miraculous'
than in the rest of the narrative. The sections which can be

assigned to P are easily distinguished as follows: 7:19–20*a*,21*b*–22; 8:5–7,15*b*–19; 9:8–12; 11:9–10; 12:1–20,28,40–51.

Aside from these two sources, there are some passages which do not fit into the patterns described. The chief feature of such passages has to do with the rôle of Moses. In them he (rather than Aaron) uses his rod as a wand to bring on the plague; in the case of the plague of darkness he appears to use his hand in the same way (10:21–22). Most scholars believe that these passages represent fragments of an E narrative; it is clear that we do not have E in anything approaching the completeness with which J and P are preserved. A few scholars think that only two sources, J and P, are to be distinguished in the account of the plagues (e.g. Noth, Rudolph, Winnett), although they find it necessary to consider as additions or glosses some of the passages generally assigned to E, or assign some of them to P instead. In our discussion we shall assume that fragments of E are preserved in the plague narratives. The details will be discussed in the treatment of the separate plagues. Only one plague, that of darkness, appears to have been preserved in E alone.

In the literary analysis it becomes apparent that none of the three sources has preserved all of the ten plagues. The following table will show at a glance how the plagues are preserved by the different sources.

		J	E	P
1.	Blood	J	E	P
2.	Frogs	J	—	P
3.	Gnats	—	—	P
4.	Flies	J	—	—
5.	Cattle plague	J	—	—
6.	Boils	—	—	P
7.	Hail	J	E	—
8.	Locusts	J	E	—
9.	Darkness	—	E	—
10.	Death of First-born	J	E	P

In this table it is immediately obvious that the three sources preserve an account of only the first and last; E's portion of the last is in fact very brief. Only P preserves a record of 3 and 6; only J preserves a record of 4 and 5. The account of the plague of darkness is only in E. It is probable that 3 and 4 are variant accounts of the same tradition; and the same may be true of 5 and 6. E's plague of darkness may be a variant of one of the others (eighth or tenth).

This listing makes it apparent that the idea of *ten* plagues leading up to the exodus is not a part of the early traditions. J has seven plagues, and E has five. P has five, or six if we count the rod wonder as a plague (as P himself may have counted it). In two of the Psalms, 78:43–51 and 105:28–36, the plagues are recounted, but the order and number varies. We must conclude that the traditions regarding the plagues grew and developed over a long period of time, during which there were variations in the number and order, as well as in the representation, of the several plagues. The present arrangement is the work of the final redactor of Exodus.

The story of the plagues is the account of a confrontation between Yahweh, God of the Hebrews, and the gods of Egypt— and Pharaoh himself was considered a god by his subjects. Yet, it is not really a contest to subdue the spirit and coerce the will of Pharaoh, for Yahweh says in advance, 'I will harden Pharaoh's heart, and though I multiply my signs and wonders in the land of Egypt, Pharaoh will not listen to you' (7:3–4). The real purpose of the plagues is expressed in the sentence, 'And the Egyptians shall know that I am Yahweh' (7:5). Sometimes addressed to Pharaoh, this idea is repeated in 7:17; 8:22, and then it is varied in 8:10; 9:14,29, to the assertion that there is no one like Yahweh, and that the earth is Yahweh's. According to 9:16, Yahweh let Pharaoh live to show Pharaoh his power, so that his name might be declared throughout all the earth.

In the narration of the plagues there is nevertheless evidence of progress, of movement toward a goal. This is most clearly evident in what is said of the attitude of the Pharaoh. He is unmoved by the rod trick and the first two plagues, which his magicians can emulate. After the third, he is willing to let the Hebrews sacrifice in Egypt (8:25), and then a short distance from the land (8:28). After the seventh, he confesses he has sinned and agrees to let the Hebrews go (9:27f.), but then hardens his heart again. Just before the eighth, he tries to negotiate with Moses to let only the men depart, but Moses will not agree (10:8–11). After the eighth the Pharaoh confesses that he has sinned against Yahweh and against Moses, and asks intercession to remove the death from him (10:16f.). After the ninth, he is willing to let them go without their flocks and herds. Finally, after the plague of death on the first-born, Pharaoh is willing to let all go as Moses has requested, and he asks a blessing from the Hebrew leader (12:31f.)! In asking a blessing, Pharaoh confesses the power of Yahweh.

There are some other signs of progress in the narrative. The first two plagues, along with the wonder of converting a rod into a snake, all appear to be magical tricks, which the Egyptian magicians also can perform. With the third, they confess that the plague is brought on by 'the finger of God' (8:19), and they cannot emulate it, and they too suffer in later plagues. This somewhat primitive conception of the plagues as magic, produced by the wand of Aaron, gives way in the later plagues to the impression that they are produced by Yahweh as they are announced by his servant, Moses. This impression results in part from the fact that the P source is not used by the redactor after the sixth plague, until the last one is reached. Yet, it is not correct to say that the plagues become increasingly severe in their effect upon the Egyptians, except in the very general sense that they culminate in the severest of all, the death of the first-born.

In their present sequence the plagues involve several inconsistencies which give evidence for the view that they were transmitted separately, or in separate groups, before being put into their present form. The final redactor has not gone to the trouble to eliminate the inconsistencies, if he noticed them. The most glaring example of this is the series of statements made concerning the animals of Egypt: in 9:6 all the domestic animals of the Egyptians die, the Israelites' animals being spared; in 9:10, in the very next plague, the animals are afflicted with boils along with the people; and finally in 9:25 the hailstorm strikes down everything that is in the field, both man and beast. We cannot eliminate the difficulties by stressing the use of different words in Hebrew, *miḳneh* and *bᵉhēmāh*, for essentially the same domestic animals must be meant in all three cases. Sometimes there are puzzling statements within the account of a single plague by the same narrator. For example, in the first plague as told by P, all the water of Egypt—in the rivers, canals, ponds, pools and even sap of the trees—is turned into blood (7:19,21b), but immediately afterward we are informed that 'the magicians of Egypt did the same by their secret arts' (7:22). To the modern mind the transformation miracle itself is incredible, and he is further inclined to ask where the water came from for the magicians to operate upon! The ancient narrator probably had no difficulty believing that the water all over Egypt was transformed into blood by Yahweh's power, then transformed back into water, and then into blood again by the Egyptian magicians! A form-critical analysis of this material is given by Dennis J. McCarthy, in 'Moses' Dealings with Pharaoh: Exodus 7:8— 10:27', *CBQ*, xxvii (1965), pp. 336–47, and in 'Plagues and Sea of Reeds: Exodus 5—14', *JBL*, lxxxv (1966), pp. 137–58. He sees 7:8—10:27 as a well-constructed unit using a complex concentric literary scheme; it is continued in 14:1–31. 11:1—12:42, on the other hand, he thinks, is a continuation of 6:2—7:7.

(P) Aaron Appointed as Prophet of Moses 7:1–7

Yahweh designates Aaron as the prophet (spokesman) for Moses. Yahweh promises that he will show many signs and wonders in Egypt, but will harden Pharaoh's heart so that he will not listen to Moses and Aaron. Yahweh will ultimately bring Israel out by great acts of judgement, and the Egyptians will know that he is Yahweh. A note is added of the ages of Moses and Aaron.

This section is entirely from P, continuing P's narrative of the preceding chapter. Moses protested in 6:12 that he was 'a man of uncircumcised lips'. After a long insertion giving the genealogy of Moses and Aaron, the protest is repeated in 6:30. 7:1 follows then as the response of Yahweh to the protest.

These verses form an appropriate introduction to the account of the ten plagues and the release of the Hebrews from Egypt, telling in advance what is to happen, and why it will happen as it does.

1. I make you as God to Pharaoh: cf. 4:15–16. These words are subject to misunderstanding. The meaning is not that Moses is to have divine power, but rather that in the dealings with Pharaoh Moses will serve in the position that a deity serves in relationship to his own spokesman: the deity places his words in the mouth of his prophet-spokesman, who then delivers them to the intended recipient. In the situation here, **Aaron your brother shall be your prophet.** This is one of the clearest indications in the *OT* that the word *nābî'* can have the basic meaning of 'spokesman'. It is significant, as observed above on 4:15–16, that in the sequel Aaron is not represented as speaking to the Pharaoh. On some occasions he does use his rod as a wand to produce wonders, but it is Moses who speaks to Pharaoh. It would be straining the evidence to say that Moses spoke in Hebrew to

Pharaoh and Aaron translated into the Egyptian language. Moses does not protest lack of knowledge of the Egyptian tongue, but lack of facility in speaking at all. The name of Aaron has been awkwardly inserted at several points—8:8,25; 9:27; 10:3,16.

3. I will harden Pharaoh's heart: this has already been said in 4:21 (E), using a different Hebrew word. The narrative of the plagues in Exodus frequently affirms in one way or another that Yahweh hardened the heart of the Pharaoh so that he refused to release the Hebrews. It is stated by R_D in 10:1 (assigned by some critics to J); by E in 4:21; 10:20,27; and several times by P (7:3; 9:12; 11:10; 14:4,8). P says in 14:17 that Yahweh will harden the heart of the Egyptians so that they will pursue the Israelites into the sea. In a few passages a Hebrew verb is used which requires that we read 'Pharaoh's heart was hard' (J in 7:14; 9:7; E in 9:35; P in 7:13,22; 8:19). This is more accurate than 'was (or remained) hardened' in *RSV*, for the verb is a *qal* form, not a passive or reflexive. Three times J says that the Pharaoh hardened his own heart (8:15,32; 9:34). J uses the *hifil* of *kābēd* in those passages, and R_D in 10:1. The most usual word in E and P translated 'harden' is a *piel* of *ḥāzaḳ*, but P once uses *hifil* of *ḳāṣāh*, 7:3).

It is not difficult to understand how the belief arose that it was Yahweh who hardened the heart of the Egyptian king. The story of the exodus included the report that Pharaoh did not readily permit the Hebrews to depart. He resisted their demands, and did not consent until after many incidents that the Israelites interpreted as constituting signs and wonders of their God. In the course of re-telling the exodus story and reflecting upon it, they came to believe that the will of Yahweh could not in any sense be thwarted by the will of the pagan ruler. Thus there arose the belief that the heart of Pharaoh was stubborn precisely because that was the will of the Hebrew God, who hardened Pharaoh's heart. As the story of the exodus was told and re-told, the Israelites came to believe more and more in the complete sovereignty of their God. The final redactor of Exodus did not remove J's assertions that the Egyptian king hardened his own heart. The tension between divine determinism and human freedom is not actually resolved, but the balance is in favour of the former.

In the subsequent events we thus do not have a true contest of wills between Yahweh and Pharaoh. Pharaoh is not really free to oppose the will of Yahweh—at least in the dominant tradition. The 'signs and wonders' have the effect of enhancing the glory and the power of Yahweh, although the record subtly represents Pharaoh as gradually relenting. At the very end, however, Yahweh hardens the heart of the Egyptians, so that they rush to their own death in pursuit of the fleeing Israelites (14:17).

4. my hosts: my armies. See comment on 6:26.

great acts of judgment: see comment on 6:6.

5. the Egyptians shall know that I am the LORD: they will learn that the will of Yahweh is supreme as they see him acting in the history of Israel, to bring Israel out of Egypt. The phrase, 'you (they) shall know that I am Yahweh' is very frequent in Ezekiel, occurring more than fifty times (6:7,10,13,14; 7:4,9 etc.). Ezekiel and P show many affinities in literary style and ideas.

7. Moses' lifetime, according to the later tradition, was 120 years, divided into three periods: forty years in Midian, and forty years each during the exodus and in wandering in the wilderness (see Dt. 34:7 and comment on 2:11). Aaron is represented as the older brother by three years (cf. 4:15 and comment there).

(P) THE MIRACLE OF TRANSFORMING RODS INTO SERPENTS
7:8-13

Pharaoh requests a miracle from Moses and Aaron. Aaron casts down his rod, and it becomes a serpent. The magicians of Egypt are able to perform the same wonder, but Aaron's rod swallows up their rods. Still Pharaoh's heart is hard and he will not heed their request.

This narrative, like the preceding, is wholly from P. This incident is related to 4:1-4(J), but the present section has a few differences in detail. In the former narrative, Moses is instructed in the serpent sign that is to be performed before the people of Israel (or the elders) to prove that he has had a vision of Yahweh. After the rod is transformed into a serpent, Moses is able to turn it back into a rod. Here the wonder is performed by Aaron in the presence of Pharaoh and his court, in response to the King's request. The serpent is not changed back into a rod, but at the end Aaron's serpent-rod swallows up the serpent-rods of the Egyptian magicians, thereby proving his superior magical power received from Yahweh.

9. Prove yourselves by working a miracle: this is a slight over-translation of the Hebrew, but a valid interpretation. The Hebrew is literally, 'give for yourselves a wonder', the personal pronoun being reflexive, or in the 'ethical dative'. On the word **miracle,** see the extended comment on 4:21. A rendering such as 'wonder', 'marvel', or the like would be better.

serpent: here and in verses 10, 12, the Hebrew is *tannîn*, whereas *nāḥāš* is employed in 4:3 and 7:15. *tannîn* is used of various large reptiles (cf. Gen. 1:21; Dt. 32:33), but is more frequently employed of mythological dragons or monsters (Job 7:12; Ps. 74:13; Isa. 27:1; 51:9; Jer. 51:34). *nāḥāš* is the ordinary word for snake. The use of *tannîn* here gives the impression of a greater marvel being performed.

11. The wonder is performed also by the **magicians of Egypt.** The names of Jannes and Jambres were given to these magicians by Jewish tradition of a much later time (see 2 Tim. 3:8, Jerusalem Targum etc.). The Hebrew word for 'magicians', *ḥarṭummîm*, is used (always in the plural) only in this section of Exodus (7:22; 8:7,18,19; 9:11), in the story of Joseph (Gen. 41:8,24), and in Dan. 1:20; 2:2. It is derived from an Egyptian word, *hry-tp*, which meant originally 'chief lector-priest' (see J. Vergote, *Joseph en Egypte* [1959], pp. 66–73). Originally in Egypt it applied to religious functionaries who took part in the liturgy, but the liturgy included spells, incantations, and the like, especially in funerary ceremonies. In Egypt religion and magic were closely associated, as also in Babylonia.

13. Still Pharaoh's heart was hardened: see extended comment on 7:3. It would be more accurate to render the Hebrew verb, *yeḥᵉzaḳ* simply as 'was hard', for there is no reflexive or passive idea in it.

THE FIRST PLAGUE: FOULING OF THE WATERS OF EGYPT

7:14–24

Yahweh sends Moses to Pharaoh to tell him that, because he has not obeyed Yahweh's command to let his people go, Yahweh will strike the water in the Nile. The Nile will be turned to blood, the fish will die, and the Nile water will become foul, so that the Egyptians will loathe to drink it. The plague is carried out in such a manner that all of the waters of Egypt become blood. The magicians of Egypt do the same by their secret arts, and the Pharaoh remains obdurate. Because they cannot drink the Nile water, the Egyptians dig round about the Nile for water to drink.

In its present form the account of the first plague is filled with confusion. Anyone who reads it as a straightforward story will come to the end wondering how the plague was brought about— directly by Yahweh, by the rod of Moses, or by the rod of Aaron? He will also wonder how much of the water of Egypt was turned into blood, and what is the relationship between the transformation of the water into blood and the death of the fish. The literary analysis of the story answers most of these questions, showing that three separate accounts have been woven together, but not successfully in every respect.

The J narrative is 7:14–15*a* ('. . . river's brink'), 16–17*ab* ('. . . in the Nile'), 18,21*a* ('. . . from the Nile'), 24. The P narrative is 7:19–20*a* ('. . . his servants'), 21*b*–22. This leaves us fragments of the E narrative that have been unsuccessfully woven in: 7:15*b* ('and take . . .'), 17*cd* ('with the rod . . .'), 20*b* ('he lifted up . . .'), and 23. In the J account, Yahweh strikes the Nile water, so that the fish in it die and the Egyptians loathe to drink it; the Egyptians dig for water around the Nile. In E, Moses strikes the Nile with his rod and the Nile is turned into blood. In P, Aaron stretches his rod out over the waters of Egypt, and the waters all over the land of Egypt become blood; the magicians of Egypt are able to do the same by their magic. J and P have been preserved almost intact.

The first plague has a superficial resemblance to the third sign which Moses is taught, in 4:9. There, Moses is instructed to take some water from the Nile and pour it on the dry ground; the water, he is told, will become blood on the dry ground. That account is from J, but the plague as told by J is quite different.

14. Pharaoh's heart is hardened: see comment on 7:3. J here uses a form of the verb *kābēd*, 'to be heavy'.

15. as he is going out to the water ; wait for him by the river's brink: the purpose of Pharaoh's going to the bank of the Nile is not known; cf. 8:20. In 2:5 the Egyptian princess goes to the river to bathe. Since the Nile river was deified by the Egyptians, and the Pharaoh presided at ceremonies honouring the Nile particularly at the time of its annual overflow, he may have been going for such a purpose.

which was turned into a serpent may be a gloss to explain which rod; E does not tell the story of the rod being changed into a serpent (cf. 4:1–4 J; 7:9–12 P).

16. that they may serve me in the wilderness: this means to go into the desert to worship at the mountain of the theophany. This is the regular demand in J, sometimes specifying that the Hebrews be allowed to go in order to 'sacrifice to Yahweh' (3:18; 5:3,8). In P, the demand is for unconditional release.

17. you shall know that I am the LORD: cf. comment on 7:5. This expresses the principal goal of the plagues.

I will strike the water that is in the Nile with the rod that is in my hand: this is an awkward statement in a word of Yahweh. The confusion arises from the combination of part of E with J's account. In J Yahweh must have said that he would strike the Nile water and make the fish die (cf. 7:25); in E, Moses must have said virtually the words of 17*b*.

18. the fish in the Nile shall die: since fish were an important factor in the food of the Egyptians, this in itself would have created hardship. However, nothing is said as to why they died, and their death is related in J only in order to account for the fouling of the Nile water.

19. In P the plague requires that all of the waters all over Egypt become blood.

both in vessels of wood and in vessels of stone: this is partly interpretation by *RSV*, and may not be correct. The Hebrew is literally, 'in trees and in stones'. There is no word in either case meaning **vessels of.** The meaning is probably that the turning of water into blood all over the land will be so complete that even the sap in the trees and the springs arising in stony places will become blood. In any event, trees were rare in ancient Egypt, and 'vessels of wood' would have been very rare. Note the parallel to this plague from Mesopotamia, mentioned below after the comment on verse 24. In that story the groves and gardens are saturated with blood.

20. he lifted up the rod and struck the water that was in the Nile: for E the subject was Moses. Aaron was commanded to stretch his rod out over all the waters of Egypt (19).

22. But the magicians of Egypt did the same by their secret arts: how they could do this after all the waters of Egypt had become blood is not explained. P probably thought of the transformation from water into blood as a magical trick that occurred instantaneously, and perhaps he thought the transformation back into water occurred instantaneously. Cf. comment on 7:11.

23. Pharaoh turned and went into his house: he is ap-

parently thought of as remaining out of doors on the bank of the
Nile while the wonder is being performed, and then returning to
his palace all in the same day. This verse is usually assigned to E,
but this is not entirely certain.

**24. And all the Egyptians dug round about the Nile for
water to drink:** this verse has an important bearing upon the
question of the historicity of the plague, or its 'natural' explanation.
Attempts to explain this plague have usually taken one of two
forms: (i) It is pointed out that when the Nile begins to rise,
usually in the latter part of June, it often has a dark reddish hue
because of the presence in the water of red mud picked up by the
river as it flows through the mountains of Abyssinia. (ii) The
reddish hue is explained as caused by micro-organisms—flagellates, algae, or the like—which might be effective also in killing
the Nile fish. Both of these explanations, as commonly given,
assume that the Nile was in flood stage, or approaching flood
stage. But it would not have been possible for the Egyptians to
dig **round about the Nile** in order to find water at a time when
the river was flooding. Furthermore, the discolouration of the
river water through mud does not make it undrinkable, and is
not an unusual occurrence.

We should note carefully that the earliest tradition (J) regarding
the first plague says nothing of the water of the Nile or any other
body of water becoming blood; it says that the fish died and the
water became foul, so that the Egyptians could not—or would
not—drink the water (verses 18,21). Verse 24 is from the same
source. The death of the fish in the river, at least in a limited
area, could have been caused by some epidemic disease; the dying
of the fish in large numbers in that area would be sufficient to
make the water malodorous and difficult or impossible to drink.
The later traditions speak of the water *becoming* blood, not of its
becoming red in colour.

There is an interesting parallel to this plague from Mesopotamia
of the third millennium B.C. The Sumerian goddess Inanna
became angry with a gardener, Shukallituda, and to punish him
sent three plagues against the land of Sumer. One of the plagues
was to fill all the wells of the land, and saturate all its groves and
gardens, with blood (S. N. Kramer, *History Begins at Sumer* [1958],
pp. 110–14).

The Second Plague: Frogs 7:25—8:15

7:25—8:4(J). *Seven days after Yahweh struck the Nile with the first plague, he commands Moses to go again to Pharaoh. This time he is to announce a plague of frogs out of the Nile if the Pharaoh refuses to let the Hebrews leave.*

8:5–7(P). *Aaron is told to stretch his rod over the rivers, canals and pools of Egypt and bring frogs upon the land. He does so, and frogs cover the land of Egypt. The Egyptian magicians are also able to bring frogs, by their magical arts.*

8:8–15(J,P). *Pharaoh summons Moses and Aaron, and asks them to intercede with Yahweh to withdraw the frogs, and then he will let the Hebrews go. At an agreed time the next day Moses intercedes, and the frogs die, but Pharaoh hardens his heart and refuses to let them go.*

This account is from the two sources J and P. J is found in 7:25—8:4,8–15a, and P in 8:5–7,15b ('and would not . . .'). The principal difference, apart from the role of Aaron, is that in J the frogs come up only from the Nile, while in P they come out of the various rivers, canals and pools of the land (cf. P in the first plague, 7:19). J's account of the actual bringing of the plague is not preserved; its place is taken by verse 6.

Frogs were common in ancient Egypt, particularly after the flooding of the Nile river. In that country the frog was associated with the goddess Heqt, who assisted women at childbirth; thus the frog was considered as the embodiment of a life-giving force. Here the plague of frogs is not represented as a danger to life, but only as a great inconvenience and nuisance. The second plague is less serious than the first, but the second is represented as being a greater inconvenience to Pharaoh himself.

Frogs are seldom mentioned in the Bible, probably because the frog was not particularly common in Palestine. The two other *OT* occurrences, Ps. 78:45; 105:30, refer to this plague in Egypt. In *NT* the only occurrence is in Rev. 16:13.

7:25. Seven days passed: J probably means to say that the first plague lasted for seven days—that is, the fouling of the water consequent upon the dying of the fish persisted for that length of time.

8:1. that they may serve me: see comment on 7:16. In 8 below, Pharaoh says he will let the people go 'to sacrifice to the Lord'.

3–4. The plague of frogs is described as being very thorough-going. The frogs will enter even into the **bedchamber** and the **bed** of the Pharaoh, and they will **come up on you**. The frogs are to be a great nuisance to Pharaoh himself, as well as to all the people of his land.

6–7. The statement that the magicians of Egypt can do the same by their secret arts is somewhat artificial, after we have been told that the frogs **covered the land of Egypt** (6). Cf. comment on 7:11.

8. Like the prophets of a later time (cf. Am. 7:2,5; Jer. 7:16; 27:18), Moses and Aaron are requested to serve as intercessors before Yahweh. In asking them to entreat Yahweh that he remove the frogs, the Pharaoh is recognizing the power of Yahweh. **Aaron** is an addition to the J narrative here and in verse 12. Note that in 9 Moses alone replies, and in verse 13 he alone entreats Yahweh.

10. Moses agrees to make his entreaty at a specific time, so that Pharaoh may know that it is really Yahweh who destroys the frogs. Then the Pharaoh will **know that there is no one like the LORD our God:** cf. 7:5,17, and later 8:22; 9:14,29.

12. as he had agreed with Pharaoh: the translation is uncertain. *RSV* mg. has another interpretation. The Hebrew is literally 'which he put to (or for) Pharaoh'. The subject of the verb is uncertain.

13–14. In response to the entreaty of Moses, Yahweh causes the frogs to die immediately, so that the people pile up the dead frogs in heaps. In the first plague, nothing was said about withdrawing the plague. Here the plague is withdrawn as suddenly as it had been brought, in both cases by the power of Yahweh.

15. Pharaoh . . . hardened his heart: only J says that Pharaoh hardened his own heart, here and in 8:32; 9:34. See the extended comment on 7:3.

and would not listen to them; as the LORD had said: this is from P. The same or very similar words are in 7:13*b*; 8:19*b*; 9:12*b*, all P.

(P) THE THIRD PLAGUE: GNATS **8:16–19**

Yahweh tells Moses to order Aaron to stretch out his rod and strike the dust, so that it may become gnats throughout the land of Egypt. Aaron does so, and all the dust becomes gnats. The magicians are not able to reproduce this wonder, but declare, 'This is the finger of God'. Pharaoh's heart is still hard, and he refuses to let the people go.

This plague is entirely from P, and is a good example of the form in which P recounts the plagues. It is brief and direct. There is no record of an interview with Pharaoh, either before or after the plague, and there is no mention of the removal of the plague. It is probable that this plague is a variant of the fourth which follows, told entirely by J.

16. that it may become gnats: the Hebrew word *kinnîm* refers to some kind of small insect. The translation as 'gnats' is supported by LXX and Vulgate. Philo also uses the word for gnats (*sknīpes*) and says that this insect is very small and troublesome, for it not only produces an unpleasant and noxious itching, but gets into the nostrils and ears, and flies into and damages the pupils of the eyes (*de vita Mos.* 1.xix.108). Other insects have been suggested as translation. *JB* and *Am. Tr.* have 'mosquitoes'. Other renderings are 'lice' (*AV, RV*), 'sand flies' or 'fleas' (*RV* mg.) and 'maggots' (*NEB*). In any event a country like Egypt, with its hot, dry climate, has always been troubled by numerous small insects.

This is another transformation wonder, like the rod wonder and the first plague, for we are told here that the dust will *become gnats*, and in 17*b* that 'all of the dust of the earth *became* gnats etc.'.

17. all the dust of the earth became gnats throughout the land of Egypt: notice how widespread the plague of gnats is described as being. This is characteristic of P; cf. 7:19; 8:5.

19. 'This is the finger of God': the magicians are not able to perform this wonder, and they recognize that the plague of gnats has been caused by the power of a deity. This is not just a magical trick, but something based on divine intervention. They do not necessarily recognize Yahweh as God by this statement. In Exod. 31:18 and Dt. 9:10 reference is made to the two tables of stone as written by the finger of God; in Ps. 8:3 'thy fingers' is used in association with creation. In Lk. 11:20 Jesus implies that he casts out demons 'by the finger of God'. B. Couroyer, *RB*, LXIII (1956), pp. 481–95, suggests that the sentence in the present context is an Egyptianism, and that the magicians mean to identify the rod of Aaron with the finger of God. He quotes Egyptian texts in which a wooden object, the translation of which is usually uncertain, is identified with the finger of a specific deity—e.g. *Book of the Dead*, ch. 153. This is an interesting suggestion, but it seems unlikely that such an Egyptianism would occur in P. Even if it is correct, ultimately the meaning is the same, for the rod of Aaron was believed to be a symbol or agent of divine power.

Pharaoh's heart was hardened: see comment on 7:3.

THE FOURTH PLAGUE: SWARMS OF FLIES 8:20-32

8:20-24(J). *Yahweh sends Moses to Pharaoh to threaten him with swarms of flies if he does not let the Hebrews go. The plague is brought on, so that Egypt is ruined because of the flies.*

25-32(J). *Pharaoh summons Moses and Aaron, and offers permission for the Israelites to sacrifice in the land. Moses objects that their offerings would be abominable to the Egyptians. Pharaoh then agrees to let them go into the desert, but not far away. Moses makes entreaty for Pharaoh, and the plague of flies is removed. Pharaoh still hardens his heart, and refuses permission for the exodus.*

This account is completely by J, whose hand extends without interruption through 9:7. This section demonstrates admirably the characteristics of J, except that for the first time mention is made of the exemption of the Hebrews living in the land of Goshen; also the interviews between Pharaoh and Moses are longer than with the former plagues. This plague is very likely a variant of the preceding, told completely by P.

20. as he goes out to the water: probably, as he goes out to the bank of the Nile; see comment on 7:15. He is apparently back in his palace the next day, according to 8:25.

21. I will send swarms of flies: the Hebrew is ʿārōḇ, which is a collective noun meaning 'swarm(s)', literally 'a mixture'. The word might cover swarms of various kinds of insects. LXX translates by kunómuia, 'dog-fly'. Philo in describing that insect says that it has the audacity of both the dog and the fly and is 'a creature venomous and vicious, which comes with a whirr from a distance, hurls itself like a javelin, and, with a violent onrush, fastens itself firmly on its victim' (*de vita Mos.* i.xxiii.131).

The fly was so common in ancient Egypt that it is used as a symbol for Egypt (and Ethiopia) in Isa. 7:18; 18:1.

22. the land of Goshen was that part of Egypt in which the Hebrews were settled, according to Gen. 45:10; 46:28 etc. It was a fertile area in the NE. part of the delta, in the area of the Wadi Tumilat. All of the references to it are in J; see below, 9:26. It is otherwise called 'the land of Rameses' (Gen. 47:11 [P]).

that you may know that I am the LORD in the midst of the earth: see comment on 7:5.

23. I will put a division between my people and your people: Yahweh is to treat the Hebrews differently from the Egyptians. Nothing is said in the preceding plagues regarding the exemption of the Hebrews. *RSV* follows LXX and Vulgate in rendering 'a division', where the Hebrew has a word that usually means 'a redemption', *peḏûṭ* (cf. Isa. 50:2; Ps. 111:9; 130:7). Here such a meaning seems out of place, but we should note that in 6:6 the verb 'redeem' is used to describe the forthcoming exodus. The text here is usually emended to *pelûṭ*, 'division'.

By tomorrow: this is the first time that Pharaoh is given an ultimatum with a specific period of time attached; cf. 8:10, where the frogs are to be killed 'tomorrow'.

24. And the LORD did so: in J, Yahweh brings the plagues directly without intervention of the rod or hand of Moses or Aaron.

25. and Aaron is a secondary addition; he plays no part in the action or dialogue of this plague.

26. we shall sacrifice to the LORD our God offerings abominable to the Egyptians: the Hebrews probably would offer animal sacrifices in the main if not exclusively, especially animals from their flocks. The Egyptians did on some occasions offer whole animals, including sheep and goats, but more often vegetable offerings with pieces of poultry or meat. Thus we cannot say that animal sacrifices in themselves would be abominable to the Egyptians. Their sacrifices would, however, have differed from these of the Egyptians in their manner and the accompanying ritual to such an extent that the latter would consider them abominable.

There is the implication here that the Hebrews did not offer sacrifices to Yahweh in Egypt. The whole tradition of the plagues and the exodus indicates the belief (at least of later times) that Yahweh's power extended into Egypt so that he could exercise control over Pharaoh. Though Moses is represented as praying to Yahweh in Egypt, we must suppose that the Hebrews believed that sacrificial worship could be made to him only in the desert, probably at a specified place or places.

There is a minor inconsistency here in J's narrative: if the Hebrews live apart in the land of Goshen, why must they be concerned about the reaction of Egyptians to their sacrifices? In

some other respects J is not completely consistent in his view that
the Hebrews dwelt apart in Goshen (e.g. 5:12).

27. This is the demand customarily made by the Hebrews, or
Moses, in J's account. See 3:18; 5:3; 7:16; etc.

28. For the first time the Pharaoh consents to let the Hebrews
leave Egypt, but he specifies, **only you shall not go very far
away.** This is apparently considered by Moses to be a satisfactory
reply. Pharaoh says to Moses, **Make entreaty for me,** as in 8:8,
but rather abruptly here. In making such a request he recognizes
the power of Yahweh, and the rôle of Moses as intercessor with
Yahweh.

29. Moses agrees to pray for the removal of the swarms of flies,
but he recalls that Pharaoh had once before gone back on his
word (8:15), and so he says, **let not Pharaoh deal falsely again
by not letting the people go to sacrifice to the LORD.**

32. Pharaoh hardened his heart this time also: see
comment on 7:3.

(J) THE FIFTH PLAGUE: PLAGUE ON CATTLE 9:1-7

*Yahweh sends Moses to Pharaoh to say that, if he does not let the people
go, a severe plague will fall on the cattle of the Egyptians. The next day is
set as the time, and the plague comes as promised. All the cattle of the
Egyptians die, but none of the Israelites' cattle. Still the heart of the
Pharaoh is hard, and he refuses to let the Hebrews go.*

The source here is J. It has many of the characteristics of that
narrator, but it lacks some of the elements of the pattern by which
J usually describes the plagues. Verses 2-3 sound as if they are a
word of Moses, speaking about Yahweh in the third person, and
not a direct word of Yahweh, as verse 1 is. There is no interview
with Pharaoh after the plague has struck. The whole account is
shorter than J usually is; cf. the account of the preceding plague
which is also by J. The nature of the plague called for a shorter
account, for *all* of the cattle were killed; it was hardly appropriate
for the Pharaoh to negotiate with Moses for their re-vivification,
and no use to describe the cessation of the plague when *all* of the
cattle had been killed.

3. The **very severe plague** is not described in such a manner
that we can identify the nature of the disease on cattle involved.
The Hebrew *déber* is a very general word for plague or pestilence.

'Murrain' (*AV*, *RV*) is likewise a general term, now usually restricted to plague in cattle. Some have conjectured that the disease was anthrax, but this cannot be demonstrated.

cattle: the Hebrew is *miḳneh*, a very general word for domesticated animals. Since the English word 'cattle' is now employed almost exclusively for domesticated bovine animals, the term 'livestock' (used in several modern translations) would be more appropriate here. It includes the animals enumerated in the remainder of the verse.

the horses: the horse and chariot were introduced into Egypt by the Hyksos, in the seventeenth century B.C. Horses were probably used at the time of the plagues only for pulling chariots; the earliest mention of cavalry horses (in Mesopotamia) is in the twelfth century. It is not likely that horses were plentiful in Egypt at this time.

asses had been domesticated in the third millennium B.C., and were widely used in the Near East thereafter for various forms of work and for riding.

camels may be an anachronism for the period of the plagues, but we cannot affirm this with certainty. It is likely that they were not domesticated—at least in great numbers—before the twelfth century B.C. Yet, camels are mentioned in the patriarchal narratives (see especially Gen. 24), and the bones of camels have been found in houses at Mari (in northern Syria) of the eighteenth century B.C., and evidence for their existence in the second millennium has been found sporadically at other places. Camels are almost completely absent from Egyptian art and literature until Ptolemaic times. It is not impossible that domestic camels existed in Egypt at this time, but the mention of them here may reflect their presence in Palestine at the time J wrote.

the herds: the Hebrew word *bāḳār* is often rendered 'cattle' in the usual modern sense, domestic bovine animals.

4. The **distinction** is made possible by the fact that the Hebrews live apart in Goshen, as explained in 8:22; 9:26. See comment on 8:22. It is not probable that the Hebrews possessed camels and horses; see the preceding note. It is particularly unlikely that they owned horses, for they were used at this time only for drawing chariots, and a horse and chariot were very expensive. The Hebrews were slow to adopt the use of horses even after they entered Canaan: Joshua hamstrung the chariot horses he captured (Jos. 11:6,9), and David hamstrung most of those he took

(2 Sam. 8:4). It was not until the time of Solomon that the Israelites kept them on a large scale (1 Kg. 10:26-29).

5. **Tomorrow the LORD will do this thing in the land:** cf. the same period of time in 8:23. The Lord acts directly, as is customary in J.

6. This verse seems to imply that all the animals died immediately. The narrator does not have in mind a natural disease, but a supernatural and very deadly plague inflicted by the hand of Yahweh.

7. **The heart of the Pharaoh was hardened:** see comment on 7:3.

(P) THE SIXTH PLAGUE: BOILS ON MAN AND BEAST 9:8-12

Yahweh directs Moses and Aaron to take handfuls of ashes from the kiln, and Moses is to throw them into the air in the presence of Pharaoh. They will become fine dust that in turn will become boils breaking out in sores on man and beast all over Egypt. They do so, and the plague comes. The Egyptian magicians are unable to reproduce this wonder, but they also suffer from the boils. Yet, Yahweh hardens Pharaoh's heart, and he still refuses to let the Hebrews go.

This section is entirely from P. It has the characteristics of P with one important exception: the plague is brought on, not by Aaron's rod, but by Moses, casting ashes into the air. Some scholars have conjectured that this plague is only a variant of the fifth, told entirely by J. There are similarities between the two, but in the present plague both men and animals suffer, and it is not said that the animals perish, as in the plague on cattle in the preceding section.

In the preceding plague we are told that all the cattle of the Egyptians died (9:6), and one is naturally left to wonder where the animals came from to be afflicted by the sixth plague. This is evidence that the stories of the plagues circulated independently, or in independent groups, before they were put together by the redactor of the book, who either did not notice the discrepancies or did not bother to eliminate them.

8. The word for **ashes**, *pîᵃḥ*, is a *hapax legomenon;* some translate it as 'soot'. The root of the noun is a verb that means to 'blow' or 'breathe'.

the kiln was one such as might be used for baking pottery, or for making lime or charcoal. The word *kibšān* occurs elsewhere only in 19:18 and Gen. 19:28, in both of which there are references to smoke of the kiln.

let Moses throw them toward heaven in the sight of Pharaoh: in P it is usually Aaron who brings on the plagues by holding out his rod. Here Moses has the rôle of the wonder-worker. This plague is more like a magical trick than some of the others. It involves a double transformation of ashes (or soot) into dust and then into boils. It takes place at Pharaoh's court, in the presence of the King, and the magicians are standing by to attempt to reproduce the trick. The setting is similar to that in 7:8–13, when Aaron's rod turns into a serpent.

9. boils, the Hebrew word, *šeḥîn,* may be singular or collective. It is used of the sickness of Hezekiah (2 Kg. 20:7) and of Job (2:7); in Lev. 13:18–20 it is used of boils that may be leprous. Boils were so common in Egypt that the term 'boils of Egypt' is listed as an affliction in Dt. 28:27. We do not have enough information to identify the nature of the disease. It is apparently considered here as very troublesome, but not necessarily fatal.

sores: the word occurs only here; it apparently means blisters, small boils or sores, pustules, or the like.

beast: Hebrew *beḥēmāh,* a different word for animals than the one rendered 'cattle' in the preceding plague, but it must have included the types of livestock listed in 9:3. *Beḥēmāh* may be used of animals in general, including wild animals, but most often refers to domesticated animals. It would seem to refer to the latter in the present instance.

11. The magicians of Egypt, who had been able to reproduce the first two plagues, are now not only unable to reproduce the plague of boils, but they suffer with the rest of the Egyptians. There is sly humour here. In the case of the third plague they confessed that it was brought on by 'the finger of God' (8:19). They are not mentioned in connection with the fourth and fifth plagues, both told by J; it is only in P that the magicians appear. See comment on 7:11.

12. But the LORD hardened the heart of Pharaoh: see comment on 7:3.

THE SEVENTH PLAGUE: HAILSTORM 9:13–35

13(J). *Yahweh instructs Moses to go to Pharaoh and demand that he let the people go, that they may serve Yahweh.*

14–16(P). *This time, Yahweh says, he will send all his plagues upon Pharaoh, his servants and his people, that they may know there is none like him in all the earth. He could have destroyed the people with pestilence, but has preserved Pharaoh in order to show him Yahweh's power.*

17–21(J). *Moses is to announce the sending on the morrow of a great hailstorm, such as has not been known in Egypt since its founding. Some of the people, upon being instructed to do so, take their cattle from the fields into safe shelter.*

22–26(E,J). *Moses stretches forth his rod toward heaven, and a mighty hailstorm begins, with thunder and lightning. It strikes down all men and animals in the field, and all plants and trees. The Israelites in Goshen are spared.*

27–35(J,E). *Pharaoh calls Moses and Aaron, confesses he has sinned, and asks them to entreat Yahweh to remove the plague. Moses goes out from the city, stretches his hands to Yahweh, and the hailstorm ceases. But Pharaoh adds to his sin by hardening his heart again, and he refuses to let the Hebrews go.*

The basic narrative of this plague is from J, but there are fragments of E, and one or more passages may be attributed to redactors. The primary evidence for E is in verses 22–23a, where the plague is brought on after Moses stretches forth his rod toward heaven. In verses 24–25 the description of the plague seems repetitious and overloaded with detail. We should probably assign verses 24a, 25a to E. It appears that E mentions hail, thunder, and lightning together, whereas J speaks only of hail until verses 28ff., when he speaks of hail, thunder and rain. Verse 35 is from E; J has already told of the hardening of Pharaoh's heart in his own phraseology in verse 34.

Verses 14–16 constitute a passage curious in its present context. It is too reflective for J, and it comes in awkwardly at this point, since this is not the last plague. Here someone explains the purpose of the plagues, and apparently he has in mind 'all my plagues' (14). We may attribute these verses to a late strand of P. Verses 19–21 and 31–32 have been attributed by critics to one or another supplementer or redactor; since there is not sufficient evidence to determine what redactor may be responsible for them,

we may simply attribute them to J, who could have known the
details they contain as well as anyone.

We thus have the following source analysis for this account:
J—9:13,17–21,23*b*,24*b*,25*b*,26–34; E—9:22–23*a* ('. . . earth'), 24*a*
('. . . the hail'), 25*a* ('. . . beast'), 35; P—9:14–16.

13. The wording is almost precisely the same as 8:20 (J).

14–16. These verses are widely attributed to a redactor by
critics, and we assign them to a late strand of P (see above).
This is really an apology for all of the plagues, explaining why
Yahweh sent so many plagues against Pharaoh and did not just
destroy him with pestilence at the outset; Yahweh's purpose was
to show the Pharaoh his power (or, show his power in Pharaoh;
see below), and thus make it possible for Yahweh's name to be
declared throughout all the earth. This is theology of the sixth
century B.C. or later—hardly of the time that J wrote. It goes
beyond the purpose expressed by both J and the original P, that
the Egyptians and Pharaoh may 'know that I am Yahweh' (7:5,17;
8:22), or that Pharaoh may 'know that there is no one like
Yahweh our God' (8:10 J), or that he may 'know that the earth
(or, the land?) is Yahweh's' (9:29). This last assertion seems close
to the idea expressed in the present verse, but it does not call for
the proclamation of Yahweh's name in all the earth.

14. I will send all my plagues upon your heart: we should
emend *el libbᵉkā* to *ēlleh bᵉkā*, and translate, 'I will send all these
plagues of mine upon you, and upon your servants . . .'. The
wording then is similar to that of 8:4,9,11,21,29; for 'these
plagues of mine' cf. 'these signs of mine' in 10:1. The Hebrew
word for plagues, *maggēpōṯ*, is used only here of the Egyptian
plagues.

15. pestilence: the same word is used in 9:3 for the severe
plague on cattle, *déḇer*. Yahweh could have destroyed men as well
as animals by his plague.

16. to show you my power: LXX and some other versions
read, 'that I may show my power in you', and that is the form in
which this verse is quoted in Rom. 9:17. Since it requires only a
slight emendation of the Hebrew, it may be correct. In Rom.
9:14–18, Paul quotes this verse and 33:19 to show that God 'has
mercy upon whomever he wills, and he hardens the heart of
whomever he wills'.

17 should be closely connected with the following verse.
We might render it, 'Since you are still exalting yourself against

my people, and will not let them go, behold, tomorrow about
this time . . . '.

18. I will cause very heavy hail to fall: hail develops when
there is violent turbulence in fully developed clouds, the raindrops
being carried to great heights where they freeze before falling.
The phenomenon is very rare in Egypt, much more than in
Palestine. Hailstorms are likely to be accompanied by thunder,
lightning and great downpouring of rain, and the hail can be
very destructive. The description given here may have been
influenced by acquaintance with hailstorms in Palestine.

19-21 has been considered by many critics to be a secondary
addition to J; this is possible, but there is no decisive evidence for
it. If anything here is secondary, it is only verses 20-21. This
section is perhaps somewhat concerned to show that some of the
men and animals were saved, so that they might be hit by the last
plague! It also shows that some of the Egyptians were obedient to
the word of the LORD in getting their cattle and slaves into
places of safety. Verse 20 indicates that it was the **slaves** working
out in the open fields who were most endangered by the
hailstorm.

22-23. It is characteristic of E that Moses uses his rod (or perhaps
his hand alone, 10:22) in bringing about a plague; cf. earlier his
action in striking the Nile with his rod to make the water turn to
blood, 7:20, and later, stretching out his rod to bring on the
locusts in 10:13. We assign 22-23a (. . . **down to the earth**) to
the E narrator. It appears that this narrator thought of the
storm as consisting of hail, thunder and fire; J mentions only
hail alone until 28, when there is mention of hail and thunder,
and later rain is mentioned in 33. See comment on verse 18.
thunder: lit. 'voices' (*ḳōlōṯ*); the Hebrews believed that thunder
was the voice of the deity (cf. 19:16; 20:18; Job 28:26; 38:25).

25. The hail struck down everything . . . : the word used for
struck here often means 'to kill', 'to slay with a single blow'
(*nākāh* [*hifil*]), and that is apparently the meaning here, if we
interpret in the light of verse 18, where it is said that men and
animals left in the fields will *die*. It is not likely that a natural
hailstorm would be so destructive; the author must have had in
mind a great supernatural hailstorm, unlike anything ever
experienced by man before or after. We should note that all of the
livestock were killed by the plague in 9:6 (J), and both men and
animals were afflicted with boils in 9:10 (P). The stories of the

various plagues were transmitted independently, or in separate groups, and inconsistencies such as this are not unusual.

26. The Hebrews living in **the land of Goshen** were spared the terrors of the hailstorm; see comment on 8:22.

27. and Aaron is a secondary addition here, as in numerous other places. In the context Moses alone replies to Pharaoh, and he alone goes out from the city and makes entreaty for the King. This time Pharaoh confesses that he has sinned, and that Yahweh **is in the right, and I and my people are in the wrong.** In doing so he admits the power of Yahweh, and goes a step farther than he had done in 8:8,25ff.

29. I will stretch out my hands to the LORD: the characteristic posture of prayer in the *OT* is to stretch out or lift up the hands toward heaven while standing (cf. 1 Kg. 8:22; Ezra 9:5; Isa. 1:15; Pss. 28:2; 63:4; Lam. 2:19 etc.).

that you may know that the earth is the LORD'S: cf. 8:10; 9:14.

31-32 are an explanatory passage, properly placed within parentheses by *RSV*. The position here is awkward; a more natural position would be directly after 25.

These two verses are generally considered to be an explanatory gloss by a secondary hand, but there is disagreement as to who the glossator was. The position of the verses is awkward, and it seems that the author of these verses had in mind a natural hailstorm that would only damage the ears and buds, whereas 25 suggests a much more destructive hail. However, we may note that in 10:5,15 (see below) the narrator of the locust plague refers to that which has been left by the hail. Thus this passage may be from J, who placed it awkwardly. We cannot, however, be certain of the origin of 31-32.

This passage explains that not 'every plant of the field' (9:25) was damaged or destroyed. **The flax and the barley** had begun to ripen and thus had ears and buds that could be destroyed by hail. **The wheat and the spelt,** on the other hand, were not far enough along in the process of growth for such damage. The month was probably January, when flax and barley normally ripen in Egypt; wheat and spelt are about a month later in growth.

Egypt was famous in the ancient world for the fine linen made from the fibre of flax. Barley thrived in the dry climate, and was used as food for both men and animals.

spelt: an inferior and coarse type of wheat. It is not certain,

however, that the Hebrew *kussémeṭ* is specifically 'spelt'. The word
occurs elsewhere only in Isa. 28:25; Ezek. 4:9. It may refer to
emmer, another type of wheat. Emmer has been found in ancient
Egyptian tombs, but there is no evidence for the cultivation of
spelt in Egypt and Palestine in ancient times.

34–35. Pharaoh sins again and hardens his heart, refusing to
let Israel go. The two-fold statement of the hardening of the
King's heart is evidence for two different sources, J and E (see
comment on 7:3). The last clause, **as the LORD had spoken
through Moses,** is like P's concluding statement in 7:13; 8:15,19;
9:12. It is such a simple, straightforward statement that it could
be from E.

THE EIGHTH PLAGUE: LOCUSTS 10:1–20

1–2(J,R_D). *Yahweh tells Moses to go to Pharaoh, for Yahweh has
hardened his heart so that he may show these signs and Moses' descendants
may learn how Yahweh made sport of the Egyptians, and so that 'you may
know that I am the LORD'.*

3–6(J). *Moses and Aaron go to Pharaoh, and announce that Yahweh
will bring locusts upon the land if he does not let the people go.*

7–11(J). *Pharaoh's servant pleads with Pharaoh to let the Israelites go
so that Moses may not continue to be a snare to them. Pharaoh calls Moses
and Aaron back; he offers to let only the men of the Hebrews go. When
Moses refuses to agree to this, they are driven out of the Pharaoh's presence.*

12–20(J,E). *Moses stretches forth his rod over the land and a dense
swarm of locusts comes upon Egypt, darkening the land and eating the
plants, the fruits of trees, and every green thing. Pharaoh hastily calls
Moses and Aaron, confesses he has sinned, and asks them to entreat
Yahweh to 'remove this death from me'. Moses entreats the Lord, who
sends a strong west wind to remove the locusts. But the Lord had hardened
Pharaoh's heart, and he will not let the Israelites go.*

The basic source of this narrative is J, but there are some indications of E and of a redactor. E's narrative is preserved in verses
12–13*a*, where Moses brings on the plague of locusts by stretching
out his rod over the land; it continues with the description of the
coming of the locusts in 14*a* ('. . . all the land of Egypt'), 15*b* ('and
they ate . . . hail had left'), and the conclusion in 20. 10:1*b*–2,
beginning with 'for I have hardened . . .', is considered by several
critics to be from a redactor, although others assign it without
question to J. It is an explanation for the plagues somewhat like

9:14–16, and it comes awkwardly at this point in a word of Yahweh to Moses. Some critics consider it as the work of the redactor of J or JE; others assign it to a Deuteronomic redactor (Beer, Rylaarsdam, and W. H. Bennett in the first edition of this commentary). In its terminology it is closer to J than to P, and the idea that Pharaoh's heart is hardened so that Yahweh may show his signs and the descendants of Moses may learn about this series of events reminds one of Deuteronomy, with its interest in the education of children and the handing on of tradition (Dt. 4:9; 6:7). We thus prefer to assign verses 1*b*–2 to the Deuteronomic redactor (R_D). Details regarding the vocabulary and the ideas present in this section are given below.

In Egypt and other Near Eastern lands, locusts have often appeared in great swarms to cause enormous damage. They are less frequent in Egypt than in Palestine. The *OT* has many references to locusts, and the book of Joel gives a detailed description of a locust invasion. The locust which is believed to have caused most of the widespread plagues in ancient and modern times in the Near East is the desert locust (*Acridium peregrinum*). This locust is capable of multiplying with appalling rapidity; it is gregarious and swarms in enormous masses; it has a wandering instinct which frequently leads it into lands far distant from its breeding grounds; and thus it is capable of periodically inflicting frightful damage upon cultivated vegetation. Those who have experienced locust plagues in modern times say that the description in the present chapter contains little exaggeration, and conforms in general to the course of a locust invasion. However, a locust invasion is not likely to have devastated the whole of Egypt.

1. for I have hardened his heart and the heart of his servants: as noted above, this begins a secondary addition by R_D, extending to verse 2. It is an explanation of the plagues, similar to 9:14–16. The plagues show the power of Yahweh, and throughout the course of them he is in complete control. The word used here for 'hardened' is the word used by J, *kābēd*, but J elsewhere speaks only of Pharaoh's hardening his own heart (8:15,32; 9:34); unlike P and E, he does not say that Yahweh hardened the King's heart. Nowhere else is it said that the heart of the servants of Pharaoh is hardened, but in 14:17 (P) Yahweh hardens the heart of the Egyptians. What R_D says here about the servants is not consistent with verse 7 below.

that I may show these signs of mine among them: the signs (*'ōṯōṯ*) are the plagues, as in both J (4:8f.; 8:23) and P (7:3).

2. that you may tell in the hearing of your son . . . : this interest in the transmission of the tradition of the exodus from Egypt, and the education of children, is found especially in Deuteronomy—see Dt. 4:9; 6:7. *I* **have made sport of the Egyptians:** the verb used here, *hiṯ'allaltî*, often means to deal ruthlessly or wantonly with someone. *JB* renders it, 'I made fools of the Egyptians'. Cf. the explanation of the plagues in 9:16.

that you may know that I am the LORD: 'you' is plural, addressed to the Israelites (the pronoun at the beginning of the verse is singular, addressed to Moses). This statement of purpose is often addressed to Pharaoh or the Egyptians, but to the Israelites in 6:7. It is used both by J (7:17; 8:22) and by P (7:5).

3. and Aaron is an addition here, and also in verse 8. Careful reading will show that Moses alone speaks and acts. Note especially 'this man' in verse 7, which refers to Moses.

4. tomorrow I will bring locusts: the same period of time as in 8:23; 9:18.

5. the face of the land: lit., 'the eye of the land'. The Hebrew expression is uncommon, and occurs elsewhere only in verse 15 below, and in Num. 22:5,11 (JE).

what is left to you after the hail: 9:25 speaks of the hail striking down 'everything that was in the field . . . every plant of the field . . .', but 9:31–32 explains that the wheat and spelt were not ruined. See note on 9:31–32.

6. In addition to the harm done to growing plants and trees, locusts can be a very great nuisance to human beings, as they pass over all obstacles.

7. Pharaoh's servants said to him: for the first time the servants of Pharaoh try to persuade him to accede to the demand of Moses. The **servants** of Pharaoh are the various persons at his court, including officials of the government. *Am. Tr.* and *JB* appropriately render the word here and frequently as 'courtiers'. These courtiers are represented as appreciating the damage being done to the land of Egypt by the stubbornness of the king. Some of them earlier paid attention to Moses, 9:20.

this man: i.e., Moses.

8. For the first time in the course of the plagues, the Pharaoh attempts to negotiate with Moses in advance, to prevent a plague from coming upon his land.

9. Moses' request is that the whole company of the Israelites, with their young and old and all of their flocks and herds, be allowed to go out into the wilderness to worship Yahweh. He never relaxes this demand.

for we must hold a feast to the LORD: see comment on 5:1.

10. The LORD be with you: sarcastic in the mouth of Pharaoh. He is willing to let only the adult males go, wishing to keep the women and children as hostages to insure the return of the men.

11. serve the LORD, for that is what you desire: the rendering of the second half of this is uncertain; the Hebrew is literally, 'for it (feminine) you are seeking'. Perhaps only the adult males would actually participate in the feast (as was the practice at a later time; see 23:17; 34:23; Dt. 16:16), and Pharaoh is saying that only the men need to go if the true purpose of the Israelites is to hold a feast for their God.

they were driven out from Pharaoh's presence: Moses refuses to accept the offer that only the men go.

12. This verse, as well as verses 13a, 14a, and part of 15, is from E. It is characteristic of E that Moses produces the plagues by lifting his rod; cf. 7:20 (striking the Nile), 9:22 (the hailstorm), and 10:21–22 (see below). If the material assigned to E in these verses is read continuously, it gives a complete account of the coming of the plague.

13. the LORD brought an east wind: it is characteristic of J that Yahweh brings on the plagues directly, without intervention by Moses or Aaron, and often by 'natural' means. It has often been observed in modern times that winds can carry locusts long distances; it was noted in ancient times by Livy, Strabo and others. In J's account the locusts are removed by a strong west wind that drives them into the sea (10:19). In J's account of the crossing of the sea, it is a strong east wind that dries up the sea and makes the crossing possible (see below 14:21). An east wind would bring the locusts from the desert regions of Sinai and Arabia, where the desert locusts breed under favourable conditions.

15. the land was darkened: swarms of locusts are sometimes so dense that they produce temporary darkness. This statement may have led to some confusion between the plague of locusts and the plague of darkness; see below on 21–23.

16–17. and Aaron is secondary; in verse 18, it is Moses who entreats the Lord. This time Pharaoh says, **I have sinned against the LORD your God, and against you,** thus recogniz-

ing Yahweh and going further than he had in 9:27. For the fourth
time he requests, **entreat the LORD your God** (cf. 8:8,28;
9:28).

19. See above on verse 13.

drove them into the Red Sea: the *yām sûp* is not properly the
Red Sea as we know it today, but the 'sea of reeds'. See excursus
below after chapter 14.

not a single locust was left in all the country of Egypt: it is
characteristic of the desert locust that it does not reproduce in
areas into which it wanders for food, because in such areas it
does not reach sexual maturity. Thus locust plagues tend to be
periodic, and an area may be completely free of them between
times of invasion from outside.

20. The LORD hardened Pharaoh's heart: see comment on
7:3. This verse is probably from E (cf. 9:35; 10:27).

THE NINTH PLAGUE: DARKNESS 10:21-29

21-23(E). *Yahweh tells Moses to stretch out his hand toward heaven
that darkness may come over the land of Egypt. Moses does so, and a thick
darkness covers the land for three days. Egyptians cannot see one another
nor move about, but the Israelites have light in their dwellings.*

24-29(J,E). *Pharaoh summons Moses and tells him to go and worship
Yahweh, but leave behind the Israelites' flocks and herds. Moses explains
that they must take their flocks and herds with them, so that they may
select from the animals for sacrifice. Yahweh hardens Pharaoh's heart, and
refuses to let the people go. He orders Moses from his presence, and tells
him never to see his face again. Moses leaves, saying that he will not see
Pharaoh again.*

The sources here are J and E. The account of the bringing of the
plague and its duration is from E (21-23); it has the characteristic
use of Moses' rod as a wand to bring the plague. The statement
concerning the hardening of Pharaoh's heart is also from E (27).
The rest of the section is from J (24-26, 28-29).

Several scholars have argued that the J narrative here originally
belonged with the eighth plague, and that it is therefore out of
place as the sequel to the plague of darkness. This is very probably
correct. We have already been told in verses 22-23 that the
darkness lasted for three days; hence the interview recorded in
verses 24ff. cannot be a negotiation for the ending of the plague of
darkness. Also, Pharaoh asks in 17 that Moses and Aaron pray

'only this once', suggesting that this is the last plague to be endured. Furthermore, verse 24 is a rather abrupt beginning for an interview between the Pharaoh and Moses. If one reads the J material in the latter half of this chapter, omitting the E material (20–23, 27), he will see that J has a good, continuous narrative. It should also appear to him that the E material has been awkwardly placed; verse 27 is especially awkward in its present position. The E material was very likely placed where it is because of the mention in verse 15 of the darkening of the land in the locust plague. J must not have had a plague of darkness in his series.

E begins abruptly in verse 21 with the instruction by Yahweh to Moses to stretch out his hand; he has no interview before the plague in which the plague is announced, nor after the plague has begun, for Pharaoh to negotiate for its cessation or for any other purpose. It seems very probable that the E account of the individual plagues was brief, consisting only of the instruction to Moses, description of the plague, and statement of the hardening of Pharaoh's heart. If E had an account of an interview before the plague, or if J had a record of a plague of darkness in his usual form, it is probable that the redactor would have included an announcement of the plague from one or the other.

The plague of darkness is often explained as resulting from a strong southerly wind called in modern times *khamsîn*. The *khamsîn* frequently occurs in Egypt in the spring (its Arabic name, meaning literally 'fifty', is derived from the fact that it comes during the fifty days of spring). It usually springs up suddenly as a strong wind, bringing intense heat, sand and dust, and causing darkness where it goes. It usually lasts only two or three days. While the account of the ninth plague resembles this superficially, we cannot really account for it in that way. Only the darkness is mentioned, and it is a very thick darkness. For the ancient Egyptians, such darkness would not just be an inconvenience, but would cause great terror. Like most peoples of the ancient Near East, they considered the darkness as the realm of evil spirits that could cause many kinds of evil, even death. An intense darkness lasting for three days would cause anxiety that the powers of darkness and chaos had conquered, and there would be no more light.

21. Stretch out your hand: this probably means that Moses was to stretch out the rod in his hand, in spite of the fact that the rod is not mentioned either here or in the following verse. In both 9:22–33 and 10:12–13, Moses is instructed to stretch forth his hand, and then the account says he stretched forth his rod. In 14:16,21 (also E), the situation is reversed: he is instructed to lift up his rod, and the record is that he stretched out his hand. In all such cases it is most likely that E intended to say that Moses used his rod as a wand.

a darkness to be felt: the translation is not certain, but this is more probable than the alternative which is sometimes preferred, 'so that men shall grope in darkness'.

22. there was thick darkness: the Hebrew has two different words meaning darkness, *ḥōšek̲-ᵃp̲ēlāh*. In translating this, LXX uses three Greek words, the first two of which mean darkness, the third meaning 'storm' (*thúella*). The LXX translator may have been one of the first to associate the plague of darkness with the *khamsîn* mentioned above.

23. all the people of Israel had light where they dwelt: the Hebrew is literally, 'in their dwellings'. Since E usually represents the Israelites as dwelling among the Egyptians, not specifically in Goshen, as J does, it may be that E means that the Israelites had light in their separate houses. This would be a most miraculous situation indeed!

24. Pharaoh goes beyond his offer in verse 11. He is now willing to let all the Israelite people go, provided they leave behind their flocks and herds. They could serve as hostages to insure the return of the people.

25-26. This should not be interpreted as a genuine request by Moses that the Pharaoh give them animals for sacrifice, in addition to letting them take their own flocks and herds. The words of Moses may be paraphrased as follows: '*You* would have to provide us with sacrifices and burnt offerings for our worship if we did not take along our own livestock. Furthermore, we cannot choose in advance from our own flocks and herds the animals to be sacrificed, and leave behind the rest, for we will not know which will be needed until we arrive at the place of sacrifice'. The Israelites apparently had no customary rules for their offerings at this time, depending upon divine instruction—perhaps through oracles—at the time of sacrifice.

27 is from E. For the phraseology cf. 9:35; 10:20.

28-29. Moses does in fact have a later audience with Pharaoh. An audience is recorded in 12:31-32, and implied in 11:4-9.

THE TENTH PLAGUE: DEATH OF THE FIRST-BORN **11:1—13:16**

In the account of the tenth plague, the literary patterns used for the preceding plagues are not followed. This is due in part to the fact that the tenth plague is successful in securing the release of the Israelites by Pharaoh, and in part to the fact that the account of this plague has been worked over in such a manner as to include laws of the Passover and Festival of Unleavened Bread, and the Law of Firstlings.

In this long section there is more material from P than any other source. P gives regulations for Passover and Unleavened Bread, and a brief statement about Firstlings. The viewpoint of P is unmistakably that of a later time, when Israel is settled in Canaan and can observe the feasts in leisurely fashion over a period of eleven days, with two holy assemblies of the 'congregation of Israel'. It is a time also when the Israelites own slaves, and have foreigners living in their midst (12:43–49). The Priestly writer is not relating what happened in Egypt, but giving the regulations for the feasts in his own time (fifth century B.C.); yet he does include features that are very ancient (see 12:7–8 especially). Passover and the Festival of Unleavened Bread have been combined into a single observance. The P material is in 11:9–10, 12:1–20,28,40–51; 13:1–2.

J contains the announcement of the coming plague (11:4–8). He alone tells about the inflicting of the tenth plague upon the Egyptians and Pharaoh's release of the Israelites (12:29–34), and about the beginning of their journey (12:37–39). This is prefixed by J's record of Moses' instructions to the elders to kill the Passover lamb and perform the blood-rite (12:21–23).

There is very little E material in this section. 11:1–3 and 12:35–36 are usually assigned to E, as is the preceding passage that forecasts the despoiling of the Egyptians by the Israelites (3:19–22). We may note, however, that Noth assigns all of these to J, and thus sees no E material in the present section. If E had an account of the Passover and the tenth plague, it was apparently not sufficiently different from J's account to be preserved.

Two passages show the marks of a redactor with Deuteronomistic characteristics (R_D): 12:24–27a and 13:3–16. These are of a prescriptive nature, like much of the P material.

The source analysis is thus as follows—J: 11:4–8; 12:21–23,

27*b*,29–34,37–39; E: 11:1–3; 12:35–36; P: 11:9–10; 12:1–20,28, 40–50; 13:1–2; and R_D: 12:24–27*a*; 13:3–16.

The principal biblical passages bearing on the history of the Passover and Unleavened Bread are the following: Exod. 34:18,25 (J); Dt. 16:1–8; Ezek. 45:21–25; Lev. 23:5–8 (H); Num. 9:1–14 (P); and the historical passages, Jos. 5:10; 2 Kg. 23:21–23; 2 Chr. 30:1–27; 35:1–9; Ezra 6:19–22. The Mishnah tractate *Pesaḥim* gives the regulations for the Tannaitic period, which is roughly the period of the New Testament. The Jews of that time made a distinction between 'the Passover of Egypt' and 'the Passover of the generations'. The former included features which were believed to have been carried out only in Egypt, and not required of future generations: the securing of the lamb on the tenth day of the month, the sprinkling of blood on the lintel and doorposts, and the eating of the Passover in haste in one night (*Pesaḥim* 9:5).

ANNOUNCEMENT OF THE TENTH PLAGUE 11:1–10

1–3(E). *Yahweh tells Moses that he will bring one more plague upon Pharaoh and Egypt, and then Pharaoh will let the Hebrews go. Before they leave, the Israelites are to ask of their neighbours jewelry of silver and gold. Yahweh gives the people of Israel favour in the sight of the Egyptians, and the Egyptians consider Moses to be very great.*

4–8(J). *Yahweh announces that about midnight he will go through the land of Egypt and slay the first-born of all the people and of the cattle. No harm will come to the Israelites. The servants of Pharaoh will come to Moses and tell him and the people to leave.*

9–10(P). *Yahweh tells Moses that Pharaoh will not listen, so that Yahweh's wonders may be multiplied in Egypt. Moses and Aaron do the wonders, but Yahweh hardens Pharaoh's heart.*

The sources in this chapter are clear. Verses 1–3 are from E; they seem to presuppose that the Israelites are living among the Egyptians, not apart in Goshen. Verses 4–8 are from J, and may have originally stood directly after 10:29. Verses 9–10 are from P.

1. Yet one plague more: the Hebrew is literally 'stroke' (*négaʿ*), a different word from those used in 9:3 (*déḇer*), 9:14 (*maggēp̄āh*), and 12:13 (*négep̄*). E does not tell what the plague is to be. Very little E material is preserved in chapters 11–13; the only other E passage is 12:35–36.

when he lets you go, he will drive you away completely: see 6:1 (J). The implication is that Pharaoh will be glad to be rid

E

of the troublesome Hebrews. *NEB* renders this clause as follows: 'he will send you packing, as a man dismisses a rejected bride'. This involves emending the M.T., apparently changing *kālāh gārēš* to *kallāh gᵉrušāh*. The Hebrew here is difficult, and this emendation is possible; however, the comparison of Israel with a rejected bride does not seem appropriate to the situation.

2. Similar instructions are given in 3:21–22. They are carried out, according to 12:35–36; see comment *in loc.*

3. And the LORD gave the people favour in the sight of the Egyptians: in 12:36 this means that the Egyptians gave them what they asked.

Moreover, the man Moses was very great in the land of Egypt: he was respected and feared by the Egyptians, as a result of the plagues. Cf. Num. 12:3, 'Now the man Moses was very meek, more than all men that were on the face of the earth'.

4–8 are from J. These verses follow naturally after 10:29, and probably originally constituted the conclusion of the interview which is reported in 10:24ff. Some critics think 4–6 are addressed to the Israelites. However, they are more likely addressed to Pharaoh, as is indicated by the use of the second person singular in 8. It hardly seems probable that Pharaoh would have granted Moses another audience after the words of 10:28, and Moses' reply in 10:29.

4. About midnight I will go forth in the midst of Egypt: see 12:23,29. This vivid anthropomorphic language is characteristic of J; cf. Gen. 3:8; 11:5; 18:22; Exod. 7:17.

5. all the first-born in the land of Egypt shall die: cf. 4:23; 12:19. This plague is one which brings about the death of all the first-born of the people of Egypt, and of their livestock.

7. that you may know: Hebrew is second person plural, but the Samaritan text and LXX are probably correct in reading singular. In verse 8 Moses clearly is speaking to Pharaoh.

the LORD makes a distinction between the Egyptians and Israel: the same verb is used in 8:22 and 9:4 of the separation of the Israelites in the land of Goshen, and their special treatment.

8. these your servants shall come down to me: 'your' is second person singular; Moses is speaking to Pharaoh. The servants are the courtiers of Pharaoh (see comment on 10:7).

9–10 are from P, but both seem rather awkward in their present position. In 9 **my wonders** are those which are yet to be done, in the tenth plague and the release of the Israelites. In 10

these wonders are the wonders of the first nine plagues; Moses and Aaron have no direct part in the final plague, which is the work of Yahweh alone.

10. The LORD hardened Pharaoh's heart: cf. 4:21; 7:3; 9:12; 10:1,20,27. See comment on 7:3.

INSTRUCTIONS FOR OBSERVING PASSOVER AND UNLEAVENED BREAD
12:1-28

12:1-12(P). *Yahweh gives instructions to Moses and Aaron for keeping the Passover. On the tenth day of the first month, a year-old unblemished animal from the sheep or goats is to be selected, and kept until the fourteenth day. On the fourteenth the animal is to be killed, some of the blood is to be placed on the doorposts and lintels of the houses, and the flesh is to be eaten roasted, with unleavened bread and bitter herbs, on that night. When Yahweh passes through the land of Egypt to slay the first-born, he will pass over the Israelites and no plague will fall on them.*

13-20(P). *Unleavened bread is to be eaten for seven days. On the first day all leaven is to be put out of the houses. A holy assembly is to be held on the first day, and again on the seventh day. This feast is to be in remembrance of the day that Yahweh brought Israel out of Egypt.*

21-23(J). *Moses calls the elders and gives them instructions to kill the Passover lamb, and put some of its blood on the lintel and two doorposts of each house. When the Lord passes through to slay the Egyptians, he will pass over the door and not allow the destroyer to enter the houses of the Israelites.*

24-27(RD,J). *Instructions to observe this rite as an ordinance forever. When children ask, 'What do you mean by this service?' the answer is to be that it is Yahweh's Passover, because he passed over the houses of the Israelites when he slew the Egyptians.*

28(P). *The people of Israel do as Yahweh had commanded Moses and Aaron.*

1. These regulations are given **to Moses and Aaron in the land of Egypt:** according to P, they are the only prescriptions given in Egypt, before the promulgation of the law at Sinai.

2. This month is the spring month corresponding to March-April. In the older Israelite calendar, borrowed from the Canaanites, it was called ʾabib (13:4; 23:15; 34:18; Dt. 16:1). When the Mesopotamian names of the months were taken over in the late seventh century, it was called Nisan (Neh. 2:1; Est. 3:7). In post-exilic times it was customary to call months by their number; this is the **first month** in the system borrowed from Mesopotamia.

3. Tell all the congregation of Israel: the common expression in P for Israel as an organized religious community is *'ēḏāh*, used more than a hundred times. The selection of the animal **on the tenth day of this month** was not observed in Mishnaic times (*Pesaḥim* 9:5; see above). The word for **lamb** is *śeh*, which means a single animal of either the sheep or the goats, as is made clear in verse 5 below.

a lamb for a household: the Passover is here a domestic rite, although in Dt. 16:1–8 it is a Temple rite, to be observed in the Temple in Jerusalem. In making it a household rite, P is undoubtedly returning to the practice in very early times, before the feast was observed in sanctuaries (if indeed it was observed at all before the time of Deuteronomy). According to the regulation of later times, at least ten were required to make a 'congregation' (Josephus, *Jewish War* vi.ix.3). The next verse provides for two adjacent households to share a lamb if necessary.

4. according to what each can eat . . . for the lamb: the meaning is expressed in the words of the *Am. Tr.:* 'charging each household for the proportionate amount of the sheep that it ate.'

5. Animals for sacrifice were usually required to be **without blemish;** cf. Lev. 22:19,21; Dt. 17:1.

6. The Passover animals were to be killed on the fourteenth day of the first month **in the evening.** The last phrase is literally 'between the two evenings'. This is a technical expression frequently used by P; it has been given three interpretations: (i) the period between sunset and the time when the stars become visible; (ii) the period between the time when the sun first begins to decline to the west and shadows begin to lengthen (shortly after noon) and the beginning of night; and (iii) the period between the time when the heat of the sun begins to decrease (about 3 p.m.) and sunset. The last is the explanation adopted by the Pharisees and Talmud, and it seems to be supported by the Mishna (*Pesaḥim* 5:1) and Josephus (*Jewish War* vi.ix.3).

7. On the rite described here, see verse 22 below. This is doubtless a very ancient rite—perhaps the most ancient rite of the Passover—which P seeks to revive in the home ceremony. It is not prescribed in Dt. 16:1–8. In the Mishnah this is one of the features belonging to 'the Passover of Egypt' which was not observed by later Jews (*Pesaḥim* 9:5).

8. The Passover sacrifice was **roasted** whole (see the next verse). According to Dt. 16:7, it was to be boiled, as were other sacrifices which were eaten by the worshippers. P is probably reverting here to the primitive custom; in the nomadic stage the animals would have been roasted whole over an open fire. It was eaten **with unleavened bread**; this too was probably a very primitive custom, for unleavened bread is still the ordinary fare of the Beduin. The **bitter herbs** were probably originally the wild desert plants which the nomads would pick to season the meat. The Mishnah lists five herbs that may be eaten to fulfill this obligation: lettuce, chicory, pepperwort, snakeroot, and dandelion (*Pesaḥim* 2:6; see Eng. transl. by H. Danby [1933], p. 138). According to later interpretation, they ate the bitter herbs 'because the Egyptians embittered the lives of our fathers in Egypt' (*ibid.*, 10:5; cf. Exod. 1:14).

9. Some critics think that in the most primitive times the sacrificed animal was eaten **raw,** but there is no real evidence for this.

10. This is a regulation generally followed with sacrifices, to prevent the profaning of sacred flesh; cf. Exod. 23:18; 34:25; Lev. 7:15 (cf. verse 17).

11. The Israelites are to eat the Passover in haste, ready for departure; cf. verses 33, 34, 39 (J). Noth and some other scholars think that the Passover was originally a cultic ceremony of wandering shepherds performed in the spring, just before their departure for summer pasturage. This accounts for some of the features of the ceremony, such as those suggesting haste. In time, according to Noth, it acquired a historical reference as a cultic representation of the one great departure from Egypt. This may be valid as a partial explanation of the origin of the rite, but see further on verses 22–23 below.

It is the LORD's Passover: the Hebrew for 'Passover' is *pésaḥ*, which may be used of the feast, the victim, or the sacrifice. *pésaḥ* has come into English (through Greek) as the adjective 'paschal'. The origin of the word is not known. Attempts have been made to associate it with the Akkadian *pašāḫu*, 'to be appeased, to be placated'; but the idea of propitiation or expiation is not prominent in the rite, if present at all. B. Couroyer has sought to prove that the Hebrew is an adaptation of an Egyptian word, *p3 sḥ*, meaning 'the stroke' (*RB*, LXII [1955], pp. 481–96). It is true that the tenth plague is considered as the final, climactic stroke of Yahweh (*néga'*, 11:1), and that it was the direct action of Yahweh without human aid, but it is doubtful that the Hebrews would have

adopted an Egyptian word for the event that meant their deliverance from Egypt. Also, the rite very probably antedates the
sojourn of the Hebrews in Egypt (see below on 21-23). A meaning
such as 'protection' would fit the very early purpose of the rite
and the probable meaning of the verb *pāsaḥ* in Isa. 31:5 (see
comment below on verse 13, and excursus, pp. 144-46).

12. The slaying of the first-born in Egypt is forecast in 4:23 and
11:5, and related in 12:29.

on all the gods of Egypt I will execute judgments: the same
idea is expressed in Num. 33:4 (P). Yahweh will show his superiority over the gods of Egypt (which included the Pharaoh,
whom the Egyptians considered to be divine) and punish them for
resisting the demand made by Moses. On the phrase 'execute
judgments', see comment on 6:6.

13. I will pass over you: the Hebrew verb is *pāsaḥ*, related in
some manner to *pésaḥ* (see above on verse 11). This verb in this
sense occurs only in 23 and 27, and in Isa. 31:5, where *RSV*
translates, 'he will spare [Jerusalem]'. Hebrew has a verb *pāsaḥ*
which means 'limp, do a limping dance' and the like (2 Sam. 4:4;
1 Kg. 18:21,26). The adjective *pissēaḥ* means 'lame, crippled'
(2 Sam. 9:13; 19:26; Dt. 15:21 etc.). Some scholars believe that
this is the same verbal root, and interpret the present verse to
mean that Yahweh 'leaps' or 'skips over' the Israelites. This seems
somewhat far-fetched. It may be an intentional play on the word
pésaḥ as the name of the ceremony. There is no evidence that the
Passover was celebrated with a 'limping dance' such as is referred
to in 1 Kg. 18:26. Some believe the two verbal roots to be entirely
separate.

no plague shall fall upon you to destroy you: The Hebrew is
literally, 'there shall not be upon you a plague as a destroyer', the
last word being *mašḥîṭ*, the same word used in verse 23; see
comment *in loc*.

14-20 give P's regulations for the observance of Unleavened
Bread, joined rather loosely to the preceding. By the time P
wrote, Passover and the Feast of Unleavened Bread had been
united into a single spring feast, but the Unleavened Bread
feast had a different origin from Passover. Passover originated, in
all probability, among nomadic shepherds in pre-Mosaic times
(see comment on 21-23). The Feast of Unleavened Bread, *maṣṣôṭ*,
was in all likelihood adopted by the Israelites from the Canaanites
after they entered Canaan. It was an agricultural ceremony,

celebrating the beginning of the barley harvest in the spring in which the new grain was eaten without any leaven from the old crop. It marked a time of new beginnings. The Feast of Unleavened Bread is prescribed as one of the three annual pilgrimage feasts in 23:15 (E) and 34:18 (J). Both of the feasts occurred in the spring, Passover at the time of the full moon of the vernal equinox and Unleavened Bread at the beginning of the barley harvest; it was a short step for the two to be combined into a single observance, as they were in Dt. 16:1-8, and perhaps earlier (see Jos. 5:10-12; at Gilgal the people eat 'unleavened cakes and parched grain' on the day after the Passover observance).

14. This day shall be for you a memorial day: the first day of Unleavened Bread is a memorial of the exodus from Egypt.

you shall keep it as a feast to the LORD: this celebration was a pilgrimage-feast (*ḥag*, which is used here) from the beginning, celebrated at the sanctuaries, whereas Passover was originally a domestic feast.

15. unleavened bread: Hebrew *maṣṣôṭ* is better translated 'unleavened cakes'. The word is plural, and refers to flat, round cakes made of the new grain without leavening from the old dough. Such cakes were probably the normal fare of nomads (as they are of the Beduin today), and were eaten in connection with the nomadic Passover (see verse 8). The use of *maṣṣôṭ* in both feasts was another element that made it easy to combine the two into a single observance (see above). J explains the origin of the use of *maṣṣôṭ* on the basis of the haste of the Hebrews in leaving Egypt (verse 39).

leaven: *śe'ōr* was usually a piece of fermented dough from a previous batch. The oldest codes forbade the offering of sacrifices to Yahweh with leaven (23:18; 34:25), and the cereal offering was not leavened (Lev. 2:11; 6:17); offerings which were to be eaten by the priests or others could be leavened (Lev. 7:13; 23:17). In the Bible leaven is generally a symbol of corruption (see especially Mt. 16:11; 1 Cor. 5:6-8).

what is leavened: Hebrew *ḥāmēṣ*, a general term for anything made with leaven.

that person shall be cut off from Israel: frequent in P. It is usually connected with neglect of a ceremonial prescription, and is the equivalent of 'excommunication', accompanied by the expressed or implied threat of divine punishment.

16. The first and seventh day were to be days of **holy assembly:**

a convocation of all the people for religious observance, on which no work was to be done.

21-23 is the oldest account of the Passover, from J. Here the primary emphasis is on the apotropaic blood rite, designed to ward off death from the homes of the Israelites in Egypt. We can most probably detect here the origin of the Passover rite. It very likely originated among the nomadic shepherds of pre-Mosaic days. It was a spring rite in which they killed animals from their flocks, then put some of the blood on the tent-poles to keep away demonic powers, represented by the 'destroyer' (*mašḥît*) of 12:13, 23. The purpose was to promote the fecundity and welfare of the flocks, and the welfare of the people. Although it is not stated in this section, we may assume that the animals were eaten, probably very much as prescribed in verses 8-9: roasted whole, and eaten with unleavened cakes and wild herbs picked in the desert. It is never said anywhere in the regulations for the Passover that the animals were the first-born, and this was probably not required. The eating of the flesh may have been designed to establish communion with the deity, but there is no hint in the biblical records of a covenant.

21. Moses called all the elders of Israel: they play a prominent role in J's account; see 3:16,18; 4:29 etc.

according to your families: J makes the Passover a family rite, as also does P (3, 4 above); in Dt. 16:1-8 it is a Temple rite.

22. hyssop was a very small, bushy plant, probably the Syrian marjoram (*Origanum maru* L.). It was used in other cultic rites (leprosy cleansing [Lev. 14:4ff.]; the red heifer rite [Num. 19:6ff.], and is referred to figuratively in Ps. 51:7. It is spoken of as 'the hyssop that grows out of the wall', the smallest of plants, in 1 Kg. 4:33. The present verse is the only reference to a 'bunch' of hyssop. The putting of the blood on **the lintel and the two doorposts** of each house (originally on the tent-poles) would serve to ward off the 'destroyer' of verse 23.

none of you shall go out . . . until the morning: presumably there would be danger to those who left the protection of the marked houses; this prescription is not given elsewhere, but cf. 12:46.

23. the LORD will pass over the door: see comment on 13 for the word rendered 'pass over'.

the destroyer (*mašḥît*): a survival from the very ancient, pre-Mosaic idea that demonic powers might attack those who were

not protected by the blood. In the Yahwistic faith he was probably
conceived to be a destroying angel carrying out the will of Yahweh
(cf. 2 Sam. 24:16; 2 Kg. 19:35; Heb. 11:28). The *mašḥit* occurs
also in verse 13; see the comment *in loc.*

The J account as now preserved does not go on to give instructions for the eating of the Passover lamb. It may have originally
done so, giving the same instructions as 8–9, possibly 10–11.
If so, these were displaced by 24–27*a*, which are from a Deuteronomic editor. The conclusion of J's narrative in 21–23 is now in 27*b*.

26–27. The interest in telling the children of future generations
the significance of what is done is characteristic of Deuteronomy
and the D editors. For the same literary form as here, see Dt.
6:20–25; Jos. 4:6–7,21–24; and see also Exod. 10:2 (R_D), Dt. 4:9;
6:7.

And the people bowed their heads and worshipped:
virtually the same words are at the end of 4:31, forming the
conclusion to an interview between Moses (and Aaron) and the
elders of Israel. Here they originally formed the conclusion to J's
account of the instructions given by Moses to the elders.

28, which is from P, is the conclusion to P's account in verses
1–20.

THE TENTH PLAGUE, AND RELEASE OF THE ISRAELITES
12:29–36 (J,E)
*Account of the tenth plague, and the release of the Israelites by Pharaoh.
At midnight Yahweh smites all the first-born of Egypt, and there is a great
cry throughout all the land. Pharaoh rises in the night; he summons Moses
and Aaron, and orders them to go and worship Yahweh, taking along their
flocks and herds. The people of Israel go in haste, taking their dough before
it is leavened. They despoil the Egyptians of articles of silver and gold.*

29–34 are from J, **35–36** from E.
29. Only J tells of the actual coming of the tenth plague, which
meant the death of the first-born of the people of Egypt and of
their livestock, including even the first-born of the Egyptian
King. Such a plague, striking only the first-born of the Egyptians,
sparing those of the Hebrews, and striking also the first-born of the
livestock of the Egyptians, would be miraculous in the extreme;
no one has successfully given a 'natural' explanation of this
plague, such as can be offered for many of the first nine (see
Appendix). Some critics take the view that this plague was a

disease of some nature that took the life of Pharaoh's first-born; they see in 4:23 the implication that the final stroke is to be the death of the King's first-born son. This is possible, and the death of the first-born son by a disease that took his life very quickly could have been interpreted by Pharaoh, as well as by the Israelites, as a 'stroke of Yahweh'. See further the discussion below after 13:16.

31–32. The Pharaoh finally summons Moses and Aaron and orders them to leave, taking along their flocks and herds, as they had insisted they must (10:25–26). This is more than mere permission. He is now anxious to have them leave in order to spare the Egyptians and himself of more deaths, and he drives them away as had been predicted in 6:1 and 11:1.

bless me also! is not sarcastic in this situation. Pharaoh recognizes at last the overwhelming power and the divinity of Yahweh; as the Israelites worship their God at the sanctuary to which they are going, they are to ask the blessing of Yahweh upon the Egyptian king.

35–36 are assigned to E. The passage appears to assume that the Israelites were living in various parts of Egypt among the Egyptian people, not isolated in Goshen, as J represents them. Instructions to ask the Egyptians for certain articles are given in 3:21–22 and 11:2. If the incident is historical, these objects were perhaps intended for use in the celebration of the festival in the wilderness which the Hebrews said they were going three days' journey to celebrate. It is very difficult, however, to imagine that the Egyptians would actually give up such articles to the enslaved Hebrews. The incident may be aetiological, to explain the source of the materials for the golden calf (32:2–4) and the tent of meeting (35:22–24). In a much later time, the spoliation of the Egyptians was explained as retaliation upon the Egyptians for the enslavement of the Hebrews, and as a slight wage for their time of service (Philo, *de vit. Mos.* i.xxv; Jubilees 48:18; and some early Church Fathers). In early Christianity the spoliation of the Egyptians became an example or metaphor for the appropriation of the culture of the Greeks by the Christian faith (cf. Augustine, *On Christian Doctrine* ii.xl). Cf. the discussions by J. Morgenstern, *JBL*, LXVIII (1949), pp. 1–28 and G. W. Coats, *VT*, xviii (1968), pp. 450–57.

jewelry of silver and gold: since *keͅlîm* is a very general word meaning 'articles, objects, things', the rendering **jewelry** may be too specific. 'articles of silver and gold' would be better (including of course jewelry, ornaments, and the like).

THE JOURNEY FROM RAMESES TO SUCCOTH **12:37-42**

37-39(J). *The Israelites journey from Rameses to Succoth, numbering about 600,000 men on foot, besides the women and children. Also with them are a mixed multitude, and very many livestock. They bake the unleavened cakes and eat them as they hurriedly leave Egypt.*

40-42(P). *The period of the Israelites' sojourn in Egypt is given as 430 years.*

37. The first part of this verse (... **Succoth**) is assigned by many critics to P. It may be from that source, but J could have contained the information. **Rameses** is probably to be identified with modern San el-Hajar, and **Succoth** with Tell el-Maskhuta; see detailed comments on 1:11.

about six hundred thousand men . . . and children: this would make a total of some two or three million persons leaving Egypt. The same figure is given in Num. 11:21 (J), and P has a similar figure in Num. 1:46; he gives 603,550, excluding Levites, as the total arrived at in a census taken in the wilderness of Sinai. Such figures are not credible, in the light of the number of Hebrews who went down to Egypt, the number that could have been employed in Egypt, and—above all—the number that could be supported in the desert between Egypt and Palestine. The correct figure is more likely to be a few thousand; tradition has exaggerated the number in the years that intervened between the exodus and the earliest narrative.

38. **A mixed multitude also went up with them:** this probably consisted mostly of other slaves who had worked at forced labour in Egypt, and now identified themselves with the Hebrews, seeking a better life outside Egypt. Some may have been Egyptian slaves.

39. J here explains the use of unleavened cakes as due to the haste with which the Hebrews left Egypt. They had taken their kneading bowls with them (verse 34), and now baked and ate unleavened cakes. J apparently thinks of the unleavened cakes as being eaten for only one or two days, not the seven days of the *maṣṣôṭ* festival. We have suggested that unleavened bread, as the ordinary diet of nomads, was eaten with the Passover sacrifice (see 8-9).

40. four hundred and thirty years: this is from P's chronology. The figure 'four hundred' for the same period in Gen. 15:13 is probably from a redactor of E. It is inconsistent with other data: in Gen. 15:16 (E) the promise is given to Abraham that in the fourth generation his descendants will return from Egypt; and the P genealogy in Exod. 6:13–25 allows only four generations from the sons of Jacob to Aaron and Moses. P's chronology is late and artificial; some interpreters suggest that he counted 100 years as a generation. See Introduction, pp. 40–42.

42. night of watching: often rendered a 'night of vigil(s)'. There is here a play on the word *šāmar*, which means 'watch', but also 'keep, protect, observe' and the like. On this night Yahweh watched over Israel to protect and keep them, bringing them safely out of Egypt (cf. the meaning in Ps. 16:1; 91:11 and frequently); on the Passover night the Israelites are to watch for Yahweh by keeping this festival and obeying him (cf. the meaning in Exod. 12:17; 23:15; 34:18 etc.).

FURTHER REGULATIONS FOR PASSOVER **12:43–51**

This section is from P, continuing his regulations for Passover from 12:1–20 and concluding with two summary verses.

43–49 were obviously not written for the Israelites in Egypt, but for a much later time when they were settled in Palestine, owned slaves, and had foreigners living among them. This section shows clearly the close tie between nationality and religion in ancient Israel. The general principle is that no foreigner is to eat of the Passover, unless he submits to circumcision; if he submits to circumcision then he is virtually an Israelite, participating in the religion of Israel and in its life.

44. every slave that is bought for money: such a slave would be a foreigner bought by an Israelite. The other type of slave, one 'born in the house', would be circumcised on the eighth day; see Gen. 17:12,23,27. Thus, any slave who had been circumcised could eat of the Passover.

45. sojourner: the precise meaning of *tôšāb* is not clear. He is different from the *gēr*, 'stranger', of verses 48–49. Most likely the *tôšāb* was a less permanent resident or visitor among the Israelites than the *gēr*. 'Visitor' or 'transient alien' might give the right connotation. *Am. Tr.* renders it as 'serf'.

hired servant: a foreigner hired as a day labourer, and thus less permanent than a slave or a *gēr*.

46–47 stress the idea of unity in the Passover: it is to be eaten in
one house (cf. 22); it is roasted whole, no bone of it being
broken (cf. 9); it is to be kept by **all the congregation of Israel.
you shall not break a bone of it:** quoted in Jn. 19:36, in connection with the crucifixion.

48. stranger is Hebrew *gēr*. He would be an alien residing
more or less permanently among the Israelites, who wished to
come under their protection and participate in their religious
observances. The *gēr* is given no special legal status in JE and Dt.,
but P continually seeks to place the *gēr* on virtually the same level
as the native Israelite, enjoying the same rights and subject to the
same laws; see passages such as Num. 35:15; Lev. 19:34; 22:18;
24:16. P repeats several times the rule stated in the next verse.

**49. There shall be one law for the native and for the
stranger who sojourns among you:** see Lev. 24:22; Num.
9:14; 15:15f. LXX renders it *prosēlutos* here and frequently.
Am. Tr. here translates it as 'proselyte'. In P the *gēr* is a convert to
Judaism, for all practical purposes, but we are hardly to assume
that there was active proselytization in the early post-exilic
period.

51. by their hosts: see comment on 6:26.

REGULATIONS CONCERNING FIRSTLINGS AND UNLEAVENED BREAD
13:1–16

13:1–2(P). *Yahweh gives to Moses the general principle that 'whatever
is the first to open the womb among the people of Israel, both of man and
beast, is mine'.*

3–10(RD). *Further regulations concerning the keeping of Unleavened
Bread. It is a memorial of the time that Yahweh brought Israel out of
Egypt.*

11–16(RD). *Regulations concerning the offering of Firstlings. All that
first opens the womb is to be set apart to Yahweh, with these exceptions: the
firstling of an ass is to be redeemed, or its neck broken; and the first-born of
men is to be redeemed. This is to be a memorial of the time when Yahweh
slew the first-born of the Egyptians, and brought the Israelites out of Egypt.*

This is an appendix that is attached, somewhat loosely, to the
preceding account of the release of the Israelites. 1–2, 11–16 give
instructions regarding the consecration of the first-born in Israel,
emphasizing the fact that Yahweh had slain the first-born of men
and livestock in Egypt. 3–10 contain instructions regarding the
Feast of Unleavened Bread, slightly at variance with the preceding.

1–2 are probably from P, but the rest has a strong Deuteronomic colouring in vocabulary and ideas; it is probably from a Deuteronomic redactor, like 12:24–27*a*. It may, however, be built up on a small nucleus of J material (such as verses 12–13).

2 states the general principle concerning the consecration of the first-born:

whatever is the first to open the womb among the people of Israel belongs to Yahweh. This is subsequently defined more closely as referring to males only (12–13). The Hebrew here and elsewhere uses a technical term, *pĕṭer* (*rĕḥem*), 'that which opens (the womb)'. Yahweh is the giver of fertility in men and animals, as well as of the land; the first-born and the first-fruits belong to him (for first-fruits of the soil, see 23:19). Apart from the present chapter, the following are the passages regarding consecration of the first-born: J, 34:19f; E, 22:29*b*–30; Dt. 15:19–23; and P, Num. 3:11–13,40–51; 8:16–18; 18:15–18. It is never stated that the Passover sacrifice was a first-born animal.

3–4 use the second person plural, whereas the second person singular is employed in 2 and 5ff.

the month of Abib: this is the old Canaanite name for the first month, equivalent to March-April (see comment on 12:2). It is used in Dt. 16:1.

5. the land of the Canaanites ... Jebusites: see comment on 3:17. Lists of peoples such as this are particularly frequent in Deuteronomy and the D history of Joshua (Dt. 7:1; 20:17; Jos. 3:10; 9:1; 11:3; 12:8; 24:11).

keep this service: cf. 12:25.

6–7 say nothing of the two days of holy assembly on the first and seventh days, as does 12:16. 12:14 seems to imply that the first day was the day of the feast (*ḥag*, pilgrimage-feast, cf. Lev. 23:5–8).

8. See comment on 12:27 and the references there given.

9. as a sign on your hand and as a memorial between your eyes: see verse 16 below. Note that the 'memorial' of this verse becomes 'frontlets' later.

that the law of the LORD may be in your mouth: a Deuteronomic emphasis (cf. Dt. 6:7; 11:19; Jos. 1:8).

12. set apart to the LORD: the verb is an unusual verb for this idea, its literal meaning being 'cause to pass over'. It is the verb regularly used for sacrificing children to Molech or other foreign gods (2 Kg. 16:3; 23:10; Lev. 18:21; Jer. 32:35 etc.).

firstlings of your cattle: all the livestock, a better rendering for *bᵉhēmāh* (see comment on 9:9). The firstlings of livestock except the asses, which would be cows, sheep and goats, were doubtless in early times slaughtered and the flesh eaten by the worshippers. Deuteronomy specifies that the unblemished firstlings are to be eaten at a sacrificial meal at the central sanctuary, the blemished ones being eaten in secular manner (15:20–23). According to P, the blood and fat are to be offered on the altar, and the flesh given to the priests (Num. 18:17f.).

13. Because the ass was a valuable work animal (see 9:3), and probably considered unclean, it was to be redeemed with a lamb; if not redeemed, it was to be put to death by having its neck broken (so that the blood would not be spilled), and it was not to be worked (cf. Dt. 15:19). P provides for the redemption of all unclean animals at a price of their valuation plus one-fifth (Num. 18:15; Lev. 27:27); somewhat inconsistently, or in another strand of P, it says that the livestock of the Levites are to be taken instead of the firstlings of the Israelites (Num. 3:41,45).

Every first-born of man among your sons you shall redeem: in 22:29b (E) no provision is made specifically for the redemption of first-born children. Some critics take this as an indication that in earliest times the first-born were actually sacrificed; others think that redemption is there taken for granted. The present verse says nothing as to what is to be given as redemption for the child; probably an animal was sacrificed. In Num. 18:16 (P), the redemption price is set at five shekels, 'according to the shekel of the sanctuary'. In Num. 3:40ff., the Levites are taken as substitute for the first-born of the Israelites. The number of the first-born exceeded the number of the Levites by 273, and for those a redemption price of five shekels apiece was paid.

14–15. For this Deuteronomic emphasis and literary form, see comment on 12:26–27 and references given there.

16. as a mark on your hand or frontlets between your eyes: in Dt. 6:8 and 11:18, the Israelites are told to take the words given to them and 'bind them as a sign upon your hand, and they shall be as frontlets between your eyes'. The Jews of later times (the Mishnaic period if not earlier) took the Deuteronomic passage literally and made for themselves *tᵉpillîn*, two cubical leather boxes which were worn on the head and on the left arm, containing the following passages inscribed on small parchments: Exod. 13:1–10,11–16; Dt. 6:4–9; 11:13–21. These are very probably the 'phylacteries' of Mt. 23:5. They were worn particularly at daily morning prayer. The use of the mark probably grew out of the very early custom of placing a tattoo or brand upon the hand as a symbol of the deity to whom one was dedicated and whose protection was sought. The frontlet was in origin a similar badge, or amulet, used for protection and dedication.

The two verses here, 9 and 16, are used as scriptural warrant for the use of the *tᵉpillîn*. In 9, the word *ʾôṭ* is rendered 'sign' rather than 'mark' as here; and 'memorial' (*zikkārôn*) appears instead of 'frontlets' (*ṭôṭāpōṭ*). In these two verses the words are most likely intended to be taken figuratively; it is very difficult to see how the words could be taken literally in connection with the rite of the Unleavened Bread or the rite of Firstlings. In Deuteronomy it is the *words* of Yahweh that are to be bound upon the hand and used as frontlets, and there the literal interpretation is not unnatural.

EXCURSUS: *The Historicity of 11:1—13:16, and the Origin of Passover and Unleavened Bread*

The question of the historicity of 11:1—13:16 has been very much debated by *OT* scholars, and no general agreement has been reached.

On the one hand, some scholars hold that there is a historical nucleus to this narrative. They think that there was a severe epidemic in Egypt which took the lives of many Egyptians, including the first-born son of the King—the Crown Prince who was destined to succeed him. Perhaps it was a very severe and dramatic disease that took only the Crown Prince's life. The Hebrews in Egypt took advantage of the situation to make their escape from slavery; possibly they were even permitted to do so by the frightened Pharaoh. The departure of the Hebrews took place at or near the time of their observance of the Passover rite in the spring; hence, in the years to come they more and more associated that rite with their deliverance from Egypt, and with the rite was combined the Feast of Unleavened Bread. The story of the first nine plagues arose to give a greater aura of wonder to the narrative.

On the other hand, there are scholars who hold that the 'historical' features of this narrative are an invention, designed to form a part of the 'legend' of the Feast of Passover and Unleavened Bread. Liturgy was the mother of history. The story of the striking of the first-born of the Pharaoh and the Egyptians, and even of their cattle, was told to reinforce the law of the offering of the first-born in the Passover ceremony. Sometimes the whole of Exodus 1–15 is considered to be the legend of the Passover ceremony as observed by the Israelites in Canaan (see Introduction, pp. 30–32).

Both of these points of view contain some truth, but neither by itself is fully satisfactory. Our commentary has shown that these chapters have undergone a long period of development; the earliest written material is that of J (Solomonic era), and the latest is that of P (around 400 B.C.). It is clear that P includes much material that is intended to regulate the observance of Passover and the Feast of Unleavened Bread, and the D material in 16:3–16 is designed to give instructions regarding Unleavened Bread and the offering of Firstlings. But some of P contains ancient regulations, and most of J clearly purports to be history rather than rules for the observance of any rites.

The point of view adopted in this commentary may be summarized as follows; on some of the details it is impossible to be precise, but the general course of development can be sketched. (Cf. especially Fohrer, *Überlieferung und Geschichte des Exodus*, pp. 89–97; Roland de Vaux, *Ancient Israel*, pp. 484–93).

The Passover originated in pre-Mosaic times among nomadic shepherds, the ancestors of those who in a later time were to be called Hebrews and Israelites. It was a ceremony performed in the spring, at the time of the full moon of the vernal equinox, and involved the offering of animals from the flock. Great emphasis was placed upon the blood rite in which some of the animal's blood was placed on the tent-poles in order to keep away hostile, demonic powers ('the destroyer'), that could bring sterility or death in the night. The flesh would have been eaten, for nomadic shepherds would not have missed the opportunity to eat meat. Perhaps the flesh was eaten with the seasoning of wild desert plants, and with unleavened cakes. The original Passover did not involve sanctuary, altar or priest, and centred in family life.

The Hebrews took this rite with them into Egypt, where no doubt some continued to live as semi-nomads, although many became settled. There came a year when a series of calamities occurred in Egypt, probably from an unusually heavy inundation of the Nile, culminating in a severe epidemic that took the lives of many Egyptians, prominent as well as humble, and even the life of the Crown Prince. The Hebrews took advantage of the situation and made their escape from their 'house of bondage'. (It could have been a flight rather than a permitted departure, for the Egyptian king tried to overtake them, without success.) Their escape came at the time of the Passover, which was fixed according to the moon, either just at the time of the rite, or very near that time.

When the Israelites settled in Canaan, they adopted the Feast of Unleavened Bread from the Canaanites, who were farmers rather than pastoralists. The Feast of Unleavened Bread was a spring barley harvest ceremony, and as a pilgrimage-feast was observed at the sanctuaries. Its date was fixed by the beginning of the barley harvest, and may have varied in various parts of the country. Yet both Passover and Unleavened Bread came in the spring, near each other. At some time they were united—at least by the time of Deuteronomy, which made them a pilgrimage-feast in the Jerusalem Temple. It is possible that they were united much earlier in the pre-monarchial period; Jos. 5:10–12 may be an indication of that. The tradition more and more 'historicized' the two feasts, Passover and Unleavened Bread, connecting them with the deliverance from Egypt and the death of the first-born of that land. The Deuteronomic redactor inserted regulations concerning offering of the firstlings in Exodus 13, because of the tradition concerning the death of the first-born in Egypt. But the Passover was not an offering of the first-born. This is nowhere stated in the *OT*. There are passages in the *OT* which place regulations concerning the offering of first-born or firstlings near those that concern Passover or Unleavened Bread (Exod. 34:18–20,25–26; Dt. 15:19—16:8), but those are only literary connections. The offering of first-born and firstlings is very ancient, and was in no way based in its origin upon the tenth plague in Egypt.

The history of the traditions concerning the Passover, Unleavened Bread, and Firstlings illustrates two characteristics of Israelite cultic life: (i) the tendency to 'historicize' ceremonies that did not originate with historical events, and (ii) the development of the cultus to meet changing conditions in the life of the Israelite people. The history of many centuries is mirrored in this narrative.

EXODUS FROM EGYPT AND CROSSING OF THE SEA

13:17—15:21

13:17-19(E). *God leads the Israelites out of Egypt, not by way of the land of the Philistines, but by way of the wilderness. They leave Egypt equipped for battle.*
20-22(J). *They move from Succoth to Etham. Yahweh goes before them in a pillar of cloud by day and a pillar of fire by night, so that they may travel by both day and night.*
14:1-4(P). *The people are instructed to turn back and encamp at Pi-ha-hiroth. Yahweh says he will harden Pharaoh's heart so that he will pursue them, but Yahweh will get glory over Pharaoh.*
5-9(J,E,P). *When the king of Egypt hears that the Israelites have fled, he makes ready his chariot and army to pursue them. He overtakes them by Pi-ha-hiroth.*
10-14(J). *When the Israelites see the Egyptians, they are afraid, and cry out to Yahweh. They complain to Moses that he has brought them into the wilderness only to die. Moses tells them not to fear but to be firm, and they will see the salvation which Yahweh will work for them.*
15-18(E,P). *Yahweh tells Moses to order the Israelites to move forward. He tells Moses to lift up his rod and stretch out his hand over the sea; it will divide so that the Israelites can cross over on dry ground. Yahweh promises that he will get glory over Pharaoh and his army.*
21-25(J,P). *Moses stretches out his hand over the sea, Yahweh drives the sea back by a strong east wind, and the Israelites are able to cross the sea on dry ground. The Egyptians pursue the Israelites into the sea.*
26-31(P,J). *When Moses stretches out his hand again, the sea resumes its customary flow and overwhelms the Egyptians. The Israelites see the Egyptians dead on the sea-shore, and thus witness the great work which Yahweh has done against the Egyptians.*
15:1-19(P). *Moses and the people sing a song praising Yahweh for his victory over the Egyptians at the sea, and for leading Israel through the wilderness into the land of promise, even to the sanctuary which his hands established.*
20-21(J). *Miriam and all the women go out with timbrels and dancing, singing a song for Yahweh's victory over the Egyptians.*

The literary analysis of this section is complicated, but it well illustrates some of the characteristic features of the different narratives, especially J and P. The most obvious difference is in the manner of the Israelites' crossing of the sea. In J, Yahweh drives the sea back by a strong east wind, so that the sea becomes dry land and the Israelites cross over; Yahweh discomfits the Egyptian army and clogs their chariot wheels; the sea returns to its wonted flow and Yahweh routs the Egyptians. In P, Moses stretches out his hand over the sea and the waters are divided, allowing the Israelites to cross over between two walls of water. Moses again stretches out his hand, and the waters return, destroying the Egyptians. J characteristically speaks frequently of Yahweh acting directly for the Israelites: Yahweh fights for them, controls the sea by means of the wind, discomfits and routs the Egyptians, and through it all he saves Israel. Israel looks on and sees the salvation which Yahweh works. In P, on the other hand, Moses is a wonder worker, and the crossing of the sea is a more 'supernatural' occurrence than in J. Only fragments of E are preserved, particularly in 14:16, where the rod of Moses is referred to, and in 14:19a, where we read that the angel of God led the host of Israel. In J, Israel is led by the pillar of cloud by day and the pillar of fire by night (13:21f.; 14:19b). J's narrative may be read as a continuous and complete account of the events recorded here; it is the basic narrative, and probably has been preserved intact. P is an almost complete account. Little of E is preserved (according to some scholars, not even fragments of E are to be found).

The analysis is as follows: J—13:20-22; 14:5-6,10-14,19b-20, 21b ('and the Lord drove . . . dry land'), 24-25,27b ('and the sea returned . . . midst of the sea'), 30-31; 15:20-21; E—13:17-19; 14:7,16 ('Lift up your rod'), 19a; P—14:1-4,8-9,15,16b-18,21a,c, 22-23,26-27a ('. . . over the sea'), 28-29; 15-1:19. The poems in 15:1b-18 and 15:21 are each older than the narratives in which they have been used (P and J). See below on 15:1-21.

Yahweh's leading of Israel out of Egypt through the Red Sea was considered by them as the climactic and decisive act of salvation for the people. It acquired greater and greater significance as time went on, as Yahweh's mightiest act of salvation and redemption. Modern critics have often sought to determine what actually happened, and where the crossing took place. It is apparent that the J narrative presents the events recorded here in a more 'natural' manner than the later narratives. Nevertheless, we cannot now take them at their face value, and we cannot determine with accuracy either what happened or where it happened. The earliest tradition saw the crossing of the sea as the result of Yahweh's direct action on Israel's behalf. That tradition was not interested in representing the event in the same manner as a modern historian would describe it. Furthermore, the tradition does not offer clear evidence of the location for the event, not even where the earliest tradition represented it as taking place. The place and manner of the crossing are discussed further in an excursus below, pp. 156–61.

JOURNEY FROM SUCCOTH TO THE SEA 13:17—14:4

13:17. God did not lead the Israelites **by way of the land of the Philistines:** this was probably the military route that led along the shore of the Mediterranean Sea into the SW. sector of Palestine, called by the Egyptians 'the Ways of Horus'. It began at the frontier fortress of Zilu and ran to Raphia in SW. Palestine. This was the nearest route, if the Israelites were in fact setting out for Canaan, or for a mountain located just to the south of Canaan. E represents God as rejecting such a route, lest the Israelites come into contact with the war-like and well-equipped Philistines and then wish to return to Egypt. If the exodus took place in the thirteenth century B.C. or earlier (see Introduction, pp. 143–44), 'land of the Philistines' is anachronistic. The Philistines settled in Canaan after their decisive defeat by Ramses III in 1188 B.C.; there were, however, some Philistines in Palestine before that time, but hardly enough to give rise to the designation of a 'land' after them; cf. G. E. Wright, 'Fresh Evidence for the Philistine Story', *BA*, xxix (1966), pp. 70–86.

18. They went out of Egypt **equipped for battle:** P represents the Israelites as going out of Egypt as an army in battle array (see comment on 6:26). While that would be artificial for a group of people who had been slaves in Egypt, we may well believe they left Egypt with some arms in order to combat resistance at the border fortresses. This verse is from E.

19. See Gen. 50:25 (also E).

20. Succoth is probably to be identified with modern Tell el-Maskhuta in the Wadi Tumilat; see detailed comment on 1:11, and also 12:37.

Etham cannot be identified. Num. 33:6 also refers to it as **on the edge of the wilderness,** and Num. 33:8 refers to a 'wilderness of Etham', presumably the wilderness area which it adjoined. It may have been the site of an Egyptian fortress on the eastern border of Egypt, and thus east of Succoth.

21–22. J represents Yahweh as leading the Israelites by going before them **by day in a pillar of cloud** and **by night in a pillar of fire;** thus they are able to **travel by day and by night** (cf. 14:19-20, and Num. 14:14). E and P have somewhat different representations of the cloud. E says that when Moses would enter the tent of meeting, a pillar of cloud would descend and stand at the door of the tent as Yahweh spoke with Moses (Exod. 33:7-11; Num. 11:25; 12:5,10; Dt. 31:15). There is no mention of a fiery cloud at night, for the cloud is not for the purpose of guiding the people, but to indicate the presence of Yahweh at a particular place. According to P, a cloud covered the tent of meeting, or Tabernacle, when it was finished, and then 'the glory of the Lord filled the tabernacle'. Moses was not able to enter it because of this cloud. Whenever the cloud would ascend from above the Tabernacle, the Israelites would go onward in their journey, resting when it came to rest. At night the cloud had the appearance of fire (Exod. 40:34-38; Num. 9:15-16). P thus agrees with E in associating the cloud with the tent of meeting, and with J in making it a guiding cloud. There have been various conjectures as to the origin of this tradition. Some have thought it originated from the custom, attested in ancient times and among modern Arabs, of carrying braziers filled with burning wood at the head of an army or caravan to indicate the line of march. Others believed that the tradition arose from the phenomena of thick clouds and lightning associated with Mount Sinai that suggest volcanic activity (see 19:16-18; 24:15-18). The latter is more probable.

14:1-2. The Israelites are instructed to **turn back,** presumably from Etham, a border fortress which they failed to pass (see 13:20 above) and **encamp in front of Pi-ha-hiroth.** Verses 1-4 are from P, with characteristic phraseology and specific detail, but unfortunately the sites are difficult or impossible to identify.

Pi-ha-hiroth: Hahiroth in Num. 33:8, and Num. 33:7 says it was 'east of Baal-zephon'. Here and in verse 9, LXX renders it by *epaulis*, meaning 'encampment' or 'unwalled city' (possibly from a Hebrew text that had *ḥaṣērôṭ*). The name may be a corruption of the Egyptian place-name Pr-Ḥthr 'House of (the goddess) Hathor', but it cannot be identified.

Migdol: a name of Semitic origin meaning 'tower' or 'fortress'. Towns with the same name are mentioned in Jer. 44:1; 46:14; Ezek. 29:10; 30:6, all in northern Egypt, but we cannot be certain that all are the same. Migdol is often identified with modern Tell el-Her, just south of Pelusium, but the biblical text suggests a place west of that point, probably north of Succoth and near Tell Defneh.

Baal-Zephon: of Semitic origin, meaning 'Lord of the North' or 'Lord of (Mount) Zaphon'. This deity was associated particularly with the mountain in Syria north of Ugarit. Two suggestions have been made for identification of the site. One is modern Tell Defneh, classical Daphnae, Egyptian Tahpanhes. A papyrus letter of the sixth century B.C. which mentions 'Baal-zephon and all the gods of Tahpanhes' suggests that a temple of that deity existed at or near Tahpanhes. The other identification is with the Graeco-Roman Casium, modern Ras Kasrun, about 25 miles E. of Mohammediyeh on the thin strip of land separating the Mediterranean Sea from Lake Sirbonis. This site seems, however, to be too far to the east and too close to the 'way of the land of the Philistines' which the Hebrews are said to have avoided. See the excursus below, pp. 151–61.

3. They are entangled in the land: the meaning is perhaps best given by *Am. Tr.*: 'They are wandering aimlessly in the land; the desert has shut them in'. Their wanderings suggested to Pharaoh that they did not know where they were going, and were having difficulty getting out of Egypt. They had to contend with the Egyptian border fortresses and the perils of the desert as well as with the sea.

4. I will harden Pharaoh's heart: see comment on 7:3.

I will get glory over Pharaoh and all his host: the terminology and idea are characteristic of P, who emphasized the honour that comes to Yahweh from the display of his power over the Egyptian army; see verses 17f. below, and, for the phraseology, Lev. 10:3.

the Egyptians shall know that I am the LORD: see comment on 6:7.

PURSUIT BY THE EGYPTIANS **14:5-20**

5. The first clause of this verse is considered by some critics as a remnant of the earliest tradition concerning the departure from Egypt, differing from the account in chapter 13 in indicating that the Israelites fled hastily from the land without the permission of Pharaoh. Thus it is assigned to E, or to an early strand of J. However, we assign verses 5–6 to J, because they are not entirely inconsistent with the account of J in 12:33-34,39 which says that the Israelites left in great haste. It is likely that the Israelite departure was a hurried one, but it may have been with the Egyptian king's consent. The belief that Pharaoh gave his consent became more and more prominent, however, in the tradition concerning the plagues and the exodus, with extensive negotiations between Moses and the Egyptian king. Many critics think the exodus was really a secret escape, without the king's consent. See remarks in the Introduction, pp. 44-45.

7 is E's duplicate of 6.

with officers over all of them: the literal meaning seems to be, 'with three (men) in each of them'. The writer may have in mind here the practice known among the Hittites, Assyrians and Syrians, and presumably the Hebrews, of having three men in each chariot—a driver, a warrior, and a third man who was shield-bearer and aide for the warrior. In Egypt each chariot customarily had only two occupants—a driver and a warrior. However, it is quite possible that *šālîš* had acquired the general meaning of 'officer', 'captain', or the like (cf. Exod. 15:4; 2 Kg. 7:2,17,19; 9:25; 10:25; 15:25).

8-9 is from P, continuing verses 1-4. The first clause of 9 may be a fragment of J. On the location of **Pi-ha-hiroth** and **Baal-zephon,** see comment on 14:1.

11-12 is similar to complaints found in 16:3; 17:3; Num. 11:4-6; 14:2-3; 16:12-14; 20:3-5; 21:5. The murmuring of the Israelites against Moses is a persistent element in the tradition of the exodus and the wilderness wandering. Many of the Israelites recalled their life in Egypt, and thought it was better than the hardships they experienced in the desert. It is a tribute to the patience and leadership of Moses that he was able to keep the Israelites on their way. See below, introductory comments on 15:22—18:27, pp. 170-71.

13-14. Moses assures the Israelites that they have only to **stand firm, and see the salvation of the LORD, which he will work for you. . . . The LORD will fight for you, and you have only to be still.** It is J who emphasizes the divine initiative and activity in the exodus: Yahweh works for the salvation of his people and fights directly for them. In the ancient Israelite concept of 'holy war', Yahweh was the warrior for Israel; the duty of the Israelites was to stand still and see what Yahweh would do. P places more stress upon human activity, but sees the event as primarily Yahweh's act.

16. Lift up your rod is probably a small fragment of E's account of the departure from Egypt. In the accounts of the plagues, E several times has Moses lifting his rod (or hand) to bring about the miracle (7:20; 9:23; 10:13,22). It is uncertain whether the further references in this chapter to Moses' stretching his hand over the sea to divide it, or to bring the waters back again, are from E or from P. With most critics we have assigned them to P. In the accounts of the plagues, P speaks several times of Aaron producing a wonder by means of his rod or outstretched hand (7:19; 8:5,16), but Aaron does not appear at all in the narrative of the crossing of the sea.

17-18 expand the message in verse 4.

19. The first half of this verse is from E, the second half from J. E represents the Israelites as being led by the **angel of God**; cf. other references to the angel of God by E in Gen. 21:17; 31:11; Exod. 32:34; Num. 20:16. On the **pillar of cloud,** see 13:21f. above, and the comment *in loc.*

20. The Hebrew text of the second half of this verse is corrupt. *RSV* follows LXX in reading **the night passed.** A literal rendering of the Hebrew is: 'And the cloud was and the darkness, and it illumined the night. And no one drew near to another all the night'. With emendation of the Hebrew, reading *heḥᵃešiḳ* instead of *haḥōšeḳ*, and *wayyaᶜaḇᵉrû* instead of *wayyāʾer*, we may render: 'The cloud grew dark, and they passed the night without one (army) coming near the other'. Jos. 24:7 refers to this event, saying 'And when they cried to the Lord, he put darkness between you and the Egyptians'. The meaning is that the pillar of cloud, which led the Israelites by day, grew dark, the pillar of fire did not appear, and thus darkness stood between the Egyptian and Israelite armies. The Egyptians were thus unable to attack the Israelites on that fateful night, and the Israelites crossed the sea during the night.

CROSSING OF THE SEA **14:21-31**

21 is a combination of P and J. According to P, **Then Moses stretched out his hand over the sea, and the waters were divided.** According to J, **the LORD drove the sea back by a strong east wind all night, and made the sea dry land.** In P, Moses is a wonder-worker; in J, Yahweh works directly to drive the sea back by an east wind.

strong east wind: in 10:13-15, an east wind brings the swarm of locusts that cause great devastation and also darken the land. In the 'Song of the Sea' in chapter 15, we read in verse 10 of Yahweh blowing with his wind, and in verse 8 of the blast of his nostrils piling up the waters. This strong east wind has been used by many modern critics as the key to a 'rational' explanation of the event here described. They say that a strong east wind (or perhaps, more precisely, a north-east wind) could dry up the waters of a lake or a bay of the sea (either of the Mediterranean or of the Gulf of Suez), especially if it was a hot, dry wind off the desert. With the subsiding of the wind, or its change of direction, the sea would return to 'its wonted flow' (verse 27) and overwhelm the Egyptians. Concerning this explanation we may say, first, that the J tradition certainly did not look upon this as a natural event, but as a mighty display of Yahweh's power; and second, that as a natural explanation it is cogent only if the 'sea' referred to here was a very shallow body of water or only a wet marsh. This latter is possible; see the excursus below, pp. 156-61.

22-23 are from P, a continuation of verse 21. This highly miraculous account of the crossing may have been influenced, in the course of the development of the exodus tradition, by the tradition concerning the Israelites' crossing of the Jordan river. According to Jos. 3:17 the Israelites crossed over the Jordan 'on dry ground'. In Ps. 114:3,4 the 'sea' and the Jordan are brought together in a psalm that briefly treats together the exodus from Egypt and the conquest of Canaan.

24-25 are from the J tradition. Here the emphasis is on the panic produced among the Egyptians when Yahweh **looked down** upon them. Ps. 77:16-20, which describes the passage through the sea, speaks of rain, thunder, lightning and earthquake. The tradition implies a theophany which struck terror in the enemy. Thus Yahweh **discomfited the host of the Egyptians.** The verb employed here (*hāmam*) is used when Yahweh is said to cause panic or confusion in an enemy of Israel (cf. 23:27; Jos. 10:10; Jg. 4:15; 1 Sam. 7:10). This took place at the time of **the morning watch,** the third division of the night, approximately 2 a.m. to 6 a.m. Originally this may have expressed the idea that the Egyptians were put into a panic during the time of great darkness referred to in verse 20.

clogging their chariot wheels so that they drove heavily: the Hebrew text here has a verb meaning 'remove' or 'turn aside'

(*sûr*). The Samaritan text, LXX, and Syriac apparently have a
different root meaning 'bind', from which the *RSV* translation is
derived. If this is correct, the words suggest that the Egyptian
chariots were bogged down in the mud or quicksand over which the
Israelites had been able to pass easily. However, this clause comes
too early in the account, for there is no reference to the return of
the waters until verse 27. Some scholars thus consider this to be a
fragment of E or an early strand of J, or a secondary addition to J.
It is an item of the tradition that has not been well integrated with
the rest of the narrative, either of J or of P.

the LORD fights for them: the Egyptians recognize that
Yahweh fights for the Israelites, as promised in verse 14. This is
the concept of 'holy war', in which Yahweh fights on behalf of his
people, who have only to stand and watch him win the victory
(cf. verses 14, 27, 31).

26-27a (. . . hand over the sea) are P's continuation of the
account, following 23. Moses' outstretched hand had caused the
waters to be divided; now it brings them together again to overwhelm the Egyptians. The rest of 27 is the continuation of J's
narrative, following 25. J does not say what caused the sea to
return to its bed. Presumably the wind died down or changed its
direction; there may have been a storm (see excursus below,
pp. 156-61).

its wonted flow: these words suggest to some readers the return
of a tide. This would be possible if the crossing took place, for
example, near modern Suez, across the northern arm of the Gulf
of Suez, where the tide is affected by the winds; or perhaps at the
southern end of Lake Menzaleh. The Hebrew word used here,
ᵓêṭān, is twice used adjectivally to refer to 'ever-flowing' streams
(Am. 5:24; Ps. 74:15; cf. Dt. 21:4).

the Egyptians fled into it: taken literally, this suggests that the
Egyptians had reached the eastern side of the sea, and now
they fled back into the sea where they were overwhelmed.
In the tradition of J, the look of Yahweh caused panic in the
Egyptian army (verse 24) and caused them to flee back into
the sea. If 25a is an original part of this tradition, but out of place,
we may assume that the Egyptians fled back into the sea-bed,
where their chariots became bogged down in the wet mud or
quicksand.

28-29 are P's continuation of the narrative, following 27a. In
this tradition the waters of the sea were considered to have

overwhelmed the Egyptians as they attempted to pursue the Israelites.

30–31 are J's conclusion to the whole episode. It stresses the initiative and activity of Yahweh in saving Israel from her enemy, the Egyptians. As they saw the great work of Yahweh on their behalf they believed in him and in Moses. Thus the doubts expressed in 10–14 are overcome.

his servant Moses: within the Pentateuch the designation 'servant' is used for Moses only here and in Num. 12:7f.; Dt. 34:5. It is frequent in the book of Joshua.

EXCURSUS: *The Site and Manner of the Israelites' Crossing of the Sea*

We have seen that the story of the Israelites' crossing of the sea comes to us from differing traditions, principally J and P, and that there are some inconsistencies within the tradition of J. This is one of the reasons why it is difficult for us to determine what actually happened, and where it occurred. Another difficulty arises from the uncertainty in identification of sites mentioned in the narrative, and from our ignorance as to some of the ancient topographical features of the region involved.

We have seen that the biblical account lays emphasis on the belief of the Israelites that their crossing was made possible by a great act of Yahweh, who on their behalf fought and destroyed the Egyptian army. Little is said of human effort; Moses had only to raise his arm to make the waters divide, and raise it again to make them come together. Nevertheless, we must view the crossing of the sea as a historical event—that is, a happening in space and time, in which human beings acted and were acted upon. It is not presented as a mythological event; Yahweh does not fight against the sea, but against a human foe. The essence of the historical happening was the unexpected defeat of an Egyptian force, made possible by something that occurred at a 'sea'. Thus the Israelites were enabled to escape from the land of Egypt.

In discussing this subject, two things should be kept in mind, one a fact, the other a probability.

The fact is that it was not absolutely necessary for the Israelites to cross a body of water in order to travel from Egypt into the Sinai peninsula. Many persons imagine that Egypt in ancient times was separated from that peninsula by a continuous body of water, as it is today. But the Suez Canal was dug in the nineteenth century A.D. The isthmus of Suez at its narrowest is about 70 miles from north to south. Of this distance, about forty miles are covered by lakes, the rest being land. The lakes from north to south, counting all of those from the modern Port Said to Suez, are Lake Menzaleh (an arm of the Mediterranean), the Balaḥ Lakes, Lake Timsaḥ, and the (two) Bitter Lakes. There were very probably in ancient times marshy lagoons on some of the regions between these lakes. However, at a point north of Lake Timsaḥ the isthmus reaches a height of 52 feet above sea level, and there are other high points along the way. In ancient times Egyptian border fortresses guarded some of the land areas, if not all of them.

We can only conjecture the reason why the Israelites found themselves faced with the necessity of crossing water. Perhaps they did not know their way and found themselves accidentally trapped; this may be the meaning of Exod. 14:3. Or they may have pursued such a course intentionally in order to trap the Egyptians, with their heavy chariots. Or, as a third possibility, they may have been pushed into such a trap by the Egyptian army. They were apparently faced with the necessity of either fighting their way past an Egyptian fortress, or making their way through a body of water.

The probability which we must keep in mind is that there was a military encounter between the Israelites and the Egyptians. This is never stated by the narrative, since the Israelites believed that it was Yahweh himself who fought against their foe, but it is implied in various ways. P represents the Israelites as marching out of Egypt 'by their hosts', in battle array (6:26; see comment there). E says that they were 'equipped for battle' (13:18). There are several references to the Israelites camping or being in an encampment (13:20; 14:2,9,19,20; the Hebrew words are ḥānāh and maḥᵃneh). The Egyptians are pictured as pursuing the Israelites with royal chariotry, headed by Pharaoh himself (14:5–10). All of this evidence, as well as common sense, suggests to us that the Israelites themselves left Egypt with some weapons of war, such as slaves could afford to buy or make, and that they were pursued by a much better armed Egyptian force, equipped with chariots. If it was not actually a royal army, it was a force from one of the Egyptian border fortresses.

As to the place at which the crossing occurred, we must note first that some modern critics believe any attempt to determine the place is futile. Their belief is based in part on the general nature of the narratives which, as we have seen, had little interest in the event as a historical occurrence. It is based specifically on lack of confidence in the topographical data given in Exod. 14:2. This is in a P section, and is believed by some critics to be only a late attempt to localize the crossing, and thus to have no historical value (cf. Martin Noth, 'Der Schauplatz des Meereswunders', *Festschrift Otto Eissfeldt*, ed. J. Fück [1947], pp. 181–90). However, it is quite possible that P has preserved an ancient tradition, and we must make the best use we can of the topographical data at our disposal.

In chapter 14 the place of crossing is always referred to only as 'the sea'. Hebrew *yām* is a very general word which may be used of a lake, a sea (such as the Mediterranean), a river (such as the Nile, Isa. 19:5) or possibly other bodies of water. However, in Exod. 13:18 a body of water is referred to as the Red Sea, and that is the designation often used in other passages which speak of the crossing of the sea (Exod. 15:4,22; Dt. 11:4; Jos. 2:10; 4:23; 24:6; Ps. 106:7,9,22; Neh. 9:9 etc.). The Hebrew in such passages is *yām sûp*, which means literally 'sea of reeds', or 'sea of rushes'. In Exod. 2:3,5 *sûp* is used of 'the reeds' in which Moses was placed. *Yām sûp* could well be rendered 'Reed Sea'. The translation in *RSV* by 'Red Sea' is based upon the rendering in LXX, *eruthra thalassa*, and Vulgate, *mare rubrum*. In antiquity 'the Red Sea' was a general term including the Indian Ocean, the Persian Gulf, and perhaps even more. Today it is applied to the large body of water which separates Arabia from Africa, extending from the Gulf of Aden to the Gulfs of Suez and Aqaba. It was certainly not this large body of water which the Israelites crossed.

The *OT* uses *yām sûp* with more than one meaning. In 1 Kg. 9:26 it clearly refers to the Gulf of Aqaba, and probably also in Num. 21:4; Dt. 2:1. In Num. 33:10 (P) *yām sûp* obviously means the Gulf of Suez, and is distinguished from 'the sea' through which the Israelites had passed just after leaving Hahiroth (33:8). An Egyptian text says that near the city of Raamses-Tanis (see Exod. 1:11) there was a body of water called 'lake of reeds', using the Egyptian word from which Hebrew *sûp* was derived.

The earliest tradition of the exodus from Egypt may have related only the crossing of a 'sea', which was later identified with the *yām sûp*, on the basis of its occurrence in 'the Song of the Sea', at Exod. 15:4. The early identification may have been based on the proximity of the place of crossing to the Gulf of Suez, or possibly confusion with the Gulf of Aqaba. Another possibility is that several bodies of water were called *yām sûp*, and the place of crossing was one.

Several suggestions have been made as to the place of the actual crossing of the isthmus of Suez:

(i) Across the southern end of the isthmus, either in the arm of the Gulf of Suez which is near the modern town of Suez (where the tide is greatly influenced by winds from the N. or NE.), or somewhere between the Gulf of Suez and the Bitter Lakes. It was formerly believed that the Gulf of Suez extended in ancient times as far north as the Bitter Lakes, but modern archaeological findings at the head of the two gulfs of Suez and Aqaba have proved that the water level has not changed appreciably in the last 3,500 years. This theory places the crossing too far from the land of Goshen and the most probable sites of the places mentioned in the narrative.

(ii) Across the centre of the isthmus in the vicinity of Lake Timsah, near the modern town of Ismailiya or at the southern end of that lake. This theory has the advantage of placing the crossing just W. of the land of Goshen (Wadi Tumilat) and the site of Succoth. However, after encamping at Etham, which was on the edge of the wilderness, the Israelites were told to 'turn back' and encamp in the vicinity of Pi-ha-hiroth and Baal-zephon, between Migdol and 'the sea' (Exod. 13:20; 14:1–2; cf. Num. 33:5–8). Though we cannot identify Etham with certainty, it was probably the site of an Egyptian fortress which the Israelites were unable to pass. Thus they must have 'turned back' either to the N. or to the S., to attempt their exit at another point. There were probably marshy lagoons at both ends of Lake Timsah, and the lake itself may have been no more than a large marsh at times.

(iii) Across the northern end of the isthmus—that is, at the southern end of Lake Menzaleh, or in the marshy lagoon just S. of it. This seems to us to be the most likely place of crossing, if our identification of Baal-zephon with Tell Defneh is correct (see comment on 14:2). The terrain here is such that there could have been a body of water to be crossed that was called *yām sûp*, 'Sea of Reeds'. The passage would then have been within the neighbourhood of the modern town of Qantara.

(iv) Across the narrow strip of sandy land which separates Lake Sirbonis (modern Lake Bardawil) from the Mediterranean Sea. That strip may have been the 'tongue of the sea of Egypt' of

Isa. 11:15. In this view the *yām sûp* was Lake Sirbonis, which was surrounded in various areas by reeds. The Israelites fled across the narrow strip, but a strong E. wind caused a break-through of the strip, and the Egyptians were overwhelmed by water. Baal-zephon is then identified with modern Ras Kasrun, about 25 miles E. of Mohammediyeh, and Migdol with Tell el-Her. This is an attractive theory which is held by several modern scholars. It seems to us, however, to place the crossing too far to the NE., and too close to the 'way of the land of the Philistines', which they were to avoid (13:17). Also, we prefer the identification of Baal-zephon with Tell Defneh, as indicated above.

If we turn now to discuss the manner in which the Israelites crossed the sea, we may conjecture that it took place as follows. A strong, hot wind from the E. or NE. blew for several days, and dried up the water in a marshy lagoon around the southern end of Lake Menzaleh, which was the 'sea' the Israelites were to cross. A wind such as this in the spring could not only succeed in drying up such a lagoon, or at least in reducing its water level appreciably, but also cause considerable darkness by the sand and dust blown up. This could be the darkness of Exod. 14:20. (The Egyptian *khamsîn* was caused by a southerly wind; see comment on 10:13-14 and 13:22). The Israelites were able to cross the 'sea' because they were only lightly armed infantry. The east wind suddenly died down. Exod. 14:24, which says that Yahweh looked down upon the Egyptian army in a pillar of fire and cloud, and threw them into a panic, suggests that there may have been a sudden violent storm, with rain, thunder and lightning (suggested also by Ps. 77:16-20). Such a storm would have brought water into the marsh and frightened the Egyptians, who could now say that Yahweh was fighting for Israel (14:25). The Egyptians may have first succeeded in crossing the 'sea' from west to east when the water was low, but as they attempted to cross back to Egypt in panic, their chariot wheels were bogged down in the mud or quicksand. Many of the Egyptians were drowned in the water or killed by the Israelites, who could easily overcome them as they were bogged down in the mire. Then the Israelites made good their escape to the east.

This reconstruction is, of course, quite speculative. We can be sure, however, that something took place which led the Israelites to believe that Yahweh had saved them from the Egyptians. In our view, that which happened was a combination of natural

forces, the strong east wind and a storm, and their own effort in
military encounter with the Egyptians.

To some extent we can trace out influences which led to the
development of the tradition from this historical event to the form
in which it occurs in Exodus, chapter 14, and other places in the
OT, particularly Exod. 15:1-12; Ps. 77:16-20; 106:7-11;
136:13-15. That which had occurred over a space of several days,
including the duration of the east wind, was compressed into a
single night perhaps for cultic reasons, or because of the influence
of the single Passover night (Exod. 12:29ff.). The event was
interpreted in the light of the concept of 'holy war', which
developed in the pre-monarchial period in Canaan. The event
became more and more 'supernatural', with Moses as a wonder-
worker, as can be seen in other parts of the Exodus narrative.
The story of the passage through the sea was probably influenced
by the tradition concerning the crossing of the Jordan 'on dry
ground'; the two crossings are mentioned together in Jos. 4:23
and Ps. 114:3,5.

The story as told in Exod. 14 has little if any mythology. The
enemy of Yahweh is not the sea, but the Egyptians under Pharaoh;
Yahweh uses the wind and the sea to overwhelm the Egyptians.
In the course of time, however, the passage of the sea came to be
interpreted in mythological terms as a conflict between Yahweh
and the Sea, as Canaanite and other Near Eastern mythology had
depicted creation as resulting from conflict between a deity and
Chaos or the Sea; cf. Isa. 51:9f.; Ps. 77:16-20; 106:9, and perhaps
Exod. 15:8.

Finally, we may say that if the original tradition told only of the
crossing of a 'sea' (which may have been in fact a marshy lagoon),
the identification of this as the *yām sûp* may be a part of the
development of tradition, as the event became localized. Of this
we cannot be sure, since *yām sûp* could have been the name of
several different bodies of water (on this, cf. especially N. H.
Snaith, '*Yām sûp*: the Sea of Reeds: the Red Sea', *VT*, xv [1965],
pp. 395-98).

Two Victory Hymns Praising Yahweh 15:1-21

The account of the crossing of the sea is followed by two poems
which celebrate the victory of Yahweh over the forces of Egypt.
The first poem, 1a-18, is followed by a short prose summary or

F

explanation; the second consists of only one verse, 21. It is generally believed that the first, the Song of the Sea, is an elaboration of the second, the Song of Miriam. If this is correct, the 'Song of Miriam' may be much older than the 'Song of the Sea'.

THE SONG OF THE SEA 15:1–19

This poem is called by a variety of names: 'Song of Moses', 'Song of the Sea', 'Victory Hymn of Moses', 'Song of the Reed Sea', and even 'Song of Miriam'. Because the song in Dt. 32 is also attributed to Moses, the first designation is likely to be ambiguous. We prefer to call it simply 'Song of the Sea'.

This is one of the finest poems in the Pentateuch. It is vivid, is carefully composed by strophes, and makes excellent use of assonance, repetition, and climax. The metre is usually 2:2, but is occasionally 3:3; good discussion of the literary composition and probable liturgical use is James Muilenburg, 'A Liturgy on the Triumphs of Yahweh', *Studia Biblica et Semitica Theodoro Christiano Vriezen dedicata* (1966), pp. 233–51. For a more recent form-critical analysis, see G. W. Coats, 'The Song of the Sea', *CBQ*, XXXI (1969), pp. 1–17.

It seems probable that this poem was used in the cult, and various suggestions have been made as to the occasion on which it was employed. The most frequent suggestion is Passover, but it has also been connected with the supposed annual Festival of the Enthronement of Yahweh. The former view is more likely, because of the close association of this poem with the account of the first Passover, but it may have been used liturgically on various occasions because of the central importance of the theme of the crossing of the sea.

There is no agreement among scholars regarding the date, and the widest divergence can be found in the various treatments. According to F. M. Cross and D. N. Freedman, the poem in its original form dates from the twelfth century B.C., and in its present form from the eleventh century ('The Song of Miriam', *JNES*, XIV [1955], pp. 237–50). This date is maintained also by Cross in his later article, 'The Song of the Sea and Canaanite Myth', *JTC*, V (1968), pp. 1–25, although he excludes verse 2 as a secondary interpolation. At the other extreme, R. H. Pfeiffer dated it in the second half of the fifth century, and considered it to be 'a homiletic and devout paraphrase' of Miriam's Song by 'a pseudo-poet' (*Introduction*, p. 281). G. Fohrer also considers it to be post-Exilic, influenced in verse 18 by Second Isaiah (Sellin-Fohrer, *Introduction*, p. 189). The poem is often assigned to the seventh century; Beer, for example, thought it was a cantata composed for the great celebration of the Passover in the time of Josiah, 621 B.C. We believe that verses 1–12 may be very old, or at least incorporate very old material, possibly as old as Cross and Freedman maintain, but that verses 13–18 presuppose the conquest of Canaaṇ and probably the erection of Solomon's Temple. In its present form this 'Song of the Sea', which should be interpreted as a unit, is therefore not earlier than the time of Solomon; it may have been composed at that time or soon thereafter. The poem was inserted in its present position by the one who wrote verse 19, that is, by P or by someone who knew the P tradition of chapter 14. It may, of course, have existed independently for a long time before then, but we cannot assign it to the J or E source. It could have been composed in the seventh century.

The general outline of the 'Song of the Sea' is clear: verses 1*b*–11 (or 12) treat the overthrow of the forces of Egypt in the Sea; 12(or 13)–17 celebrate the leading of the Israelites by Yahweh into the promised land; 18 is the final ascription of praise to Yahweh as King. Muilenburg offers the following analysis of the poem: It opens with a hymnic introit (1*b*). This is followed by four main divisions. The first three divisions are 2–6, 7–11, 12–16*b*. Each of these has three parts: hymnic confession (2–3, 7–8, 12–14), epic narrative (4–5, 9–10, 15–16*b*), and hymnic response (6, 11, 16*cd*). The fourth main division (17) celebrates Yahweh's occupation of the land and enthronement in the sanctuary; it stands outside the earlier structural divisions because it was designed to 'bring the worshipping congregation to the present' (*loc. cit.*, p. 249). The poem closes with a coda: 'Yahweh will reign forever!', probably a closing acclamation by the people. Muilenburg thinks the liturgy was used in the autumnal festival in the sanctuary, the participants being the person who played the role of Moses in the cult, the people, and perhaps the Temple choirs.

1. The first two lines of the poem, which serve as an introduction or liturgical introit, correspond almost precisely to the 'Song of Miriam' (verse 21); see comment *in loc.* The only difference is that here the opening words are **I will sing to the LORD,** whereas verse 21 has a plural imperative, 'Sing to the Lord'. Both forms occur in Hebrew poems. The first person occurs in the 'Song of

Deborah' (Jg. 5:3), and in Ps. 89:1; 101:1; 108:1. The 'I' is Moses, or the person taking the role of Moses in the cult, or the personified community.

his rider: *RSV* mg. 'its chariot' is to be preferred. It is not likely that horses were ridden by the Egyptians at this time. Cf. comment on 9:3, and see verse 4 below.

2. my song: Cross and Freedman suggest this should be rendered 'my defence', on the basis of comparison with South Arabic and with Amorite proper names. This is appropriate here.

my father's God: For parallels to this expression see 3:6, where Yahweh says to Moses, 'I am the God of your father'; and 18:4 where the explanation of the name of Moses' child, Eliezer, is, 'The God of my father was my help, and delivered me from the sword of Pharaoh'. See excursus above, pp. 78–81.

3. The LORD is a man of war: the phrase is used of human soldiers (Jg. 20:17; 1 Sam. 16:18; Isa. 3:2 etc.). Yahweh was viewed as fighting for Israel in order to save them from the Egyptian army, 14:14,25.

4. picked officers: on the meaning see comment on 14:7.

Red Sea: chapter 14 always speaks of the body of water crossed by Israel only as 'the sea'. For the meaning of *yām sûp*, here rendered Red Sea, see excursus at the end of chapter 14, above. 'Reed Sea' is a better rendering.

5. The floods cover them: this corresponds with the P account in 14:28.

6 is perhaps to be considered, with Muilenburg (see above), as a hymnic response, or refrain, like 11 and 16*b*.

glorious in power: Cross and Freedman render this 'is awesome in power', considering *ne'dārî* to be an infinitive absolute used for a finite verb.

8 is similar in its conception to the P account in 14:22,29. The **floods** and **deeps** are here perhaps the subterranean waters, and the conflict between Yahweh and the waters may thus be conceived in mythological terms, under the influence of the ancient Near Eastern myth of a primeval combat between a deity and Chaos or the Sea (cf. the Babylonian myth of creation, *ANET*, pp. 60–72, and the Ugaritic myth of the conflict between Baal and Sea, *ANET*, pp. 129–31). If the poem is early, the P account may be a literalizing of the mythological account.

10. thy wind: Cf. the 'strong east wind' of 14:21, and also 15:8. *Rû*a*ḥ* may mean wind, breath, or spirit. The

Hebrews considered the wind to be the breath of God; cf. Isa.
40:7; 59:19.

11 is perhaps to be considered, with Muilenburg (see above),
as a hymnic response, or refrain, like verses 6 and 16. The literary
device of a rhetorical question is frequently used to express the
incomparability of Yahweh; cf. Ps. 35:10; 71:19; 89:6-8; Isa.
40:18,25; Mic. 7:18.

among the gods: ʾēlîm in this context does not mean high gods,
but 'heavenly beings', like the 'sons of god' in passages such as
Ps. 29:1; 89:7; Dt. 32:8, *RSV.*

majestic in holiness: it is perhaps better to follow LXX and
Syro-hexaplar, which presuppose *keḏōšîm* instead of *ḳōḏeš,* and
render, 'majestic among the holy ones'. This fits the parallelism.
The background of this verse is the idea of a heavenly council,
which was found in Near Eastern religion and is evidenced in a
number of *OT* passages such as Isa. 6:1ff.; 40:1-11; Jer. 23:18,22;
Job 1:6ff.; Ps. 58:1; 82:1; 86:8. Yahweh was conceived as
presiding over a heavenly council which consisted of himself and
lower divine beings, angels, holy ones, or the like.

12. the earth swallowed them: this has been interpreted by
some scholars as referring to the incident described in Num.
16:1-32, in which the earth opened its mouth and swallowed
Korah, Dathan, and Abiram, with their households, because of
their rebellion against Moses (cf. Ps. 106:17). With this interpretation, verse 12 is related to the verses that follow. However, it
is better to translate ʾéreṣ as 'underworld', a meaning it has in
Gen. 2:6; 1 Sam. 28:13; Isa. 29:4; Jon. 2:6, and possibly other
passages. The cognate has that meaning sometimes in Ugaritic
and Akkadian. With this interpretation, verse 12 is related to
verses 7-11. The verb here translated **swallowed them** is
tiḇlāʿēmô. This is an example of a verb which appears to be imperfect in form, but is in reality an archaic preterite, used in past
narration (a similar verbal form exists in Ugaritic, and one may
compare the Akkadian preterite *iprus*). It is possible that the
verbs in verses 5-7 and 14-16 which *RSV* renders by the present
tense belong to the same verbal form; they are rendered by past
tense by Cross, *loc. cit.,* pp. 13-16, and see note 55. It is difficult
to determine whether these are genuinely archaic forms or
only archaizing forms; they alternate with Hebrew perfects
without any consistent principle that is obvious. The poem
contains other archaic or archaizing linguistic features, such as

the suffix -*mô* (verses 7, 9–11, 15, 17) and the relative particle *zû* (verses 13, 16).

13–16. Moses and the people are here represented as looking forward to the time when Yahweh will lead Israel through the wilderness and into the land of promise. It is most probable that these verses were written only after the Israelites had come into the land of Canaan, and even after the building of the Temple of Solomon.

The description of the leading of Israel into the promised land here is unrealistic. The people of Transjordan did not allow the Israelites to pass through out of terror, and the inhabitants of Canaan did not simply melt away! It took Israel about three centuries to 'conquer' Canaan. This is poetry rather than sober history. Some scholars think it is unrealistic because it was written long after the entrance of Israel into Canaan. On the other hand, it may be unrealistic because it was influenced by early Israelite conceptions of the 'holy war'. The Israelites believed that their God Yahweh fought for them, striking terror and panic into the hearts of the enemies of his people. Cf. 14:14 and comment there.

13. the people whom thou hast redeemed: see comment on 6:6 for use of the word 'redeem' for Yahweh's activity in leading Israel out of Egypt. The use of *gāʾal*, 'redeem', for the exodus is rare before Second Isaiah. However, the word *pādāh* in that sense is frequent in Deuteronomy (7:8; 9:26; 13:6; 15:15; 21:9).
thy holy abode: *nāweh* was originally an encampment or abode for sheep and shepherds, and came to mean pasture and abode in general. The phrase here has been given a great variety of interpretations: Sinai, Kadesh, the battle encampment at Shittim (Cross, *loc. cit.*, p. 23), the land of Canaan as a whole (cf. Jer. 10:25; 23:3; Ps. 79:7), or Zion, or the city of Jerusalem (cf. 2 Sam. 15:25; Isa. 27:10). If the phrase is to be taken here as the first in a series of geographical designations, continued by the references to Philistia, Edom, Moab, and Canaan, then we would most naturally think of Sinai as being the 'holy abode' of Yahweh to which he led the Israelites after the crossing of the sea. Sinai was conceived as being in some sense the dwelling place of Yahweh (cf. Jg. 5:5; Dt. 33:2; Ps. 68:9), although *nāweh* is not used of it. Kadesh would be much less likely. On the other hand, the biblical parallels given above, in which the word *nāweh* is used, suggest that the reference may be to Jerusalem or, more likely, to the

whole of the land of Canaan conceived as the special abode of
Yahweh. See also Ps. 78:54, 'his holy territory', $g^e \underline{b}ûl$ $ko\underline{d}\check{s}\hat{o}$.
Perhaps the most natural interpretation in the context is the first,
Sinai.

14. Philistia is very probably anachronistic here. Cf. comment
on 13:17. There is some evidence for the presence of 'Sea Peoples',
probably including some known specifically as Philistines, in the
Palestinian region in the latter part of the thirteenth century B.C.,
but it was not until after their defeat at the hands of Rameses III
in 1188 B.C. that the Philistines were settled in the south-western
corner of Palestine (cf. G. E. Wright, *BA*, xxix [1966], pp. 70–86).
Furthermore, the historical narratives record no conflicts of the
Israelites with the Philistines until after their entrance into Canaan
from the east. It is hardly necessary to re-arrange the lines, as
some critics do, for this is a poetic description, not a historical
record. Perhaps Philistia is mentioned here first because it was
near the peninsula of Sinai and the land of Egypt.

15. the chiefs of Edom are dismayed: Edom was in the
extreme southern part of Transjordan. Its leaders were not actually
dismayed before Israel; according to Num. 20:14–21 the Edomites
steadfastly refused to allow the Israelites passage through their
land, so that they had to journey around that land.
Moab was just N. of Edom. For Israel's conflicts with Moab, see
Num. 21–32.
all the inhabitants of Canaan: rendered 'the enthroned of
Canaan' (i.e. the rulers of Canaan) by Cross and Freedman,
parallel to the **chiefs** of Edom and **leaders** of Moab. Many of the
Canaanites did not melt away, but gave vigorous battle to the
invading Israelites; the same idea, however, is expressed in
Jos. 2:9,24.

16. the people . . . whom thou hast purchased: the verb
kānî\underline{t}ā could better be translated, 'thou hast created'. *RSV* thus
translates the same verb in Dt. 32:6; Prov. 8:22 (cf. 'maker' in
Gen. 14:19,22).

17 is of crucial importance for the interpretation and dating of
the 'Song of the Sea'. This verse says to Yahweh that he will
bring in his people and **plant them on thy own mountain,**
har naḥ^alā\underline{t}kā, lit. 'the mountain of thine inheritance'. This is
followed by two additional phrases: **the place . . . which thou
hast made for thy abode,** and **the sanctuary . . . which thy
hands have established.** The three phrases are taken by some

critics to be synonymous. Noth interprets all three as referring to the land of Canaan, into which Yahweh brought the people of Israel. The first phrase is used for the whole land because Israel settled chiefly in the hilly regions of Canaan. Beer, on the other hand, thinks the three phrases are synonymous references to Zion; in his opinion it is not the whole land, for then the verse would only repeat what was said in verse 13. One of these interpretations is necessary if we must take **plant them** in a somewhat literal sense, for Yahweh could be said to 'plant' his people in the land of Canaan (cf. 2 Sam. 7:10; Am. 9:15; Jer. 24:6; 32:41; 42:10; Ps. 44:3) or—less likely—on Zion, but hardly to 'plant' them in the Temple. The difficulty with Noth's interpretation is that the land is nowhere said to be the 'sanctuary' of Yahweh; in Ps. 114:2 the land of Judah is the 'sanctuary' of the people of Israel.

It is probable, however, that in poetry such as this the verb is not to be taken so closely with all three phrases. The first phrase, 'the mountain of thine inheritance', could readily refer to the hill-country of Palestine, or to the whole land of which the hill-country was a prominent part (cf. Dt. 3:25; Isa. 11:9; Ps.78:54). The other two phrases could naturally refer to a temple, and most probably to the Temple of Solomon in Jerusalem. In the poem used at the dedication of Solomon's Temple, according to 1 Kg. 8:13, the same phrase is used as here: $mākôn\ l^e\check{s}ibt^ek\bar{a}$, 'a place for thy dwelling'. It is used of heaven as Yahweh's abode in 1 Kg. 8:39,43,49; Ps. 33:14. The temple built by Solomon is often referred to as a 'sanctuary', $mikdā\check{s}$, and Ps. 78:69 says that Yahweh 'built his sanctuary like the high heavens', just as here he makes his own sanctuary. It would not be unnatural, then, to suppose that the second and third of the phrases used here are not synonymous with the first, but refer to Solomon's Temple. Cross has suggested, in line with his early dating of the poem, that the sanctuary which the poet had in mind was the early sanctuary at Gilgal, where he thinks there was a festival of the spring New Year at which the events of exodus and conquest were re-enacted in a cultic ceremony. He thinks that later the verse was assumed to apply to the Temple 'mount' in Jerusalem (*loc. cit.*, pp. 21, 24).

18 is an affirmation of the eternal kingship of Yahweh. It may have been in the liturgy a closing shout of the people. This is the only direct affirmation of the kingship of Yahweh in the Song, and it is from this verse that the connection with the festival of the enthronement of Yahweh is derived, along with the fact that the

Song as a whole affirms the sovereignty of Yahweh over nature
and over the history of Israel. One may compare the words of
Ps. 93:1; 96:10; 97:1; 99:1; all in psalms thought by some critics
to have been used in that festival. Here the verb is imperfect to
express the future, to conform to the fiction that Moses sang this
Song immediately after the crossing of the Sea.

19 was probably written by P as an explanation or summary of
the 'Song of the Sea': he is responsible also for 15:1a. The conception here of the manner in which Yahweh overthrew the Egyptians
agrees with that of P in 14:22,28–29. It is not unusual for poems in
the *OT* historical books to be placed within a prose framework, or
to be explained or commented on in prose. See, for example, how
the poem in which Joshua addresses the Sun and Moon, Jos.
10:12b–13a, which was taken from the 'Book of Jashar', is explained
in verses 13b–14.

THE SONG OF MIRIAM **19:20–21**

This section is probably from the oldest source, J, for the poem
appears to be ancient. However, the phrase **the sister of Aaron**
is probably a gloss, since Aaron may not have appeared originally
in the J narrative, but he has been secondarily introduced into
that narrative in 4:29,30; 5:20; 8:8,12,25; 9:27; 10:3,8,16;
see comment on 4:14 (E).

20. the prophetess: Miriam was considered to be an ecstatic
prophetess. For the association of music with ecstatic prophesy,
see 1 Sam. 10:5; 2 Kg. 3:15.

**all the women went out after her with timbrels and
dancing:** this presupposes the custom whereby the women went
out from their homes to meet their husbands as they came back
victorious from battle, dancing and singing a song of victory, as in
1 Sam. 18:6–8, of the time of Saul and David (cf. Jg. 11:34).
This would not have been appropriate to the time of the actual
crossing of the sea.

21. The Song here is very brief. It consists of a single strophe of
two couplets (or bicola), in 2:2 metre. It was probably from this
ancient brief song that the 'Song of the Sea', 15:1a–18, was
developed. In the opinion of Cross and Freedman this short
poem is only the title of the long poem in 1b–18, taken from a
different cycle of traditions. Thus they call the longer poem the
'Song of Miriam' (loc. cit., p. 237). In his later article Cross calls it
'Song of the Sea'.

the horse and his rider he has thrown into the sea: this way of depicting the overthrow of the Egyptian forces is closer to the J account in 14:24–25,27 than to the P account, which depicted the sea as being divided, and then overwhelming the Egyptians as the waters came back together, 14:23,28.

THE JOURNEY FROM THE SEA TO SINAI
15:22—18:27

After the wondrous victory over the Egyptians at the Sea, the Israelites go into the desert east of Egypt, into the peninsula of Sinai. There they come face to face with the realities of a harsh life in the arid desert, with which they are poorly equipped to deal as former slaves in Egypt. Their journey is represented as a series of crises, brought on by thirst, hunger and enemies. They murmur against their leaders and blame them for their plight, but each crisis is dealt with by Yahweh in such a way as to demonstrate his concern and power, and his presence with Moses and the Israelites.

Several of the individual narratives in this section have aetiological motives. Three of them, by play on Hebrew words, explain the origin of the place-names Marah (15:23–25) and Massah-Meribah (17:7), and the name of the manna (16:15,31). The account in 17:8–16 is intended in part to explain the perpetual enmity between the Israelites and Amalekites. The presence of these motives does not prove that the events are not historical, but it does make their interpretation as history somewhat precarious.

The route of the Hebrews through these chapters is very problematic. The earliest tradition, as has long been recognized, may have had the Israelites going directly from the Sea, a journey of about three days, to the region of Kadesh; see the commentary on 15:25*b* and 17:7. If our contention is correct that Sinai was located near Kadesh (see excursus below, pp. 203–07), they may have gone to Sinai in the vicinity of Kadesh. At any rate, several of the incidents recorded below fit better *after* than *before* the halt at Sinai, as the detailed comments will show. Some of the stories have parallels or duplicates in Numbers, such as the stories of the quails in Num. 11, and of Meribah in Num. 20:1–13. It is very difficult to locate a number of the geographical sites mentioned, especially those preserved in the late tradition of P (15:22a,27; 16:1; 17:1a), which are considered by some critics as having little historical value.

A motif which occurs several times here, as well as in Numbers, is that of the murmuring or rebellion of the people against Moses, or Moses and Aaron, or even against Yahweh (15:24–25; 16:2–3, 8; 17:1–7). The motif has already been seen in Exod. 14:10–14 and it occurs in Num. 11:1–6; 14:2–3; 16:13–14; 20:2–13; 21:4–5; cf. Dt. 1:26f.; Ps. 78:17–42; 95:8–11. In these accounts the Israelites complain against their leadership and want to return to the fleshpots of Egypt; some accounts seem to indicate outright rebellion. But Yahweh responds by providing the people with their needs. This is a view of the desert period which is at variance with the view of passages such as Jer. 2:2 and Hos. 2:17, which represent the desert period as one of deep faithfulness of Israel to Yahweh. For form-critical studies of this motif, see G. W. Coats, *Rebellion in the Wilderness* (1968) and S. De Vries, 'The Origin of the Murmuring Tradition', *JBL*, LXXXVII (1968), pp. 51–59. It is not improbable that this tradition has its root in actual history. The Hebrews who had been slave labourers in Egypt must have found life in the desert very hard indeed, and some at least must have wanted to return to Egypt. It is a tribute to the leadership and resourcefulness of Moses that he was able to lead them successfully through the desert.

HEALING OF THE WATER AT MARAH 15:22–26

22–25a(P,J). *Moses leads Israel from the Red Sea into the wilderness of Shur, where they come to Marah. The water there is bitter, and for that reason it is named 'Marah'. Moses sweetens the water by throwing into it a tree, at the command of Yahweh.*

25a–26(R_D). *There Yahweh makes a statue for Israel and proves them, promising to be their healer if they will heed his commandments.*

The literary analysis is clear: 22b–25a are from J, 22a from P, and 25b–26 from a Deuteronomic redactor (R_D). The terminology of the latter is characteristic of D, as is also the interest in the diseases of Egypt (cf. Dt. 7:15; 28:27,60).

22. the wilderness of Shur was apparently a general name for the Sinai desert east of Egypt or some portion of it. Num. 33:8 (P) has for the same region 'wilderness of Etham'; see comment on

13:20. Shur is mentioned in Gen. 16:7; 20:1; 25:18; 1 Sam. 15:7; 27:8. Because Shur can mean 'wall' (Gen. 49:22; 2 Sam. 22:30; Ps. 18:29), some scholars believe that it was a line of frontier fortresses built to keep invaders from the east out of Egypt. Others think the name was applied to a range of white cliffs parallel to the coast about twelve miles E. of the Gulf of Suez, called Jebel er-Rahah. The biblical information does not allow us to identify the region precisely.

three days in the wilderness: according to 3:18; 5:3 (J), the Hebrews asked Pharaoh for permission to go into the wilderness 'a three days' journey' to sacrifice to their God.

23. Marah is often identified with ʿAin Hawarah, about fifty miles S. of the northern end of the Gulf of Suez. There were doubtless many wells and pools with brackish, unpalatable water in the desert. A location more directly E. of the place of the cross- ing of the Sea would be preferable. This story is primarily an aetiological legend, designed to explain the name 'Marah', which in Hebrew means 'bitterness'.

24. The murmuring of the Israelites against Moses, or Moses and Aaron, is a frequent theme in these narratives; see comment on 14:11-12, and above, p. 171.

25. The **tree** which Moses threw into the water was probably a desert bush or shrub, since Hebrew ʿēṣ is a more general word than our 'tree' (cf. Jg. 9:8ff., where it includes vines and brambles, and Ezek. 15:2,6). A similar miracle is recorded in 2 Kg. 2:21: Elisha throws salt into a spring of water to make its bad water wholesome. The latter is a case of 'homeopathic magic'; perhaps the action of Moses can be assigned to the same category. For the Israelites it meant that Yahweh made provision for them through Moses their leader.

he proved them: the root of the Hebrew verb (nāsāh) is the root also of the name 'Massah', in 17:7. This brief section, 25b–26, which is clearly from a Deuteronomic hand in its present form, may contain a misplaced fragment which at one time had some relationship to the story now told in 17:1-7. Some critics think that originally there stood here the account (from J or E) of the incident at Massah-Meribah now contained in 17:1-7 (cf. Num. 20:1-13). Then, because Meribah is located in the vicinity of Kadesh (see comment on 17:7), they draw the further conclusion that the early tradition had the Israelites going directly from Egypt to Kadesh, this being their original intention when they demanded permission to go three days' journey into the wilderness. This view could be correct, but it must be pointed out that Kadesh was more than an actual three days' journey from the border of Egypt.

ENCAMPMENT AT ELIM 15:27

This single verse is probably from P. It tells only that the Israelites came to Elim, where there were twelve springs of water and seventy palm trees, and there they encamped.

Elim has been identified with Wadi Gharandel, where there are palms, vegetation, and abundant water, about 63 miles SE. of the town of Suez. The name means 'terebinths' or, just possibly, 'gods'. It was probably an oasis that was also a sacred place with many sacred trees. Some scholars associate it with Elath, or Eloth, which was situated at the northern end of the Gulf of Aqaba, modern Tell el-Kheleifeh. However, the name of that site was more probably Ezion-geber at that time (Num. 33:35f.; cf. *IDB*, art. 'Ezion-geber').

twelve springs of water and seventy palm trees: there was probably a symbolic significance in these numbers—such as one spring for each of the twelve tribes of Israel, and one palm tree for each of the seventy elders (Num. 11:16).

THE GIFT OF MANNA AND QUAILS IN THE WILDERNESS OF SIN 16:1-36

1-3(P). *The Israelites journey from Elim to the wilderness of Sin. They murmur against Moses and Aaron, wishing they had died in Egypt where they had plenty to eat.*

4-5(J). *Yahweh promises to Moses that he will rain bread from heaven, and the people are to gather a day's portion every day. On the sixth day, it will be twice as much as they gather on other days.*

6-12(P). *Moses (and Aaron) promise that the Israelites will be given flesh in the evening and bread in the morning; thus they shall know that it was Yahweh who brought them out of Egypt, and see the glory of Yahweh.*

13-21(J,P). *In the evening quails come up and cover the camp; in the morning the manna comes. Yahweh commands them to gather as much as each man can eat, an omer apiece. When some is left until the next day, it becomes foul.*

22-30(P). *On the sixth day they gather twice as much bread, so that* *they may observe the seventh day as a holy sabbath to Yahweh, and rest on that day.*

31–34(P). *The Israelites call the name of the bread 'manna'. Moses gives instruction for an omer of manna to be kept in a jar 'before the* LORD' *throughout the generations.*

35–36(P). *The Israelites eat manna forty years until they come to the border of Canaan. It is explained that an omer is the tenth part of an ephah.*

The present chapter is mainly an account of the giving of the manna to the Israelites, and its relationship to the Sabbath; the quails are mentioned, but only briefly. In Num. 11 there is an account of both manna and quails, with more space given to the latter (11:31–33).

A number of points in the present account suggest that this incident may have taken place *after* the giving of the law on Mount Sinai. Verse 10 seems to have in view the existence of a sanctuary. Of more importance is the fact that in verses 32–34 Moses gives an order for a jar of manna to be placed 'before the LORD' or 'before the Testimony', that is, before the Ark, whereas the Ark was not made until the people came to Sinai (Exod. 37:1–9). Either this incident has been erroneously placed on the journey to Sinai, or the redactor who placed it in its present position was unaware of the anachronisms involved.

The literary analysis is difficult, and scholars differ widely in their views. The narrative is made up mostly of P material, with J material to be found in 4–5, 13*b*–15*a* ('. . . know what it was'), 21 and 27–30. But the material assigned to P is not well unified; there are duplicates or repetitions. For example, 6–8 and 9–12 are almost duplicates; at least, 6–8 is better read after 9–12 than before. It is probable that the P narrative has been supplemented at some points by a redactor (or redactors). The interest of the Priestly redactors in the Sabbath may have attracted their attention to this chapter and caused them to supplement it. There is no E material in this chapter.

1. all the congregation of the people of Israel is a phrase characteristic of P.

the wilderness of Sin: mentioned only here and in 17:1, Num. 33:11f. By those who locate Mount Sinai at Jebel Musa in the southern part of the Sinai Peninsula, it is identified with plain Debbet er-Ramleh, which is on the western fringe of the Sinai plateau. It is to be distinguished from the wilderness of Zin (Num. 13:21; 20:1 etc.) which was SE. of Judah.

fifteenth day of the second month: in the chronology of P, the Israelites observed Passover and fled from Egypt on the night of the tenth day of the first month (12:2f.,51). Apparently it was thought that within a little over a month they had consumed the provisions with which they left Egypt, and were now faced with hunger.

2-3. The Israelites frequently murmured against Yahweh and their leaders; see comments on 14:11-12; 15:24; 17:3 etc., and above, p. 171.

4-5 are J's account of the promise of the manna. In this tradition it was conceived as **bread from heaven** that fell like rain or the dew (verses 13-14 below). Cf. Ps. 78:24; 105:40. In Jn. 6:31ff., Jesus is 'the true bread from heaven'.

6-8 are out of place, and could be more appropriately placed after 9-12. They may be from a Priestly redactor, who wished to emphasize the fact that the murmuring was against Yahweh rather than against Moses and Aaron; otherwise the content is virtually the same as 9-12.

9. Come near before the LORD: these words suggest coming to a sanctuary to 'appear before the Lord'.

10. the glory of the LORD appeared in the cloud: this seems to presuppose the idea, found in P, that a cloud covered the Tabernacle, and this meant that 'the glory of the Lord filled the Tabernacle' (Exod. 40:34-38; cf. Num. 9:15-16). See comment on 13:21-22 for the conception of the cloud in the various traditions. Here the existence of the tent of meeting, or Tabernacle or some kind of sanctuary, is presupposed; this is one of the reasons for thinking that the incidents of this chapter, if historical, occurred after the events of Sinai, rather than before.

12. At twilight: the Hebrew is literally 'between the two evenings'. See the discussion of this phrase at 12:6. In verse 6, the usual word for 'evening' is used.

13. quails came up and covered the camp: a more detailed description of the quails is given in Num. 11:31-33 (cf. Ps. 78:27-31). There they come in on a 'wind from the Lord' in very great numbers, so that they lie two cubits (three feet) deep on the ground! The people gather and eat them in great numbers, and are stricken with a great plague. In that passage the quails are not sent as an act of grace to relieve hunger, but as the result of Yahweh's anger at the people's complaints.

In the Mediterranean area, the quail winters in Africa and

Arabia, and migrates north in the spring in very large flocks. They return in the early autumn. Some fly over the peninsula of Sinai. The birds migrate in stages, and their flights are very exhausting. They are easily caught, and are a delicacy. Neither biblical passage speaks of the coming of the quails as an annual occurrence, but they could in fact have been used at various times by the Hebrews as meat in their desert wandering.

The first half of this verse is from P; it is the fulfilment of the promise of flesh made in 8 and 12. The different representation in Num. 11 is from J. Here, 13*b*–15*a* are from J.

14. a fine, flake-like thing, fine as hoarfrost on the ground: the first description of the manna; for others, see verse 31 and Num. 11:7–8. The word rendered 'flake-like thing', *meḥuspām*, occurs only here and its meaning is not certain. It is usually thought to mean scale-like or flake-like, but *JB* translates it 'powdery'.

It has long been observed that a substance appears in parts of the Sinai peninsula that may have given rise to the story of the gift of manna. Josephus said, 'To this very day all that region is watered by a rain like to that which then, as a favour to Moses, the Deity sent down for men's sustenance' (*Ant.* III.i.7). In modern times it has often been observed that a granular substance appears in the early summer in some regions of the Sinai peninsula, particularly on and under a species of tamarisk. The Arabs gather it in the early morning, boil it, strain it, and use it like honey. Their name for it is *mann*. This substance was long thought to be a secretion of the tamarisk, but F. S. Bodenheimer has shown that it is really the honeydew excretion of two scale insects, *Trabutina mannipara* Ehr. and *Najacoccus serpentinus minor* Green, which live on the twigs of the tamarisk. The excretion is mainly from growing larvae and immature females, which feed on plant saps that are rich in carbohydrates and poor in nitrogen. They excrete a sweet, sugary substance that turns white, brown or yellow. The granules drop and accumulate mostly in the night, but in the daytime are collected by ants after the soil becomes warm. The quantity of the *mann* varies according to the amount of winter rainfall. It is said that the annual crop does not exceed several kilograms, but that the extraordinary sweetness of the substance makes it extremely attractive to nomads of the desert. For further details, see F. S. Bodenheimer, 'The Manna of Sinai', *BA*, x (1947), pp. 2–6.

While it is quite possible that the Hebrews in the desert knew this substance and used it, and thus the story of the manna arose, there are many features of the manna as described in the biblical passages which do not fit the modern *mann:* the great quantities in which it could be gathered, its automatic adjustment to the needs of each person, its failure to appear on the Sabbath, its being made into cakes, its putrefaction if kept until morning, and its ability to feed the Hebrews over a period of forty years. That which was a natural supplement to the desert nomads' diet, very welcome because of its sweetness, has become 'bread from heaven' that was the mainstay of their food supply.

15. 'What is it?' Hebrew *mān hû'* can be thus rendered, or 'It is manna', or 'Is it manna?' The Hebrew for 'manna' is *mān;* our English 'manna' is derived from the LXX translation in Num. 11:6-7. In the present verse the rendering of the text of *RSV* is to be preferred in view of the immediate context, as well as the LXX translation, *Ti estin touto.* However, there is difficulty in this translation, because the Hebrew word for 'what?' is *māh,* not *mān.* In Arabic and Aramaic, *man* (with short *a*) means 'who?' *Mān* (with long *a*) means 'what?' in Syriac and late Aramaic, but it cannot be demonstrated that it is an ancient Aramaic form. In any event, the present verse gives only a popular etymology, which may have intentionally used an irregular form.

16. omer: a dry measure used only in this chapter. According to verse 36 it was one-tenth of an ephah, and thus slightly more than two quarts (about 2.3 litres). This was considered the ration of one person for one day.

17 is quoted by Paul in 2 Cor. 8:15 in a plea for Christian generosity.

18-19. The literal meaning of 18 is difficult to determine, but clearly the main point of these verses is that God provided what each person needed for each day, but no more. The Israelites were to depend upon him entirely for their 'daily bread'.

20. it bred worms and became foul: this does not in fact happen with the modern *mann* found in the Sinai peninsula. Bodenheimer explains that the ants in great numbers collect the *mann* in the daytime, and believes this may have given rise to the statement concerning worms (see comment on verse 14 above).

21 is from J, continuing 13*b*-15*a*.

when the sun grew hot, it melted: some observers have reported that this happens with the modern *mann,* but Bodenheimer

denies it, and thinks the idea results from the collection of the
granules of the *mann* by ants (see comments on verses 14 and 20).

22-26 is P's account of the first observance of the Sabbath.

23. bake what you will bake and boil what you will boil:
This implies that the manna itself could be boiled or baked.
Cf. Num. 11:8. The modern *mann* is not made into cakes, but can
be used like honey on bread.

27-30 is the continuation of J's account, after verse 21. Some
critics assign 28 to R_D, but the verse is necessary to the context;
J may originally have told about the giving of a law concerning
the Sabbath (cf. end of verse 4). This is the earliest mention of the
Sabbath, and also the earliest observance of the Sabbath by the
Israelites (the account in Gen. 2:2-3 of the founding of the
Sabbath is from P, written much later than J, and it does not use
the word 'Sabbath'). It is significant that here the Sabbath is
considered to be a day of cessation from labour; that seems to be
the oldest conception of the Sabbath, which eventually became a
day of religious observance.

Little is known of the actual origin of the Sabbath, and the
question has been much debated by scholars. Its origin has been
traced to Mesopotamia, to Canaan, or to the Kenites. Some
scholars think, however, that it is a very ancient institution that
goes back to the nomadic days of the Israelites, not borrowed
from any other culture.

The present account reflects the Israelites' belief that the keeping
of the Sabbath goes back to the time even before the giving of the
law on Mount Sinai, unless—as we have noted—the chapter is out
of place and originally stood at a point after the sojourn at Sinai.
In the latter case, the present account presupposes the law of the
Sabbath promulgated at Sinai (20:8-10; 23:12; 31:14-16; 35:2-3).
We must observe, however, that the present account—even in its
J form—does not inspire much confidence as a historical record.
The keeping of the Sabbath is closely associated with a conception
of the gift of manna which is artificial, requiring that a double
portion be given on the sixth day and the withholding of the
manna on the seventh day.

31. This is another description of the manna; cf. verse 14 and
Num. 11:7-8.

coriander was an umbelliferous plant whose fruit (usually called
seed) were used for seasoning very much as caraway and sesame
are used today. The seed were small, globular, and greyish. Here

the comparison is for the size. According to this verse, it was
white; according to Num. 11:7 the appearance of manna was
'like that of bdellium'. The colour of the modern *mann* varies;
see comment on verse 14.

32–34. A jar containing an omer of the manna is to be kept as a
memorial for all generations.

before the LORD, or **before the Testimony** means before the
Ark of the Covenant, since 'Testimony' was sometimes used by P
for the Ark itself (30:36; Num. 17:4–10); he also used the word
for the tablets containing the ten commandments (25:16,21;
40:20). According to Heb. 9:4, the Ark of the Covenant in the
holy of holies of the Tabernacle contained a golden urn holding
the manna, along with Aaron's rod and the tables of the covenant.
This is not attested in the *OT*.

35. According to Jos. 5:12, the manna ceased when the Israelites
came to Gilgal, and there began to eat the products of the land of
Canaan.

36. See comment on verse 16. The size of the omer is given in
relationship to that of the **ephah,** a dry measure commonly used
in the *OT*.

WATER FROM THE ROCK AT MASSAH-MERIBAH **17:1–7**

1a(P). *The Israelites move on from the wilderness of Sin by stages,
and camp at Rephidim.*

1b–3(J,E). *The people have no water to drink and murmur against
Moses. He asks, 'Why do you find fault with me? Why do you put the
Lord to the proof?'*

4–6(E). *At the command of Yahweh, Moses strikes the rock, and water
comes out of it for the people to drink.*

7(J,E). *He calls the name of the place Massah ('proof') and Meribah
('fault-finding').*

This is another aetiological story, similar to the one in 15:22–26,
told in order to explain the origin of a place called Massah and
Meribah. The literary analysis shows that it is in reality a combination of two stories, with the same theme but with two different
names. It cannot be determined whether they originally concerned
two different places where the same incident occurred, or whether
the place is the same with different names in the two stories.
The latter is more probable, but in the desert the Hebrews

must have often had to contend with the problem of securing sufficient water. It is not surprising that several stories of this kind arose.

One account plays on the verbal root *rîḇ*, which means 'find fault', and applies to the name Meribah; this one is from E. The other story plays on the verbal root *nāsāh*, which means 'put to the proof, test, try', and applies to Massah; this one is from J. The analysis of the section is as follows: J: 2*b* ('Why do you put the Lord to the proof?'), 3, 7*a*, *c* (And he called the name of the place Massah . . . because they put the Lord to the proof by saying, 'Is the Lord among us or not?'); E: 1*b*–2*a*, 4–6, 7*b* (Meribah, because of the fault-finding of the children of Israel); P: 1*a* (. . . at Rephidim).

This story should be compared with the similar story in Num. 20:1–13, also designed to account for the name Meribah (a P narrative). The action there took place at or near Kadesh. In that narrative, Moses is commanded to speak to the rock, but instead he strikes it twice. The water comes forth in abundance, but for his lack of faith Moses is denied the privilege of leading Israel into the promised land.

Various indications suggest that the present story, like others in chapters 15–18, took place near the end of the journey through the wilderness, at or near Kadesh. See the comment below on Meribah, verse 7.

1. This verse through **Rephidim** is from P; the rest comes from E. Rephidim is usually identified with the Wadi Refayid, in the southern part of the peninsula of Sinai, near Jebel Musa, the traditional site of Mount Sinai. However, the information from P concerning the stopping-places of the Israelites in their desert wandering has little independent value. It is more likely that Massah-Meribah is to be located at or near Kadesh, on the southern border of Palestine.

2. the people found fault with Moses: the verb is from the root *rîḇ*, which means 'find fault, contend (in or outside a court of law)'. It is related to the word Meribah, which (in the opinion of Noth) originated from the time when nomadic shepherds assembled there to settle their 'disputes at law'.

Why do you put the LORD to the proof? The verb here is from the root *nāsāh* (*piel*), which means 'put to the proof, test, try'. It is related to the word Massah. Cf. 15:25, where the same root is used in what may be a fragment of this or a related story.

3. the people murmured against Moses: this is a frequent theme in the wilderness wanderings; cf. 14:11; 16:2f., etc.

4. They are almost ready to stone me: stoning was a common expression of the anger of a mob, sometimes leading to death (1 Sam. 30:6; 1 Kg. 12:18; Mt. 21:35; 23:37; Jn 10:31; Ac. 14:5). In the laws several offences were punished by stoning (Exod. 21:28–32; Lev. 20:2–5; 24:15–16; etc.).

5. take in your hand the rod with which you struck the Nile: see 7:17,20. It is characteristic of E that Moses uses the rod; in P the wonders are done with the rod in the hand of Aaron. **and go:** Moses is not told where to go. It is possible that we have only a portion of the original account. In the opinion of some scholars the original continued with 'to Horeb'; see next verse.

6. Behold, I will stand before you there: Yahweh promises to appear to aid Moses. Little is made in this account of the theophany, but it proves the presence of Yahweh with Israel to counter the complaint quoted at the end of verse 7.
at Horeb: the mention of Horeb here is puzzling, for Horeb is the name usually employed by Deuteronomy and E (see 3:1; 33:6) for the sacred mountain which is called Sinai by J and P. Sometimes the name seems to apply to a somewhat larger area than the mountain, including what is called the wilderness of Sinai (Dt. 4:10; 9:8; 18:16). But, as the narrative now stands, the Israelites do not arrive at the sacred mountain and the wilderness of Sinai until 19:1. It is very probable that **on the rock at Horeb** is a gloss by a scribe who thought that Yahweh could appear only at the sacred mountain. In 33:21–23, Yahweh tells Moses to 'stand upon the rock' (apparently of Sinai) and see the back of the deity as he passes by. The end of verse 5 may have originally contained the name of the place to which Moses should go; in verse 6 Yahweh promises that he will stand before Moses there: the scribal gloss sought to explain what was meant by 'there'.
you shall strike the rock: this rock became very famous. Jewish tradition developed the view that this rock, with its water supply, followed the Israelites on their journey to the promised land. Paul obviously refers to this tradition when he says that our fathers 'all drank the same supernatural drink. For they drank from the supernatural Rock which followed them, and the Rock was Christ' (1 Cor. 10:4).

7. Massah is derived from the root *nāsāh*, used in the second question of verse 2. It is sometimes a common noun meaning

'a proving, test, trial'—e.g. of the trials by which Yahweh brought
Israel out of Egypt, Dt. 4:3; 7:19; 29:3. As the name of a place it
occurs alone in Dt. 6:16; 9:22, referring to the present incident;
it occurs with Meribah in Dt. 33:8; Ps. 95:8. Strangely, Dt. 33:8
speaks of the testing *of Levi* at Massah and the waters of Meribah.
Meribah is derived from the root *rîb*, used in the first question of
verse 2. It also is sometimes a common noun, meaning 'strife,
contention'—e.g., of the 'strife' between the herdsmen of Abram
and Lot, Gen. 13:8. As a place name it occurs usually in the
phrase, 'the waters of Meribah' (Dt. 33:8; Num. 20:13; Ps. 81:7;
106:32). The place at which the incident recorded in Num.
20:1–13 occurred must have been in the wilderness of Zin, at or
near Kadesh, on the southern border of Palestine. This is clearly
indicated by Num. 20:1, and the name 'Meribah-Kadesh',
meaning Meribah of Kadesh (that is, by or near Kadesh) occurs
frequently (Num. 27:14; Dt. 32:51; Ezek. 47:19; 48:28). While
it is not impossible that there were two places with the same name,
the similarity of the incident recorded here and in Num. 20 makes
it very likely that they are only variant traditions of the same
incident. The present account is a combination of J and E,
whereas Num. 20:1–13 is from the Priestly narrative. The latter
narrative seeks to change the basic motif from the testing of
Yahweh by the people to Yahweh's testing of the faith of Moses.

In the light of the probability that Meribah was located on the
southern border of Palestine, in the neighbourhood of Kadesh, it
is likely that this incident should be placed near the end of the
journey of the Israelites, *after* rather than *before* the halt at Sinai.
The location of Massah-Meribah near Kadesh is cited by some
scholars as evidence for the location of Sinai-Horeb in the vicinity
of Kadesh (see excursus at the end of chapter 19).

VICTORY OVER AMALEK 17:8–16

8–9(E). *The Amalekites attack the Hebrews, who prepare to defend
themselves.*

10–13(E). *Moses, Aaron and Hur go to the top of a hill. Whenever
Moses holds up his hand, the Hebrews prevail; when he lowers it, Amalek
prevails. When his hands grow weary, Aaron and Hur hold them up, and
Joshua is able to defeat the Amalekites.*

14(Rᴅ). *Yahweh instructs Moses to write this as a memorial in a book,
that he will utterly blot out the remembrance of Amalek from under
heaven.*

15–16(E). *Moses builds an altar and calls its name 'The Lord is my banner', saying that Yahweh will have war with Amalek from generation to generation.*

This section is mostly from E. It is assigned to that source because of the prominence of Aaron and of the rod of Moses. Verse 14 is from a Deuteronomic redactor; cf. Dt. 25:19. It is a parallel to 16, which is an integral part of the E account.

The narrative here is an aetiological story, designed to explain the origin of the perpetual hostility between Israel and Amalek, and also the origin of an altar, probably in the vicinity of Kadesh, which had the name 'Yahweh is my banner'.

The Amalekites were a wide-ranging desert tribe, or confederation of tribes, who are uniformly represented as enemies of Israel. The Israelites associated them in origin with the Edomites; the genealogy in Gen. 36:12 makes Amalek a grandson of Esau. In Num. 24:20 they are called in an oracle of Balaam 'the first of the nations', an indication of their great antiquity. They are listed in Num. 14:43–45, along with Canaanites, as peoples with whom the Israelites had to fight as they tried to push northward from Kadesh. Both Saul and David had to fight against them (1 Sam. 15 and 30), and the Amalekites were apparently not finally overcome until the monarchy was firmly established. According to 1 Chr. 4:43 it was in the time of King Hezekiah that 'the remnant of the Amalekites' was finally destroyed. The memory of antagonism to the Amalekites survives in the book of Esther, where Mordecai is pitted against Haman, called the Agagite, after Agag, a noted king of the Amalekites (1 Sam. 15:32–33).

8. at Rephidim: this notice is dependent on verse 1 which, being from P, was not an original part of the story in verses 1–7; see comment on verse 1. While we cannot deny that the Amalekites may have wandered as far as the southern part of the peninsula of Sinai, where Rephidim is traditionally located, it seems more probable that the conflict with Amalek took place at or near Kadesh, like the incident in verses 1–7. The Amalekites were associated especially with the southern part of Palestine and the neighbourhood of Kadesh (see, e.g., Gen. 14:7).

9. Joshua is here introduced for the first time, as if he were a well-known figure. He is usually represented as a minister of Moses, especially in attending the tent of meeting (24:13; 32:17; 33:11; Num. 11:28). This is the only place in the Pentateuch where he is represented as a warrior. According to Num. 27:18–23 (P), he was commissioned by Moses to be his successor, shortly before Moses died.

with the rod of God in my hand: the rod in the hand of Moses is a characteristic feature of E, but it is not clear what rôle the rod plays in the present narrative. It is not mentioned in the verses that follow, and some critics consider this clause to be a secondary gloss. However, the rod is such a prominent feature in many of the wonders performed by Moses (or Aaron) that we should be slow to eliminate it from the original narrative here. In verse 11, the Hebrew text says that when Moses held up his *hand* (singular; several ancient versions have the plural), Israel prevailed; but when he lowered his *hand*, Amalek prevailed. Now, in preceding narratives we sometimes read that Moses is ordered to stretch forth his hand toward heaven, and when he obeys the order the record says that he stretched forth his rod toward heaven (9:22–23 and 10:12–13; cf. 10:21–22, where only 'hand' occurs, and 14:16 where both occur; the usual verb is 'stretch out', but 'lift up' occurs in 7:20; 14:16). Thus the natural interpretation of verse 11 is that Moses held up his hand with the rod in it. The difficulty arises in verse 12, where we are told that Moses' *hands* (plural) grew weary, and Aaron and Hur held them up, one on each side of Moses. Perhaps he alternated his hands in holding the rod. Or do we have here the conflation of two traditions, one emphasizing the rod in the hand of Moses, the other his lifting up of both hands alone?

10. Hur is mentioned as if he were a well-known person; he occurs also in 24:14. He may have played a prominent rôle in early traditions which are now lost to us. There are several other persons in the *OT* with the same name.

11–12. Moses is here the wonder-working magician. It is not the courage and energy of Joshua and his men that produce victory, but Moses holding up his hand(s). Thus this act has some intrinsic efficacy as a channel of the power of Yahweh, working on behalf of Israel.

14 is from the Deuteronomic redactor, who wrote after the danger from the Amalekites had been overcome and it was thought that Yahweh had utterly blotted out their remembrance. The terminology of Dt. 25:19 is very similar: 'you shall blot out the remembrance of Amalek from under heaven; you shall not forget'. **Write this as a memorial in a book:** one of the few references to Moses' writing in the Pentateuch. In 24:4 and 34:27 he writes the words of Yahweh; in Num. 33:2 he writes down the starting-places of the Israelites; in Dt. 31:9,24 he writes 'this law', and in Dt. 31:22, 'this song'.

A similar incident may be that reported in Jos. 8:18,26, which says that Joshua stretched out his hand with a javelin in it toward Ai, and did not draw it back until he had completely destroyed the inhabitants of Ai. In that case, however, the language may be only figurative for his fighting against the people of Ai.

15. This account of the building of an altar by Moses was probably inspired by the presence in the vicinity of Kadesh of an altar, which was believed to mark the place where a battle with Amalekites had occurred. There are several examples of altars that had special names; see Gen. 33:20; Jos. 22:34; Jg. 6:24; cf. Gen. 35:7.

The LORD is my banner: Hebrew, *YHWH-nissî*. *nēs* has a variety of meanings: standard, banner, ensign, signal; the sail of a ship (Isa. 33:23); the pole on which Moses erected the bronze serpent (Num. 21:8–9); and even warning (Num. 26:10). A banner or standard was often used to rally an army; see especially Ps. 60:4, and cf. Isa. 5:26; 11:12; 13:2; 18:3; 49:22; 62:10; Jer. 4:6,21; 51:12,27. Nothing is known definitely of the appearance of such banners among the Israelites; on the standards of the troops in Egypt, Mesopotamia and other countries, representations of animals or of deities were common (see *IDB*, s.v. 'Banner'). Here the implication is that Yahweh himself is the Banner around which Israel rallies. In fact it was probably the hand(s) of Moses (with the rod uplifted?) which was originally considered to be the banner, and then the altar.

16. 'A hand upon the banner of the LORD!': The Hebrew is very obscure, reading 'For a hand upon *kēsyāh*'. The last word has no obvious meaning. *RSV* emends it to read *nēs-Yāh*, 'banner of Yah(weh)'. Vulgate's *solium Domini* suggests a text such as *kissēʾ-Yah*, 'throne of Yahweh', and both Samaritan Text and Syriac read 'throne'. If this is the correct reading, it suggests the altar may have been considered as the stone on which Moses sat, thought of as the 'throne of Yahweh'. Or it may suggest an oath of loyalty taken by the 'throne of Yahweh'. *Am. Tr.* has an entirely different interpretation, 'Because a hand has been raised against the throne of the Lord, the Lord will have war with Amalek from generation to generation.' All in all, the emendation made by *RSV* may be the best solution for an obscure text. The meaning of the *RSV* text as emended and punctuated is that Moses took an oath by the 'banner of the Lord' (i.e. by the altar), declaring that Yahweh would have continual war with Amalek. The hostility is declared here as existing between Yahweh and Amalek, not Israel and Amalek.

The LORD will have war with Amalek from generation to generation: this is an explanation for the continual hostility between Israel and Amalek, which had come to an end by the time verse 14 was inserted by R_D.

VISIT OF JETHRO TO MOSES 18:1–27

1–5(E). *Jethro, having heard of all that God had done for Moses and Israel, takes Zipporah and her two sons and goes to visit Moses at his encampment on the mountain of God.*

6–9(E). *Moses goes out to greet his father-in-law, and takes him into the tent. Moses tells him about what Yahweh has done in delivering the Israelites out of Egypt. Jethro rejoices for all the good Yahweh has done to Israel.*

10–12(E). *Jethro blesses Yahweh and confesses that he is greater than all gods. He then offers sacrifices to God, and eats bread with Aaron and all the elders of Israel before God.*

13–23(E). *Moses' father-in-law observes Moses as he judges the people, and tells Moses that he is wearing himself out in seeking to decide all cases himself. He advises Moses that he should continue to represent the people before God, and teach them statutes and decisions, but he should choose able, trustworthy, and honest men to assist him and decide the small matters.*

24–27(E). *Moses heeds Jethro's advice and chooses assistants to judge the people. Moses then lets his father-in-law depart, and Jethro returns to his own country.*

The narrative here is largely, if not exclusively, from E. The word ᵓ*elohim* is used twelve times, and *Yahweh* only six, all of the latter being in verses 1, 8–11. Some critics see Yahwistic additions in 1*b*–4 and 8–11, in whole or in part. Verses 2–4 may be an explanatory gloss, but there is no valid reason to consider 8–11 as originating with J, even as a secondary addition, for the Elohist sometimes used the divine name 'Yahweh' after its revelation in chapter 3. Verses 13–27 are a unified section by E, and there is no P material in the chapter.

The time of this visit by Jethro can hardly be on the Israelite journey to Sinai, for verse 5 puts the events at the wilderness where Moses is encamped at the mountain of God. This must mean the wilderness of Sinai, and Mount Sinai or Horeb (cf. 3:1), which the Israelites do not reach until 19:1. Dt. 1:9–18 places the reorganization of the judicial system at the time when the Israelites are about to leave Horeb. Furthermore verses 16, 20 seem to indicate that Moses has already given statutes to the Israelites. Therefore, it is most likely that the time of this visit was some time after the Israelites reached Sinai, perhaps as they were about ready to leave. Some scholars put the visit at Kadesh, but this makes it necessary to consider a part of verse 5 as a gloss.

A visit of Moses' father-in-law is recounted in Num. 10:29–32 (J), where he is called Hobab. There Moses tries to persuade him to serve as their guide in the desert; it is not clear whether he consents or not. That incident may have been a part of the visit related in the present chapter. However, it is not certain that Jethro and Hobab are in reality the same individual; see comment on 2:18.

For scholars who think that Yahweh was originally a Midianite (or Kenite) god, and that Moses adopted the worship of Yahweh from Jethro, this chapter is of crucial significance. Verse 12 is interpreted by them as the formal rite of initiation of Aaron and the elders of Israel into the cult of Yahweh by Jethro. Other scholars, however, see this as the conversion of Jethro to the worship of Yahweh. The best interpretation, in our opinion, is that this is the record of the making of a covenant, or treaty, between the Midianites and Israelites, a covenant between equals. Other scholars have adopted this interpretation, among them C. H. W. Brekelmans, 'Exodus XVIII and the Origins of Yahwism in Israel', *Oudtestamentische Studiën* x (1954), pp. 215–24; F. C. Fensham, 'Did a Treaty between the Israelites and the Kenites Exist?' *BASOR*, no. 175 (Oct. 1964), pp. 51–54; and A. Cody, 'Exodus 18:12: Jethro Accepts a Covenant with the Israelites', *Biblica*, XLIX (1968), pp. 153–66. Brekelmans says it is the view adopted in the commentaries of Strack (1894), von Hummelauer (1897), and Heinisch (1934). On the problem of the origin of Moses' Yahwism, see excursus, pp. 78–81.

THE SACRIFICIAL MEAL ON THE MOUNTAIN OF GOD **18:1–12**

1. Jethro, the priest of Midian, Moses' father-in-law: he is given three different names in the *OT*; see comment on 2:18.

He is never called 'priest of Yahweh', but only 'priest of Midian' (cf. 2:16). As a priest, he was probably also a chieftain.

2-4. This detailed explanation concerning Moses' family may be a secondary insertion, to explain why Zipporah and the two sons were not with Moses. They play little part in the sequel, because the narrative is not about a family reunion, but about a visit by Jethro to Moses. Earlier the narrative has recorded the birth of Gershom (2:22), but nothing has been said about the birth of the other son. We have been told of Moses' departure from Midian with his wife and sons (4:20,24–26), but not of their return to Zipporah's family in Midian. Moses may have sent them back from Egypt, or after the incident of 4:24–26. Jewish tradition says that Aaron (4:27) persuaded Moses to send them back in order not to add to the number of unfortunates in Egypt. **The God of my father was my help:** for this title of Moses' deity, cf. 3:6; 15:2. Since Eliezer means 'my God is my help', this explanation is surprising. It may represent the authentic original of the child's name. See excursus, pp. 78–81.

5. in the wilderness where he was encamped at the mountain of God: this must mean the wilderness of Sinai, the mountain being Sinai-Horeb. The Israelites reached it after the present incident, according to 19:1. It is likely, as indicated above, that the present chapter is out of chronological order. For 'mountain of God', see 3:1; 4:27.

6. Lo, your father-in-law Jethro is coming: *RSV* here follows Samaritan text, LXX, and Syriac in reading *hinnēh* instead of *ʾanî*. The Hebrew text is literally, 'I, your father-in-law Jethro, am coming'. *RSV* follows the more likely reading.

7. did obeisance and kissed him: he greets him with Near Eastern courtesy; the words do not suggest homage of an inferior to a superior. In the *OT* a kiss is usually between males who are relatives or close friends (examples of kissing between the sexes are rare).

went into the tent: some have suggested that this was the tent of meeting described in 33:7–11. However, that tent was a place where oracles were received, where Yahweh spoke to Moses. The tent here is probably Moses' own tent.

8. Moses relates to his father-in-law all the mighty acts which Yahweh had done in order to deliver Israel out of Egypt and from their hardships along the desert journey. For the Israelites, Yahweh was characteristically a God who acted in their history

9. And Jethro rejoiced: the verb here from the root *ḥāḏāh* is rarely used in the *OT*, elsewhere only Job 3:6 and Ps. 21:6. LXX translates *éxestē*, 'was astonished' (perhaps from a text that had a form of *ḥāraḏ*). This could be the correct text, indicating that Jethro was amazed and astonished at all the good which Yahweh had done for Israel.

10–11. Jethro says **Blessed be the LORD,** and recognizes that Yahweh is **greater than all gods,** because of his deliverance of Israel from the Egyptians and Pharaoh. Scholars who hold that Jethro was a priest of the Midianite god Yahweh see in this Jethro's recognition of the greatness of his own deity, who is even mightier than he had previously thought. Other scholars maintain, on the contrary, that this is evidence for the conversion of Jethro to the worship of Yahweh for the first time. It is best to see this statement of Jethro in the light of other covenant contexts in which a foreigner or foreigners come to a Hebrew to seek a covenant. When Abimelech and his army commander came to Abraham, they said, 'God is with you in all that you do'(Gen. 21:22 E), and they asked him to make an oath with them. Similarly, in Gen. 26:28 (J), Abimelech and his men said to Isaac, 'We see plainly that Yahweh is with you'. And when the Gibeonites went to Joshua to seek a covenant , they said they had come from a very far country 'because of the name of Yahweh your God; for we have heard a report of him, and all that he did in Egypt, and all that he did to the two kings' (Jos. 9:9–10). It was only natural, then, for Jethro, when he went to seek a covenant with Moses and the Israelites, to recognize the power of the Israelite God, particularly in what he had done for Israel.

when they dealt arrogantly with them: *RSV* correctly transposes this clause from the end of verse 10.

12. And Jethro, Moses' father-in-law, offered a burnt offering and sacrifices to God: as the *RSV* footnotes indicate, the Hebrew text has 'took', *wayyiḳaḥ;* so also the LXX. *RSV* follows Syriac, Targum and Vulgate to read **offered.** It is very likely that those versions were only interpreting the Hebrew, and did not have a different Hebrew text. We should thus read 'took'. A. Cody, *loc. cit.*, thinks that this means that Jethro 'accepted the sacrifices (made) to God', and in doing so he signified his acceptance of the covenant offered to him. His acceptance of the sacrifices was indicated by receiving a portion of the sacrificial victims offered to him, which he ate, as the representatives of Israel ate their portions. This is not a convincing interpretation; the parallels which he suggests to support his view, Jos. 9:14 and Gen. 21:30, are not really parallel situations. It is better to interpret this as Jethro's providing the sacrifices, which he may in fact have participated in offering. Lev. 12:8 says that a person who wishes to make an offering is to 'take' the necessary animals to the priest who makes atonement for the worshipper; the usual word is 'bring'. Also, Gen. 21:27 says that 'Abraham took sheep and oxen and gave them to Abimelech, and the two men made a covenant'; the context indicates, however, that the animals are a gift instead of a sacrifice, but a sacrifice of some kind could have been involved. That Jethro was a sheep-owner is indicated by 2:16ff.; 3:1. Sacrifices are sometimes clearly mentioned in covenant-making ceremonies; see Gen. 31:54; Exod. 24:5; and probably Jos. 8:30-35 and Dt. 27:5-7; cf. Ps. 50:5. Other Near Eastern nations sometimes had sacrifices to accompany covenants (cf. Fensham, loc. cit., p. 54; Cody, pp. 155-57). Because the **burnt offering** was wholly consumed on the altar (Lev. 1) and may have been adopted from the Canaanites, the original story probably did not tell of that type of offering. The offerings were made **to God:** this is an E passage and *'elohim* is used, but we can hardly doubt that sacrifices were made to Yahweh; they may have been made also to the deity worshipped by Jethro.

Aaron came with all the elders of Israel to eat bread with Moses' father-in-law before God: This is to be interpreted as the eating of a covenant meal by representatives of both parties to the covenant. Such meals are definitely indicated in Gen. 26:30; 31:54; Exod. 24:11, and may be implied in other covenant contexts. **Aaron,** who is prominent in E but not in J, is probably secondary in this context; we may assume that Moses played a leading part, and **the elders of Israel** play a representative rôle here similar to that we find them playing in other passages such as 3:16; 4:29; 12:21; 17:5; 24:9-11. A covenant meal was consumed by the participants **before God**—that is, before the altar on which the sacrifices had been made.

Verse 12 seems to be unusually brief, even laconic, in view of the fullness of the preceding verses. It is quite possible that some of the details in the original account have been deliberately suppressed in the text. If it did relate in clear terms the making of a covenant of friendship and peace between the Midianites and Israelites, the reason for the suppression may be found in the prohibition against making covenants with foreign nations, Exod. 23:32; 34:12–16; Jg. 2:2; these were made specifically against the inhabitants of Canaan, but were probably interpreted in a wide sense, particularly in view of the later enmity with some Midianites. (Note also the Kenites in the list in Gen. 15:19, and cf. Num. 24:21f.).

Since we have interpreted this ceremony as a covenant ceremony, we may conjecture the terms of the covenant, or treaty, made at this time between the Midianites and Israelites. Other covenants to which we have made reference in our discussion usually mention the stipulations of the covenant, in either general or specific terms. Abimelech and Abraham agreed that they would deal loyally (perform *ḥésed*) with each other, and not deal falsely, and this must have meant specifically mutual respect for water rights (Gen. 21:23). Abimelech and Isaac agreed that they would do no harm to each other, but only good, implying also respect for water rights (Gen. 26:29). Laban and Jacob agreed that they would not pass over the pillar or heap to do harm to the other (31:52). With the Gibeonites Joshua made a treaty which required him to protect them from the Israelites and from other Canaanites (Jos. 9:26; 10:6ff.).

We may conjecture that the covenant between Jethro and Moses, or the Midianites and Israelites, was a covenant of peace and friendship between equals. Perhaps one reason why Jethro came to see Moses was that he feared the Israelites might encroach upon the oases and pasture lands of his people, and thus one stipulation was that the Israelites would not encroach upon the Midianite pasture lands, and vice versa. Exod. 12:38 says the Israelites left Egypt with flocks and herds.

But the covenant apparently went further than this, involving friendship and alliance between the two peoples. Later references to the relationships between the two indicate this, if Kenites and Midianites are related. Jg. 1:16 says that the descendants of the Kenite, Moses' father-in-law, went with the tribe of Judah into the wilderness of Judah and there settled with the people. In the battle celebrated in the Song of Deborah, Sisera was killed by Jael, wife of Heber the Kenite (Jg. 4:21; 5:26). Later, when Saul was about to attack the Amalekites, he called upon the Kenites to separate themselves from the Amalekites 'for you showed kindness [performed *ḥésed*] to all the people of Israel when they came up out of Egypt' (1 Sam. 15:6). And finally, David in his outlaw days sent some of the spoils of war to his friends, including those 'in the cities of the Kenites' (1 Sam. 30:29).

Thus, a treaty of peace and friendship between the Israelites and Midianite-Kenites seems to have been made at some time, and the most likely time is the event recorded in this passage. This assumes that the Kenites were related to the Midianites, probably as a subdivision of that large group, or as a clan that was at one time associated with them. This is the prevailing opinion of scholars today; see comments on 2:15,18, and *IDB*, s.v. 'Kenites', 'Midianites'. In a recent article, de Vaux maintains that the Kenites and Midianites were different ethnic groups, and that the *OT* contains two quite different traditions concerning Moses' marriage: one a Kenite tradition which originated in southern Palestine, where the Kenites settled with Judah in the region of Arad, and the other a Midianite tradition which is closely linked with the exodus from Egypt. He thinks that Israelite Yahwism came from neither group; see his 'Sur l'origine Kenite ou Madianite du Yahvisme', in *Eretz-Israel*, IX (1969), pp. 28–32.

ADVICE ON JUDICIAL ADMINISTRATION **18:13–26**

Moses is here represented as accepting the advice of Jethro for establishing a system of judicial administration that relieves him of much of the burden of judging the people himself. In Num. 11:16–17,24–30, Moses chooses elders to assist him, and they receive some of his spirit and prophesy; it is not said that they act as judges. Dt. 1:9–18 is probably dependent upon the present account.

It is widely recognized that the system as described here, particularly the appointment of 'rulers of thousands, of hundreds, of fifties, and of tens', would not be suitable to the desert, and that such a system sounds more like a military arrangement than a judicial system (see comment on verses 21, 25). This account has, therefore, often been interpreted as providing justification and legitimation for a system of judicial administration of some later time, by claiming that the system was established by Moses.

Noth thinks that this tradition originated in the period soon after the settlement of the Israelites in Canaan, when there were still friendly relations between the Midianites and the southern Israelite tribes. He sees it as accounting for the separation of 'civic' justice from sacral justice.

It is more likely, however, that this account comes from the time after the monarchy was established, when the system of judicial administration was more elaborate than would have been the case in pre-monarchial times. Rolf Knierim, *ZAW*, LXXIII (1961), pp. 146–71, has made a good case for the view that this narrative provided the aetiology for the reforms of King Jehoshaphat of Judah in the ninth century B.C. According to 2 Chr. 19:5–11, that king appointed judges in all the fortified cities of Judah, and appointed in Jerusalem a court of appeal consisting of Levites and priests and heads of families of Israel. The difficulty in this theory is that we cannot be certain of the historicity of the Chronicler's account of Jehoshaphat's reforms. A similar system of courts is provided for in Dt. 16:18–20; 17:8–13. Some scholars have thus placed the present account in the time of Josiah, but that is probably too late.

This narrative may have a historical nucleus. It would have been natural for Moses, as a leader of the Israelites, to serve as judge, very much as modern Beduin sheikhs do. Also, it would not have been unnatural for him to seek advice in matters of this nature from Jethro, an older man who, as a priest and chieftain among the Midianites, probably also served in a judicial capacity. The Midianites were more experienced in the organization required in the desert than were the Israelites.

There is no necessary connection between the covenant ceremony of verses 1–12 and this section, except that it would have been easier for Jethro to give advice to Moses after forming a covenant with him than before.

15. to inquire of God: this phrase usually means, in a context such as this, to secure answer to a specific question through a divine oracle; cf. Gen. 25:22f.; 1 Sam. 9:9; 1 Kg. 22:8; 2 Kg. 3:11; 8:8; 22:13,18. According to Exod. 33:7–11, Moses would enter the tent of meeting and there 'the LORD would speak with Moses.' This may have been the method by which Moses inquired of Yahweh in judicial cases, but we cannot be certain.

16. I make them know the statutes of God and his decisions: the former are probably regulations and laws such as are attributed to Moses later in the Pentateuch. The word for **decisions** is *tôrōt*, plural of *tôrāh*, often translated 'law'. A *tôrāh* in the present sense was probably a decision, often secured through a divine oracle, on a specific question presented to the judge. In later times, the giving of *tôrāh* or *tôrōt* was frequently considered the

G

prerogative of the priests (Dt. 33:10; Jer. 18:18; Ezek. 7:26; 22:26; Hag. 2:11ff.; Mal. 2:6–9).

19. I will give you counsel, and God be with you: the last clause is better translated, 'that God may be with you'. Hebrew jussive with simple *waw* here expresses purpose.

21. and place such men over the people as rulers . . . of tens: this arrangement is suitable to military administration, but not to judicial organization; cf. 1 Sam. 8:12; 2 Kg. 1:9ff., but note that the military administration does not carry it down to 'rulers of tens'. This is probably a secondary addition in the narrative, motivated by the fact that the Hebrew *śārîm*, 'rulers', did at times function both as military leaders and judges (cf. Knierim, *loc. cit.*, pp. 155, 167–71).

22. every great matter they shall bring to you, but any small matter they shall decide themselves: this may be the heart of Jethro's practical advice. Moses was to decide the more important and more difficult matters, perhaps especially those requiring consultation of the divine oracle, whereas the lesser judges were to decide the ordinary cases for which there was known precedent and custom. For later times, this perhaps meant that the judges in the towns would decide ordinary matters and less difficult cases, whereas difficult matters and those for which there were no precedents or the precedents were not clear would be taken to the appeal court in Jerusalem. This probably does not mean simple distinction between 'religious' and 'civic' cases.

23 seems to presuppose that the people of Israel are settled in the land, not in the desert. *Am. Tr.* renders the second half of the verse: 'and also, this whole people can then have their cases settled near home.' This is paraphrastic, but may be a legitimate interpretation.

25. The second half of this verse is probably secondary; see comment above on verse 21.

DEPARTURE OF JETHRO TO HIS OWN LAND 18:27

The covenant between the followers of Jethro and those of Moses did not provide for them to dwell together, at this time at least, but Jethro leaves Moses and goes to his own country. On the possible relationship of this visit to Num. 10:29–32, see comment above, p. 187.

EVENTS AND LAWS OF MOUNT SINAI 19:1—40:38

At the beginning of this section the Israelites arrive at Sinai, and there they remain throughout the period narrated in the rest of this book and up to Num. 10:11, where it is said they set out from the wilderness of Sinai. All of the events, laws, and instructions recorded in the book of Exodus after 19:1 have their setting at Sinai.

In this section, Yahweh appears to the Israelites on Sinai, gives to them his covenant and laws (the Decalogue and the Covenant Code), and issues various instructions regarding the cultus. After the formation of the covenant and giving of the laws, the Israelites break the covenant by making a golden calf, but the covenant is subsequently restored. The Israelites carry out the instructions which they received regarding the cultus.

The literary analysis of this section presents unusual difficulties. There are two large blocks of Priestly material, 24:15—31:18 and 34:29—40:38. In the first of these the cultic instructions are given, and in the second they are carried out. Most of the rest of the material is from J and E, but the separation of the two is difficult, and there is little agreement among modern scholars as to their analysis.

There are at least two reasons for the literary difficulties in this section. One is that this part of the book of Exodus, especially chapters 19–24 and 32–34, was of crucial importance to the Israelites, because it contained an account of the formation of the covenant between Israel and Yahweh and of the commands on which it was based. Thus the section was subject to much reworking and expansion.

The other is the probability that this material concerning Sinai, or a part of it, was used in the cult. For example, Gerhard von Rad has advanced the view that the Sinai *pericope* (Exod. 19—24) was originally a festival legend used at Shechem in a ceremony of covenant renewal, at the time of the Festival of Booths (*sukkôt*). He sees here a preparatory ritual purification and sanctification of the people (19:10–15); their approach to God at the sound of the trumpets (19:13b,16); Yahweh's revelation of himself in a theophany in order to declare his will (19:18; chapters 20—23); and, finally, the ratification of the covenant and the people's sacrifice (chapter 24) (von Rad, *The Problem of the Hexateuch and*

Other Essays, pp. 21ff.). Earlier, Sigmund Mowinckel had connected the Sinai *pericope* with the New Year's festival, which was also a ceremony of covenant renewal (*Le Décalogue*, pp. 121ff.). It is quite possible that some of the materials here were used in the cult in some manner, but we should not assume that they were developed only within the cult and that they have little or no historical value. Also, we must note that von Rad's view is based upon the Sinai *pericope* in its finished form and that is rather late, containing as it does some redaction by the Deuteronomic redactor. For discussion of von Rad's views on the Sinai materials and their relationship to other materials in the Hexateuch, see Introduction, pp. 32–36.

FORMATION OF THE COVENANT 19:1—24:18

One of the most characteristic features of Israelite religion was the belief that it rested upon a covenant made between Yahweh and the people of Israel whereby he became their God and they became his people, promising to worship him and obey his commands. Only the early traditions, J and E, tell of the formation of the covenant in the time of Moses, for according to P the decisive covenant had been made at an earlier time with Abraham (Gen. 17). The book of Deuteronomy and the books of the *OT* which were edited by the Deuteronomists lay much emphasis on the concept of the covenant; the seventh century B.C. saw a great interest in this idea and institution. However, the word and the concept appear much earlier, as passages within the present section show, and there can be little doubt that the concept goes back to early times, most probably to the Mosaic age.

In the literary analysis of this section there are certain criteria, in addition to the employment of the divine names, Yahweh and *ᵓelohim* (not always decisive criteria after the revelation of the name Yahweh in 3:14ff.), which seem to be helpful: (i) in E, God dwells on the mountain (19:3), whereas in J he descends from heaven to the mountain (19:11,18; cf. 34:5); (ii) E calls the sacred mountain simply 'the mountain', but it is 'Mount Sinai' in J; (iii) in J, the theophany has the characteristics of volcanic activity (19:18), whereas in E it has the features of a violent storm (19:16; 20:18); (iv) in J, the people must be severely warned not to go up the mountain or touch its border (19:12–13,21–23), but in E they

appear to be naturally afraid, and ask Moses to serve as mediator
with God (19:16; 20:18–20).

The literary analysis is as follows: J—19:9–16a, 18, (20–24 J
supplementer); 24:1–2,9–11. E—19:2b–3a,16b–17,19,25; 20:18–
21; 24:3,4b–6,8,12–14,18b. R_D—19:3b–8; 20:22; 23:20–33;
24:4a,7. P—19:1–2a; 24:15–18a. The ethical Decalogue (20:1–17),
and the Covenant Code (20:22—23:19) should be considered as
separate units that have their own history. The ethical Decalogue
was probably placed in its present position by E, and the Covenant
Code in its present position by R_D, as we shall see in the discussion
below. 20:18–21 is now out of position; its original place was
apparently before chapter 20, as will be shown. The Deuteronomic
redactor played an important part in putting this section into its
present form, after J and E had been separately formed and then
combined. In addition to putting the Covenant Code in its present
position, he wrote 23:20–33 as the conclusion to that code,
provided the account of the theophany at Sinai with the introductory exhortation, 19:3b–8, and made certain adjustments in
chapter 24 (verses 4a, 7) to make it fit its present position immediately following the Covenant Code.

In discussing the form of the present section, as well as the
origin of the covenant and particularly of the Ten Commandments,
some recent scholars have pointed out parallels in form, and to
some extent in content, to ancient Near Eastern international
treaties, especially those known as 'vassal treaties' in which the
king of a great nation made a treaty with a vassal state. English
translations of such treaties may be found in *ANET*, pp. 203–06,
529–41, 659–61; the treaty between Rameses II of Egypt and
Hattusilis III of the Hittites, *ibid.* pp. 199–203, is a 'parity treaty'
between nations of equal rank, exhibiting many of the same
features. For a thorough discussion of these treaties and their
possible relationship to the *OT*, see D. J. McCarthy, *Treaty and
Covenant* (1963). He shows that such treaties were known not only
among the Hittites of the fourteenth to twelfth centuries B.C.
(roughly including the Mosaic age), but also earlier in Mesopotamia, and in the first millennium B.C. in Syria and Assyria.
He shows also that the clearest evidence for the possible influence
of the vassal treaty form can be seen in the core of Deuteronomy.

The full form of the vassal treaties is as follows: (i) the name and
titles of the king of the superior nation; (ii) a historical prologue
concerning the past relationships of the two countries, designed to

produce gratitude in the vassal and serve as warning to him; (iii) stipulations as to what both parties must do (mutual help in cases of aggression, extradition of refugees, etc.); (iv) statement that copies of the treaty are to be placed in temples and read periodically before the king and the people of each country; (v) a list of the witnesses, including deities of both countries; (vi) the blessings and curses that will ensue from observance or non-observance of the terms of the treaty. Items (i), (iii), (v) and (vi) are invariable elements, but the others are sometimes left out.

As an example of a scholar who sees the influence of the Hittite treaties in the present section, we may refer to W. Beyerlin, *Origins and History of the Oldest Sinaitic Traditions* (1965). He thinks that the covenant was formed at Kadesh, some of the tribes that entered into it having been at Sinai. At Kadesh the Ten Commandments were first written, as the terms of the covenant. A copy of the Ten Commandments was placed in the Ark (Dt. 10:1–5; cf. 31:26), and they were periodically read in the cult (cf. Dt. 31:10–11). Beyerlin thinks that the Israelites of this period knew the Hittite treaty form, and that influence of that form can be seen in the Ten Commandments and some other parts of the Sinai narrative.

Such a theory, in the opinion of the present writer, goes too far. It sees relationships to the Hittite treaty form that are only very slight (e.g. in comparing Exod. 20:2*b* with the historical section of the treaties), and it has to draw upon elements in the tradition concerning Sinai that are late (e.g. the deposit of the law in the Ark, and its periodic reading). Some elements of the vassal treaties are entirely lacking. Furthermore, one must ask the question: how and where could Moses or anyone of his age have learned the treaty form? This form was known by officials and scribes in the chancelleries of several countries, but would it have been known to Hebrew slaves in Egypt, or nomads in the desert? Although there is an Egyptian copy of the treaty between Rameses II and Hattusilis III, the treaty form was not really at home in Egypt. We may grant that there are possible traces of the treaty form in the finished form of the Sinai *pericope* in Exod. 19–24, after it left the hands of the Deuteronomic redactor (with the appended blessings and implied curse in 23:20–33), but the earlier forms of the narrative, including the ethical Decalogue, have little resemblance to the treaties. Only in Deuteronomy (and possibly in Joshua 24) is the influence of the treaty form

really evident, when the form had been used for a long time in
other nations.

The spirit and content of the Sinai narrative are very different
from the international treaty. Here we do not have a great king
making a contract with a vassal, but a sovereign deity manifesting
himself and making his will known to his chosen people. He calls
them to be loyal to him because of what he is and what he has
done for them, and unites them with himself in rites that are
designed to create a union of kinship between the two parties.
Not contract, but theophany· and rite, are here dominant.

THEOPHANY ON MOUNT SINAI 19:1–25

19:1–2(P,E). *The Israelites leave Rephidim and arrive at the wilderness of Sinai in the third month after their departure from Egypt. They
encamp before the mountain.*

19:3–8(E,R_D). *Moses goes up to God, and Yahweh calls to him out of
the mountain. Moses is to tell the Israelites that, if they will keep Yahweh's
covenant, they will be Yahweh's possession, and a kingdom of priests and
holy nation. Moses tells this to the elders of Israel, and the people agree that
they will do what Yahweh has spoken.*

19:9–15(J). *Yahweh promises Moses that he will come to him in a
thick cloud. Moses is to go down and instruct the Israelites how to consecrate
themselves before they come to the mountain. He does so, making the people
ready for the third day.*

19:16–19(J,E). *On the third day Yahweh appears on the mountain as
the people stand at the foot of it. Moses speaks to God, who answers him in
thunder.*

19:20–25(Js,E). *Yahweh calls Moses to the top of the mountain.
He tells Moses to warn the people not to break through to gaze, lest they
perish. The priests also are to consecrate themselves, lest Yahweh break out
upon them. Moses is also to bring Aaron up with him. Moses goes down to
the people and tells them.*

This chapter is clearly composite. This can be seen in the various
statements about the movements of Moses, if nothing else: in
verse 3 Moses goes up to God—that is, up the mountain; in both
verses 8 and 9*b* he reports to Yahweh; in verse 14 he goes down
from the mountain to consecrate the people, but in verse 19 he is
apparently on the mountain; in verses 20–24 he is called to the
top of the mountain, and told to go down and bring up Aaron;
in verse 25 he goes down to the people.

The literary analysis of the chapter is as follows: J—19:9*a*,

10–16a,18; E—19:2b–3a,16b–17,19,25; P—19:1–2a; R_D—19:3b–
8. Verses 9b and 20–24 appear to be late additions; the latter has
characteristics of a Judaean tradition, and thus is assigned to the
J supplementer (Js).

1–2a (**. . . encamped in the wilderness**) are from P. Verse 2
should logically precede verse 1, and that may have been the
original order. This is P's chronology, continuing the chronological
data of 12:1–2; 16:1.

1. the third new moon is the first day of the third month.
This may have been an attempt by P to associate the Sinai
tradition with the Feast of Weeks (Dt. 16:9–12), and there may
be a relationship to the late passage (2 Chr. 15:10–14), which
tells of a covenant renewal ceremony in the reign of King Asa in
the third month of his fifteenth year. See comment above, pp. 195f.
the wilderness of Sinai: the plain in the immediate vicinity of
Mount Sinai; cf. 'wilderness of Sin' in 16:1.
Rephidim: see 17:1,8.

3b–8 are from the Deuteronomic redactor (R_D). Some scholars
attribute these verses to E, but verses 5–6 are filled with Deuteronomic terminology, and the whole section anticipates the conclusion of the covenant which comes later. The redactor has
placed here at the beginning of the Sinai *pericope* an exhortation
which summarizes in admirable fashion the covenant theology.
The language is elevated and in part poetic, with parallelism of
lines in verses 4–6. R_D may have enlarged an E passage which
originally stood here. Such an exhortation as we have here would
form an excellent beginning for a cultic ceremony using the Sinai
tradition.

4. how I bore you on eagles' wings: cf. Dt. 32:11.
5. my own possession: cf. Dt. 7:6; 14:2; 26:18; Ps. 135:4;
Mal. 3:17 (the last passage refers to the future). Hebrew *s^egullāh*
is a king's private treasure in 1 Chr. 29:3; Ec. 2:8. It is related to
the Akkadian *sikiltu*, which means a private fund, a private
accumulation.

6. a kingdom of priests: a similar idea is expressed in Isa.
61:6, but the phrase does not occur elsewhere in the *OT*. In the
NT the idea appears in 1 Pet. 2:5,9; Rev. 1:6; 5:10; 20:6. As a
'kingdom of priests' the Israelites were all to have access to
Yahweh, and the nation was to serve as priest for the rest of the
nations of the world.
a holy nation: cf. 'holy people' Dt. 7:6; 14:2,21; 26:19; Isa.

62:12. 1 Pet. 2:9 uses the term employed here. As a holy people or nation, the Israelites were set apart from other nations for the worship and service of Yahweh.

9-15 is basically J's account of the preparations for Yahweh's appearance, continued by verse 18, J's account of the theophany. The people are to consecrate themselves and be ritually pure, and they are forbidden to go up the mountain or touch its border upon pain of death.

9. **you** in this verse is second person singular: Yahweh will come to Moses and speak with him, in order that the people may believe him. The general viewpoint of J is that Yahweh appears only to Moses, and the people are forbidden to come near or to look upon Yahweh (cf. verse 21). Yet, verse 11 says that Yahweh will come down 'in the sight of all the people', while they are waiting at the foot of the mountain. On the people's believing Moses, cf. 14:31. They are to believe him **for ever**: the Mosaic covenant is an eternal covenant.

Then Moses told the words of the people to the LORD: this is a misplaced variant of the last sentence of verse 7.

12. **whoever touches the mountain shall be put to death:** the mountain is sacred, or as we might say, 'taboo'. If anyone does touch the mountain, then no other hand is to touch him for fear of the *tabu* passing to him. Anyone violating the prohibition was thus to be stoned or shot.

13. **When the trumpet sounds a long blast, they shall come up to the mountain:** this seems to be a liturgical direction, and is adduced by some critics as evidence for the use of this pericope in the cult. The Hebrew for trumpet is *yōḇēl*, lit. 'ram's horn'. Another word, *šōp̄ār*, is used in 19:16,19; 20:18. The trumpet was a signalling instrument, often used to sound the alarm in war, but sometimes to summons the people to a cultic ceremony or assembly (Lev. 25:9; Ps. 47:5; 81:3; 2 Chr. 15:14; Isa. 27:13). The blast of the trumpet represented the presence of Yahweh. Because of the use of the word **they,** some scholars consider this passage to be a small fragment of a tradition which may have had some connection with 24:1-2,9-11, where we read that Moses went up the mountain, taking Aaron, Nadab, Abihu, and seventy elders. The *RSV* rendering here assumes that 'they' are to come 'up to the mountain'—that is, to the foot of the mountain—at the sound of the trumpet; however, the Hebrew could better be translated, 'they shall come up the mountain'.

15. do not go near a woman: sexual relations were prohibited to the men, because they were believed to make the men unfit for sacred duties; cf. 1 Sam. 21:5.

18. Here the theophany is represented with phenomena associated with volcanic activity: **fire, smoke . . . like the smoke of a kiln,** and the quaking of **the whole mountain.** Because this representation is more unusual than that of the storm, this probably reproduces the earlier tradition regarding the appearance of Yahweh on Mount Sinai. It has led some scholars to suggest that Sinai was a volcanic mountain; see discussion below on the location of Sinai.

the LORD descended upon it in fire: in J, Yahweh descends upon the mountain, whereas in E he is conceived as having his permanent abode on the sacred mountain.

and the whole mountain quaked greatly: nine Hebrew manuscripts and LXX read 'and all the people trembled greatly.' This is adopted as the correct reading by some (e.g. *Am. Tr.*), but the text of *RSV* is more likely to be correct. While it is true that the verb is not elsewhere used of the quaking of a mountain, it is used with inanimate objects as subject in Isa. 41:5; Ezek. 26:18 (both metaphorically of fear).

19. Because the Hebrew uses two verbs in the imperfect here, representing repeated action, we should render: 'And as the sound of the trumpet grew louder and louder, Moses kept speaking, and God kept answering him in thunder'.

in thunder: the Hebrew is 'in a voice', but thunder was often considered to be the voice of God (Ps. 29:3–5,7–9; 46:6; Job 37:4; etc.).

20–24 is an addition to the original accounts of the theophany. It is repetitious within itself, and repetitious of what has preceded, especially of verses 12–13. The reference here to the priests is anachronistic, as no account has yet been given in the book of Exodus to the setting apart of priests; this occurs first in chapter 29. This section, which rests generally upon Judaean tradition, must be considered as a commentary on verses 12–13, added in order to deal with the question later raised whether the priests were included in the prohibition announced in those verses.

24. Go down, and come up bringing Aaron with you: this instruction is not literally carried out, unless 24:9 is to be considered as fulfilling it. There we read that Aaron went up on the mountain with Aaron, Nadab, Abihu and seventy elders, in

response to the instruction given in 24:1. Meanwhile, in 20:21
Moses draws near to God alone.

25. This verse breaks off abruptly, ending 'and he said to them.'
The original ending has obviously been lost.

EXCURSUS: *The Location of Mount Sinai*

The name of the sacred mountain in the J and P narratives is
'Sinai', but E and D call it 'Horeb'. This was the 'mountain of
God' (3:1; 18:5). The name Sinai may be related to the name of
the ancient Semitic moon-god, Sin; Horeb means 'desolate
region'. In most passages these two names apparently refer to the
same mountain, but in a few passages in Deuteronomy 'Horeb'
may designate a wider region (4:10; 9:8; 18:16). The oldest
tradition apparently used the name 'Sinai'.

It is not possible for us now to locate Sinai with confidence,
because the data in the *OT* upon which we must depend are
in conflict. We cannot make all the data fit one location.
Three different localities have been proposed as the site of Sinai-
Horeb.

(i) The traditional ·site is in the mountainous region at the
southern end of the peninsula of Sinai. That peninsula has been
described as 'a huge wedge-shaped block of mountains, intersected
by numerous gorges and valleys, lying between the gulfs of Suez
and Akaba' (Driver, p. 177). The mountains in the south are
rugged and very high. The Christian tradition which locates
Mount Sinai in that region can be traced back to the fourth century
A.D., when Christian monasteries were being built there; but no
earlier. The famous convent of S. Catherine was erected by
Justinian in the sixth century, but it is said to have been built on
the site of a small church erected by the Empress Helena two
centuries earlier. The mediaeval legend of Catherine of Alexandria
held that, after her martyrdom, her body was carried to the top of
the mountain that now bears her name. Mount Sinai is usually
identified specifically with Jebel Musa, 'Mountain of Moses',
which rises about 7500 ft. above sea level, or Jebel Katarin,
'Mountain of Catherine', about a thousand feet higher. Some
scholars identify it with Jebel Serbal, twenty miles to the NW. of
the latter.

There is evidence that this region may have been the goal of
pagan pilgrimages even before the Christian identification of it
with Sinai. Nabatean rock inscriptions of the second and third

centuries A.D., found especially near Jebel Serbal, indicate that a mountain shrine in this region was the goal of Nabatean pilgrims. Since sacred places have a tendency to persist for a long time, and to pass from religion to religion, it has been maintained that this region may have been the object of pilgrimages in pre-Christian Jewish religion, even going back to Israelite times (Noth, pp. 155f.).

An argument advanced against the traditional site is that at the time of the exodus of the Israelites from Egypt this region was under the control of the Egyptians, who for a long time had worked the mines of copper and turquoise especially at Serabit el-Khadem, NW. of Jebel Musa. Would the Israelites have gone to such a region when they wished to escape from the Egyptians? Also, would they have taken such a circuitous route if their real object was to return to Palestine? It must be pointed out, however, that in the thirteenth century B.C. (when the exodus probably occurred), Egyptian control over the Sinai peninsula was weakened, and the mines were not exploited as vigorously as they had been earlier. The discovery at Serabit el-Khadem of Semitic inscriptions (the Proto-Sinaitic Inscriptions) from c. 1500 B.C. has no bearing on the problem of the location of Sinai.

(ii) Another region proposed for the location of Mount Sinai is in the north-western part of Arabia, to the SE. of the gulf of Aqaba. The strongest argument for this location is the presence in the region of volcanic mountains. The J tradition of the theophany on Mount Sinai suggests a volcanic eruption, particularly 19:18, which speaks of fire, the ascending of smoke like the smoke of a kiln, and the quaking of the whole mountain. There is no evidence for the existence of volcanoes in the peninsula of Sinai, but there are volcanoes still active in the vicinity of Tebuk, which is on the great pilgrim road that goes down to Mecca and Medina. Those who locate Sinai in this region do not point out any particular mountain that is identifiable with Sinai, but only the general area. Scholars who oppose the location of Sinai in this region say that the description of the theophany makes use of traditional metaphors, and does not necessarily reflect literal volcanic phenomena.

Another argument for the location of Sinai in the region E. of the Araba and the gulf of Aqaba is derived from references in three poems of the OT, which are in part very ancient. In the 'Song of Deborah' (Jg. 5:4), Yahweh is said to 'go forth from Seir', and 'march from the region of Edom', and Sinai is mentioned in 5:5. In the 'Blessing of Moses' (Dt. 33:2), we read that Yahweh 'came from Sinai . . . dawned from Seir . . . shone forth from Mount Paran.' Hab. 3:3 says that 'God came from Teman, and the Holy One from Mount Paran.' Teman is located E. of the Araba near modern Petra, and Seir-Edom was the region E. of the Dead Sea and the Araba, but no doubt at times covering some territory W. of the Araba. This is, of course, somewhat north of the region in which volcanic mountains are found, but nearer than the traditional site in the peninsula of Sinai. (Paran is very difficult to locate, but the Wilderness of Paran apparently included Kadesh-barnea, and the references to it are used to support the third identification, discussed below.)

A third argument for this identification is that Sinai was located in the land of Midian (2:15; 3:1), which is often located specifically to the east of the gulf of Aqaba. However, the Midian-ites were wide-ranging nomads, and it is perilous to try to locate their 'land' precisely (see comment on 2:15).

(iii) A third location suggested for Mount Sinai is the region immediately S. of Palestine, somewhere in the vicinity of Kadesh-barnea. The latter is identified with ʿAin Qedeis or ʿAin el-Qudeirat, about 50 miles SSE. of Beersheba. Some scholars point specifically to Jebel Helal, some 30 miles to the W., as the site of Sinai. The location of Sinai near Kadesh was favoured by R. Kittel, *Geschichte des Volkes Israel*, 6th ed. (1923), pp. 343–49.

An argument which has been adduced in favour of this identi-fication is the statement, apparently in the oldest tradition, that the Hebrews left Egypt in order to make a journey of three days to Sinai. In Exod. 3:18 Yahweh instructs Moses and the elders to demand of Pharaoh that he allow the Hebrews to go a three days' journey into the wilderness in order to sacrifice to their God— presumably meaning to the sacred place at which Yahweh has just appeared to Moses. Such a demand is made in 5:3 and 8:27. Then, in an obscure passage in 15:22 we are told that the Israelites went three days in the wilderness and, finding no water, came to Marah. Then in 17:1–7 they are at a place called Massah and Meribah. In a related tradition recorded in Num. 20:1–13, Meribah is located near Kadesh, and there are several references to Meribath-Kadesh, or Meribah of Kadesh (see comments on 15:22 and 17:1–7). These data are by no means clear and compelling, and Kadesh is farther than a three days' journey from the Egyptian border. But Kadesh was an extremely impor-

tant place for the Hebrews in the period of the wilderness wandering, and the location of Sinai nearer to Kadesh than Jebel Musa
would solve a number of difficulties. In the commentary it has been
shown that many of the incidents recorded in chapters 16–18 could
more logically have taken place after the events at Sinai rather
than before; hence a journey directly to Sinai, near Kadesh, after
the crossing of the Red Sea would seem more probable.

The poetic passages referred to above, Dt. 33:2; Jg. 5:4–5;
Hab. 3:3, are sometimes used as evidence by those who favour the
location of Sinai in the region immediately S. of Palestine, as well
as by advocates of the second view. They point out that Seir-
Edom sometimes included territory to the W. of the Araba (see
Num. 20:16), and that the Wilderness of Paran included the
region of Kadesh-barnea (see Num. 13:3,26). Teman, however, is
not to be located in such a region, but it occurs only in the
Habakkuk poem, which may not be ancient.

The location of Sinai in the vicinity of Kadesh-barnea cannot
be reconciled with the statement in Dt. 1:2 that it was an eleven
days' journey from Horeb by way of Mount Seir to Kadesh-
barnea. That statement can more easily be reconciled with the
traditional location. However, since it occurs only in Deuteronomy,
it is probably not an early element in the tradition.

We must conclude by repeating what was said at the outset: no
location of Sinai can be made to fit all the *OT* data. The biblical
writers did not have a primary interest in geographical data, and
in making precise statements concerning geographical locations.
They were interested in relating the events in the light of the
meaning which they attributed to them. Furthermore, the
materials concerning the period of the exodus and the wilderness
wandering have gone through a long process of oral tradition and
editing which extended over many centuries.

It is the opinion of the present writer, however, that the
traditional site at the southern end of the Sinai peninsula has less
to recommend it than the other two. Either of the other two
seems to be more in harmony with the earliest tradition, as it can
be discovered through literary criticism and the analysis of the
history of tradition. The third identification suggested above may
be the correct one, in view of the 'three days' journey' tradition,
the likelihood that the Israelites were really seeking to return to
Palestine, and the tremendous importance of Kadesh-barnea in
the history of the 'wilderness wandering'. It is unfortunate that

advocates of this view cannot point to a specific mountain as imposing and awe-inspiring as Jebel Musa.

THE TEN COMMANDMENTS **20:1–17**
God speaks 'all these words', giving to the Israelites for the first time the Ten Commandments, sometimes called also the ethical decalogue to distinguish it from a supposed 'ritual decalogue' of 34:17–26. These may be the 'ten words' which Moses wrote upon the two tables of stone (34:28; Dt. 4:13; 10:4).

This decalogue is sometimes referred to as the E decalogue, but it is a mistake to do so. The word *ʾelohim* rather than Yahweh is used in verse 1, and this section is followed by E material in verses 18–21, but there is nothing that specifically marks this decalogue as Elohistic in its origin. Exod. 20:1–17 should be looked upon as a unit having a history of its own apart from the usual sources. It may have been placed in its position by E or R$_{JE}$ (some scholars think rather by D), but it is not impossible that the J narrative included it at some point, perhaps originally in chapter 34; see discussion below *in loc.*

It is likewise a mistake to think of the Ten Commandments as being law or a law code. They certainly do not comprise a law code, for they are not comprehensive enough for that: they deal with general principles rather than with detailed cases, and they specify no punishments (implying only that those who broke the commandments would incur the wrath of Yahweh and of the community). The Ten Commandments were 'the words of Yahweh' that the Israelites accepted as their obligation when they entered into covenant with him. They may have been the original 'Book of the Covenant' of 24:7 (see comment *in loc.*); the Covenant Code of 20:23—23:19 is a secondary insertion. Willing acceptance of, and obedience to, the Ten Commandments marked Israel as the people chosen by Yahweh as his own people.

When seen within the context of the covenant relationship between Yahweh and Israel, the Ten Commandments cease to be 'law' in any legalistic sense, as commands which must be kept for their own sake or out of fear of punishment. As the offering of the covenant was an act of grace on the part of Yahweh, so was the promulgation of the Ten Commandments. Israel freely accepted them and responded to them from a sense of gratitude for what Yahweh had done for her.

This interpretation of the Ten Commandments does not in itself answer the question whether they originated with Moses, or at a later time. This is a question which has been much debated by scholars, and there is no scholarly consensus at the present time. Wellhausen and many critics after him thought that this decalogue was not from Moses, because they thought it shows the influence of the Hebrew prophets; they placed it after the beginning of the classical prophetic movement in the eighth century, some putting it as late as the Babylonian Exile. Hos. 4:2 was sometimes considered the first evidence for the existence of a decalogue, and Jer. 7:9 was cited as evidence that it had been formed, or was in the process of formation.

Since about 1930, however, an increasing number of critical scholars have been willing to attribute the decalogue to Moses, or at least to consider it as an ancient, pre-prophetic document. This view has arisen for a number of reasons. It has been pointed out that the decalogue does not really exhibit the concern for social problems found in the prophets, and the general course of the development of Israelite religion is now viewed in a different light from that of Wellhausen. The prophets are seen not as innovators, but rather as reformers who wished to revive some of the ideals of an older age which went back in part to Moses. Detailed discussions of the problems involved may be found in J. J. Stamm and M. E. Andrew, *The Ten Commandments in Recent Research* (1967); H. H. Rowley, 'Moses and the Decalogue', in his *Men of God* (1963), pp. 1–36; and Eduard Nielsen, *The Ten Commandments in New Perspective* (1968).

The view of the present writer is that the ethical decalogue, in a brief and succinct form, *could* have originated with Moses. It is not possible to offer definitive proof or disproof of this view, but we believe that, if the *OT* contains anywhere the 'ten words' of Yahweh spoken through Moses, they are in the ethical decalogue.

There is nothing in the Ten Commandments which could not have originated with Moses. It does not show, as some other supposed 'decalogues' do, the influence of an agrarian background such as we would expect if it originated after the entrance into Canaan. There is nothing in it which is clearly cultic. The Sabbath in 20:8–11 was not originally a day for cultic observance but rather for rest from work.

The Ten Commandments do not deal with individual acts and their punishment, but rather with general principles. It calls for respect for and right relationship with God on the one hand, and on the other for respect for the neighbour—his life, his property, his good name, and his marriage bond. When viewed as a whole, the Ten Commandments contain surprisingly little that is uniquely Israelite. The unique elements are the worship of Yahweh rather than of any other deity, and the worship of him without the aid of idols. It is precisely the emphasis upon the worship of Yahweh that we associate especially with Moses. He is depicted in the *OT* as the type of vigorous and dedicated leader who would have been capable of issuing a general set of commandments such as these, designed to hold together the disparate elements in the early Israelite community, and bind them to their deity. Most of the commandments are by no means new, for every civilized community must have regulations to protect the life, property, and good name of its members.

The commandments were promulgated at the outset for Israel only, and they had at the outset a limited application to the Israelite community. Yet they contained from the beginning elements of universality and general applicability that made it inevitable for them to become a foundation stone for Judaeo-Christian ethics.

They are expressed in the second person singular; this is not obvious in the *RSV*, which uses 'you' for both singular and plural. They are addressed to the individual within the Israelite community. All of them have the 'apodictic' form, as distinguished from the 'casuistic' form which appears frequently in the Covenant Code—e.g. 21:2-14,18-36; 22:1-17. On the difference between these forms, see A. Alt, 'The Origins of Israelite Law', translated in his *Essays on Old Testament History and Religion* (1966), pp. 79–132. The apodictic form is categorical and absolute. All of the Ten Commandments are expressed in the negative, as prohibitions, except those regarding the Sabbath and the honouring of father and mother. Some scholars believe that the negative form was originally used in all the commandments, but this cannot be proved. Alt believed that the apodictic form indicated native Israelite law. However, subsequent study has shown that this form was used frequently outside Israel—e.g. in Hittite treaties, and in Egyptian and Mesopotamian wisdom literature. In itself the form does not indicate origin.

They may have been read periodically in the cult, as suggested by von Rad and others (see above, pp. 195f), but it is not probable that they originated in the cult. They are much more likely to have originated in the customs and regulations of the families and clans of pre-Mosaic times, as handed down by heads of families and clans, elders, and wise men. In this sense some of the commandments are 'pre-Mosaic' in origin. Moses' work was to select them, put them in succinct form, and relate them to the covenant.

The code is reproduced also in Dt. 5:6–21. There are numerous minor differences between the Exodus and Deuteronomy forms of individual commandments in the Hebrew; some of these will be pointed out in the comments. Generally the Exodus form is more ancient, but it shows traces of both Deuteronomic and Priestly editing—the latter particularly in verse 11. In their original form the individual commandments were doubtless brief and succinct, like the commandments in verses 3, 13–16. All of the expansions appear to have been made by the Deuteronomic redactor, except verse 11, which is a P addition (cf. Gen. 2:2–3).

The method of ordering the commandments varies in various communions. The Roman Catholics and Lutherans count verses 3–6 as the first commandment, and divide verse 17 to make two commandments (ninth and tenth) concerning coveting. Jews and most Protestants count verse 3 as the first commandment, verses 4–6 as the second, and verse 17 as the tenth. The latter method is more logical, and is the method we follow in numbering the commandments.

2 is an introduction or prologue to the Ten Commandments. **I am the LORD your God:** this might be translated 'I, Yahweh, am your God', and such a translation is preferred by some modern scholars. The *RSV* rendering follows that of LXX and Vulgate. 'I am Yahweh' is a phrase found especially in P, Ezekiel, and 2 Isaiah. Cf. Exod. 6:2, 6,7,8, and the comments on 3:15.

who brought you out of the land of Egypt, out of the house of bondage: this phrase is compared today with the historical prologue often found in international treaties of the ancient Near East, especially the Hittite (see above, pp. 179–99). However, this is too brief to be a real parallel to the treaty forms. This phrase identifies Yahweh as the God who delivered Israel from slavery in Egypt; such deliverance is the foundation of Yahweh's right to issue commands to his covenant people.

3. The rendering of the last phrase, ʿal pānāy, is uncertain: *RSV* gives **before me,** but notes in mg. an alternative possibility,

besides me. In some *OT* passages *ʿal pᵉnê* has a hostile undertone, meaning 'over against'; see Gen. 16:12; 25:18; Dt. 21:16. Thus the meaning may be: 'You shall not prefer other gods to me'. In any event, this commandment does not enjoin monotheism, the belief in only one God for the whole world. In fact, it seems to presuppose the existence of other gods. The viewpoint is that of henotheism or monolatry, a type of theism which asserts that each nation or people may have its own god in which it believes and which it worships, but the existence of many deities is not denied. Yet, from the beginning the Israelites believed that Yahweh was a jealous God (see verse 5 and 34:14). Thus the first commandment suggests 'a dynamic monolatry which had the seeds of monotheism within it' (Stamm and Andrew, p. 81).

4. You shall not make yourself a graven image: this was probably the original form of the second commandment, the rest being an interpretative expansion by R_D. The rendering of *pésel* by 'graven image' may be too precise. Strictly, it did mean an image that could be carved or hewn, and thus be made of wood or stone. This is the type of image the Israelites might have had in their earliest period. However, *pésel* sometimes has a broader meaning, including molten images of metal as well (Isa. 40:19; 44:10). That is probably the meaning here; certainly it was the meaning accepted by the one who gave the extensive interpretation in the rest of the commandment. Images are prohibited in several early passages: 20:23; 34:17 (J); Dt. 27:15. In spite of the fact that this prohibition was sometimes not observed, it is likely that Israelite Yahwism forbade images from the beginning. An image was considered in the ancient Near East as a means by which a deity manifested himself; it was not believed that the image *was* the deity. As early as the 1st Dynasty of Egypt, in the document known as 'The Theology of Memphis', it was pointed out that the gods entered into their bodies of wood, stone, clay and the like (*ANET*, p. 5). The second commandment intends to say that Yahweh is the kind of deity who cannot properly manifest himself in any kind of image; Yahweh was to the Israelite a God manifesting himself in his word and in history. Those who made images sought to control the gods for their own purposes, but Yahweh could not be used or manipulated by man. This commandment was originally directed against images of Yahweh, but later included foreign idols, which of course were forbidden by the first commandment.

the water under the earth: the great subterranean abyss, according to Hebrew cosmology (Gen. 49:25; Ps. 24:2; 136:6).

5. I the LORD your God am a jealous God: Yahweh is a God who is jealous of his position. The idea is very close to that expressed in the word 'zealous'. It is an old concept, as indicated by 34:14 (J), but is found especially in Deuteronomy (Dt. 4:24; 6:15; Jos. 24:19).

7. You shall not take the name of the LORD your God in vain: probably the original form of the third commandment, the rest of the verse being a later comment (RD). The knowledge and use of the name of a deity was very important in ancient times, for it could be uttered to gain the power of the deity. This prohibition was directed primarily against the wrong use of the name of Yahweh in oath-taking, blessings and curses, and sorcery; more broadly, it was directed against any insincere and evil use of the name. Thus it was not especially concerned with what in modern times is called 'profanity' or 'swearing'. The *OT* enjoins the Hebrew to swear—that is, take oaths—in the name of Yahweh, and to do so with sincerity, not falsely (Jer. 4:2; 5:2; 7:9; Lev. 19:12; Zech. 5:3; Mal. 3:5). The basis for this prohibition is similar to that of the preceding commandment: man cannot secure power over Yahweh and use him or his name for his own purposes.

8. Remember the Sabbath day to keep it holy: this was probably the original form of the fourth commandment, the remainder, to verse 10, being from RD, and verse 11 from P. The form of this commandment in Dt. 5:12–15 differs considerably from the present form. It uses 'observe' instead of 'remember'. At the end of the first sentence it adds, 'as the LORD your God commands you'. The enumeration of animals in verse 10 is more detailed. The motive for the commandment in Dt. 5:15 is, 'You shall remember that you were a servant in the land of Egypt, and the LORD your God brought you out thence with a mighty hand and an outstretched arm; therefore the LORD your God commanded you to keep the Sabbath day.' It is likely that the motivation in Exod. 20:11, which emphasizes the imitation of God's rest on the Sabbath (Gen. 2:2–3), has been substituted by P for a motivation similar to that of Deuteronomy.

This commandment enjoins the Israelite to keep the Sabbath holy as a day set apart to Yahweh, as the other days are profane or secular. Some scholars insist that its original form was negative, such as the following: 'you shall not do any work on the Sabbath day.' It is not necessary to make this change, but early references to the Sabbath or seventh day make it a day of cessation from work: see the other references in Exod. 16:30 (J); 23:12; 34:21 (J); 35:2 (P). It is not known when the Sabbath originated, but it could be of Mosaic origin; see comment on 16:27–30. This last passage indicates that the Israelites believed it originated even before the giving of the law on Sinai. In origin it was a taboo day, on which work was forbidden, rather than a day for religious festival.

12. **Honour your father and your mother:** this was the extent of the original commandment, the rest clearly being from the Deuteronomic redactor (cf. Dt. 4:40; 5:33; 6:2; 11:9; 22:7; 30:18; 32:47). This is the only commandment that in its present form has a promise for obedience. The position of the fifth commandment is significant: it comes immediately after commandments which inculcate proper worship and respect for Yahweh, and before the commandments concerning neighbours. The importance of filial respect is thus underlined by its position, and the commandment forms a bridge between those concerning God and those concerning the neighbour.

This commandment inculcates obedience and respect for parents, and must have applied both to young children, and to adults living in the same household with their aged parents. In ancient Israel there must have often been three or even more generations within a single household. Young children were to give obedience and respect to their parents; adult children were to express their respect for aged parents by supporting and caring for them and giving them proper deference. That parents were sometimes maltreated is indicated by passages such as Prov. 19:26; 28:24. Other passages indicate that death was the penalty for cursing or striking a father or mother (Exod. 21:15,17); a stubborn and rebellious son was subjected to stoning by the community (Dt. 21:18–21).

It is worthy of note that here and in other passages it is said the mother should be honoured equally with the father. In Lev. 19:3, the mother is placed before the father. The book of Proverbs contains numerous verses concerning respect for both parents.

Some scholars think that this commandment originally had a negative form, like most of the others. On the basis of Exod. 21:17 and Dt. 27:16, they suggest the original form was, 'You shall not curse [or, dishonour] your father and your mother'. While this is

possible, it cannot be proved. The injunction is sometimes framed
positively, as e.g., Lev. 19:3, 'Every one of you shall revere his
mother and his father', and often in Proverbs.

13. You shall not kill. The verb which is used here, *rāṣaḥ*, is
used much less often than two other verbs meaning to kill, *hārag*
and *hēmît* (*hifil* of *mût*). Careful studies have shown that it is
nearly always used of the killing of a personal enemy; it is not
confined, however, to intentional murder, but is occasionally used
of unintentional homicide (e.g. Dt. 4:41–43; 19:1–13). Later laws
made provision for the right of asylum in case of involuntary
homicide: Exod. 21:12–13 provides for asylum at an altar (cf.
1 Kg. 1:50; 2:28), and Num. 35:9–34 (P); Dt. 19:1–31 provide
for cities of refuge. The purpose of the sixth commandment was to
prohibit any kind of illegal killing that was contrary to the will
and the best interests of the community. Thus its real import was
to prohibit murder, in spite of the fact that this meaning is not
specifically derived from the verb employed. It originally had
nothing to do with capital punishment (administered by the
avenger of blood or by the community), killing in war which was
certainly sanctioned by the *OT*, or the killing of animals. In the
course of history, this commandment has been broadened to
apply to killing in war, capital punishment, and the like. The
prohibition against killing was based upon Hebrew belief in the
great value of human life (Gen. 9:6). Later law provided that no
ransom could be made for murder (Num. 35:31–33 P).

14. You shall not commit adultery: for the ancient Hebrew,
adultery was not any form of extra-marital sexual union, but the
voluntary cohabitation of a married or betrothed woman with a
man who was not her own husband. The penalty for adultery in
the later laws was death for both the man and the woman (Lev.
20:10; Dt. 22:22–24, which specifies death by stoning; cf. Jn 8:5).
Thus, adultery did not include extra-marital relationships of a
man with an unmarried woman, though penalties were exacted in
some cases (22:16f.; Dt. 22:28–29). Adultery was considered,
therefore, a violation of the sanctity of the marriage bond; it was
an offence against the husband, who was entitled to exclusive
sexual possession of his wife. It was considered also as a sin against
God (Gen. 20:6; 39:9; Ps. 51:4). In the history of the interpretation of this commandment, it has been widened to include
various types of extra-marital relationships, and has been
spiritualized (cf. Mt. 5:27–28).

15. The eighth commandment is usually interpreted as for-
bidding all manner of stealing, but some scholars believe that the
verb originally had an object, as in Exod. 21:16 and Dt.
24:7, and read, 'You shall not steal a man'. It was thus a prohibition
against the kidnapping of a free Israelite man (A. Alt, *Kleine
Schriften*, 1 (1959), pp. 333-40). The tenth commandment is then
interpreted as a prohibition, not of envy or inordinate desire, but
rather of action taken to appropriate the property of others.
The difference between the eighth and tenth commandments is
then said to be a difference in the object stolen: the eighth forbids
the stealing of a free Israelite man, while the tenth forbids the
stealing of a woman, child, slave, or any other possession. This
narrowing of the eighth commandment, while possible, is not
necessarily correct. The kidnapping of free Israelite men must have
been rare in ancient times, and it is doubtful that the ethical
decalogue would have contained a prohibition against so rare an
occurrence, when the other commandments are general in nature.
Also, it is not easy to understand why the commandment was
shortened if it was originally longer. See further below on verse 17.

16 may be literally rendered, 'You shall not answer against
your neighbour as a lying witness [*ʿēḏ šéḵer*]'. The corresponding
commandment in Dt. 5:20 has 'as a witness of emptiness [*ʿēḏ šāwʾ*]'.
The Exodus form is the more original, since the phrase 'lying
witness' occurs elsewhere in the *OT* (Ps. 27:12; Prov. 6:19; 12:17;
14:5; 19:5,9; 25:18), and the phrase *ʿēḏ šāw* occurs only in
Dt. 5:20. This commandment was originally directed against the
giving of false testimony in a judicial trial, not against all forms of
lying or untruthfulness. The language of the verse is that of the
law court. Hebrew *ʿānāh* ('answer') was a technical term meaning
to testify, give testimony in a court, as in Num. 35:30; Dt. 19:16,
18. In ancient Israel, where judicial proceedings were somewhat
informal (at least in earliest times) and free Israelites were often
called upon to act as judges or witnesses, truthfulness in the
giving of testimony was of extreme importance—as indeed is true
in all legal systems. The penalty for false testimony by a witness
for the prosecution is given in Dt. 19:16-19: he was to be dealt
with by the law of retaliation.

17. The corresponding commandment in Dt. 5:21 reverses the
order given here; the commandment not to covet a neighbour's
wife precedes the command not to covet his house, field, man-
servant, maidservant, ox, ass, or anything else. It is most likely that

the Exodus form is original, and that the earliest form of the tenth commandment was simply: **You shall not covet your neighbour's house,** the last word meaning the household and those possessions usually found in it—wife, slaves, animals, and the rest. This is the usage, e.g., in Gen. 7:1; 12:17; 15:3; Dt. 6:22; and elsewhere. In Num. 16:32; Dt. 11:6, it is used even of people who are dwelling in tents. The remainder of the verse is a later expansion which explains what was meant by 'house'.

covet: we have seen above, in discussing verse 15, that some scholars interpret this word to mean not simply envy or inordinate desire, but rather action (and intrigue) taken to appropriate someone else's property (Stamm and Andrew, pp. 101–05). This is not supported, however, by all the passages adduced to prove it. Those such as Dt. 7:25; Jos. 7:21; and Mic. 2:2 prove rather the opposite, for each of these contains the word for 'covet' and a word for taking that which is coveted; these are successive and not parallel activities. Furthermore, we should note that LXX renders the verbs both here and in Dt. 5:21 by *epithumēseis*; and that the second verb in Dt. 5:21 is *tit'awweh*, which means 'long for', 'lust after', and the like, as an inner disposition.

The evil of covetousness was known and condemned long before the time of Moses, in Egyptian wisdom literature. As examples note the following: the Instruction of the Vizier Ptahhotep, purporting to come from the Pyramid Age and certainly very ancient, says, 'Do not be covetous at a division. Do not be greedy, unless (it be) for thy (own) portion. Do not be covetous against thy (own) kindred. . . . It is (only) a little of that for which one is covetous that turns a calm man into a contentious man' (*ANET*, p. 413). In the Instruction for King Meri-ka-re, *c.* 2200 B.C., the author says to his son and successor, 'He who is covetous when other men possess is a fool' (*ANET*, p. 415). In the 'Tale of the Eloquent Peasant', from the Middle Kingdom, the peasant says to the Chief Steward: 'That great one who is covetous is not really great. . . . One may fall a long way because of greed. The covetous man is void of success; (any) success of his belongs to failure. Though thy heart is covetous, it is not (of avail) for thee' (*ANET*, p. 409). These passages, to which others could be added, show not only that covetousness was considered as an evil before the time of Moses, and thus it was not too 'advanced' for him to condemn, but also that covetousness was a matter of the heart or mind, synonymous with greed or avarice. In this sense covetousness

could not be perceived or punished unless it issued in action, but
the decalogue is not concerned with penalties for the breaking of the
commandments it contains.

THE PEOPLE REQUEST A MEDIATOR 20:18-21

The Israelites are afraid and tremble as they observe the phenomena of Sinai, and they stand afar off. They ask Moses to speak to
them, but not let God speak to them, lest they die. Moses replies
that God has come to prove them, and the fear of him will keep
them from sinning.

This small section is from E. Verse 18 only repeats what has
been said in 19:16-17, and the general outlook is that of E.
However, this section is apparently not in its original place.
It seems strange for the Israelites to ask for a mediator just after
Yahweh has spoken the Ten Commandments. The original place
of this section must, therefore, have been *before* rather than *after*
20:1-17. 20:18*b*-21 ('and they stood afar off . . .') may have stood
originally immediately after 19:19. If that is correct, when these
verses became separated from their original position, 18*a* was
written to summarize what had gone before.

18. the people were afraid: *RSV* here follows LXX, Vulgate
and Samaritan text by reading 'were afraid'. This involves
revocalizing M.T., which reads 'the people saw'. *RSV* is more
appropriate to the context.

20. Do not fear: Moses enjoins the people not to have that kind
of fear which leads them to tremble and have dread in the presence
of Yahweh; the proper **fear of him** will lead them to respect him
and will keep them from that disobedience which is sin. The
proper 'fear' of Yahweh is based upon faith and upon reverence in
his presence. Thus Yahweh has come to Israel in order to **prove**
her, to test the sincerity of her faith and protestations of obedience
(cf. Dt. 8:2).

THE BOOK OF THE COVENANT 20:22—23:33

The title 'Book of the Covenant' is derived from Exod. 24:7; on its
origin, see comment *in loc*. The Book of the Covenant consists of a
brief introduction (20:22), a group of cultic regulations (20:23-
26), a title (21:1), a group of laws, admonitions and regulations
(21:2—23:19), and finally closing promises and exhortations
(23:20-33). It should not be considered as part of E (as is
customary), nor of any of the generally recognized literary

sources. Like the Ten Commandments, the Book of the Covenant has a history of its own. It represents in the main the oldest law of the *OT*, most of it coming from the pre-monarchial period. Its age can be demonstrated in part by comparison with other codes, such as Deuteronomy, the Holiness code, and P. Furthermore, it comes from a society that was primarily agrarian. The inhabitants kept sheep, oxen, and asses, but not horses or camels. They practised slavery. There was some trade and a limited money economy, based on pieces of silver weighed out, not minted coins. There is never any mention of a king or court. If Noth is correct, the *nāśîᵓ* ('ruler') of 22:28 was a tribal representative in the sacral federation. (However, even in later codes the king usually plays only a limited rôle, for Hebrew law was primarily administered through local courts.)

The Book of the Covenant has had a complex history, only part of which we can trace out. It is most probable that it was placed in its present position by the Deuteronomic redactor, who supplied the title in 21:1 (in an awkward position!) and the concluding exhortations in 23:20–33, and possibly a few passages such as 22:21*b*,31; 23:8,9*b*. (See comments on 23:20–33; 24:4*a*,7). Various conjectures have been made as to the original position of the Book of the Covenant in the *OT*. For example, Beer and Weiser think it originally stood in Jos. 24 (see Jos. 24:25–26, with the reference to 'the book of the law of God'). This can be only conjecture.

The term 'Covenant Code' is usually applied to 20:23–26; 21:2—23:19, that is, to the 'legalistic' sections of the Book of the Covenant. It should be said at once, however, that this is not a law code in the modern sense. In the first place, it is fragmentary and incomplete, not including by any means all that one would expect to find in a genuine law code. Important details are missing in some of the laws, and some are compact to the point of obscurity. Important matters usually dealt with in a law code are missing; for example, relatively little is said about marriage law and custom. The marriage laws of Dt. 22:13–29 have been considered by some scholars as having been at one time a part of the Covenant Code, or of its source—or an expansion of what was in that source.

In the second place this is not a law code in the modern sense because it includes not only laws as generally understood (with specified penalties), but also admonitions concerning social morality, and religious and cultic regulations. Yet, the source of all of these is Yahweh, the God of the Israelites. Throughout the *OT* it is Yahweh who is the source of 'law' and not the king, as was true in other countries of the ancient Near East. Moses mediated the law, but Yahweh was its author, as he was also the source of ethical admonitions, cultic regulations and the like.

Many special studies have been made of the Book of the Covenant. Two fundamental studies are those of Alfred Jepsen, *Untersuchungen zum Bundesbuch* (1927), and Albrecht Alt, in his *Essays on Old Testament History and Religion* (1966). Both are concerned with form-critical analysis of the Book of the Covenant, with the origin of the constituent parts, and with the origin and nature of the whole. Our discussion, particularly in the following paragraphs, owes much to these two studies, but does not follow either in all details.

The Covenant Code can be readily divided into two major divisions: (a) 21:2—22:20, civil and criminal laws; (b) 20:23-26; 22:21—23:19, miscellaneous admonitions concerning social morality, and religious and cultic regulations. The first division is generally well unified and systematically arranged. The second is quite varied in its contents, and is not arranged systematically. It can be divided into several subdivisions, and these will be indicated in our detailed commentary below.

The laws of the first division follow a definite literary form, if we exclude for the present 21:12-17; 22:18-20. These are genuine laws which express conditions and corresponding penalties or consequences. They have the form now usually called casuistic, a conditional form appropriate to case law. In Hebrew the main condition is introduced by *kî*, usually rendered by *RSV* as 'when', and the subordinate conditions are introduced by *'im*, rendered 'if' (*RSV* is not entirely consistent in these renderings, as in 22:1,7, 10,14,16, which should begin with 'when'). The form can be easily recognized in the first law which concerns slavery: '*When* you buy a Hebrew slave, he shall serve six years. . . . *If* he comes in single, he shall go out single; *if* he comes in married, then his wife shall go out with him . . .' (21:2ff.). These are *secular* laws dealing with slavery, injury to persons and animals, and damage to property. Only occasionally is it necessary for litigants to come to a sanctuary to take oaths 'before God' in order to determine guilt (22:8,9,11; cf. 21:6). There were no officially appointed judges at this time, and justice was administered by laymen (priests

being involved perhaps only in the cases just referred to). Alt calls
these 'ordinances for the administration of justice by the local
secular jurisdiction. These would be read out to the men gathered
in the gate to form a court whenever they had to try and give
judgement in cases of the particular kind a given law dealt with'
(op. cit., p. 92).

There can be little question as to the origin of these laws.
They have remarkable similarities to other ancient Near Eastern
law codes, particularly the Code of Hammurapi (see below).
Yet there can be no question of *direct* borrowing from that or any
other known ancient code, for there are numerous differences in
detail. There must have been a general body of ancient Near
Eastern law, with many local variations to suit the various
societies. It is generally believed that the Israelites received these
casuistic laws from the Canaanites, although at present no
Canaanite law code has been discovered. Most of them would
have been taken over after the settlement of the Israelites in
Canaan in the thirteenth century B.C. and following, but we cannot
eliminate the possibility that the Israelites may have adopted some
in the patriarchal period when they were in direct contact with
northern Mesopotamia. Jepsen calls these casuistic laws 'Hebrew
mishpatim [ordinances]', distinguishing them from 'Israelite
mishpatim', on the basis primarily of the reference in 21:2 to a
Hebrew slave. He thinks that 'Hebrew' there means the same as
ḫabirū, and speaks of the borrowing of these laws from the *ḫabirū*,
and even calls them 'Amorite laws'. However, this is doubtful, in
view of all we now know about the *ḫabirū*. The term designates a
social class, not an ethnic group, that was known in many parts of
the ancient Near East over the span of many centuries. See
comment on 21:2, and Introduction, pp. 39–42.

It is remarkable that these casuistic laws have been adopted
from the Canaanites with virtually no editing, and that there
is little that is specifically Yahwistic about them. In 21:6; 22:8,9
the word *'elōhîm* which was probably in the Canaanite code has
been retained; only in 22:11 has the change to 'Yahweh' been
made.

Within the verses we have excluded from the above discussion
of the first major division in the Covenant Code, the following
verses follow another specific form: 21:12,15,16,17; 22:19,20.
Each of these has (or had in its original form) only five short
Hebrew words, each beginning with a Hebrew participle. For

example, 21:12 reads in Hebrew: *makkēh ʾîš wāmēt môt yûmāt*,
'Whoever strikes a man and he dies shall surely be put to death'.
All end with the same two words. Alt says: 'The five short words
must be spoken very slowly and emphatically, with a caesura
between the subject and the predicate, that is, between the third
and fourth words, as in the metre of a five-beat Hebrew verse'
(op. cit., p. 109). Alt finds evidence for a similar form (sometimes
changed or interpolated) in 31:14f.; Lev. 20:2,9–13,15–16,27;
24:16; 27:29. All carry the unconditional death penalty, perhaps
administered by stoning by the community (Lev. 20:2,27; 24:16).
They have similarities in both form and content to the list of
twelve curses in Dt. 27:15–26.

These laws generally deal with matters not dealt with in the
casuistic laws; they have to do mostly with a man's relationship
to the divine, and to members of his family. In all probability
these should be considered as native Israelite law, because of the
nature of the matters with which they deal, because of the
severity of the penalty which they demand, and because of the
form. Alt classifies them as apodictic laws, but we think it better
to give them a different classification according to their form, and
call them 'Hebrew participial laws'. They are, of course, apodictic
and unconditional, but we prefer to reserve the designation
apodictic for those laws or admonitions which are in the
second person, to be discussed below. (Jepsen included the *lex
talionis* [21:23–25] in the same group with these laws, designating
them as 'Israelite *mishpatim*'. However, it does not have the same
form as the others, and is not a uniquely Israelite law, being
generally Semitic; see below on 21:23–25.)

The second major division contains a miscellaneous group of
admonitions concerning social morality, and regulations concerning religion and the cult. Within this group form-critics
recognize another specific literary form which should properly be
called 'apodictic'. It is categorical and unconditional, like the
Hebrew participial form, but it is in the second person (most
often singular) and usually is a negative command or prohibition,
expressed by the strong Hebrew negative *lōʾ* (some scholars think
the form was originally always negative). This is the form we have
recognized in the Ten Commandments in chapter 20.

Within the second major division Jepsen has isolated a small
group of religious and ethical prohibitions, which he thinks are
native Israelite and very old, though their precise date cannot be

determined. Each of these has a definite form: object of the verb + the negative *lo'*+a single verb. Each therefore has only three words in Hebrew (though a little variation on this point can be observed). His list is as follows, giving a literal translation in each case:

A sorceress thou shalt not permit to live (*22:18*)
And a stranger thou shalt not wrong (*22:21a*)
God thou shalt not revile (*22:28a*)
And a ruler among thy people thou shalt not curse (*22:28b*)
And a bribe thou shalt not take (*23:8a*)

To this list he thinks possibly 23:2,7*b* should be added, and 23:9*a* as a variant of 22:21.

In his discussion of this literary form, Alt has an almost identical list: 22:18,21*a*,22*b*,28*a*,*b*. To this he adds two other groups of apodictic laws that have received several interpolations: 23:1–5, 6–9.

In his discussion of the apodictic laws (in which he includes those having the participial form), Alt expressed the opinion that the apodictic law was native Israelite law, and that the casuistic law was borrowed from Canaanites. Subsequent studies have shown, however, that the apodictic form (conceived broadly) is found in other literatures outside Israel; for example, in the Hittite treaties, in Egyptian and Mesopotamian wisdom literature, and sporadically even in the Near Eastern codes (cf. Hammurapi Code, 36, 38–40; Middle Assyrian Laws, A, 40, 57–59; B, 6). Also, the apodictic form—if we do not interpret it it too narrowly as containing only prohibitions and always addressed in the second person singular—is found in many of the cultic laws of the Covenant Code which were borrowed from the Canaanites. Indeed most of the material in the second major division of the Covenant Code is expressed in the apodictic style. Some have a mixed, or quasi-casuistic, form: 20:25; 21:13–14,23–25; 22:25–27; 23:4–5. Some scholars have seen a considerable amount of prophetic influence, or influence of the Deuteronomists, in the second major division. This, however, is not extensive. R$_D$ may be responsible for 22:21*b*,31; 23:8,9*b*.

In the second major division of the Covenant Code there occur numerous verses in which Yahweh is represented as speaking in the first person, or in which a reason is given for the observance of a certain law. W. Beyerlin has called these the 'parenetic elements' (*die Paränese*) in the Book of the Covenant and devoted an essay to discussion of their origin (*Hertzberg Festschrift*, ed. H. Reventlow, pp. 9–29). These parenetic elements sometimes give promise of Yahweh's blessing (20:24) or a warning from him (20:26), or exhort the people to give full obedience to his laws (23:13). Most often they give the motive for the keeping of a specific law or regulation—20:25*b*; 22:21*b*,23–24,27,31*a*; 23:7*c*, 8*b*,9*b*,15*b*. Such elements are not found in the large division 21:2—22:17, except in 21:13–14 (a secondary addition to a participial form). According to Beyerlin, these parenetic elements in the Book of the Covenant are not the result of Deuteronomic editing, as thought by several scholars, but they originated in the pre-monarchial period, along with the laws and regulations of the Covenant Code, and had their setting particularly in the three annual pilgrimage festivals of ancient Israel, listed in 23:14ff. In such times the Israelites could have conceived of Yahweh as appearing to those from all the tribes who went to the festivals, addressing them sometimes as Thou and sometimes as You. Yahweh's purpose for them is expressed in 22:31: 'You shall be men consecrated to me (*ʾanšê ḳōḏeš*)'. The laws and the parenetic elements are thus to be understood within the context of the covenant between Yahweh and his people.

Beyerlin's view is very attractive, but it must be said that our solid information concerning tribal organization and cultic practices in the pre-monarchial period is not extensive. It is indeed difficult to decide on the origin of many of the elements in the second major division of the Covenant Code. This division is much more imbued with the spirit of Yahwism than the other division, and some of its admonitions sound as if they were influenced by the prophets or by the Deuteronomists. However, it is our view that most of the Covenant Code did originate in the pre-monarchial period (though we question the existence of a genuine amphictyony in that time). We assign 22:21*b*,31; 23:8,9*b* to R_D, but we cannot be certain even of them.

We have had occasion above to make brief reference to codes of law of Near Eastern countries outside Israel, and in our comments below we shall point out numerous comparisons with individual laws within them.

The longest, and the one which has been known for the longest time, is the Code of Hammurapi (also spelled Hammurabi, but the former is probably the correct ancient form). He was an Amorite who ruled Babylonia from 1728 to 1686 B.C.

But three codes earlier than Hammurapi's are now known. The oldest is that of Ur-Nammu, the founder of the III Dynasty of Ur who began to reign *c*. 2050 B.C. This code was written in Sumerian, and is preserved only in fragmentary form on a clay tablet. The next is the Code of Lipit-Ishtar, a Sumerian ruler of the Isin dynasty, about two centuries later. From about the same time is the work known as the Laws of Eshnunna, an Amorite kingdom, written in Akkadian. It is not called a 'code', because it does not now have the three-fold form of the other codes: prologue, laws, and epilogue.

Following the time of Hammurapi, two sets of laws are known: the Middle Assyrian Laws, on clay tablets of the twelfth century B.C.; and the Hittite Laws, on two tablets of the fourteenth century B.C. The Hittites were a non-Semitic, Indo-European people.

All of these can be found in excellent translation in *ANET*, pp. 159–97, 523–25.

To the present time no law code has been discovered in Egypt. The reason usually given for this is that in Egypt the king was considered to be a god, and his spoken word was final and was always available. However, there must have been a body of 'custom' to which the king and his officials adhered, and the king himself was obligated to abide by and promote *ma‘at*, which embodies such concepts as right, order, truth, justice, and right-eousness. Egyptian literature contains some references to the writing of a code, and eventually one may come to light. It is not likely, however, that Egyptian law influenced that of Israel as deeply as did the law of the peoples of Mesopotamia and Syria. For study of the Near Eastern parallels to Exod. 21:2—22:16, see especially S. M. Paul, *The Book of the Covenant* (1965), chapter 5.

Introduction **20:22**
The introduction to the Book of the Covenant follows naturally from what has just preceded; the words which Yahweh instructs Moses to speak to Israel continue without interruption to the end of chapter 23. However it is not likely that this verse is from E, J, or any other generally recognized source. Yahweh here says: **You have seen for yourselves that I have talked with you from heaven.** The viewpoint of J is that Yahweh descends upon Mount Sinai and there speaks with Moses (19:9,11,18,20; 34:5), and in E Yahweh is believed to have his abode on Mount Sinai in

the thick cloud (19:3; 20:21*b*). The point of view here is independent of both those representations, and is from R$_D$ (cf. Dt. 4:36).

This introduction is designed in part to authenticate the whole
of the Book of the Covenant that follows, and in part to give the
specific motive for the following verse which forbids the making of
other gods. The Hammurapi Code, for example, has a long
prologue of 301 cuneiform lines. It tells how the gods Anum and
Enlil chose Hammurapi 'to make justice prevail in the land, to
destroy the evil and the wicked, and keep the strong from oppressing
the weak. . . .' The greater part of what follows is taken up with
the king's self-laudatory description of himself and his accomplish-
ments.

Cultic Regulations **20:23-26**
This section is concerned with regulations concerning altars,
except the first verse. It is somewhat puzzling that this section
introduces the Covenant Code, preceding the title in 21:1. The
regulations concerning altars must be very old, for they describe
the most ancient types of altars and presuppose the existence of
numerous sanctuaries. We can only assume that the redactor who
placed this section here must have deemed it to have great
importance, for he placed it at the beginning of the Covenant
Code. It is not wholly inconsistent with Deuteronomic ideas (see
Dt. 27:5-6).

23 forbids the making of **gods of silver to be with me** and
gods of gold. It is thus a prohibition of the making of images of
Yahweh; cf. 20:4ff.; 34:17; Dt. 27:15 (see comment especially at
20:4ff.) The phrase **to be with me** (Hebrew *'ittî*) is apparently
meant also to prohibit Israel's worship of other deities—that is, to
promote monolatry, not necessarily genuine monotheism (see
comment on 20:3).

24. An altar of earth you shall make for me: this must have
been one of the oldest types of altar. It is not clear whether it
means an altar made of packed earth, or one made of sun-dried
mud bricks. Altars of mud bricks have been found in Canaanite
sacred places (e.g. at Megiddo, Shechem, Lachish, and Alalakh,
Syria; see K. Galling, 'Altar', *IDB*, I, pp. 96–100). However, it
would be difficult for archaeologists to identify an altar of packed
earth, since it would not be likely to survive erosion and could
easily blend with the surrounding earth. On **your burnt offerings
and your peace offerings,** see 24:5.

H

**in every place where I cause my name to be remembered
I will come to you and bless you:** this assumes a multiplicity
of places of sacrifice, either temples or open-air sanctuaries, and
agrees with the evidence of the historical books regarding practices
in Israel before the centralization of worship in the Jerusalem
Temple in the time of Josiah (621 B.C.). Deuteronomy and the D
redactors often speak of the Temple (in Jerusalem) as the place
where Yahweh places his name, or causes his name to dwell
(Dt. 12:5,11; 1 Kg. 8:29 etc.).

25. If an altar of stone is made (and in Palestine, where stones
are plentiful, such altars were doubtless often built), it is not to be
built of hewn stones; **for if you wield your tool upon it you
profane it.** The word here rendered tool (*ḥéreḇ*) most often means
a sword; in Ezek. 26:9 the plural is rendered by *RSV* as 'axes'.
It must be here a general term for any tool that could be used to
cut, dress, or carve out a stone. The reason for this prohibition is
explained in various ways by scholars. According to some, the
altar of natural stones had the sanction of antiquity; according to
others, the stones should be used only in their *natural* state (as only
unblemished animals were to be sacrificed); according to others,
the use of a tool would drive out the spirit or *numen* in the stone, in
accordance with primitive religious notions; a still further possibility is that this was an anti-Canaanite measure, for the
Canaanites made altars of both types, of natural stones and of
hewn stones (e.g. at Hazor from the Late Bronze Age there was
found an enormous altar made of a single block weighing about
five tons, having a part of the top hollowed out perhaps for burnt
offerings, and another hollowed out to form a rectangular basin
for blood or liquid offerings). The true reason may have been a
combination of these. This prohibition is referred to in Jos. 8:31;
Dt. 27:5f.; 1 Mac. 4:47. However, it is most unlikely that all later
altars were made of unhewn stone. This could not have been true
of the altars with horns (1 Kg. 1:50; 2:28), of the altars of incense
(1 Kg. 6:20; 7:48), of which numerous archaeological examples
have been found, and very probably not of the great altar of
sacrifice in front of the Temple of Solomon. That altar is not
described in the principal description of the Temple in 1 Kg. 6–7,
but the brief description in 2 Chr. 4:1 may be authentic, and the
description of the altar in Ezek. 43:13–17 may refer to one which
actually existed, such as that installed by King Ahaz (2 Kg.
16:10ff.).

26. And you shall not go up by steps to my altar, that your nakedness be not exposed on it: it does not seem likely that the reason given here for prohibiting steps to an altar is the original one. There would hardly be any danger of exposing the nakedness of the sacrificer (priest or layman) by his going up only some two or three steps. This is probably a prohibition which arises from opposition to Canaanite practice. Some of the discovered Canaanite altars were approached by steps, usually very few in number (e.g. at Lachish, Megiddo, Beth-shan, and Ugarit). At any rate, some of the later altars must have had steps. Lev. 9:22 speaks of the priest coming down from making the offerings, and the description of the altar in Ezek. 43:13–17 says plainly, 'The steps of the altar shall face east.' Some reconstructions of that altar show it as having some twenty or more steps. The second half of the present verse is perhaps the reason for the provision in 28:42 and Lev. 6:10 that the priests must wear linen breeches when they minister at the altar. According to Josephus (*Jewish War*, v, v, 6), the altar of Herod's Temple was approached by a ramp, apparently in deference to this prohibition of steps.

A Title **21:1**
This title seems to the modern reader to be awkwardly placed, since some of the regulations of the Covenant Code have already been given in 20:23–26. It is not certain whether this title is intended to serve for the rest of the Covenant Code, up to 23:19, or whether it serves for only a portion of what follows, extending perhaps to 22:20. The word 'ordinances' (*mišpāṭîm*) seems more appropriate for the shorter section just mentioned, since most of the verses or paragraphs after 22:20 are admonitions without expressed penalties, rather than specific laws with penalties. It is possible that this title is from the Deuteronomic redactor (R_D), who intended for it to cover only the section through 22:20. The word *mišpāṭ* occurs frequently in the *OT* with a wide variety of meanings, but it is significant that it is frequently used (in the plural) by Deuteronomy and D redactors, often in connection with other words meaning 'statutes', 'commandments', and the like (Dt. 4:1,5,8,14,45; 5:1,31; 6:1; 7:12; 30:16; 2 Kg. 17:37 etc.). The word occurs frequently also in P, but this verse is hardly as late as P.

Laws on Slavery **21:2-11**
These laws regarding slavery are concerned primarily with the
term of bondage required of Hebrew slaves, and the conditions
under which they might be released. Cf. the later laws on this
subject, Dt. 15:12-18; Lev. 25:29-54.

The basic law was that a male Hebrew slave should serve six
years and be released in the seventh without compensation. But
he might become a permanent slave of his own volition, and
undergo the ceremony described in verse 6. A female slave,
however, was treated differently, for she was normally expected to
become the wife or concubine of the master. He might do one of
three things with a female slave: (i) take her for himself; (ii) give
her to his son as wife; or (iii) let her be redeemed, presumably by
her own family. Provision was made that if he took a second wife,
he must not diminish the food, clothing, and conjugal rights of the
first. If he did so, she could go free without compensation.

Among the ancient Israelites a person might sell himself or his
wife or children into slavery because of poverty or specifically for
non-payment of debt (2 Kg. 4:1; Neh. 5:1-5; Amos 2:6; the case
in Exod. 22:3*b* of enslavement for theft is actually a case of
enslavement for inability to pay the restitution required). Most
slaves were apparently defaulting debtors, and probably served as
domestic workers. The slave was considered as a chattel, the
property of his owner, but it was also recognized that as a human
being he had certain rights.

2. When you buy a Hebrew slave: the law here concerns
only native slaves. Captives of war also became slaves, but they
were largely the property of the state, and were taken into permanent bondage. 'Hebrew' here is the equivalent of Israelite, as
also in Dt. 15:12. It is not likely that at this time it had the more
general meaning of *ḫabiru* or *ᶜapiru*. Jepsen and Alt ascribe to it the
broader meaning, but this is not probable. The P writer of Lev.
25:39-54 seeks to confine slavery to foreigners, but he represents
idealization rather than the actual situation.

he shall serve six years: the Code of Hammurapi (117) limits
the period of bondage to three years in the case where a man, for
default of debt, sells his wife, son, or daughter, or goes into
bondage himself.

he shall go out free, for nothing: he becomes a freeman, without payment of any compensation. The later law in Dt.

15:13f. requires that the owner shall not let him go out empty-handed, but provide him liberally so that he may begin life anew.

4. This provision protects the right of the owner, since in the case described here the wife and children would belong to the master. A slave born in slavery was known as a 'homeborn slave' (Gen. 17:12–17,27; Lev. 22:11; Jer. 2:14).

5. Many a slave must have preferred permanent slavery with his family than to be separated from them, and also to face the possibility of destitution even though he was free. But he could only of his own free will become a permanent slave.

6. The ceremony described here is not known elsewhere, except in Dt. 15:17, which is very similar to the present law. The ceremony has been interpreted in two different ways. Some think that it symbolized the permanent attachment of the slave to the household of the master, and that the ceremony is more likely to have taken place at the door of the master than at a local sanctuary (S. R. Driver, pp. 211–12). Others think that the hole was bored in the ear of the slave in order to receive a ring or cord to which was fastened a tag made of clay or metal, indicating ownership of the slave (see I. Mendelsohn, art. 'Slavery in the OT', in *IDB*, IV, p. 385). The latter interpretation seems the more probable, in view of the fact that the hole itself would soon become almost invisible. Slaves were usually marked in some manner in the ancient Near East—with a tag or label, a brand, a tattoo, or the like.

shall bring him to God: since the Hebrew here is *hā-ʾelōhîm,* this could be translated, 'shall bring him to the gods'—i.e. the gods of the local sanctuary or of the household. It would have had this meaning for the Canaanites, but the Hebrews would have interpreted it as meaning Yahweh. We cannot determine for certain whether the ceremony was performed at a local sanctuary or in the home of the owner, in the presence of his household deity. The mention of the **door or the doorpost** leads many critics to think it could refer only to the house of the owner. However, in the Eshnunna Laws (37), it is said that in case of a dispute over loss of deposited property, 'the owner of the house [where the deposit was lost] shall swear an oath for him in the door [*bab*] of the Temple of Tishpak' (cf. F. C. Fensham, *JBL*, LXXVIII [1959], 160f.). This indicates that oaths before a given deity were sometimes taken at the door of that deity's temple, and makes it possible that this was a temple ceremony. See further 22:8,9,11.

7. The sale of a daughter into slavery brought about different conditions from those surrounding a male slave, for it was assumed that the female slave would become the wife (or concubine) of the owner or his son. This section reflects customs similar to those which prevailed in the city of Nuzi in Mesopotamia, in the middle of the second millennium B.C., as has been shown by I. Mendelsohn, *JAOS*, LV (1935), pp. 190–95. Contracts from Nuzi contain almost precisely the same conditions as are here depicted. The present passage seems to assume that all sales of daughters would conform to these stipulations, but we cannot be certain of that, since the Covenant Code is not a complete code of laws. Perhaps in some cases the owner could give the slave to one of his male slaves, as verse 4 may imply. The purpose of these provisions was to insure that the female slave would not become merely a prostitute in the owner's possession. In Dt. 15:12 both male and female slaves are to serve only six years, no distinction being made between them.

8. If the daughter pleased the owner, he might marry her himself. If not, he could **let her be redeemed,** presumably by a near kinsman (cf. Lev. 25:48–54).

he shall have no right to sell her to a foreign people: this probably does not mean a foreign nation (for that would not often be a realistic prospect), but to a family or clan other than her own.

9. She might be given in marriage to the owner's son, in which case the owner must **deal with her as with a daughter.**

10. If the owner takes another wife, he must protect the rights of the first wife. He must not diminish **her food, her clothing, or her marital rights.** The third item here is Hebrew *ʿōnātāh*, and occurs only here. Its meaning is very uncertain. S. M. Paul has suggested that it means 'oil, ointments' or the like, because in many Sumerian and Akkadian texts the three items of 'food, clothing, and oil' are the main necessities of life, mentioned particularly as the prerequisites of a wife (op. cit., pp. 82–87). This could be correct. It is usually taken to mean right of sexual intercourse.

11. these three things very probably refers to the three things just enumerated that the owner must continue to supply to this first wife. Some critics take it to refer to the three possibilities open to the owner in dealing with the female slave: marrying her himself, giving her to his son, or allowing her to be redeemed.

A List of Capital Offences **21:12–17**
This is a list of offences for which the penalty is death—murder, striking of one's father or mother, stealing a man, and cursing of one's father or mother. Verses 12, 15–17 are in the Hebrew participial form; for discussion of this form, see above, pp. 220f, and cf. 22:19,20. In no case are we told how and by whom the death penalty was administered. In some cases it was probably the community, and the method stoning (cf. Lev. 20:2,27; 24:16; Num. 15:35f.). In the case of murder, the penalty was probably administered by a near kinsman of the murdered victim (cf. Dt. 19:12; Num. 35:19).

13–14 are additions to the original law of verse 12, designed to make it possible for a distinction to be made between murder and accidental homicide. The form is very different from verses 12, 15–17. God is represented as speaking here, saying **I will appoint for you a place** and **you shall take him from my altar.** The place referred to in verse 13 is the altar of a local sanctuary. See 1 Kg. 1:51; 2:28 for examples of the use of altars for sanctuary. In later times at least, there were provisions for cities of refuge; see Dt. 19:1–13; Num. 35:10–34. Some scholars believe that the cities of refuge are ancient institutions that existed alongside the sanctuary-altars, since it must have been necessary to provide for longer protection for the accidental manslayer than the local altars could afford (see *IDB*, *s.v.* 'City of Refuge'). The present passage does not indicate how or by whom a decision would be made as to whether a given case was premeditated or accidental, but that subject is dealt with in the later laws. In Dt. 19:11–13 the decision is made by the elders of the city, and in Num. 35:22–28 by the congregation.

15 must concern assault upon one's father or mother, since murder of parents would come under the preceding law. The Code of Hammurapi (195) has a less severe penalty: the son who strikes his father is to have his hand cut off.

16 concerns slave-trading, probably with a foreign nation, or kidnapping a free man in order to enslave him for one's own purposes. Cf. Dt. 24:7. However, the clause **or is found in possession of him** is very awkward syntactically in the Hebrew, and is probably a secondary insertion within the original law, which contained only five short Hebrew words.

17 shows clearly both the importance of respect for parents and the strength attributed to a curse. The death penalty applies to the cursing as well as to the striking of one's parents. Cf. Lev. 20:9.

Laws Concerning Injury **21:18–32**
The laws in this section concern mainly bodily injuries, in most cases by persons, but in the last by animals. In some cases the injury results in death. We have here the classic statement of the *lex talionis* (verses 23–25), but many of the laws specify that compensation is to be paid rather than strict retaliation meted out. The nature and amount of the compensation depends in part upon the nature of the injury, and in part upon the social rank of the injured party. There are many interesting parallels in the Code of Hammurapi and other ancient codes. While Hebrew society recognized only two classes, freemen and slaves, Babylonian society recognized three: *awīlum*, *muškēnum*, and *wardum*. The last of these is clearly the slave, but it is difficult for us to determine precisely the nature of the two upper classes; we translate them as 'nobleman' and 'commoner', the latter with T. J. Meek in *ANET*. Sometimes the word *awīlum* is used for both ranks of freemen. On *muškēnum*, see E. A. Speiser, *Orientalia*, xxvii (1958), pp. 19–29.

18–19 set forth the penalty for bodily injury in a quarrel, in which one of the parties involved is injured sufficiently to be confined to bed. The one causing the injury **shall pay for the loss of his time, and shall have him thoroughly healed—** that is, pay for his treatment. The Code of Hammurapi (206) says that if one freeman injures another in a brawl, he must swear, 'I did not strike him deliberately', and pay for the physician. The Hittite Laws (I, 10) provide that, if anyone bewitches another so that he falls ill, he must provide a man to look after the house of the injured man until he recovers, then give him six shekels of silver and pay the physician's fee. F. C. Fensham (*VT*, x [1960], pp. 333–35) compares the Hittite Law, and emends the Hebrew of the next to last clause to *bešibtô yittēn* and renders, 'he shall provide [someone] in his place.'

20–21 contain the law concerning injury to a slave. If the slave dies instantly, the owner is to be punished, but if the slave survives a day or two, there is no punishment.

he shall be punished: the nature of the punishment here is vague. The Samaritan Text reads, *môt yûmāt*, 'he shall be put to death', as in verses 12, 15–17. This reading may have been influenced by the previous verses, or it may be the original reading here. In any event, it seems unlikely that an owner was actually executed for the death of a slave. The last clause, **the slave is his money,** recognizes the fact that the owner suffers a loss in the death of a slave, and that is sufficient punishment. Other Near Eastern laws make no provision for punishing owners who mistreat slaves.

22–25 deal with situations in which a pregnant woman is caused to have a miscarriage, and in some cases suffers injury to herself. It is apparently assumed that the woman is hurt when she interferes in a strife between men. If there is no harm to herself, but she has a miscarriage, then the one who hurt her is fined as much as the woman's husband lays upon him. The text then says, **he shall pay as the judges determine,** but the translation and meaning of that clause is very obscure. The Hebrew is *nāṯan biṗᵉlilîm*. S. M. Paul renders it, 'the payment to be based on reckoning'—that is, according to the estimated age of the embryo. He points to a possible parallel in the Hittite Laws (17): 'If anyone causes a freewoman to miscarry—if (it is) the tenth month, he shall give 10 shekels of silver, if (it is) the fifth month, he shall give 5 shekels of silver, and pledge his estate as security' (op. cit., p. 100; cf. E. A. Speiser, *JBL*, LXXXII [1963], p. 302f.). This is very probably correct.

The Code of Hammurapi has a long section dealing with a similar subject (209–14). If a man strikes a pregnant woman and causes miscarriage, and she does not die, he pays a sum of money—ten shekels of silver if she is of the nobility, five if a commoner, and two if a slave. If the woman dies, then the penalty also varies: if she is of the nobility, then the daughter of the assailant is put to death; if a commoner, he pays one-half mina of silver; if a slave, one-third mina. The Middle Assyrian laws are severe. One of them (A, 21) states that if a man causes the daughter of a freeman to have a miscarriage, he must pay two talents thirty minas of lead, be flogged fifty times with staves, and do the work of the king for one full month. If the woman dies, the assailant is to be put to death (A, 50). The Middle Assyrian laws also prescribe that, if a woman has a miscarriage by her own act, 'they shall impale her on stakes without burying her' (A, 53). All of these laws show the great importance attached to the causing of a miscarriage, indicating that it was considered almost the equivalent of murder. Yet such occurrences may have been fairly common, since women must have often continued their usual occupations while pregnant.

23–25 give the fullest statement of the law of retaliation (*lex talionis*) to be found in the *OT*. It is repeated in shorter form in Dt. 19:21; Lev. 24:19f. Here it is only loosely attached to the law regarding miscarriage. Some scholars think that it is more appropriate following verse 19. However, it is in any case a secondary interpolation in its present position. The *lex talionis* was an advance over the much earlier custom of unlimited blood revenge, represented by Gen. 4:23f. Yet, it is not really applied with strictness here in the Covenant Code, or in the other codes. In many cases money compensation was allowed for various types of injury. The principle of retaliation was known to other Semitic peoples of antiquity, but it was also loosely applied at the advanced stages from which we have law codes. The Code of Hammurapi has a long section (196–214) dealing with various cases of assault and injury. In some the talion is strictly applied, but in many cases not. For example it says that if a nobleman destroys the eye or breaks the bone of another nobleman, then his own eye is destroyed or bone broken. But if the injury is to a commoner, he pays the sum of one mina of silver; if to a slave, he pays one-half the value of the slave (presumably to the owner). If a man strikes the cheek of someone of superior rank, he is to be beaten sixty times with an oxtail whip in the public assembly; but if he strikes the cheek of someone of the same rank, he pays one mina of silver. In various ways the *lex talionis* was modified to suit conditions of the society.

26–27 deal with certain injuries to one's own slave. If a man strikes the eye or knocks out the tooth of his slave, then he must let the slave go free, for the sake of the tooth or the eye. This is a humanitarian law which has no exact parallel in the Code of Hammurapi. In that Code (199), as has just been noted, the penalty for destroying the eye or breaking the bone of a slave is payment of one-half of the value of the slave, but this obviously has to do with injury to another man's slave, not to one's own. Cf. the Hittite laws (8).

28–32 contain the laws concerning the goring of a person by an ox. In any case in which an ox gored a person, the ox was to be put to death—that is, treated as if it were a responsible person.

If the owner of the ox had been warned that his ox was accustomed
to gore and had not kept it in, then he too had to suffer the penalty
of death, unless a ransom was laid on him, presumably a sum of
money which he could pay in lieu of his own death. The law here
does not specify by whom the ransom would be laid or the amount
determined; probably it was the nearest of kin of the deceased
person, in consultation with a local court. In the case of the
goring of a slave, the owner would pay to the master of the slave
thirty shekels of silver. There are laws concerning goring in other
ancient Semitic codes, but in none of the others is the ox itself
considered responsible, nor is the death penalty demanded of the
owner. The Code of Hammurapi (251-52) states that if an owner
has been notified by his city council that his ox is a gorer, and he
has not padded its horns or tied it up, and it gores a freeman, the
penalty is one-half mina of silver; if a slave, the penalty is one-third
mina of silver. In the laws of Eshnunna (54-55) the penalty for the
death of a freeman is two-thirds mina of silver, and for a slave,
fifteen shekels of silver.

28. its flesh shall not be eaten: the flesh was considered as
taboo, because it had blood-guilt upon it. The ox comes under the
principle stated in Gen. 9:5 (P), 'For your lifeblood I will surely
require a reckoning; of every beast I will require it and of
man'.

29. its owner has been warned: probably by some local
authority (in the Code of Hammurapi, it is by the city council; in
the laws of Eshnunna, by 'the authorities'). If he does not keep
his ox in, he is guilty of negligence rather than of premeditated
murder.

32. thirty shekels of silver: doubtless the average price of a
slave at the time of the compilation of the code. In Lev. 27:3ff., in
the P narrative, the value of a free Israelite is given as fifty shekels.
Joseph was sold to the Ishmaelites for twenty shekels of silver
(Gen. 37:28). Because we know so little of the purchasing power
of the shekel at various times (the shekel being in these instances
weights, not coins), it is idle to suggest modern equivalents.
On the weight of the shekel, see comment on 30:13.

Laws Concerning Damage to Property **21:33—22:17**
These laws deal with damage to various kinds of property through
negligence, theft, fire, breach of trust, and the like. The types of
property which these laws are designed to protect are those which

would be found particularly in an agricultural society—oxen, asses, sheep, fields, vineyards, and the like. The last of the group concerns the seduction of a virgin daughter, and is included in this section because the daughter was considered as the property of her father.

33–34 specify that a person who by negligence in leaving a pit open contributes to the death of an ox or ass must pay money, presumably to the value of the animal, to the owner, but he would receive the carcass of the dead animal. This was an important law inasmuch as pits were dug as cisterns for water, for storage of grain, and the like, and if left uncovered could be very dangerous for animals. The man who received the carcass could use or sell the animal hide and possibly in early times could eat the flesh of the ass or ox. The later law of Dt. 14:21 forbids the eating of anything that dies of itself, though allows it to be given to a resident alien or sold to a foreigner (cf. Lev. 17:15). The ass was considered as an unclean animal, not to be eaten, according to the specifications of Dt. 14:3–8 and Lev. 11:3–8, but the Israelites were known in times of dire need to use this animal as food (2 Kg. 6:25).

35–36 deal with situations in which one man's ox gores to death the ox of another. The Laws of Eshnunna contain a law (54) that is very similar to verse 35 in both content and wording: 'If an ox gores another ox and kills it, the owners of the two oxen shall divide the price of the live ox and the value of the dead ox.' The law in Exodus appears to mean that they divide the carcass of the dead animal, whereas the Eshnunna law provides for them to sell the carcass and divide the receipts.

22:1,3b–4. *RSV* here restores 3b to its original position immediately following verse 1. The penalty for theft of an animal is restitution, fivefold for an ox and fourfold for a sheep. Being a work animal, the ox was more valuable than a sheep. If the thief cannot make restitution, he must go into slavery for non-payment of debt, and then the law of 21:2–6 applies. The laws in the Hammurapi Code for theft vary, probably representing practices in different ages. According to paragraphs 6, 7, 22, the penalty for theft, or for purchasing or receiving stolen property (without witnesses and contracts) was death; but another law (8) requires thirtyfold restitution if the property belonged to the Temple or the State, tenfold if to a private citizen. Yet, if the person could not make restitution he could be put to death. The Hittite laws (57ff.) provide various degrees of restitution, from thirtyfold down.

2–3. The question of bloodguilt for the killing of a thief who is caught breaking into one's property rests upon the difference between theft at night and theft in the daylight. At night, when the intruder's intentions could not be judged (he might be intending to murder someone) and the property-owner could not clearly identify the intruder and take care only to restrain him, there was no bloodguilt. In the daytime, however, bloodguilt could be imputed, because then the intruder's intentions could be determined and the property-owner could take pains to refrain from killing the intruder. One law in the Code of Hammurapi (21) is more severe: it says that if a freeman makes a breach in a house, he is to be put to death in front of that breach and be walled in. The laws of Eshnunna 12–13 also make a distinction between crimes committed in the daytime and those committed at night.

5. The translation of this verse is uncertain. The principal verb used here, *bāʿar*, usually means to burn rather than to eat or consume, the causative of it meaning cause to burn or kindle, rather than cause to eat or graze. The verse may be translated, possibly (though not certainly) with a slight change of the Hebrew text, as by the *Am. Tr.*: 'If a man in burning over a field or vineyard lets the fire spread so that it burns another man's field, he must make restitution etc.' *NEB* is similar, with the alternative rendering in the margin. The situation then is one in which an owner is burning over his own field or vineyard to destroy stubble or weeds, and the fire spreads to another field. This rendering is supported by the fact that one would not ordinarily graze livestock in a vineyard, which would usually be protected by a stone fence (Isa. 5:5). Whatever the rendering, the principle is that the one who causes the damage to another man's field must make restitution. If the above rendering is correct, then this verse is closely connected with verse 6. The Hammurapi Code (57) requires that a shepherd who pastures sheep on a pasture without the owner's consent must make a payment in grain at the time of harvest (cf. also 58).

6. The general situation is similar to that of verse 5. In this verse the verbal root involved in the phrase **he that kindled the fire** is the root *bāʿar*, just referred to in verse 5.

7–8. In a simple society such as that of the early Israelites, where there were no banks or other commercial places for deposit or storage of money or articles, one might deliver to a neighbour **money or goods to keep,** as when he needed to go away on a journey. The principle is that the one receiving the deposit is responsible for it. If it is stolen and the thief is found, the thief must pay double, as in verse 4. If the thief cannot be found, then the owner of the house, to whom the deposit had been given, is required to **come near to God**—that is, go to a local sanctuary— and there take an oath declaring that he has not **put his hand to his neighbour's goods.** It is assumed here that an oath in the presence of a deity is so strong that the person would not swear to a false oath.

goods: *kēlîm* is a very general word, meaning articles or objects of all kinds.

9 is closely related to the preceding, but is more general. It applies to any kind of stolen or lost article over which there is a dispute, apparently including deposited articles. In such situations, **both parties shall come before God; he whom God shall condemn shall pay double to his neighbour.** Both parties go to a local sanctuary and there, through an oath, a divine decision is rendered, and the one convicted of taking the property of another must make double restitution, as in verses 4 and 7. The Code of Hammurapi contains laws relating to the deposit and safekeeping of articles of various kinds (120–26). It insists that in any kind of safekeeping arrangement there must be witnesses and contracts; in cases where they do not exist, there is no claim (122–23). If a person denies receiving something and it is proved against him, he must pay double (124). In certain cases there is a trial 'in the presence of the god' (126), as in these two verses. See also laws of Eshnunna, 36–37.

10–13 deal with the responsibilities of one to whom has been delivered an animal to keep. This probably has to do mainly with animals given into the hand of a shepherd or herdsman—at least in the case of sheep and cattle. We can receive aid in understanding some of the details of this law from the Code of Hammurapi, paragraphs 261–67, which deal with the responsibilities of a herdsman hired to pasture cattle or sheep. The first paragraph fixes his wage at eight *kur* of grain per year. If he loses an ox or sheep, he must make it good, ox for ox and sheep for sheep. If he alters the brands on the animals and sells them, he must make tenfold restitution. If, however, there is a 'visitation of god' in a sheepfold (probably sudden illness, lightning, death from eating poisonous herbs, or the like—any 'act of God' beyond the control of the shepherd), or if a lion kills an animal, then the shepherd must prove himself innocent 'in the presence of a god', and the owner is to receive the stricken animal.

10. is driven away: the verb usually means to be taken captive—hence probably taken by raiders, as in Job. 1:15,17, using another verb. However, this may be a mistake in the Hebrew text, a careless dittography of the preceding verb (the two are similar *–nišbar* and *nišbāh*). In verse 12, the herdsman must make restitution for stolen animals.

11. an oath by the LORD shall be between them: cf. verses 8, 9 above, where the LXX has 'god', as here. This probably is the original reading here, which would have been the reading in the law taken over from the Canaanites; here the change to 'Yahweh' has been made, but this would have been understood by the Israelites in any case.

and the owner shall accept the oath: the Hebrew has no object for the verb, reading only 'and the owner shall take'. Probably he took the carcass of the dead animal, or the injured animal, if available, as in the Hammurapi Code (see above). Even the carcass of a dead animal would have some value, for its hide if nothing else; cf. 21:23,35 above.

13. If it is torn by beasts, let him bring it as evidence: cf. 1 Sam. 17:34f.; Am. 3:12. The herdsman could bring whatever remained of the torn animal as evidence that it had been so lost. Similarly a Babylonian shepherd did not have to make restitution for whatever was killed by a lion (see above).

14-15 are difficult to interpret, because the language is very compressed, and the law may be incomplete. It probably has to do with the hiring of work animals, such as asses and oxen. The Hebrew has at the beginning, 'When a man asks from his neighbour', with no object for the verb; but the following language, **and it is hurt or dies,** suggests an animal as the object. The Syriac and one edition of the LXX have 'animal' as the object, although the Vulgate has 'anything of these'. The Hammurapi Code and some other ancient codes contain laws that specify fees for the hiring of animals and the responsibilities of the borrower. **the owner not being with it:** in some cases doubtless the owner was employed to handle a work animal, to drive a wagon or plough, or the like. If he was not with the animal, the borrower was responsible; but **if the owner was with it,** the owner would look after the animal, and the borrower would not have to make restitution. The Code of Hammurapi provides that, if the borrower causes the death of an ox through carelessness or beating, or if he breaks its foot or cuts its neck tendon, he must make good ox for ox (245-46). For lesser injuries, such as destroying an eye or breaking a horn, the borrower had to pay a specified fraction of the value of the ox to the owner (247-48). Like a shepherd, he did not have to make restitution if an animal was killed by a lion, or if 'a god struck it'. In the latter case he had to make an oath by a god to prove himself innocent (249; see a similar provision in the Hittite Laws, 75).

15. if it was hired, it came for its hire: the translation and interpretation of this very compact sentence are uncertain. The *RSV* seems to suggest that a distinction was made between that which was simply borrowed, without payment, and that which was hired. If an animal was hired, it came for its hire— possibly meaning that any injury was covered by the payment made. This, however, is not likely, and is not borne out by comparison with the other ancient codes. A different translation is possible. *śāḵîr* can mean 'hired labourer', and that is in fact its most frequent meaning (12:45; Dt. 15:18; 24:14; Lev. 19:13; etc.). Thus we can render: 'if a hired labourer (was employed), it came with his wage'—meaning that the hired labourer was responsible for damage to an animal, and any restitution required could be taken out of his wage. This seems unrealistic, and has no parallel in the other codes. The most likely rendering is simply, 'if a hired labourer (was employed), he came for his wage'—that is, if a hired labourer was employed, instead of the owner, to handle an animal and perhaps drive a wagon or the like, then the borrower must pay also the wage of the hired labourer (cf. Hammurapi Code 271, 273; Eshnunna Laws, 3, 10).

16-17 contain the law concerning the seduction of an unbetrothed virgin. If a betrothed virgin was seduced, the offence was against the husband and was treated as adultery (Dt. 22:23-29). If she was not yet betrothed, she was considered as still the property of her father and her seduction was an injury to him. If the father was willing, the offender could **give the marriage present for her, and make her his wife.** This is the *mōhār*, mentioned elsewhere only in Gen. 34:12 and 1 Sam. 18:25. Some scholars consider this as being originally the price paid to the father for the bride, but this is not certain. At this time it was considered as a compensation to the family, or a **marriage present.** It was not a dowry. In Dt. 22:29 the amount is fifty shekels silver, but it probably was not so high in the earlier period. The father could, however, utterly refuse to allow his daughter to be married, but the offender must nevertheless pay the *mōhār* to the father. The Middle Assyrian law (55) was similar but more severe. If the offender had a wife of his own, the father of the virgin could take her and give her to someone to be ravished, and then refuse to return her to her husband and take her for himself. The father could then give the daughter in marriage to the offender. If the latter had no wife, he had to make a payment to the father, and could never divorce her (cf. Dt. 22:29). The father could, on the other hand, refuse to give his daughter in marriage to the offender, and give her to anyone he wished, while still requiring payment from the offender.

Three Capital Offences 22:18–20

18. This law concerning a sorceress has the apodictic form, second person singular, but has the death penalty prescribed. Sorcery was widely condemned in Israel and the ancient world. Dt. 18:9–12 forbids it as one of several 'abominable practices' introduced by the nations whom the Israelites conquered in Canaan. In the Code of Hammurapi (2) sorcery is punished by drowning in a river, through an ordeal; the Middle Assyrian Laws (A, 47) prescribe death for one who makes magical preparations. In the Hittite laws (9–10) one who bewitches another must make a money payment to him, the amount depending upon his status, and pay the physician if he is made ill. (This biblical law was the basis for the execution of witches in England and America as late as the eighteenth century.)

19 has the Hebrew participial form, like 21:12,15–17. See the introductory comment on the Book of the Covenant (pp. 220f). Bestiality is forbidden also in Dt. 27:21; Lev. 20:15f. The latter prescribes death for the animal as well as the man or woman. According to the Hittite laws (187–88, 199), one who does evil with a sheep, a cow, or a pig, must be brought to the king's court; the king may order him to be put to death or pardoned. (The same law does not apply to bestiality with a horse or mule; II, 200.)

20 also has the Hebrew participial form, but it diverges considerably from the others noted in the preceding verse. Alt is probably correct in saying that the original form here was: *zōḇēᵃḥ lēʾlōhîm ʾᵃḥērîm môṯ yûmāṯ*, 'Whoever sacrifices to other gods

shall be put to death' (*Essays*, p. 112, n. 73). This is partly supported by some manuscripts of LXX and the Samaritan text,
which apparently read *ᵃḥērîm*, 'other', instead of *yāḥᵒrām*, 'shall be
utterly destroyed', *hofal* of a verb which means to place under the
ban (*ḥérem*). For the idea, cf. Dt. 13:12–17.

Various Humanitarian and Religious Duties **22:21–31**
Most of these are admonitions in apodictic form, in the second
person—usually singular, but sometimes plural. The reason
for their present order is not apparent, and they are quite
varied in content. These are not really laws, for no penalties are
prescribed.

**21. You (singular) shall not wrong a stranger or oppress
him, for you (plural) were strangers in the land of Egypt.**
The *gēr*, here rendered as 'stranger' but very often in *RSV* as
'sojourner', sometimes as 'alien', was usually a foreigner living
among the Israelites. In some cases, however, he could be an
Israelite who was living away from his own family and tribe
(Jg. 17:7–13; 2 Sam. 4:3). That is probably the meaning here, if
the verse comes from the pre-monarchial period, when Israel had
hardly developed a feeling of kindness toward natives of other
lands. The same admonition, with the same motivation as
expressed here, is found in Dt. 10:19; Lev. 19:33f., where the
reference is probably to resident aliens. The second half of the
verse, with its use of the second plural, may be a secondary addition
by Rᴅ. In later times *gērîm* had virtually all of the privileges, as
well as obligations, of the native-born Israelites.

22–24 forbids the affliction of widows and orphans. Second
person plural is used throughout, except in the first verb of verse
23. Widows and orphans are under the direct protection of
Yahweh, and if they are afflicted, the oppressors will be dealt with
according to the *lex talionis* (verse 24). There are many admonitions
in later literature against oppression of these two groups, often
coupled with the *gērîm* of verse 21. All three are mentioned
together in Dt. 24:17f.; 27:19; Jer. 7:6; 22:3; Zech. 7:10. Many
passages, especially in Dt. and P, enjoin kindness to widows and
orphans. Because of the use of the second person plural here, and
the similarity to later passages, some scholars consider these verses
to be secondary, probably Deuteronomic. However, we should
note that the protection of widows, orphans, and the poor is a
concern expressed in the oldest Near Eastern law codes and in

Egypt. For example, the oldest known code of law, the Sumerian
code of Ur-Nammu (c. 2050 B.C.), has a prologue in which the king
says he saw to it that 'the orphan did not fall a prey to
the wealthy . . . the widow did not fall a prey to the powerful . . .
and the man of one shekel did not fall a prey to the man of one
mina (sixty shekels)' (S. N. Kramer, *The Sumerians*, 1963, p. 84).
In the epilogue to his code, Hammurapi wrote that he had
inscribed his stela 'so that the strong might not oppress the
weak, and to give justice to the orphan and the widow' (XXIV,
59–62). These groups were under the protection of the god (usually
the sun-god Shamash in Mesopotamia and Amon-Re in Egypt),
and of the king. For further discussion and examples, see F. C.
Fensham, *JNES*, XXI (1962), pp. 129–39. Such concern may have
risen early in Israel, with Yahweh considered as the special
protector of the helpless widows and orphans.

25 forbids the exacting of interest **if you lend money to any
of my people with you who is poor.** The law is more fully
stated in Dt. 23:19–20; Lev. 25:36f. Dt. 23:20 says that interest
may be charged to a foreigner, but not an Israelite, since he is a
'brother'. Some scholars have interpreted the prohibition of
interest as applying only on loans to the very poor or poverty-
stricken—that is, on charity loans or distress loans. But in Israel,
as in other agricultural societies of the ancient Near East, farmers
must have often needed loans at the beginning of planting, to be
repaid at harvest time, and possibly also loans were necessary for
small business ventures. Dt. 23:19–20 seems to forbid interest on
all kinds of loans, even if that may not be true of the present
passage. We know a good deal about interest rates in some
ancient lands, especially Mesopotamia, from the thousands of
contract tablets discovered. Interest rates in these vary considerably, sometimes ranging up to 50 per cent. The Hammurapi Code
(88, 99) specifies 20 per cent interest on grain, and the same on
money. It has been estimated that the average rate of interest in
Babylonia, Assyria and Syria was 20–25 per cent on silver, and
$33\frac{1}{3}$ per cent on grain (I. Mendelsohn, in *IDB* IV, p. 385), though
there must have been wide fluctuations on account of economic
conditions. We do not know interest rates charged in Israel, but
the taking of interest is usually referred to with great disfavour
(Ps. 15:5; Prov. 28:8; Ezek. 18:8,13,17; 22:12; Neh. 5:6–12).
Doubtless one reason for the prohibition of interest was the high
rates charged; a man could easily become so debt-ridden that he

would have to sell himself into slavery, under such high rates. This law has been the source of embarrassment, and has led to casuistry, in both Judaism and Christianity. However, it should never have been thought applicable to a highly developed, commercial society requiring large sums of venture capital. Perhaps we should add that when the *AV* was translated, 'usury' did not mean exorbitant interest, as it does today. The biblical injunction is not against the taking of exorbitant or illegal interest, but interest of any nature.

26–27 is closely related to the preceding, and forbids keeping a poor man's **garment** (probably the large outer mantle, cf. Mt. 5:40) beyond sundown. Cf. Job 22:6; Am. 2:8; Prov. 27:13. Note that here Yahweh is the champion of the poor man: **And if he cries to me, I will hear, for I am compassionate.** In some of the ancient law codes, a person could be taken as pledge for a debt, particularly a daughter (Hammurapi Code, 114–16; Middle Assyrian Laws, A, 39, 44, 48). Dt. 24:6,10–13 places restrictions on the manner in which pledges may be taken or recovered.

28. In 1 Kg. 21:10 the penalty for cursing God and the king is death. The penalty is death for cursing God in Lev. 24:15f.; Job 2:9; likewise for cursing the king in 2 Sam. 16:9; cf. 1 Kg. 2:8f. The significance of the word here translated 'ruler' is not certain. According to Noth, the *nāśi'* was a tribal representative in the pre-monarchial sacral federation (cf. Num. 1:5–16; 13:1–15; 34:17–28). If this is correct, it is an indication of the origin of this part of the Covenant Code in that early period; but the meaning is not entirely certain. The Hittite laws (ΙΙ, 173) say that if one rejects the judgment of the king, his house shall be made a shambles; and if he rejects the judgment of a dignitary, his head shall be cut off.

29–30. The first sentence, which is very general, probably has to do with the bringing of the firstfruits of the products of the soil and wine; cf. 23:19; Dt. 26:1ff. The law regarding the offering of the first-born of sons, of oxen and of sheep is here stated in a categorical manner. Exod. 13:13 and 34:20 provide for the redemption of the first-born of sons; it does not state with what they were to be redeemed, but probably with an animal, such as a lamb. Some scholars have taken the categorical statement here as evidence for the actual sacrifice of the first-born sons in very early Hebrew history. While not impossible, this is not probable.

It may be the form in which the law was taken over directly from
the Canaanites, who apparently did practise child sacrifice.

31 is an injunction to be 'men of holiness', *'anšê ḳōḏeš*, here
rendered 'men consecrated (to me)'. The injunctions are in the
second person plural, considered by some critics as an indication
that this verse is a secondary addition (perhaps by the Deuteronomist). Cf. Dt. 14:21. For the prohibition against eating **any
flesh that is torn by beasts in the field,** cf. Lev. 7:24; 17:15.
This is probably a very old taboo; it was believed the wild animal
could transfer evil power to the torn animal. In a later time, the
rationalization was probably that the animal torn by a wild
animal had not been slaughtered in the prescribed manner, with
the blood properly drained (Dt. 12:16,23).

Admonitions Concerning Conduct in Cases at Law **23:1-9**
These are admonitions which mainly concern conduct in matters
at law. They seek to promote impartial justice, protecting the
weak and poor against the rich and powerful. They are not addressed
to professional judges, but to all free Israelites who might be
called on to testify in law courts, or to help in deciding cases in
local assemblies. These are not really laws, since they do not
specify penalties, but only admonitions. We include in this group
verses 4-5 because the 'enemy' about which they speak may be
considered as an actual or potential adversary at law, toward
whom one should conduct himself as a friend and brother.
(The application may, of course, have been broader than this,
but such an interpretation may have been the reason for placing
these verses at this point.) Most of these admonitions have the
apodictic form, using second person singular; verses 4-5 have a
mixed or quasi-casuistic form.

2. It is better to render *rabbîm* as 'majority' than **a multitude.**
The meaning is well expressed in *JB*: 'You must not take the side
of the greater number in the cause of wrong-doing nor side with
the majority and give evidence in a lawsuit in defiance of justice'.

3. Because there is usually little temptation to **be partial to a
poor man in his suit,** many scholars emend *weḏāl* to *gāḏôl*, and
translate, 'nor shall you be partial to a great man in his suit'.
This emendation is not necessarily correct. Lev. 19:15 reads,
'you shall not be partial to the poor or defer to the great'. Man
should imitate God, who is not partial in his judgments (cf. Dt.
10:17-18; Ac. 10:34-35).

4 enjoins the return of an enemy's straying ox or ass. As noted above, the 'enemy' here may be the adversary in an actual or potential legal suit—though the interpretation need not be confined to such. Dt. 22:1-3 deals similarly with various kinds of lost animals or objects belonging to a brother Israelite. The present law indicates that one is to treat the lost animal of an enemy just as he would that of a 'brother'. Some of the ancient law codes indicate that a person who finds a straying animal or a lost object, and does not return it to the owner, may lay himself open to the charge of theft. For example, in the very ancient Eshnunna Laws (50) we read that if an official seizes a lost slave or ox or donkey belonging to the palace or to a *muškēnum* [a social class closely connected with the palace or temple], and does not surrender it to Eshnunna, even if he lets only seven days pass, he shall be prosecuted for theft. Cf. also Hittite laws, 1, 71, 79, and 45 (on return of lost implements). In the light of these, the return of a lost ox or ass may not have been motivated by purely humanitarian reasons; there would have been good reason to return the animal of an enemy who might be disposed to bring a charge of theft.

5 is a humanitarian admonition, to help the ass of an enemy which may be helpless under its burden. Here there could be no thought of penalty, but simply of kindness to the animal of an enemy. Cf. Dt. 22:4 which applies to the animal of a 'brother'. Albright renders the last clause 'you shall adjust its load', giving the Hebrew the meaning of Ugaritic *ᶜdb* (*Yahweh and the Gods of Canaan*, p. 104). For other *OT* passages expressing similar sentiments of kindness to enemies, see Job 31:29; Prov. 25:21f. The injunction to 'hate your enemy' (Mt. 5:43) is never found verbally in the *OT*; it probably comes from the literature of the Qumran covenanters.

7. for I will not acquit the wicked: LXX reads, 'you (singular) shall not acquit the wicked for the sake of a bribe'. This could be correct; however, Yahweh speaks in the first person several times in this section (22:23f.,27,31; 23:13).

8 is almost verbatim the same as Dt. 16:19*b*. S. R. Driver notes that 'The prevalence of bribery in the East is notorious' (p. 238). The *OT* contains many passages condemning it.

9 is very similar to 22:21; see comment there. The first 'you' is singular, the other two being plural, possibly indicating that the second half is an addition by R_D.

The Sabbatical Year and the Sabbath Day **23:10–12**

10–11. Cf. the regulations for the sabbatical year in Lev. 25:1–7,20–22. The reason given here for allowing the land to lie fallow every seventh year is a humanitarian one: **that the poor of your people may eat; and what they leave the wild beasts may eat.** There is no suggestion here of a practical purpose: to allow the land to increase its fertility. In Lev. 25:4, the motive is that 'there shall be a sabbath of solemn rest for the land'; the land is to keep a sabbath rest as man does. Noth has suggested that behind the idea of the sabbatical year is that of the return of the land to its original state, a *restitutio in integrum*. Other scholars have suggested that, on the analogy of practices in other countries, the sabbatical year may be a relic of the ancient belief that all of the land was the property of the villagers collectively; individuals could have the use of it for only limited periods, and then at regular intervals the produce of the land would revert to the use of the community as a whole. Such an idea does not, however, seem appropriate to the practice of the *fallow* year; it would be appropriate to the practice of communal cultivation of the land in certain years. In any event, there is the question whether the law of the sabbatical year was regularly observed. Lev. 26:34f. seems to imply that it was not. Its enforcement is indicated in Neh. 10:31, and in a number of passages from the Hasmonean period—1 Mac. 6:49,53; Josephus, *Ant.* XIII.viii.1; XIV.x.6.

12. The sabbath day of rest. Here the stated reason for the sabbath is humanitarian, as in Dt. 5:14. For general discussion of the sabbath and its origin, see comment on 16:27–30.

A General Admonition **23:13**

This is a summary admonition, which may once have stood at the end of the Covenant Code, or of one of its constituent parts. Did it originally stand after verse 19? The first **you** is plural, but **your mouth** employs the second person singular. On the latter part of the verse, see 20:3; Jos. 23:7. To mention the name of a god was to recognize his existence and invoke his power.

A Calendar of Annual Feasts and other Cultic Regulations **23:14–19**

This section contains directions for the observance of the three great festivals of the year—the Feast of Unleavened Bread, at the beginning of the barley harvest in the spring; the Feast of Harvest, at the end of the spring grain harvest; and the Feast of Ingathering in the early autumn, when the summer crops (especially olives and grapes) were harvested. Most of this section, with small variations, is to be found also in 34:18–26. All of these were adapted by the Israelites from the Canaanites. As will be shown in the comments below, the source of both of these was probably an old calendar of feasts with certain appended regulations concerning sacrifices, borrowed from the Canaanites. It is not likely that either of the two *OT* sections is dependent upon the other, but rather that both go back to a common source. The form here is arranged more systematically, and is probably closer in some details to the original, than the form in chapter 34. Similar calendars of the feasts are found in Dt. 16:1–17; Lev. 23 (cf. Num. 28–29).

15. You shall keep the feast of unleavened bread: in this feast the bread was made from the first produce of the new barley crop, without the use of leaven. On the origin of the feast of unleavened bread and its relationship to the Passover, see the excursus at the end of 13:16 (pp. 144–46).

in the month of Abib, for in it you came out of Egypt: see 13:4. Here the feast is connected with the exodus from Egypt, though that was apparently not its origin. However, unleavened bread was doubtless used by the early Israelites in their nomadic stage; it is said to be the normal fare of the Arab Beduin today.

None shall appear before me empty-handed: no one should go on pilgrimage to the sanctuary without a gift for Yahweh.

16. the feast of harvest celebrated the harvest of grain in the late spring. It is called feast of weeks later, as in 34:22; see comment on that verse.

the feast of ingathering at the end of the year celebrated the harvest of the summer fruits, especially olives and grapes. (The end of the year was in September or October.) Its later name was feast of *sukkôt*, rendered as 'tabernacles', 'booths', and sometimes even 'tents' (Dt. 16:13; Lev. 23:34). It was so named because during the feast the people lived in huts or booths made of branches, as had been the custom from time immemorial during the season when the summer fruits were being gathered. According to later interpretation this was to remind the Israelites of the time when their ancestors lived in tents in the wilderness (Lev. 23:43). This feast may have its early Canaanite predecessor in the feast mentioned in Jg. 9:27. This autumn feast was the most popular and most important one in the Israelite calendar. It was a time of much joy and merry-making. Some modern scholars think that this feast included ceremonies of the renewal of the covenant between Yahweh and Israel.

17. Three times in the year shall all your males appear before the LORD God: this refers primarily to the three feasts just enumerated. Every male Israelite was expected to appear before Yahweh in one of the local sanctuaries (before the Deuteronomic reform centralized worship in the Jerusalem temple) on these three occasions as a minimum.

18. The omission of leaven from sacrifices probably rested upon the fact that in very early times all bread was made without leaven by nomads of the desert (see above on verse 15). However, Lev. 7:13; 23:17 specify that certain offerings are to be made with leavened bread. Cf. Amos 4:5.

or let the fat of my feast remain until the morning: certain parts of the fat of sacrifices were customarily consumed on the altar (Lev. 1:8,3,5). The parallel in 34:25 has an interesting variation; see comment *in loc.*

19. The first of the first fruits of your ground were considered to belong to Yahweh, as well as the first-born of men and animals (22:29-30). See also 23:16. The first fruits of the soil were to be brought to the sanctuary as an offering; according to Dt. 16:17, 'every man shall give as he is able'.

You shall not boil a kid in its mother's milk: this injunction has occasioned a great deal of comment, and it forms the biblical basis of a far-reaching principle of Jewish *kosher* laws—namely, that one must not consume in the same meal meat and a dairy product. Various explanations have been offered as the original reason for this biblical prohibition. Some have suggested that there was basically a humanitarian reason (Philo, Ibn Ezra). Others have suggested generally that this must have been prohibited because it was an idolatrous or magical rite of a foreign people. It is reported that even today among Jordanian Beduin a kid boiled in its mother's milk is a favourite dish offered to guests.

The true explanation seems to be that this rite was forbidden by the Israelites because it was a sacrificial practice of the Canaanites. This is suggested by one of the Ugaritic texts (text 52, line 14), which is mythical-ritualistic. At one point in this text we read:

'On the fire seven times the young men cook a kid in milk, mint(?) in butter.'

A part of this line is broken, but the reading and translation are fairly certain. If this text does indicate that the boiling of a kid in its mother's milk was a ritualistic practice of the people of Ugarit in the fourteenth century B.C., then it may have been known to the Israelites as a later Canaanite practice against which they revolted. Perhaps as people who had earlier been nomads they also had a natural revulsion to the practice, crystallized by observing it as a cultic rite of the inhabitants of Canaan.

Closing Promises and Exhortations **23:20–33**

   23:20–22(R_D). *Yahweh promises to send an angel before the Israelites to guard and guide them. They should give heed to him in order to receive Yahweh's blessings.*

   23:23–33(R_D). *When the angel leads them into the promised land, they are to blot out completely the peoples living there, refrain from worshipping their gods, and break down their sacred pillars. Yahweh will send his terror and hornets before them, and drive out the peoples, but he will do so only little by little. The Israelites are forbidden to make a covenant with them or their gods.*

This section is the conclusion to the Covenant Code. It assumes that Israel is now about to leave Sinai and conquer the land of Canaan. Somewhat similar passages are found in 33:1–3; 34:11–16; Lev. 26; and Dt. 28. The present passage is awkwardly placed, for the next chapter records the ratification of the covenant and subsequent chapters presuppose that the Israelites are still at Sinai; they do not leave Sinai until Num. 10:11ff. Furthermore, this section by its position seems to admonish Israel to keep the preceding Covenant Code, but verses 21–22 assume that Yahweh will speak in the future through his angel, and it is his commands they are admonished to obey.

This whole section is from the Deuteronomic redactor. He has built upon E tradition, but we cannot now disentangle his work from E. It was probably the D redactor who placed the Covenant Code in its present form and position, and compiled this section to serve as its conclusion. Virtually all of the themes, and much of the phraseology found here, occur also in Dt. 7:1–5,12–26.

   20. Behold, I send an angel before you: this is the angel (or 'messenger') who guides and guards Israel, referred to also in 14:19 (E); 32:34 (E); 33:2 (R_D); Jg. 2:1. Elsewhere we read that the Israelites were led by a pillar of cloud (13:21–22 J), or by the

Ark of the covenant (Num. 10:33–36 E). The angel here is a full
representative of Yahweh, for it is assumed that he can speak for
Yahweh and pardon transgressions.

21. for my name is in him: a characteristic feature of
Deuteronomic theology is that the 'name of Yahweh' resides in the
Temple of Solomon (Dt. 12:5,11; 1 Kg. 8:29), a way of expressing
the self-manifestation of the deity. This is the only passage in which
his name is said to be in the angel; apparently D assumed that the
name of Yahweh resided in the angel until the time that the
Temple was built.

22. Obedience to the angel—that is, to Yahweh—will bring
various blessings, such as the ones listed here and in verses 25–26.
Cf. especially Dt. 7:13–15; 28:1–14. A prominent feature of the
international treaties whose form is compared with the covenant
forms of the *OT* was the listing of various blessings or curses that
would ensue from observance or non-observance of the terms of
the treaty. Mesopotamian treaties particularly emphasize the
curses, and these are sometimes listed in the *OT*; e.g., Lev. 26:14–
39; Dt. 27:15–26; 28:15–68. No curses appear here, but one is
implied in verse 21. The epilogue to the Code of Hammurapi
pronounces blessings on any future king who shall observe the
words written on his stela and not alter the law he has enacted; on
the other hand, it pronounces curses on any who shall abolish his
law, distort his words, or efface Hammurapi's name. The curses
are much longer than the blessings.

23. For the nations listed here, see comment on 3:8.

24. break their pillars in pieces: the pillars (*maṣṣēḇôṭ*) were
associated especially with the worship of the Canaanitish deities.
They were sacred standing stones which may in some manner
have represented the deity, or they may have been memorials to
deceased heroes or ancestors. These objects are frequently
proscribed in the *OT* (e.g., Dt. 7:5; 12:3; 16:21f.; Lev. 26:1).
However, similar objects with various purposes were sometimes
erected by the early Hebrews—e.g., by the patriarchs (Gen. 28:18;
31:45; 35:14,20), by Moses (Exod. 24:4), and by Joshua (Jos. 4:20,
not specifically termed *maṣṣēḇôṭ*). The Canaanitish pillars,
suggesting idolatry, were particular objects of scorn by the
Israelite prophets and religious leaders.

26. I will fulfil the number of your days: allow you to live
out the usual number of days of a full life.

27. The words **terror** and **confusion** suggest the concept of holy war held by the early Israelites. They believed that Yahweh fought on behalf of Israel, causing such panic and confusion in their enemies that they could readily be overcome, even by small numbers. Cf. Dt. 7:23, and, for examples in the early history, Exod. 15:16; Jos. 10:10; Jg. 4:15; 1 Sam. 5:9,11; 7:10. For details of the concept, see at 'War, Ideas of', in *IDB* iv, pp. 797ff.

28. The translation **hornets** is not certain. The word *ṣirʿāh* occurs only here and in Dt. 7:20 and Jos. 24:12, always in the singular, which is usually considered as a collective. Some scholars render it 'leprosy', for which the usual word is *ṣārāʿat*, or 'discouragement'. If 'hornets' is correct, the reference is to that insect as something which was very troublesome among the inhabitants of Palestine, and was considered as an ally of the Israelites and an agent of Yahweh.

29–30. The Israelites did not conquer Canaan in a short time, as one strand of the tradition indicates (Jos. 10:28–43; 11:16–23; 21:43–45). The conquest and displacement of the natives of Canaan took place over a long period, and in various ways. One explanation devised for this fact is given here: Yahweh himself drove them out only **little by little** so that the wild beasts would not multiply in the parts of the land left desolate. Dt. 7:22 gives the same explanation. Other theories were offered elsewhere; Jg. 2:20—3:4 says that the reason was that Yahweh wanted to test the Israelites and teach them war.

31. Red Sea is here the Gulf of Aqaba, not the body of water crossed by the Israelites (see excursus at the end of chapter 14). **the sea of the Philistines:** the Mediterranean Sea, along whose coast were located the Philistine cities, in SW. Palestine. **the wilderness:** the desert on the S. of Palestine. The great territory here promised to the Israelites was not at any time ruled by them. These are the idealized boundaries of the reign of Solomon (1 Kg. 4:21; cf. Dt. 11:24). David did in fact rule over, or have alliances with the nations living in, most of the territory encompassed by these boundaries, but Solomon lost some of it.

32. The Israelites made a covenant with the wily Gibeonites (Jos. 9:3–15), but they were frequently warned against making covenants with the native inhabitants of Canaan or their gods (34:12–16; Jos. 23:12–13; Jg. 2:2). The making of covenants with them would have implied (in most cases, at least) recognition of their deities.

THE COVENANT RATIFIED **24:1–18**

1–2(J). *Moses is told to come up to Yahweh, with Aaron, Nadab, Abihu and seventy elders of Israel.*
3–8(E,R_D). *Moses tells the people, at the foot of the mountain, the words of Yahweh, and they declare that they will do the words which Yahweh has spoken. Moses writes down all the words. He then erects an altar and twelve pillars, and young men make sacrifices to Yahweh. Moses takes half of the blood and throws it against the altar, and the other half he throws upon the people, after reading the Book of the Covenant.*
9–11(J). *Moses, Aaron, Nadab, Abihu and seventy elders go up the mountain, and there see God. They eat and drink there.*
12–14(E). *Yahweh tells Moses to come up to the mountain and there Yahweh will give him the tables of stone which Yahweh has written. Moses goes up, taking Joshua, leaving the elders at the foot of the mountain, and instructing them to bring any causes they may have before Aaron and Hur.*
15–18(P). *Moses goes up the mountain, where the glory of Yahweh settles on Mount Sinai. Moses enters into the cloud, and remains on the mountain forty days and forty nights.*

It is immediately obvious that this chapter is composite. It contains two parallel accounts of a ceremony by which the covenant between Yahweh and Israel was ratified. Verses 3–8 record the reading of the 'Book of the Covenant' and a blood rite, at the foot of the mountain, whereas 1–2, 9–11 tell of Moses and a group going up the mountain, where they experience a vision of God and eat a covenant meal. The movements of Moses in the chapter also betray the composite nature of the chapter. In verse 1 he is told to come up the mountain, where he already is; again in verse 12 he is told to come up, when he is already there among a group. The subsequent verses three times tell of his going up the mountain: 13, 15, 18.

There are serious difficulties in the literary analysis, but the following seems to be the best division: J—24:1–2,9–11; E—3:4*b*–6,8,12–14,18*b*; P—15–18*a*. R_D is probably responsible for verses 4*a*, 7. This analysis is not agreed to by all scholars. Noth and Beyerlin, for example, think that, aside from the P material in verses 15–18, the chapter contains only variant E traditions with a few secondary additions. This could be correct, for some features of verses 1–2, 9–11 are not usually found in J: the presence of Aaron and his sons, and the use of 'God of Israel' in verse 9 and *Elohim* in verse 11. However, we have followed the majority of critics in assigning the verses to J, because such a division serves to point up the differences within the chapter.

The ceremony (or ceremonies) recorded here was of very great importance. It is the only ceremony in which the ratification of the covenant of Israel with Yahweh is recorded. The blood rite and the covenant meal take place at different places with somewhat different participants. If we raise the question as to the historicity of the occasion, it is impossible to determine which (if either) of these ceremonies is to be considered as historical. Both are very ancient rites. It is quite possible that the ceremony by which the covenant in the time of Moses was ratified included both a blood rite and a covenant meal, for animal sacrifices and communion meals often occurred together in ancient Israel. The blood rite described here is unique in the history of Israel.

1-2 are from J, following in that narrative after 19:18. J must have originally contained something between 19:18 and 24:1 which has been lost, or has been preserved elsewhere (see chapter 34).

Nadab and Abihu were sons of Aaron (6:23; cf. Lev. 10:1-3).

seventy of the elders of Israel were leaders and representatives of the nation; cf. Num. 11:16-25.

3 introduces the E account (3-8), and originally followed in E after 19:25, which says that Moses went down from the mountain and spoke to the people. The proclamation of **the words of the LORD** by Moses, and the response of the people declaring their intention to obey those words were probably used in the cultic ritual of Israel; cf. verse 7 and 19:4-8.

and all the ordinances is a secondary insertion, made by the Deuteronomic redactor when he placed the Covenant Code in its present position, with the concluding promises and exhortations written by him (23:20-33). The laws of the Covenant Code are designated as 'ordinances' in 21:1. In the present passage only the 'words of Yahweh' are otherwise mentioned.

4. And Moses wrote all the words of the LORD: it is surprising that Moses is here said to have written Yahweh's words, and that in verse 7 he reads from the 'Book of the Covenant' in the hearing of the people, whereas it is not until verse 12 that Yahweh promises to give to Moses the tables of stone, which are subsequently written and given to him (31:18). In Exodus it is nearly always Yahweh who writes the tables of stone (24:12; 31:18; 32:16; 34:1). Only 34:27f. says that Moses wrote them at the instruction of Yahweh (in that case, the second set of tables after the first were broken). W. Rudolph, noting this discrepancy, suggested that the original part of 24:3–11 stood originally later in Exodus, after 34:29. (Rudolph assigns 24:3,4*b*–6,8–11 to J; he denies the presence of any E material in Exodus.) It does seem plausible to suppose that the account of the ratification of the covenant once stood at a later point such as he suggests, and that 4*a* and 7 were added when the account was placed in its present position. This is likely to have been done by the Deuteronomic redactor. The account then could have originally told of the reading of the tables of stone (containing the ethical decalogue) as the basis of the covenant, but the redactor had to insert 4*a* to describe the writing of the words, and he then wrote of Moses' reading from the 'Book of the Covenant' instead of the tables of stone which, according to 34:28 (J), contained 'the words of the covenant, the ten words'. It is significant that the name 'Book of the Covenant' occurs elsewhere only in 2 Kg. 23:2,21 (2 Chr. 34:30) where it designates the book found in the time of Josiah, believed by critical scholars to have been the original core of Deuteronomy. Alternatively, the original tradition now preserved in 24:3–8 may have assumed that the 'words of Yahweh' spoken by Moses to the people were preserved in memory and delivered in oral form, not having been written down. If the basis of the covenant was the ethical decalogue of 20:2–17 in its original form, consisting of ten brief sentences, it could easily have been memorized and transmitted orally. See further the comment on verse 7 below.

twelve pillars: the function of these pillars is not described; see comment on 23:24 about them. Originally they may have been considered to be witnesses of the covenant made between Yahweh and Israel. In two other accounts of covenant-making, stones serve as witnesses: in the covenant between Laban and Jacob (Gen. 31:51f.), and in the covenant between Yahweh and Israel in the time of Joshua (Jos. 24:27). In the present account they symbolize **the twelve tribes of Israel.** Cf. 1 Kg. 18:31f.

5. Those who offer the sacrifice here are **young men of the people of Israel,** who are not designated as priests, although they serve in a priestly capacity. Moses also serves a priestly function here.

burnt offerings were wholly consumed on the altar; the later law for this type of offering is in Lev. 1.

peace offerings: $z^e\underline{b}\bar{a}\underline{h}\hat{i}m$ $\check{s}^el\bar{a}m\hat{i}m$, perhaps better 'communion sacrifices'. In later times at least (Lev. 3; 7:11–18,28–36), the characteristic feature of this type of sacrifice was that it was designed to create a union between God and the offerer. The fat of the animal sacrifice was burned upon the altar, part of the animal was given to the priests, and the rest was eaten by those who made the offering. This kind of sacrifice would have been particularly appropriate in a covenant ratification ceremony. We cannot be certain, however, that these offerings were treated at this early time just as they were later.

6–8 describe the blood rite carried out by Moses, here serving in a priestly capacity. He takes half of the blood and throws it against the altar, which represents the deity, and the rest he throws upon the people. In this manner the union between Yahweh and the people is created, since the altar and the people share the common blood. In the *OT* such a rite is never repeated, although in Israelite sacrifices the blood was sometimes thrown upon the altar (e.g. 29:16,20; Lev. 1:5,11). Rites similar to this were practised among the ancient Arabs in the making of covenants: sometimes the participants in a covenant mingled their blood, or dipped their hands into the blood of an animal, with some of the blood being applied to sacred stones representing the deity. Blood was used as the seat of life and vitality.

book of the covenant: see comment above on verse 4, where it is suggested that verses 4a and 7 may have been introduced by the Deuteronomic redactor. In the present context 'Book of the Covenant' means the preceding Covenant Code, and that would have been the intention of the Deuteronomic redactor. In all probability, however, the document which formed the basis of the covenant was 'the words of the covenant, the ten words' (34:28) inscribed upon the tables of stone, that is, the ethical decalogue of 20:2–17 (see comment below on chapter 34). We have mentioned above the possibility, however, that the terms of the covenant in the original form of the present account may have been preserved in memory and transmitted by Moses orally.

In the international treaties, which are now frequently discussed in connection with covenant forms in the *OT*, emphasis is sometimes placed upon the writing of the treaty document, its deposit in a sanctuary, and its periodic reading before the public. In two

other passages in the *OT* we are told of the writing of a document
in connection with the making of a covenant: in Jos. 24:26,
Joshua writes 'these words in the book of the law of God', and in
Dt. 27:8 Moses is instructed to set up large stones and write upon
them 'all the words of this law very plainly' (cf. 31:9,26). In the
OT there are, however, numerous accounts of the making of
covenants in which no covenant document is mentioned, and some
of them must have been based upon oral terms.

the blood of the covenant: the blood by which the covenant is
ratified or sealed. The common blood upon the altar, representing
Yahweh, and upon the people creates (or signalizes) their union.
This phrase becomes very important in the *NT* through its use at
the Last Supper; see Mt. 26:28; Mk 14:24; Lk. 22:20; 1 Cor.
11:25; Heb. 9:20; 10:29.

9–11 follow naturally after verses 1–2; this account is usually
assigned to J. Moses and certain others go up on Mount Sinai;
there they see God and also eat and drink, presumably participating
in a covenant meal.

they saw the God of Israel: it is not surprising in J for men to
see God, for he often speaks of man seeing God in one manner or
another. Generally, however, in the Sinai narrative God appears
only in a thick cloud, a fire, or the like. Exod. 33:20 (J) says, 'man
shall not see me and live'.

**under his feet as it were a pavement of sapphire stone, like
the very heaven for clearness:** the closest parallel to this is in
the vision of Ezekiel, esp. Ezek. 1:26. The sapphire (probably
really lapis lazuli) suggests the blueness of the sky, and the pavement suggests the firmament of heaven which was considered to
be solid (Gen. 1:6–8). The whole phrase implies a vision of God
in the clear, blue sky, not in a thick cloud or the like. The last
half of the verse may, however, be a late addition, influenced by
the vision of Ezekiel. The Hebrew idiom in 'the very heaven',
keʿéṣem haššāmáyim, is otherwise used only in late writings (Ezek.,P,
Job 21:23).

**he did not lay his hand on the chief men of the people of
Israel:** in the light of an idea such as is expressed in 33:20, one
might have expected that Yahweh would strike dead those who
looked upon him. The word for 'chief men', *ʾaṣîlîm*, is a rare word,
used in this sense only here.

they beheld God, and ate and drank: this was no ordinary
meal, but a covenant meal eaten by the participants in the

I

presence of God. The eating of meals is sometimes specifically
mentioned at the time of covenant-making: the covenant of
Isaac with Abimelech (Gen. 26:30), and that of Laban with
Jacob (Gen. 31:54); see also Dt. 27:7 and the comments above
on Exod. 18:12. The eating of the meal presupposes a sacrifice,
which is sometimes specifically mentioned in such passages.

12–14 must be from a different source, for in the preceding
verses Moses is already on the mountain. This section is from E.
It prepares the way for the account of Moses' receiving the tables
of stone (31:18) and of his descent from the mountain to find the
people worshipping the golden calf.

I will give you the tables of stone: see comment on verse 4.

Joshua: see comment on 17:8. In 32:17 he is with Moses. The
latter suggests he may have ascended only part way up the
mountain, Moses going to the top alone.

And he said to the elders: the instructions given to the elders
here do not presuppose the organization described in 18:13–23.
This is another indication that chapter 18 originally stood after
rather than before the making of the covenant on Mount Sinai.

Hur: see comment on 17:10.

15–18*a* are P's parallel to the account by JE in chapter 19 of
Moses' ascent on the mountain. The last preceding verses from
this source are 19:1–2. P continues in 25:1—31:18*a*.

glory of the LORD is a phrase that appears especially in P, the
Psalms and Ezekiel. The Hebrew verb from which it is derived
means 'to be heavy', 'weighty', 'honoured'. It is one of the terms
used for the visible manifestation of the Deity. Verse 17 describes
it as being **like a devouring fire;** cf. Zech. 2:5. The Priestly
narrative uses the term to express various appearances of Yahweh,
and particularly his presence in the tabernacle or tent of meeting
(16:7,10; 40:34f.; Lev. 9:6,23; Num. 14:10; 16:19; 20:6).

THE P ORDINANCES FOR THE CULT 25:1—31:18

In these seven chapters P represents Yahweh as giving to Moses
detailed instructions for the construction of the Tabernacle and
its various furnishings, as well as for the priestly garments, the
ordination of the priests, and certain other elements of the cultus.
For P, these instructions (and their fulfilment in chapters 35–40)
form a large part of the reason for Moses' being on Mount Sinai.
Chapter 25 opens with instructions for the people to bring the

materials necessary for the Tabernacle, and continues with descriptions of the Ark, the table of the Presence-Bread, and the lampstand, all of which would stand within the Tabernacle. The next chapter contains instructions for the making of the Tabernacle proper, consisting of a 'tabernacle' of very fine tapestries, a tent made of goats' hair, a wooden structure made in such a way as to be portable, a veil dividing the most holy place from the holy place, and a front screen. Chapter 27 describes the altar for burnt-offerings, the court, and the oil for the lampstand. The priestly garments are described in detail in the next chapter, and the ritual for the ordination of the priests in chapter 29. 29:35–42 describe certain offerings, and 29:43–46 seems to form a conclusion to the chapters about the making of the Tabernacle and instructions for its ministry. Chapter 30 then gives instructions for the golden altar of incense, the half shekel offering, the laver of bronze, the holy anointing oil, and holy incense. Chapter 31 gives instructions for the appointment of Bezalel and Oholiab, and commandments concerning sabbath observance. The final verse, 31:18, says that Yahweh gave to Moses the two tables of stone, written with God's finger.

As a product of P, written in the fifth century B.C. (or possibly the sixth), these chapters represent an attempt to show that regulations for the making of the sanctuary, the ordination of the priesthood, and the various offerings in the cultus, were ordained by Yahweh on Mount Sinai in instructions to Moses. The question of the historical accuracy of the chapters has centred largely around discussion of the Tabernacle and its furnishings. J. Wellhausen maintained that 'the tabernacle rests on an historical fiction' (*Prolegomena to the History of Ancient Israel* [1885], p. 39), and this has been maintained in one manner or another by most critics since his time. Attempts have been made to show that P's Tabernacle incorporates ancient elements, but his Tabernacle, taken as a whole, is an unrealistic and artificial structure that never existed except on paper!

There was in fact a historical 'tent of meeting', described in 33:7–11 (E; see detailed comments *in loc.*). It was a tent that was pitched outside the Israelite camp, and Moses would from time to time go out to it; when Moses entered it, a pillar of cloud would descend at the door of the tent, and Yahweh would speak with Moses face to face, 'as a man speaks to his friend'. Its only constant attendant was Joshua the son of Nun. P's Tabernacle, on the

other hand, was in the centre of the camp, was attended by a
large body of priests and Levites, and was a very costly, highly
ornamented structure. The cloud rested upon the Tabernacle
always (40:34–38), and Yahweh spoke to Moses especially from
above the Ark (25:22). The Tabernacle was the centre of an
elaborate cultus.

The view that such a structure as this could not have existed in
the Mosaic age, in the desert, rests upon a number of consider-
ations, which need to be only briefly enumerated: (i) There are
many obscurities and omissions, and even contradictions, in the
description of the Tabernacle. Some of these will become apparent
to any careful reader of the following chapters and their commentary. (ii) The Israelites, who could hardly have numbered
more than a few thousand (see comment on 12:37), did not have
the skill required in weaving, embroidery, carpentry, metalworking, etc. for the making of such an elaborate structure.
(iii) Likewise, they could hardly have produced or procured the
necessary materials: precious stone, linen, woollen fabric, dyes,
oils, spices, nearly a ton of gold, nearly 3¼ tons of silver, and
about 2¼ tons of bronze (38:24–31). When Solomon built his
Temple in the tenth century B.C., he had to call in skilled workmen
from Phoenicia, and contract for materials from that country
(1 Kg. 5:1–12,18; 7:13ff.; 9:10–14). (iv) The Tabernacle with its
priesthood and cultus represent theological ideas and practices
that resulted from centuries of experience of Israel in her own land.

The Tabernacle of P was conceived to be a portable sanctuary.
It is indeed an unrealistic, ideal structure, but it does rest upon two
different traditions: the tradition which goes back to the desert
'tent of meeting', very probably of the Mosaic age; and the
tradition of the Temple of Solomon and possibly subsequent
Temples (Ezekiel's Temple in Ezek. 40–43, which may be only
an ideal, or a description of the Temple of Solomon in a later
stage; and the second Temple, rebuilt under Zerubbabel). The
use of temples was borrowed largely from the Canaanites, and
conceived of Yahweh as dwelling in a permanent structure.
These two traditions are combined by P, who sought to show that
their plan or model was given by Yahweh to Moses on Sinai
(25:9,40; 26:30).

The tradition of the 'tent of meeting' is difficult to trace historically. E's tent is described in 33:7–11 and casually referred to
in Num. 11:24ff.; 12:4f.,10. These passages describe the function

of the tent, but tell us nothing concerning its size or appearance. It is never stated that the Ark stood within the tent of meeting. Only a little is related in subsequent books concerning this tent of meeting, and we cannot be certain that it is always the same structure that is referred to.

According to Jos. 18:1, the Israelites set up the tent of meeting at Shiloh (cf. 19:51; 1 Sam. 2:22). However, there are certain indications that the sanctuary of Shiloh was a permanent structure rather than a tent: 1 Sam. 1:9 speaks of 'the doorpost of the temple of the Lord', and 1 Sam. 3:15 of 'the doors of the house of the Lord'. The late references in 1 Chr. 16:39; 21:29; 2 Chr. 1:3, 13 are of dubious value. The Ark is frequently referred to in the narratives concerning Joshua, Samuel, Saul and David, but not the tent of meeting (and there is no clear evidence that the Ark was housed in the tent of meeting, see above).

David took the Ark up to Jerusalem and placed it within a tent which he had pitched for it (2 Sam. 6:17; cf. 7:2,6). Nothing is said of the size or appearance of the tent. It must have had an altar nearby, for David offered up burnt offerings and peace offerings (2 Sam. 6:17–19). There probably was a horned altar (for burnt offerings or for incense) in or near the tent-sanctuary (1 Kg. 1:50f.; 2:28); whether it was the same as the one on which David offered sacrifice we do not know.

According to 1 Kg. 8:4, the tent of meeting was brought up to the Temple of Solomon, but subsequent verses do not mention it, although they record the placing of the Ark in the inner sanctuary of the Temple. It seems very likely (as many critics believe) that the reference to the tent of meeting is a secondary gloss here. It is very difficult to see how it could have been placed in the Temple, and no subsequent accounts refer to it. If the reference is not a gloss, we can only suppose that the tent of meeting was stored somewhere in the Temple or its precincts and then only allowed to disintegrate.

In his discussion of the Tabernacle in Beer's commentary (pp. 133–37), K. Galling has pointed out that the description in Exod. 26:7–14 of a tent of goats' hair can be reconstructed as a normal nomadic tent, although of exaggerated dimensions (see comment below on 26:7–14). It is quite possible that this is the oldest part of the Tabernacle tradition, and that it preserves a memory of the Mosaic tent of meeting, or possibly of David's tent. We must emphasize, however, that none of our early sources gives us any substantial information concerning the size and appearance of either of those tents.

The other tradition preserved in P's description of the Tabernacle is the tradition represented by the Temple of Solomon, and possibly of the Temple of Ezekiel and the second Temple. The similarities to those Temples will be apparent from the subsequent commentary. Here we may only point out that the Tabernacle had a most holy place in which was placed the Ark, and a holy place in which were a table of Presence-Bread, lampstand (Solomon's had ten), and an incense altar. These correspond to the inner sanctuary and nave of Solomon's Temple, and their furnishings. The dimensions of the Tabernacle are one-half those of Solomon's Temple, except the height. Both had a surrounding court containing an altar for burnt-offering and a laver on a base (Solomon's had ten). In some respects the Tabernacle seems to resemble the second Temple more closely than Solomon's: for example, in dividing the most holy place from the holy place with a veil rather than doors (although a veil would be natural in a tent-like structure), and in having one seven-branched lampstand rather than ten lampstands.

Taken as a whole, the Tabernacle was intended by P to represent the tabernacling presence of Yahweh with Israel, as is clearly stated in 25:8; 29:45f. It accords with the promise of Ezek. 37:27: 'My dwelling place shall be with them; and I will be their God, and they shall be my people'. While Yahweh was believed to be present in the whole Tabernacle, he is represented as speaking specially with Moses from above the mercy seat of the Ark, within the most holy place (25:22). Thus is carried on the 'tent of meeting' tradition that there is a special place at which Yahweh reveals his will by speaking face to face with Moses (33:11). The Tabernacle, as a temple, was also the place where Yahweh was worshipped and where offerings were made to him by his anointed priests. P assumes the idea of the single sanctuary for the whole of Israel.

The Tabernacle is referred to by a variety of names. The commonest is 'tent of meeting', the name used by E; P uses it about 130 times. Sometimes it is called only 'the tent'. Another very common name is *miškān*. This is the word usually translated as tabernacle, following Vulgate's *tabernaculum*. In Hebrew it properly means dwelling-place, abode, and the like, and it fittingly describes the nature of the structure. The word *miškān* usually refers to the Tabernacle as a whole, but in a few places (see 26:1–6) it has a narrow meaning, referring to something which is only a part of what is usually called the Tabernacle. In our own discussions, we capitalize the word Tabernacle to refer to the structure as a whole, and use 'tabernacle' for the portion in 26:1–6. Another name used by P for the Tabernacle is 'tent of the testimony', because the decalogue was known to P as 'the testimony' and was contained in the Ark. P also employs the general term 'sanctuary' (*miḳdāš*, 25:8 etc.).

The whole of chapters 25–31 are attributed to P, and it is generally admitted that P shows considerable unity or uniformity in both its theology and its style. However, some scholars have detected two or more strata within the P material, particularly in the present chapters. K. Galling, following generally the lead of G. von Rad (*Die Priesterschrift im Hexateuch* [1934]) distinguishes in the present account three strata: Pᴬ, Pᴮ, and Pˢ (=P sequens). He thinks that in chapters 25–29 Pᴬ is responsible for the organization of the material, and Pᴮ for the minuteness of detail. Pᴮ is often responsible for the details that are the more costly (such as the abundant use of gold), and less realistic. In chapters 26–29, Pᴮ predominates. Pˢ is responsible for 30:1—31:11 (a long section believed by many critics to be a secondary addition). In the present commentary, no attempt has been made to carry through his analysis in detail, but some references are made to it when it seems relevant and enlightening. (Galling's analysis is found in his exegesis of chapters 25–31, 35–40 in Beer's commentary; see especially the table on p. 13. His analysis is more extensive and detailed than von Rad's.) For a form-critical study, see Klaus Koch, *Die Priesterschrift von Exodus 25 bis Leviticus 16* (1959).

This section of Exodus contains many obscurities, especially in the details of the Tabernacle. The reader should consult a good Bible dictionary, particularly one that contains illustrations that are reproductions of what the author thinks the Tabernacle and its details must have resembled. One of the best and most thorough is still A. R. S. Kennedy's article 'Tabernacle', in *HDB*, IV (1902), pp. 653–68. His illustrations are reproduced by many other books. For modern views, see G. H. Davies's article in *IDB*, IV, pp. 498–506; and F. M. Cross, 'The Priestly Tabernacle', *BA*, X (1947), pp. 45–68 (=*The BA Reader*, I, pp. 201–28). Cross makes stringent efforts to show that archaic elements persist in the Tabernacle, and that there is a line of continuity between it and the desert tent of meeting. His view is well summed up in these words: 'While the Priestly account is schematized and idealized, and while the Priestly writers read the theological interpretations and historical developments of later ages into their system, nevertheless, Priestly tradition must be deemed an important historical witness to the Mosaic Age' (p. 209).

THE OFFERING BY THE PEOPLE 25:1–9

Yahweh tells Moses to request that the people bring an offering of the various materials that will be needed for the Tabernacle and its furnishings. 35:20–29 describes how they brought their 'freewill offering' to Yahweh, consisting not only of raw materials, but also of jewelry, various kinds of cloth spun by the women, and the like. The purpose was that they should make for Yahweh **a sanctuary, that I may dwell in their midst.** Moses is given a **pattern of the tabernacle, and of all its furniture.**

3. gold, silver, and bronze: the failure to mention iron does not prove that the making of the Tabernacle goes back to the time before the introduction of iron. In Palestine iron was used almost exclusively for weapons and tools. 1 Chr. 22:3 is probably erroneous; cf. 1 Kg. 6:7; Dt. 27:5. **bronze** was probably usually more or less pure copper, rather than the alloy of copper and tin to which we give the name bronze.

5. goatskins: it is not certain that *tǝḥāšîm* means goats. According to some scholars, we should translate 'porpoise skins' or 'fine leather' (the latter assuming it is a loan-word from Egyptian).

acacia wood: much use was made of this wood in the Tabernacle and its furnishings in order to make it portable. It was a hard, close-grained and durable wood, very suitable for cabinet-making. Some species of it were found in Sinai as well as in Palestine. *AV* renders it 'shittim wood', merely transliterating the Hebrew name, *šiṭṭîm*.

6 is missing from LXX, and may be a secondary addition.

8. let them make me a sanctuary: *miḳdāš* is one of the numerous words for the Tabernacle; see introductory note above. **that I may dwell in their midst:** this states succinctly the primary purpose of the Tabernacle: it is to be the sanctuary in which Yahweh permanently dwells, or tabernacles, in the midst of Israel. One of the commonest names for the Tabernacle is *miškān*, 'dwelling', used in 25:9 and elsewhere about 100 times.

It is also 'the dwelling of Yahweh' (Num. 16:9 etc.) and 'the dwelling of the testimony' (38:21 etc.). Cf. 29:43–46.

9. All was to be made according to **the pattern of the tabernacle, and of all its furniture,** given to Moses by God. Cf. 25:40; 26:30; 27:8; and 1 Chr. 28:19, for the Temple of Solomon. See also Heb. 9:23–24.

THE ARK **25:10–22**

In the instructions for making the Tabernacle and its various furnishings, the Ark takes first place, although in the account of the execution of the instructions the making of the Tabernacle is described (36:8–38) before the Ark itself (37:1–9). The reason for this is that the Ark occupied a central role in the whole structure, because it was from above the Ark that Yahweh spoke with Moses (verse 22).

The Ark was originally a battle palladium leading the Israelites into battle and representing Yahweh as 'Lord of hosts' (Num. 10:35f.; 14:44). It accompanied them as they crossed the Jordan, and was installed in a sanctuary in Shiloh (1 Sam. 4). The Philistines captured the Ark in battle, but subsequently returned it (1 Sam. 4–5). David took it in a ritual procession to Jerusalem, where he placed it in his tent-sanctuary (2 Sam. 6), and it was subsequently installed in the inner sanctuary of the Temple of Solomon (1 Kg. 8:1–9). Nothing is known of its final fate; there was apparently no Ark in the Temple of Zerubbabel.

Numerous theories have been proposed as to the function and appearance of the Ark. One of the most widely held is that it was considered to be the portable throne on which the invisible Yahweh sat. This is supported in part by the fact that the Ark as a battle palladium could be addressed as 'O Yahweh' (Num. 10:35f.) and some support for this view can be found in the present section. The word *'ārôn*, however, means a chest or casket in 2 Kg. 12:10f.; Gen. 50:26.

Although this is one of the most detailed descriptions we have of the Ark anywhere, we cannot be sure it is wholly reliable. It probably represents the Ark as much more splendid than it actually was, and some of the details are difficult to understand. Noth even goes so far as to say: 'P probably knew no more than that the ark had stood in the innermost part of the pre-exilic temple, and from this made up a picture of the ark' (p. 203). The Ark was placed 'within the veil' in the most holy place of the Tabernacle (26:33). In the Temple of Solomon it was in the holy of holies, or inner sanctuary.

10. an ark of acacia wood: according to Dt. 10:3 the Ark was made of acacia wood. Apart from that passage and the numerous occurrences in this section of P, acacia is mentioned only in Isa. 41:19. The Ark was two and a half cubits long, and a cubit and a half in both breadth and height. In ancient Israel two cubits were known. One was the common cubit (Dt. 3:11) of six handbreadths, which has been calculated as being very close to 17·5 inches in length. But there was also a cubit of seven handbreadths, mentioned in Ezek. 40:5; 43:13 (cf. 2 Chr. 3:3), approximately three inches longer, or 20.5 inches. Since P is later than Ezekiel, it is possible that he uses the longer cubit, but this is not certain. For the sake of convenience in our discussion, we use a measurement of 18 inches for the cubit. If the common cubit is intended, this is very close; if the longer cubit of Ezekiel, it is a little short. Thus, we estimate the Ark measured 3¾ feet long, and 27 inches in breadth and height.

11. overlay it with pure gold: this probably means overlay with gold leaf, which would be quite possible (cf. 39:3). Some scholars believe that here and elsewhere the reference is to *inlaying* with gold.

a molding of gold: there was a similar moulding on the table (verse 25). Nothing is said as to where the moulding was; it must have been a merely decorative item. See also 30:3.

16. You shall put into the ark the testimony: *hā-ʿēḏūṯ* is P's word for the Decalogue, which he uses in various combinations ('ark of the testimony', 'tables of the testimony', 'dwelling of the testimony', etc.). According to Dt. 10:5 Moses put into the Ark the second tables of stone which he made. Before D and P, nothing is said of the contents of the Ark.

17. The translation of *kappōreṯ*, here rendered **mercy seat**, a phrase first used by Tyndale (1530), probably under the influence of Luther's *Gnadenstuhl*, is very problematic. The difficulty arises in part from uncertainty as to the root of the word. It is associated by some scholars with the root *kippēr*, meaning 'atone, make propitiation', and the like. LXX usually renders *kappōreṯ* by *hilastērion*, and the Vulgate by *propitiatorium*. Hence, many scholars prefer the English rendering, 'the propitiatory'. They point out that in the ritual for the Day of Atonement described in Lev. 16, it is said that the priest shall sprinkle some of the blood of two sacrificial animals on and in front of the *kappōreṭ*, making atonement for himself, the holy place and the tent of meeting. Yet, this Day of Atonement is a ritual that probably was introduced very late into the Hebrew cult, and it was on only this day that the *kappōreṭ* served a propitiatory function.

Other scholars associate the word with the root *kāpar*, meaning to cover, and interpret the *kappōreṭ* as a cover or lid for the Ark (*NEB* and *RSV* mg. have 'cover'). Its length and breadth were the same as those of the Ark, and it could be placed upon the Ark, not being an integral part of it (40:20).

The problem is difficult to resolve. Noth and Galling prefer the translation 'cover', but the *Am. Tr.* prefers 'propitiatory'. While it is possible that the object did have some connection with propitiation, there is nothing in the etymology of the word or description of the object to suggest a 'seat' or 'throne'. The idea could be derived from passages such as verse 22 and passages referred to above, which know the Ark as a battle palladium.

18–20. The **cherubim** were imaginary creatures conceived as part human and part animal—usually human-headed but having wings and the body of an animal, such as a bull or lion. They were widely known in Mesopotamia as guardians of temples and palaces (and the name is of Akkadian origin, *kāribu*). In the area of Syro-Palestinian art it is natural to think that they were generally conceived as human-headed, winged *lions* (see *ANEP*, nos. 128, 332, 458, 649). The cherubim are often associated with the Ark. In 1 Sam. 4:4, the Ark is called 'the ark of the covenant of the Lord of hosts who is enthroned on the cherubim'. Cf. also 2 Sam. 6:2; 22:11; Ps. 18:10; 80:1; 99:1. It is difficult, however, to derive a clear picture from the description here of the cherubim and their relationship to the 'mercy seat'. Verse 19*b* says that they were **of one piece with the mercy seat . . . on its two ends.** Could this mean they were engraved in shallow relief on the *kappōreṭ*? Verse 20, however, suggests a different picture. Galling thinks that P[B] is responsible for 19*a* and 20, and that he has been influenced by the description of the cherubim in 1 Kg. 8:7 which says that 'the cherubim spread out their wings over the place of the ark, so that the cherubim made a covering above the ark and its poles'. However, the cherubim described in 1 Kg. 6:23–28 are very large, ten cubits in height, with each having wings of five cubits each. (This is perhaps a good example of the fact that P had never seen the Ark; cf. quotation from Noth above).

22 is significant as showing why the Ark was of such great importance. It was **from above the mercy seat, from between the two cherubim** that Yahweh promised he would meet with Moses and speak with him. This apparently combines two ideas: one, that Yahweh *met with* Moses when Moses entered the tent of meeting, as described in 33:11; and the other, that Yahweh sat enthroned above the Ark as the invisible war deity.

THE TABLE OF THE BREAD OF THE PRESENCE 25:23–30

This is the table sometimes called the 'table of shewbread', after *AV's* translation of 'bread of the Presence' as 'shewbread'. It corresponds to 'the golden table for the bread of the Presence' in Solomon's Temple (1 Kg. 7:48). This was not an altar (a place of sacrifice), but an offering table such as was known in other religions of the ancient Near East (cf. *ANEP*, nos. 392, 400, 624; and Isa. 65:11; Bar. 6:30). In the Tabernacle it was placed in the holy place on the N. side (26:35). Lev. 24:5–9 describes how the priests were to place on the table every sabbath twelve baked cakes, in two rows, and also frankincense. The cakes were subsequently eaten by the priests, and the incense offered up. Verse 29 and Num. 4:7 suggest that libations were also made from the table.

The antiquity of the practice of keeping holy bread before Yahweh is indicated by the incident described in 1 Sam. 21:1–6. David demanded bread of Ahimelech the priest, and was told that he had no common bread, but only holy bread. When assured that David's men were in a state of ritual purity, he gave them the holy bread to eat. The practice probably originated in the very ancient notion that the Deity must be given food to eat, just as human beings are.

It may be possible to get an impression of the appearance of this table from the Arch of Titus, on which are depicted the objects taken by the Romans from Jerusalem; see *IDB* i, p. 464, illus. 49. The table of the second Temple was probably taken away by Antiochus Epiphanes (1 Mac. 1:23), and another was installed by Judas Maccabeus (1 Mac. 4:49). It may be the latter which is depicted on the Arch of Titus. We cannot, of course, be sure that it corresponded in detail to the table described here. See also Josephus's description in *Ant.* iii.vi.6.

23. On the length of the cubit, see verse 10. The table top measured three feet by a foot and a half, and it was 27 inches high.

25. It is difficult to know how best to render *misgéret*, here given as 'frame'. Galling thinks that 25a is P^B's duplicate of P^A's 24b, both describing the same thing. The Arch of Titus table shows on two sides cross-stays which hold the legs firm, about half way down from the table top to the bottom of the legs. This may be the object described, though it may have originally extended on all four sides. The measure, **a handbreadth**, is approximately three inches, which appears to be about the width of the cross stays on the Arch. Galling further thinks that 25b is from a later redactor who wanted to put a moulding around the 'frame'.

29. Lev. 24:7 speaks of incense being placed on the table, and Num. 4:7 mentions also the plates, dishes, flagons, and bowls here. Apparently drink offerings were involved as well as the presentation of the bread. If the practice originated in the idea of feeding the deity, such would be expected.

30. The bread placed on the table, and subsequently eaten by priests, is here called **the bread of the Presence,** *léhem pānîm,* the phrase occurring also in 1 Sam. 21:6; 1 Kg. 7:48 in addition to these chapters of Exodus. In this phrase, *pānîm,* lit. face(s), stands for the person or the self of the deity, so that the phrase virtually means 'the bread of God', just as various sacrifices are called 'the bread of God' in Lev. 21:6,8,17; 22:25. In Lam. 4:16 the *pānîm* of Yahweh is rendered by *RSV* 'the Lord himself'. The same idiom is used for persons in 2 Sam. 17:11 (of Absalom) and Prov. 7:15. Thus, this phrase is not to be interpreted as signifying that Yahweh was especially present at this table. The whole of the Tabernacle was his dwelling; if he was especially present at any point within it, that place was above the Ark (verse 22).

In post-Exilic literature the 'bread of the Presence' had various names. The commonest was *léhem hamma^ᶜᵃrékᵉṯ,* lit. 'bread of the arrangement'—i.e., bread that is arranged (or set before) God (1 Chr. 9:32; 23:29; Neh. 10:33). This could be abbreviated to *hamma^ᶜᵃrékᵉṯ,* 'the arrangement' (1 Chr. 28:16; 2 Chr. 29:18). Other names were *léhem hattāmîḏ,* 'continual bread' (Num. 4:7 P) and *ma^ᶜᵃrékᵉṯ tāmîḏ* 'continual arrangement' (2 Chr. 2:4). Jerome used the expression *panes propositionis* ('bread of the exhibition') from which apparently came Luther's *Schaubrot* and Tyndale's 'shewbread' (in Heb. 9:2, where the Greek is *hē próthesis tōn artōn,* very similar to LXX of 2 Chr. 13:11). Strangely, *RSV* itself uses 'showbread' seven times in the *OT* (in 1, 2 Chronicles and Nehemiah), but uses 'bread of the Presence' in the *NT* (Mk 2:26

and parallels, which refer to the incident of 1 Sam. 21; and Heb.
9:2).

THE LAMPSTAND 25:31–40

This section describes the lampstand (*menorah*) which was placed
on the S. side of the holy place, opposite the table (26:35). The
use of the term 'candlestick' in *AV* is anachronistic, since candles
were invented later by the Romans. In ancient Israel a lamp was
essentially a shallow bowl with one or more spouts pinched in the
rim to hold the wick(s), with oil being placed in the bowl. In the
course of time the lamp developed into a closed vessel, with a hole
in the top to receive the oil, and with one or more spouts. A great
many have been found in excavations, and the development of the
lamp is easily traced. Lampstands of clay or of metal have been
found.

The Temple of Solomon had ten lampstands in the nave
(1 Kg. 7:49), but 1 Mac. 1:21; 4:49 indicate that the second
Temple had only a single lampstand, and it is presumably that
which is described here. The Arch of Titus depicts a seven-
branched *menorah* which may give a good idea of the one which
was in the Herodian Temple. The reader is referred to the
representation of that *menorah* in *IDB* iii, p. 65, illus. 10, and also
the reconstruction from the account here by A. R. S. Kennedy in
S. R. Driver, p. 276 (from *HDB*). The description is difficult to
understand, because the meaning of some terms are poorly
understood, and the account has few verbs.

One can get much help in understanding this description if he
notes that the lampstand had numerous representations of almond-like flowers. The word 'cup' in the account means the
whole open flower; 'capital' (*kaptōr*) should be understood as
calyx, and 'flowers' (*pᵉrāḥîm*) as 'petals'.

The lampstand apparently consisted of a base (probably a
tripod), from which extended a single shaft; from the shaft there
went out three branches on each side, probably to the same height
as the central shaft. The shaft and six branches were each capped
by a whole open flower, with its calyx and petals represented.
Apparently the seven lamps were placed on top of these. In
addition, the branches and the central shaft were ornamented with
open flowers, probably totalling fifteen. (We should remark that
Galling considers the elaborate description in verses 33–36 to be
the work of Pᴮ.)

The whole lampstand is said to have been made of one piece, **of hammered work of pure gold** (36). It was surmounted by **seven lamps** (37), but we are not told whether they were ceramic or metal (the former would be more normal), nor whether each was seven-spouted, like the lamps of Zech. 4:2. Seven-spouted lamps have been found by archaeologists. No symbolical significance is given to the lampstand; its purpose was **to give light upon the space in front of it** (37).

39 A talent weighed approximately 64 lbs.

THE TABERNACLE **26:1–36**

This chapter describes in detail the structure to which we usually give the name Tabernacle. Yet, it is obvious that in verse 1 'tabernacle', *miškān*, has a narrow meaning and applied to the awning-like structure described in verses 1–7. In most other places *miškān* means the whole Tabernacle in the usual sense (25:9 etc.).

Let us first describe in simple terms the over-all structure described in this chapter, as translated by *RSV*. Details can be dealt with in the comments below. We should begin with the largely wooden temple-like structure described in verses 15–29. It consisted of 48 trellis-like frames, or boards, and twice as many bases or pedestals into which these could be fitted. The frames were held together by rings and cross-bars, and could be dismantled when the structure was moved. This building covered a space of approximately 45 by 15 feet, half the dimensions of the Temple of Solomon, not including the vestibule (1 Kg. 6:2–3). It was 15 feet high, one-third the height of Solomon's Temple.

Over three sides of this wooden structure was placed a 'tabernacle' consisting of ten curtains (or sheets) of very fine material embroidered with cherubim. These curtains had loops of blue and could be fastened with clasps of gold. It was placed over the two sides, the back, and the top, but not the front. Over the 'tabernacle' was placed a tent made of goat's hair, with less costly clasps made of bronze instead of gold. This consisted of eleven curtains. The whole structure had two coverings, one of tanned rams' skins and one of goatskins, apparently placed on top of each other (see comment on 26:14 for translation).

This Tabernacle was divided by a veil of richly embroidered material into two parts: a most holy place containing the Ark, and a holy place containing the table of the bread of the Presence and the lampstand. In front was a screen of various fine materials, embroidered with needlework, on five acacia pillars which were overlaid with gold.

It should be obvious to any reader that this is a very unrealistic structure, certainly for a group of people in the desert, as has been pointed out in the introduction to chapters 25–31. Noth has aptly remarked, 'There is no analogy to this astonishing construction anywhere in cultic history' (p. 211).

Galling believes that P^A is responsible for the description of the goats' hair tent in verses 7–14, and that P^B has added the 'tabernacle' of verses 1–6 and the wooden structure of 15–30. He thinks that a genuine historical tradition underlies the description of the goats' hair tent, for it is a nomadic tent such as has been known from time immemorial in the desert, but with exaggerated dimensions. The descriptions of P^B are largely the product of phantasy, based upon some knowledge of the Temple of Solomon and possibly subsequent temples.

Without necessarily subscribing to the literary criticism of Galling we may say that verses 7–14 must represent the oldest element of the tradition, possibly being based upon memory of the tent of meeting of E (33:7–11) or the tent sanctuary of David (2 Sam. 6:17). The rest attempts to integrate the temple tradition with the desert tent tradition. It is significant that the dimensions of the Tabernacle are approximately half those of Solomon's Temple, and it includes most of the same furnishings and basic theological ideas.

Many details in this chapter, as in other chapters dealing with furnishings of the Tabernacle, are difficult to translate or understand; reference may be made to a Bible dictionary, such as those referred to above, p. 263. It is especially helpful to look at illustrations which attempt to reconstruct the Tabernacle; Kennedy's reconstructions have been frequently reproduced by other scholars.

1–6 describe the 'tabernacle' (*miškān*), here used, as noted above, in a narrow sense. Its materials are unusually fine, including costly tapestries and clasps of gold.

1. fine twined linen: *šēš* is an Egyptian loan-word; the author may thus have in mind fine imported Egyptian linen. The **blue and purple and scarlet stuff** was woollen material principally manufactured and dyed on the Phoenician coast. The first was a bluish-purple, and the second a reddish-purple. The third, *tōlā°at*, gets its name from the insect, *Coccus ilicis*, from which the scarlet colour was secured. The **cherubim** were doubtless embroidered on the material (cf. 26:36), as cherubim were carved on the woodwork of the walls and doors of Solomon's Temple (1 Kg. 6:29,32,35).

2. The dimensions are such that the curtains of the 'tabernacle' did not quite reach the ground, being covered by the longer curtains of the goats' hair tent (cf. verses 8, 13).

7–14 describe the goats' hair tent which was placed over the object just described. According to Galling (see above), it was essentially a normal desert tent, with somewhat exaggerated dimensions, that represents the old tradition of the E tent of meeting. He reconstructs it as a tent which is held up by poles and guy-ropes (see Beer's commentary, p. 135, illus. 1).

7. for a tent over the tabernacle: Galling conjectures that this may have originally read 'for a tent of meeting'.

9. and the sixth curtain . . . front of the tent: this detail, along with verses 12–13, has caused much debate. The description in chapter 36 of the making of the Tabernacle omits 9*b*, 12, 13, probably because the author did not understand them! Galling thinks that the extra curtain of 9*b* formed a covering over the front of the tent, and that verse 12 is an unnecessary addition.

13. Since the dimensions of the curtains of the tent indicate that they were two cubits longer than those of the 'tabernacle', the goats' hair tent falls one cubit longer on each side, thus giving protection to the 'tabernacle', and reaching the ground.

14. Although the two objects thus described apparently were thrown over the top as well as three sides of the wooden structure, there are two additional coverings. One is of **tanned rams' skins.** Some scholars render this 'rams' skins dyed red' (thus *JB*), and compare it with the pre-Islamic Arabic *qubbah*, which was a miniature red leather tent, sometimes made so that it could be carried on the back of a camel, and generally containing a tribal idol of some type. Etymologically the word used here, *meʾoddāmîm*, could have such a meaning, a *pual* participle of a word meaning 'to be red'.

goatskins: for meaning see comment on 25:5. The *RSV* rendering is a little too compact, suggesting that there may have been a single covering made of the two materials. More accurately the Hebrew could be rendered (using *RSV* meanings): 'And you shall make for the tent a covering of tanned rams' skins and a covering of goatskins above that'.

15–30 describe the portable wooden structure over which were to be placed the goats' hair tent and the fine tapestry awning described in the previous verses. It was made of materials which could be dismantled and moved, but which could be made stable when the Tabernacle was set up for use.

15. upright frames: this assumes that *kᵉrāšim* were open frames rather than solid boards. Kennedy argued strongly for the view represented in *RSV*, but Galling still thinks of them as boards. If they were open frames, they would be much lighter for transportation, and also would allow the beautiful curtains of the 'tabernacle' with their embroidered cherubim to be seen from inside the building. The Ugaritic word *ḳrš*, which occurs in the Baal epic and signifies the 'pavilion' or 'apartment' of El, Father of years (J. Aistleitner, *Wörterbuch der ugaritischen Sprache*, 3rd ed., 1967, p. 283; cf. *ANET*, p. 129, line 5; p. 133, line 24) offers no help; it represents a different semantic development from the root *ḳrš* which occurs in Akkadian, Arabic and other languages with the meaning 'to divide, to cut off'.

17. two tenons: if correct, this means the two pins at the lower end of each frame that fit into the mortises of the bases. It may be better (with Kennedy) to consider *yāḏôṯ* (lit. 'hands') as the two upright arms which formed two sides of each frame, which had in addition three cross-rails, one each at the top, the bottom, and the middle (cf. verse 28).

19. bases of silver were necessary as foundations for the frames. Each must have had one mortise to receive a pin which extended down from the upright arm of the frame.

23–24 are difficult to translate and interpret. Kennedy thought that *miḳṣōᶜōṯ* of these verses meant 'buttresses' rather than 'corners'. According to the *RSV* rendering, the two frames were separated at the bottom and then joined near the top, so as to form a sloping buttress. Some scholars believe that the word *tōᵃmîm*, lit. 'twinned', should be rendered 'doubled', and that *tammîm* (**joined**) should be emended to the same word. Thus, they get a doubling at both top and bottom. In either case, the result is to secure a strengthening of the walls at the rear corners, and probably also structures that would take up the folds of the curtains at the corners.

26. bars of acacia wood: these are cross-bars of acacia, overlaid with gold (verse 29), which were designed to pass through the rings that were attached to the frames, and thus hold the frames together when the structure was set up for use.

28. The cross-bar which was designed to run through the rings on the middle cross-rails of the frames was of one piece, for each side, thus adding to the stability of the whole structure. For each of the two sides we must imagine a bar 45 feet long!

30. Cf. 25:9,40. The word for 'plan' here is *mišpāṭ*, whereas in the two other verses it is *taḇnîṭ*. This is a very unusual meaning for *mišpat*, found elsewhere only in 1 Kg. 6:38; Jer. 30:18.

31–35 describe the division of the Tabernacle into two parts by a veil. The two parts, the holy place and the most holy (place) correspond to two parts of the Temple of Solomon: 'the inner sanctuary' (*deḇîr*) (1 Kg. 6:19–23), and the 'nave' (*hêḵāl*) (1 Kg. 6:3,17, etc.). The Temple of Solomon had in addition a vestibule (1 Kg. 6:3), to which there is no corresponding part here; it was primarily an entrance porch.

31. The **veil** was made of the same materials, and ornamented in the same way with cherubim, as the curtains of the 'tabernacle' (verse 1). The two rooms of the Temple of Solomon were separated by doors of olivewood (1 Kg. 6:31). There may, however, have been a veil of this type in the Herodian Temple. In the *NT* it is said that, at the time of the crucifixion, the curtain of the Temple was rent in two, from top to bottom (Mk 15:38 and parallels; cf. Heb. 6:19f.; 10:19–22).

33. The **ark of the testimony** is placed within the veil, in the most holy place, just as the Ark was placed within the inner sanctuary of the Temple of Solomon (1 Kg. 8:6).

This verse, taken along with certain others, seems to indicate that the most holy place was a perfect cube, measuring 10 cubits, or 15 feet, in each dimension. The holy place then would have measured 30 feet in length and 15 feet in breadth and height. This is concluded from the fact that the veil dividing the two rooms was hung **from the clasps,** presumably the clasps of verse 6 which held together the two sets of five curtains each. (Since each curtain in verses 1–6 measured four cubits, five would measure 20 cubits, making a total of 20 cubits, or 30 feet.) Other computations show that the breadth and the height were 10 cubits each. In the Temple of Solomon the inner sanctuary (*deḇîr*) was also a cube, measuring 20 cubits, or 30 feet, in each dimension (1 Kg. 6:20), twice the size of the most holy place of the Tabernacle.

34. the mercy seat: see comment on 25:17.

35. the table is described in 25:23–30, and **the lampstand** in 25:31–40.

36. The **screen** is made of the same fine materials as the curtains of verse 1 and the veil of verse 31. It is **embroidered with needlework,** but cherubim are not specifically mentioned. The same word, *māsāḵ*, is used for the screen at the gate of the court (27:16), and the veil of verse 31 is sometimes called the veil of the screen (35:12; 39:34 etc.).

There is some evidence, hardly conclusive, that the second Temple may at one time have had a curtain in front, similar to the curtain here. According to 1 Mac. 4:51, when the Jews under Judas Maccabeus restored the Temple which had been desecrated by Antiochus Epiphanes, they 'hung up the curtains'. The Letter of Aristeas, sec. 86 (written sometime in the first or second century B.C.), apparently describes a curtain that was in front of the main entrance. In Josephus' description of the Herodian Temple (*War* v.v.4), there is a full-length curtain of Babylonian tapestry in front of the double doors leading into the nave.

THE ALTAR OF ACACIA WOOD **27:1–8**

The altar described here is elsewhere called 'the altar of burnt offering' (30:28; 31:9), or 'the bronze altar' (38:30; 39:39). It was an altar for offering animal sacrifices, to be distinguished from the incense altar of 30:1–10 and the table of the Bread of the Presence of 25:23–30. It was placed in the court in front of the Tabernacle (cf. 40:29). This altar corresponds to the sacrificial altar which was found also in the court of the Temple of Solomon and subsequent Temples. Strangely, that of Solomon's Temple is not described in 1 Kg. 7, but the description in 2 Chr. 4:1 may be authentic (unless the dimensions are exaggerated). Ezekiel describes an altar in his ideal Temple in 43:13–17, and Ezra 3:3 refers to the altar of Zerubbabel's Temple. The present altar was made of acacia boards, but was hollow, and was overlaid with bronze. The erection of such an altar is clearly out of harmony with the ancient instructions in 20:24–26 (see comments there). Also, one may rightly wonder whether an altar which was a hollow wooden box overlaid with bronze could have withstood the great heat necessary in the offering of sacrifices, particularly the whole burnt offerings. This is another indication of the artificiality of the accounts of the Tabernacle and its furnishings.

1. This altar was relatively small as compared with the altar of

Solomon as described in 2 Chr. 4:1, and Ezekiel's altar, 43:13–17. The dimensions are the same as the 'bronze platform' on which Solomon knelt as he prayed for Israel, according to 2 Chr. 6:13.

2. And you shall make horns for it on its four corners: the altar of Ezekiel had four horns (43:15), and archaeologists have discovered several altars (mostly incense altars) having horns. They are projections at the four corners. Using the same proportions as in Ezekiel's altar, S. R. Driver conjectures that the horns here were about seven inches high. The horns of an altar were of importance in the ritual; they were smeared with blood at the consecration of priests (29:12), in the sin-offering (Lev. 4:18ff.), and on the Day of Atonement (Lev. 16:18). In early days, before the establishing of the cities of refuge, seizing the horns of an altar gave asylum to a person guilty of accidental homicide (see comment on 21:13–14).

3. These utensils were necessary in the offering of sacrifices; cf. 1 Kg. 7:40,45.

4–5. The altar had a **ledge** that was half way down the altar, and beneath this was a **grating, a network of bronze.** The purpose of these is not stated, nor is it immediately apparent. The altar of Ezekiel had two ledges, described with a different Hebrew word (see reconstruction in *IDB*, 1, p. 98). It is usually thought that the ledge of the present altar was for the priests to stand upon as they made sacrifices on the top of the altar; some scholars, however, doubt that such would have been necessary with an altar only four and a half feet high. Perhaps it was only ornamental. The grating, too, may have been only ornamental; or, it may have been intended to prevent ashes and the like from falling upon the lower part of the altar, against which the blood was dashed.

8. You shall make it hollow, with boards: some critics have conjectured that this hollow altar was filled with earth, to fulfill the regulation of 20:24, but there is no evidence of that. Also, such an altar would have been very heavy to transport.

as it has been shown you on the mountain: cf. 25:9,40; 26:30.

THE COURT OF THE TABERNACLE **27:9–19**

The Tabernacle was surrounded by a court, just as was the case with the Solomonic and later Temples (1 Kg. 6:36 speaks of an 'inner court' for Solomon's Temple, implying there may have been more than one; the Herodian Temple had four courts of increasing sanctity—for Gentiles, Israelite men and women, and priests). The Tabernacle court measured 150 by 75 feet, and was surrounded by a wall composed of hangings of fine twined linen stretched between sixty pillars. It was entered by a gate on the eastern side indicating that the Tabernacle was oriented toward the rising sun.

9. hangings of fine twined linen: the Hebrew word for **hangings** is different from that used in 26:1ff. for the curtains of the 'tabernacle', and the material is less costly.

10. These hangings were attached to, and thus stretched between, a total of 100 **pillars,** which were placed in **bases,** both apparently **of bronze.** From the mention in verse 19 of 'all the pegs of the court' and in 35:18 of 'the pegs of the court, and their cords', we may infer that the pillars were held in place by cords used as guy-ropes, tied to pegs that were driven into the ground. **fillets:** this word (*ḥªšukîm*) probably refers to bands which surrounded each base of the capitals of the pillars. The capitals are not mentioned in the present chapter, but in 38:17. Some scholars think they were silver rods connecting the pillars, from which presumably the hangings were hung. See verse 17 below.

16. On the eastern front of the court was a **gate,** composed of a **screen,** with four pillars on four bases. The word for screen, *māsāk*, is the same word used in 26:36 for the screen in front of the Tabernacle (see comment there), and both were made of the same fine embroidered materials.

17. All the pillars around the court shall be filleted with silver: see comment on verse 10 above. The meaning is probably that the capitals of the pillars were bound around with silver bands; however, 38:19 can be interpreted as meaning that the bands were only overlaid with silver. The other interpretation suggested above is expressed in the rendering of *JB*: 'All the posts enclosing the court are to be connected by silver rods'.

19. On **pegs of the court** see verse 10 above. The vague reference here to **all its pegs** and to 'pegs of (or for) the tabernacle' in 35:18; 38:20,31 suggest that such pegs were used to fasten down the 'tent over the tabernacle' described in 26:7–14. The word is the usual word for a tent-peg (Jg. 4:21; 5:26).

OIL FOR THE LAMPSTAND **27:20–21**

Moses is told to command the Israelites to bring pure beaten olive oil for the light that is to burn continually outside the veil in the

tent of meeting. This section is almost verbatim equivalent to
Lev. 24:2-3, and is very widely considered to be a secondary
addition to P. Galling attributes it to P^S.
20. pure beaten olive oil for the light: the best of olive oil is
to be brought. Hebrew for 'light' is *māʾôr*. In 35:14 and Num. 4:9
the lampstand described in 25:31-39 is called *mᵉnōraṯ hammāʾôr*,
lit. 'the lampstand of light'. It seems very likely that here, and
also in 25:6; 35:28; Num. 4:16, the word *māʾôr* is an abbreviation
for the longer phrase. Hence, the instruction is to bring oil 'for the
lampstand'. This is borne out by the fact that in several other
passages the priests are said to take care of the *lamps* (30:8; Lev.
24:4; 2 Chr. 13:11). Lev. 24:4, which is a continuation of verses
virtually corresponding to the present section, says: 'He (Aaron)
shall keep the lamps in order upon the lampstand of pure gold
before the Lord continually'. Thus, we may assume that this section
has to do with providing for the lamps on the lampstand, in spite
of the fact that the terms used suggest at first sight a single light
or lamp.
21. In the tent of meeting, outside the veil: within the holy
place, where the lampstand customarily stood (26:33-35).
from evening to morning: this may suggest that the lamps
were lit only during the hours of darkness. In 1 Sam. 3:3 'the lamp
of God' burns only during the night. However, it is likely that
some illumination was needed in the Tabernacle in the daytime,
and that a continual light, by both day and night, is intended
(see end of verse 20).

THE GARMENTS OF THE PRIESTHOOD **28:1-43**
This chapter gives instructions for making the holy garments of
the priesthood. It is devoted almost exclusively to the vestments
for Aaron—that is, for the high priest. Only a few verses at the end,
verses 40-43, describe the far less impressive garments of Aaron's
sons—that is, the ordinary priests. In P, as is well recognized, the
priesthood is confined to the descendants of Aaron. After an
introduction (verses 1-4), this chapter describes the following
priestly garments: the ephod (5-14), the breastpiece of judgment
(15-30), the robe of the ephod (31-35), the turban and its plate
of gold (36-38), three miscellaneous items (39), and the garments
of Aaron's sons (40-43).
   Many of the details of this description are obscure, and translation of several items very difficult. In some places the description

is too meagre, while in others it seems too full. At any rate, the clothing prescribed for the high priest is likely to impress us as being costly and elaborate, and also fulsome and even heavy.

It seems probable that this is not just an ideal description by P, but that in some manner and at some times these items of clothing were worn by the high priest in the post-Exilic period. The description in Sir. 45:6–12, which agrees in most respects with the present chapter, may represent the high priest's vestments as they appeared to an onlooker in the second century B.C., when Jesus ben Sirach lived. See also Josephus' description of the priestly vestments in *Ant.* III.vii.1–6. The order of description, however, is hardly the order in which he placed them on himself. It is almost certain that the robe of verses 31–35 was placed on before the ephod and the breastpiece; otherwise their fine work and precious stones would have been covered. See below, after comments on verses 40–43.

Some of the items mentioned here were associated with the priesthood from very early times—e.g. the ephod. Others apparently represent royal insignia taken over by the priesthood after the monarchy had ceased—e.g. the breastpiece, and the crown (verse 36). In this manner the vestments of the high priest symbolized his assumption of cultic duties performed by the former kings.

The fulsomeness of this account has led some critics to resort to drastic literary criticism to separate two or more strata. Galling thinks the chapter is made up about equally of P^A and P^B elements. For example, he believes that verses 9–11 (P^A) and verses 17–21 (P^B) are doublets, both describing ornaments with settings of precious stones. However, such literary division is not wholly convincing, and in a number of places the various items are coupled together as if they were written by the same author. Nevertheless, there are no doubt some additions. The chapter may have originally described only the garment of Aaron, the only 'anointed' priest in the earliest stratum of P, with verses 1 and 40–43 being additions.

5–14 describe the **ephod**. This word is taken over directly from Hebrew, *'ēpōḏ*, because we do not know how best to translate it into English. The ephod is mentioned numerous times in the *OT*, but apparently with different meanings or purposes.(i)Sometimes it is clearly a priestly garment, such as the 'linen ephod' (*'ēpōḏ bāḏ*), worn by the boy Samuel (1 Sam. 2:18), and by David when he was conducting the Ark to Jerusalem (2 Sam. 6:14); cf. 1 Sam. 22:18. (ii) At other times the ephod seems to be a solid object of some kind, such as an image of a deity (Jg. 8:27; 17:5; 18:14ff.). (iii) In still other passages it appears to be an object used in consulting Yahweh—that is, in securing oracles. The best example is 1 Sam. 14:3,18–19,36–42 (here verse 3 has 'ephod' and verse 18 has 'ark' for what is obviously the same object; LXX reads 'ephod' also in verse 18). See also 1 Sam. 23:6–12; 30:7–8. The ephod may have contained the Urim and Thummim.

Some critics think that 'ephod' was used to describe two or more different objects. Others think that the word always refers to a garment of some nature, either placed upon an idol or worn by a priest. Sometimes an ephod in a shrine was too large to be carried around, whereas others were small enough to be carried, as in military operations. In some manner the ephod as a garment was used in consulting oracles, perhaps with a pocket or pouch containing the Urim and Thummim. For this view see G. H. Davies, 'Ephod (Object)', *IDB*, ii, pp. 118f.; cf. de Vaux, *Ancient Israel*, pp. 349–52. Another, more radical view is that of W. R. Arnold (*Ephod and Ark* [1917]). He maintained that in early Israel there were several Arks, and that the Ark was essentially an oracle-box. The ephod, on the other hand, was always a priestly garment. In the course of time the doctrine arose that there was only one Ark—namely, the one which came to be installed in David's tent-sanctuary and Solomon's Temple. Then, the word 'ephod' was substituted in the *OT* text in every place for 'ark' (the words are similar in Hebrew script), where the latter referred to any ark other than the principal one. Arnold's basic proof passage is the Hebrew of 1 Sam. 14:18 which twice mentions 'the ark of God' as being with Saul in the field at a time when the main Ark was supposedly at the home of Abinadab in Kiriath-jearim (1 Sam. 7:1f.). He says that this is the one verse which editors missed who made the substitution of 'ephod' for 'ark' in all other necessary passages. In 1 Sam. 14:18 LXX reads 'ephod' where the Hebrew text has 'ark of God'; according to most scholars this is the correct reading, but according to Arnold it is only the LXX's attempt to harmonize verse 18 with verse 3 of the same chapter. Arnold's view is attractive, but beyond the possibility of solid proof.

In any event, it is incontrovertible that the ephod was in early Israel a priestly garment; see category (i) above. It is generally

believed to have been a linen loin-cloth, or kilt-like skirt, such as
was worn at times by Egyptian priests (cf. the words of Michal in
2 Sam. 6:20). There is evidence that in very ancient times Sumerian
priests officiated nude (see *ANEP*, 597, 600, 603, 605). Ritual
tends to be conservative; the ephod of David's time was probably
a simple loin-cloth such as all men had worn at a somewhat
earlier time, and priests continued to wear when laymen had come
to have more elaborate dress.

The ephod here has been interpreted by some as being like a
waistcoat (Josephus, S. R. Driver). With more likelihood, others
have thought of it as a garment for the lower part of the body.
Am. Tr. renders it as 'apron'. It may have been something like
that, for it was attached to the breastpiece of judgment, which
was apparently above it (verses 27f.). However, the ephod here
has no oracular significance. The Urim and Thummim (see on
verse 30 below) were in the breastpiece of judgment.

5. gold: 39:3 speaks of the hammering out of gold leaf to make
it into threads.

blue and purple, etc.: these are the same materials used in the
making of parts of the Tabernacle; see comment on 26:1.

7. two shoulder-pieces were for the purpose of holding up
the ephod, and also to receive the objects described in verses 9ff.
An Egyptian tomb inscription of the VIth Dynasty shows male
dancers with two shoulder pieces on each, holding up a brief
garment like a loin-cloth (*ANEP* 210; cf. also 640 which seems to
show one strap apiece).

15–30 give instructions for making the breastpiece of judgment,
for which the Hebrew word is *ḥōšen mišpāṭ*. *JB* renders it 'pectoral
of judgment', thus using an appropriate ecclesiastical term (cf. the
pectoral cross). *Am. Tr.* translates, 'oracle pouch', which indicates
the purpose of the object. It was made of materials similar to those
of the ephod. On it were set four rows of three precious stones each,
engraved with the names of the tribes of Israel. Within it were the
Urim and Thummim.

Noth has pointed out that this object probably derives from the
royal tradition, rather than from the priestly. He refers to a royal
breastpiece found in the tomb of a king of Byblos of the Middle
Bronze Age. 'It consists of an approximately rectangular gold
plate set with precious stones and hangs from a gold chain which
is directly reminiscent of the "twisted chains" of v. 14.' (p. 222).
He says that the 'covering' of the king of Tyre in Ezek. 28:13 is to

be similarly understood; it contained only nine stones, but all of them occur in the present list.

16. The breastpiece **shall be square and double, a span its length and a span its breadth.** It was approximately 9 inches square, and doubled, or folded over, like a purse or pouch, so that it might contain the Urim and Thummim (verse 30).

17–20. The precise translation of the names of these precious stones is uncertain. For a discussion of the terminology of these and other stones in the light of both literary references and archaeological discoveries, see P. L. Garber and R. W. Funk, art. 'Jewels and Precious Stones', in *IDB* ii, pp. 898–905. For example, in verse 18, *sappîr* apparently does not mean our true **sapphire,** which would be too hard for the ancients to work, but lapis lazuli, objects made of which have been found in great numbers in Egypt and Mesopotamia, and some in Palestine. Also, *yoha̒lōm* probably does not mean **diamond,** for the method of cutting diamonds was not discovered until the fifteenth century A.D. It may have been some form of jasper.

23–28. The purpose of these arrangements was to attach the breastpiece firmly to the shoulder-piece and the ephod, so that it would lie flat on the breast. Details are obscure.

30. the Urim and Thummim were sacred lots which, in earlier times, had been used in consulting Yahweh through the oracular process. The best example, which shows rather clearly how the Urim and Thummim were employed, is to be found in 1 Sam. 14:36–42. This should be read in the *RSV*, which in the crucial verse 41 gives a correct text, following the Vulgate and LXX rather than the Hebrew. They were obviously contained in the ephod, mentioned in verse 3 (or the 'ark of God' of verse 18; see above, comments introducing verses 5–14). The Urim and Thummim are associated with the priesthood in Dt. 33:8(Levi); Num. 27:21 (Eleazar), and Ezr. 2:63 (= Neh. 7:65). See also 1 Sam. 28:6. In earlier times, they apparently were arranged in a box or pouch in such a way that a priest could put in his hand and withdraw one or the other and secure a 'Yes' or 'No' answer, or an answer deciding between two alternatives; sometimes there was no answer. We do not know what the names meant in ancient times, nor what the objects looked like. It has been suggested they were stones (of different shapes or colours), sticks, or dice. They may not have been used for oracular purposes after the time of David; thenceforth the prophets gave the word of Yahweh. They do not seem to have served any such purpose in the high priest's breastpiece here; they are a vestigial remnant of an older custom (cf. Ezra 2:63=Neh. 7:65). The word 'judgment' (*mišpāṭ*) in the name preserves the old idea that the object was somehow associated with the giving of oracles (or, more precisely, that that was the purpose of the Urim and Thummim).

31–35 describe **the robe of the ephod all of blue.** It was a long and probably sleeveless robe or mantle, usually worn over the 'coat' (properly 'tunic') of verse 39. This robe was to have **an opening for the head,** with a woven binding around it to keep it from being torn. On its skirts it was to have a series of alternating pomegranates and golden bells.

The *meʿîl* was an outer garment which was worn in earlier times only by persons of high position or social standing—e.g. by Saul (1 Sam. 24:4f.), Jonathan (1 Sam. 18:4), Samuel (1 Sam. 2:19; 15:27), Ezra (Ezr. 9:3,4), and Job (1:20; 2:12).

33. pomegranates were plentiful in ancient Palestine; in ancient art and mythology they were often symbolical of fertility but no such symbolism is apparent here. The pomegranates were to be made of the same kinds of cloth so often mentioned in these chapters, **blue and purple and scarlet stuff,** but it is not clear whether they were embroidered on the hem of the robe or were made into balls and suspended from the skirt as the **bells of gold** must have been. Josephus' description suggests the latter (*Ant.* III.vii.4).

35. its sound shall be heard . . . lest he die: originally this must have rested upon the primitive notion that the sound of the bells would frighten away any demons who might be present. In its present form, the verse means either (a) the high priest is to follow this practice **lest he die** for breach of an important ceremonial requirement; or (b) as long as the people can hear the tinkling of the bells the people know the high priest is still alive; if they cease for a long period, the people may suspect accidental death and take appropriate measures.

36–38 describe the making of the **plate of pure gold** which is to be fastened **on the turban by a lace of blue.** The plate is to be engraved with the inscription: 'Holy to the Lord'. The high priest's turban is mentioned in verse 39 as 'a turban of fine linen'.

36. a plate: the usual meaning of *ṣîṣ* is blossom, or flower (Num. 17:8; Isa. 40:7f.; Ps. 103:15 etc.). In three other passages where the same object is referred to, the word *nēzer*, 'crown', occurs: 29:6, *nēzer haḳḳōḏeš*, 'the holy crown'; 39:30, *ṣîṣ nēzer haḳḳōḏeš*, 'the plate of the holy crown'; and Lev. 8:9, *ṣîṣ hazzāhāḇ nēzer haḳḳoḏeš*, 'the golden plate, the holy crown'. In pre-Exilic times the crown (*nēzer*) had been worn by kings (2 Sam. 1:10; 2 Kg. 11:12; Ps. 89:39 etc.). The association between the crown and the idea of blossoming is suggested by Ps. 132:18 which can be literally rendered, 'His (David's) enemies I will clothe with shame, but upon him his crown will blossom' (*RSV:* 'will shed its lustre'). In the light of these passages, we must conclude that *ṣîṣ* here is meant to signify the crown or diadem of gold to be fastened to the turban of the high priest. This is further borne out by the fact that Sir. 45:12 speaks of 'a gold crown upon his turban, inscribed like a signet with "Holiness"'; and that Josephus (*Ant.* III.vii.6) says the turban of the high priest 'was encircled by a crown of gold wrought in three tiers, and sprouting above this was a golden calyx recalling the plant which with us is called *saccaron*'. He continues with a long description of that plant. If Josephus is correct, this may give another clue to the use of the term 'blossom' for the crown of gold. The *Am. Tr.* is therefore justified in translating *ṣîṣ zāhāḇ* here as 'a diadem of pure gold'. In 39:30 it translates, 'the diadem, the sacred crown', and in Lev. 8:9 'the gold diadem, the sacred crown', thus indicating that *ṣîṣ* and *nēzer* are synonyms for the same object (cf. Lev. 8:9 *RSV*).

This wearing of a crown by the high priest is another example of the adoption by the priesthood of a symbol formerly associated with the kings of Israel, like the breastpiece of judgment. **'Holy to the LORD':** the high priest has been set apart as being especially holy to Yahweh, and he represents Israel as a holy people.

38. The high priest is to accept responsibility for any involuntary ritual transgressions in carrying out the ceremonies of the cult.

39 mentions only briefly three additional items: a **coat, a turban of fine linen,** and **a girdle embroidered with needle-work.**

coat: a better rendering of *kᵉṭōneṯ* is 'tunic', as *RSV* in Job 30:18. This was the usual undergarment for both sexes. It was a long robe, usually with sleeves. The rendering **in checker work** is not certain, and is thought to be involved in the verb, *šibbaṣtā*. The verb may mean simply 'to weave'.

a girdle: 'sash' is a better modern word here. *'abnēṭ* occurs in the *OT*, aside from P passages describing this item, only in Isa. 22:21, where it is worn by a high official of the king. It is not the ordinary word for girdle or sash. Josephus gives an elaborate description of this sash, which he says had 'the appearance of a serpent's skin', and was wound twice around the body, over the tunic, the ends hanging to the ankles. (*Ant.* III.vii.2). The Talmud says it was 32 cubits long (48 feet).

40–43 describe the garments which are to be made for Aaron's sons, the ordinary priests. As noted above, this section may be a secondary addition; in any case, however, the ordinary priests must have had vestments, but we could expect them to be much less elaborate than those of the high priest.

coats: tunics; see verse 39.

girdles: sashes, the plural of the word used in verse 39. Josephus's description mentioned above applies to the word used in verse 39.

caps: *migbā'ôt* is often taken to signify conical caps, from the supposed derivation from a verb meaning 'to be high'. But the use of the verb 'bind' (*ḥābaš*) with this item in 29:9 and Lev. 8:13, and Josephus's description in *Ant.* III.vii.3, suggest that this head-gear was in reality a turban. It would no doubt have been simpler than the turban of the high priest.

42. linen breeches: these were undergarments, which we would call 'drawers' (so *NEB*). The use of them would prevent the priests from breaking the rule of 20:26. According to both Sirach (45:8) and Josephus (*Ant.* III.vii.4), these were worn by the high priest as well as the ordinary priests.

We have raised above the question as to the order in which these various items of the priestly vestments were put on. It may be of interest to note how Josephus describes their order, for he obviously is describing them in the order in which they were put on by the priests. For ordinary priests the order was: (1) the linen breeches, (2) the tunic (of verse 39), bound with the elaborate sash, and (3) the cap or turban. To these the high priest added: (4) the robe of blue material, also held by a sash as colourful and elaborate as the former, (5) the ephod and breastpiece, which he describes in the same long paragraph; and finally (6) the head-dress, consisting of a turban like that of the other priests, and a crown of gold. This seems to be a natural order, and with it the ephod and breastpiece would have been visible. Cf. the order in 29:5.

THE CONSECRATION OF THE PRIESTS **29:1–46**

This chapter contains instructions to Moses for the consecration of Aaron and his sons to the priesthood. It is assumed that Moses himself is to carry out the instructions, and thus he is to act in a priestly capacity. Lev. 8 records the carrying out of the instructions here given. We are to assume that this chapter reveals the procedure by which the high priest and the ordinary priests were consecrated in the post-Exilic period, but of course it must contain some ancient elements.

The chapter is generally well organized up to verse 25, but then occur some inconsistencies and confusion, and some sections that have nothing directly to do with the consecration of the priests. The procedure for consecrating the priests consisted of the following: (i) bringing the materials for the necessary offerings (verses 1–3); (ii) washing the priests (4); (iii) investiture and (iv) anointing of Aaron (5–7); (v) investiture of the sons of Aaron (8–9); (vi) offering up of three types of sacrifices: (a) a sin offering (10–14), (b) a burnt offering (15–18), (c) a ram of ordination (19–28, 31–34), and (d) sin offerings every day for seven days (35–36a). To this are added sections concerning the vestments for the sons of Aaron (29–30), the offerings over seven days as atonement for the altar (36b–37), the regular daily offering (38–42), and a conclusion to chapters 25–29, which gives clearly the theology of the Tabernacle (43–46).

It seems probable that Lev. 8 was known to the principal author of this chapter, and it is clear that some secondary additions have been made to it. Galling attributes most of the chapter to P^B and P^S, with P^A being responsible for only 42b–43 and 45–46.

1. The word for **consecrate** is *kiddēš, piel* (with a factitive meaning) of a verb meaning 'to be set apart'. To consecrate the priests was to set them apart from the profane sphere in order that they might perform holy duties. Note that in verse 44 Yahweh himself is the subject of the same verb; it is he who consecrates the tent of meeting, the altar, and the priests. For the word 'ordain', see verse 8.

4. wash them with water: it is generally thought that this was a washing of the whole body, but nothing is said as to where it was to take place. In the court of the Tabernacle was a bronze laver in which the priests washed their hands and feet (30:17–21).

5–6. The garments are described in detail in chapter 28. Note that **the coat** was a 'tunic' (28:39); on **the holy crown** see comment on 28:36.

7. The **anointing oil** is here poured on the head of Aaron only. It seems that in the earliest stratum of P only Aaron himself was anointed; in a later stratum, the sons of Aaron (the ordinary priests) were also to be anointed (see comment on 30:30, with references there). There is no solid evidence for the anointing of priests in the pre-Exilic period. The anointment of the priest in the post-Exilic period is another example of the assumption by the priesthood of some of the perogatives held in pre-Exilic times by the kings (see 28:15–30,36–38). The prescription for preparing **the anointing oil** is given in 30:22–33; it was to be made of spices and olive oil. On the anointing of Aaron, cf. Ps. 133:2.

8–9. On the vestments of the ordinary priests, see 28:40–43. **Thus you shall ordain Aaron and his sons:** the Hebrew is lit. 'and you shall fill the hand of Aaron and the hand of his sons'. On the origin of the idiom *millēʾ yad X*, 'fill the hand of someone', see comment on 32:29. The origin of the idiom must have been lost at an early time, so that *milluʾîm*, 'filling' (plural) came to mean 'ordination'. In verses 22, 26, 27, 31, the 'ram of ordination' is lit. 'ram of *milluʾîm*'. In the opinion of many scholars, 'install' is a better rendering than 'ordain'. *RSV* so translates the idiom in Jg. 17:5,12. The Israelite priesthood at this time was an hereditary office, not a vocation. Hence, it is more appropriate to speak of the priest as being installed in his office than as being ordained.

10–14 describe the offering up of the young bull as a sin-offering. See Lev. 4 for the general regulations for the sin-offering. Here the bull is completely burnt, either on the altar or outside the camp. In the sin-offering for a layman, part of the offering was eaten by the priest (Lev. 6:26).

15–17 describe the sacrifice of one of the rams as a burnt offering, the whole animal being burnt upon the altar. See Lev. 1. It was characteristic of this type of offering that the complete animal was consumed on the altar, none being left to be eaten by the priest or worshipper.

19–25 describe the sacrifice of the second ram, the ram of ordination. This was one of the most characteristic features of the consecration ceremony. Verse 20 describes how Moses was to take part of the blood and put it on the tips of the priests' right ears, the thumbs of their right hands, and the great toes of their right feet. A very similar ceremony was perfomed, with oil and blood, in the rite for the cleansing of lepers (Lev. 14:14,17). The words used by A. Dillmann in explaining the meaning of this ceremony have often been quoted or paraphrased. 'The priest must have consecrated ears to listen at all times to God's holy voice, consecrated

hands continually to do holy works, and consecrated feet always
to walk in holy ways' (see McNeile, p. 190). In the light of Lev.
14:14–17, this may be more homiletical than exegetical!
21 is considered by most critics to be a secondary addition.
Cf. 30:26–30; Lev. 8:30. Aaron has already been anointed in
verse 7, and all of the blood has been used up in verse 20.

22–28 describe the offering of the second ram as a **ram of
ordination**; the procedure is continued in verses 31–34, which
show that (in spite of a certain amount of confusion in the description) the offering was treated very much as if it were a 'peace
offering'. A better rendering for this type of sacrifice, *zébaḥ šelāmîm*,
is 'communion sacrifice', for it was designed to bring about a
communion with the deity through the sharing of the elements of
the sacrifice between the deity (that which is burnt on the altar),
the priest, and the worshipper (the latter two participating by
eating). See further below on 31–34.

24. The ram of ordination is also to be treated as a **wave
offering** (*tenûpāh*). The offering is waved, not from one side to the
other, but toward the altar and back, symbolical of the fact that
the offering is first given to God and then back to the priest for
his use (Lev. 7:30; 23:20). On the significance of this verse and
verse 25 for the idiom for ordination, see comments on 32:29.

26. the breast of the ram of Aaron's ordination is to be
your portion—i.e. Moses' as the officiating priest (cf. Lev. 8:29).

27–28 are apparently secondary, and somewhat inconsistent
with what has preceded, since verse 25 has implied the burning of
the right thigh (verse 22), and the breast has been given to
Aaron. On the whole question, cf. Lev. 7:31–36. There it is stated
that the breast is to be given to the priests, and the right thigh is
for the officiating priest. For earlier practice, see Dt. 18:3.

29–30. The vestments of Aaron are to be for his sons who
follow him. **30** seems to mean that it is only the son who succeeds
him as high priest who is to be invested with his holy garments
during the consecration ceremony that lasts for seven days (cf.
below verses 35–37). The verse does not mean, in any case, that
all the priests were vested in the same manner as the high priest
(Aaron).

31–34 continue the procedure for the rite of the **ram of
ordination**. Its flesh is to be boiled and the priests are to eat of it,
together with **the bread that is in the basket, at the door of
the tent of meeting.** In this manner, as indicated above, the

K

ram of ordination is treated as if it were a communion sacrifice.
For this type, cf. Lev. 3; 7:11-18; 22:18-23. See comments on
24:5.

35-37. The ritual of consecration is to last for seven days.
35-36*a* apparently means that a sin offering is to be offered every
day for the priests, but the other items of the ritual are not to be
repeated. 36*b*-37 describe regulations for consecrating the altar
(the great altar of sacrifice in front of the Tabernacle, 27:1-8).
It is to be anointed, and a sin offering is to be made for it. On the
anointing, cf. 30:26-29. Cf. also the long and elaborate ceremony
for consecration of the altar in Ezek. 43:18-26.
whatever touches the altar shall become holy: cf. comment
on 30:29*b*.

38-42 is a section that is not directly concerned with the
consecration ritual; it describes the regular daily offerings to be
made in the Tabernacle, one in the morning and one in the
evening. For pre-Exilic practice, see 2 Kg. 16:15, which prescribes
a morning burnt offering and an evening cereal offering. See also
Ezek. 46:13-15. The present section is virtually equivalent to
Num. 28:3-8.

43-46 is a conclusion to the instructions which have been
given in chapters **25-29.** Here is expressed clearly the theology of
the Tabernacle as conceived by P.

43. There I will meet with the people of Israel: at the door
of the tent of meeting (verse 42) Yahweh will meet with the
Israelites, as in E's tent of meeting Yahweh had met with Moses
(33:9 'the pillar of cloud would descend and stand at the door of
the tent'). One may, however, compare 25:22 which says that
Yahweh will meet with Moses and speak to him 'from above the
mercy seat, from between the two cherubim that are upon the
ark of the testimony'. Perhaps there is no contradiction: the place
above the mercy seat was the place of special revelation to Moses.
it shall be sanctified by my glory: the antecedent of 'it' is the
tent of meeting, or its door, of verse 42, since 'people of Israel' is
plural, lit. 'sons of Israel'. Vulgate supplies as subject 'the altar'.
LXX, Syriac, and the Targum of Onkelos presuppose a text
which read, 'I will be sanctified by my glory'. The *RSV* rendering
is satisfactory. On **my glory,** see comment on 24:16. According
to 40:34, when all the work had been finished on the Tabernacle,
'the cloud covered the tent of meeting, and the glory of the Lord
filled the tabernacle'.

45. I will dwell among the people of Israel, and will be their God: cf. 25:8. This is the part of P's theology which carries on the Temple tradition of pre-Exilic times. The Temple was considered to be the dwelling-place of Yahweh; see especially 1 Kg. 8:12-13, which incorporates a very ancient conception of the Temple as the abode of the deity.

46. And they shall know that I am the LORD their God: see comment on 6:7.

THE ALTAR OF INCENSE **30:1-10**

This section, along with the whole of chapter 30, is attributed by many scholars to a secondary stratum of P (Galling assigns it to Pˢ). There are valid reasons for this. The most natural place for the description of this altar would have been in chapter 25, where the lampstand and table of the Presence-Bread are described. Further, 29:43-46 reads very much as if it were the conclusion to the description of the Tabernacle and its furnishings. Another reason is that in most of the summary descriptions of the furniture of the Tabernacle, only one altar is mentioned, meaning the large altar for burnt offerings. The description of the making of the altar, 37:25-28, is much shorter, and is omitted in the LXX.

There was apparently a small altar of incense in the nave of the Temple of Solomon, made of cedar wood overlaid (or inlaid?) with gold (1 Kg. 6:20,22; 7:48). The passages mentioning it are believed by some critics to be secondary, and many critics since the time of Wellhausen have argued that the offering of incense did not become a legitimate part of the cult of Yahweh until the seventh century B.C., about the time of Jeremiah. The question is indeed complicated, and the evidence is ambiguous. It is complicated by the fact that incense was sometimes offered in a hand censer (Lev. 10:1; Num. 16:1ff.; Ezek. 8:11), and that a particular type of incense altar, the *ḥammān*, probably of Arabian origin, was always condemned (Lev. 26:30; 2 Chr. 14:5; 34:7; Isa. 17:8; Ezek. 6:4,6). But it is certain that there was an incense altar, or golden altar, in the second Temple (1 Mac. 1:21; 4:49; Lk. 1:11), and that would sufficiently account for the present description of such an altar in the Tabernacle, even if it should be true that there was no such altar in the Solomonic Temple.

Archaeological discoveries have been made that may help us to understand the incense altar depicted here (see K. Galling, art. 'Incense Altar', in *IDB*, II, pp. 699f.). Ceramic incense stands have been found from pre-Israelite times, but the objects that may be incense altars have been found in several places—no less than a dozen in Palestine, of which eight were found at Megiddo. These come from the tenth to the fifth centuries. Each is a relatively small rectangular block of hewn stone, often having a decorative border, with a slight depression in the upper surface and usually four horns at the corners (see *ANEP* no. 575; cf. nos. 579, 581, 583). Some show evidence of burning on the top. These are usually interpreted as incense altars, although they may usually (or always) have been used in family cultic worship rather than in temples. Some are doubtless Canaanite, but some are very likely Israelite. Nelson Glueck, 'Incense Altars', *Translating and Understanding the Old Testament*, ed. H. T. Frank and W. L. Reed (1970), pp. 325-29, maintains that all the incense altars found in Palestine should be dated between the seventh and fourth centuries B.C.

1. of acacia wood shall you make it: an incense altar made of wood is quite possible. That of the Solomonic Temple is described as made of cedar wood, overlaid with gold (see above). The incense may have been placed in a small pan or bowl (cf. 2 Chr. 26:19), and in any event the fire would not have been as hot as with an animal offering.

2. The altar was small; some of the altars found by archaeologists have dimensions similar to those given here.

its horns shall be of one piece with it: the large altar also had horns; see 27:2. Many of the archaeological objects mentioned above have horns, of one piece with the stone of the rest of the altar.

3. a molding of gold round about: there was a similar moulding on the Ark (25:11) and the acacia table (25:25). Some of the stone altars of incense mentioned above have a moulding that is a little above the mid-point of the altar. The moulding was apparently only ornamental, having no functional purpose.

6. you shall put it before the veil: within the holy place in front of the veil, apparently between the lampstand and the table of the Presence-Bread. Because of the ambiguity of the statement in 1 Kg. 6:22b and probably the phrase here, **by the ark of the testimony,** the tradition grew up that the incense altar was *within* the holy of holies, along with the Ark; see Heb. 9:4.

9. You shall offer no unholy incense thereon: $k^e\underline{t}\bar{o}re\underline{t}$ $z\bar{a}r\bar{a}h$,

lit. 'alien (or foreign) incense'. This means any incense which is
not appropriate to offering on this altar, as is described in verses
34–38; other types of incense could be made for personal perfume
(verse 38), and for use in hand-censers to be used outside the
Temple. Cf. the phrase 'ēš zārāh ('unholy fire') of Lev. 10:1;
Num. 3:4; 26:61.

10. The ritual for the annual day of atonement is contained in
Lev. 16. Verse 18 of that chapter speaks of the priest putting
blood on the horns of 'the altar which is before the Lord'. This is
usually interpreted to mean the large altar for animal sacrifice
(cf. Lev. 16:11–12). However, the Talmud (b. Yoma, 58b)
interprets this as the golden altar of incense. The directions for the
sin offering mention specifically the placing of blood on the horns
of 'the altar of fragrant incense before the Lord' (Lev. 4:7,18).

THE HALF SHEKEL OFFERING 30:11–16

When the census is taken of the people of Israel, Moses is to
demand that each one pay half a shekel as a ransom for himself, so
that there may be no plague among the Israelites. The money is
to be used for the service of the Tabernacle.

This apparently refers to the census which is reported in Num. 1,
made at the command of the Lord. The statement that the
payment was to be a half shekel, to be used for the service of the
sanctuary, is to be interpreted as justification for the annual
half-shekel Temple tax required of all Jews at a later time (Mt.
17:24). It is not known just when this tax was instituted; it may
have been in Nehemiah's time. According to 2 Chr. 24:6,9, the
tax was collected by King Joash, but this is doubtless an unhistorical
addition by the Chronicler (though it may indicate that by his
time the tax was being required). See Neh. 10:32, referred to
below.

12. **each shall give a ransom for himself to the LORD:** the
idea that the taking of a census was dangerous is found in 2 Sam.
24; Yahweh commanded David to take a census, and then
punished him for doing so. The same idea is found among many
peoples, ancient and modern. It may rest upon the notion that the
number of the people is a secret that should be known only to
God; or it may rest only upon the mundane view that a census is
usually taken for purposes of taxation, for military enrolment, or
the like.

13. **half a shekel according to the shekel of the sanctuary:**

the shekel was doubtless a weight rather than a coin (although
some Jewish coinage may be as early as the sixth century B.C.).
The ordinary shekel probably weighed about ⅖ oz. (about 11.6
grains).

the shekel of the sanctuary: this phrase, found only in P, could
be rendered, 'the sacred shekel'. It is not certain how it differed
from the ordinary shekel. R. B. Y. Scott has advanced the view that
the sacred shekel was about ⅙ smaller than the common shekel
(that is, about ⅓ oz. as against ⅖ oz.). He supports this in part upon
the basis of Ezek. 45:12 (see *Peake's Commentary on the Bible* [1962],
sec. 35a). He thus suggests that the ⅓ shekel tax of Neh. 10:32 was
approximately the equivalent of the ½ shekel payment in the
sacred shekel, assuming the former was calculated by the ordinary
standard.

14. from twenty years old and upward: in Num. 1:3 these
are described as 'all in Israel who are able to go forth to war'.

16. appoint it for the service of the tent of meeting: not
for the building of the tent of meeting, or Tabernacle, but for the
continual carrying on of its service. This was the purpose of the
later half-shekel Temple tax (cf. Neh. 10:32).

THE LAVER OF BRONZE **30:17-21**

Moses is commanded to make a laver of bronze, with a bronze
base, so that Aaron and his sons may wash before they minister in
the service. According to 1 Kg. 7:27-39 the Temple of Solomon
had ten bronze lavers, each on a very elaborate stand. The stands
are described in much detail, and the laver in more detail than is
given here. Since the Tabernacle is smaller than the Solomonic
Temple, it apparently is assumed that one laver is sufficient.
Nothing is said here of its size; the lavers in the Solomonic
Temple were large, each holding 40 baths (about 920 litres, or
200 imperial gallons).

In 38:8, where the making of the laver and its base is recorded,
the curious tradition is related that they were made 'from the
mirrors of the ministering women who ministered at the door of
the tent of meeting'. See comment below on 38:8.

20. lest they die: the priests risk death if they perform their
cultic acts in a state of ritual impurity; here bodily purity and
ritual purity are closely related. In P, death is threatened for a
number of transgressions of ritualistic regulations (28:35,43;
Lev. 8:35; 10:7).

THE HOLY ANOINTING OIL **30:22-33**

Moses is instructed how to make the holy anointing oil. With it he is to anoint the tent of meeting and its various furnishings, as well as Aaron and his sons. This oil is to be considered always as holy, and is not to be used for secular purposes.

23. Take the finest spices: spices were well-known in Israelite times, and were used for various purposes. It seems likely that most of them were imported through Arabia, but that country was not necessarily the source of all of them. **myrrh** was made from the resin of *Commiphora myrrha;* that it was known in liquid form as well as in its solid form is indicated also by Ca. 5:5,13. **cinnamon** is still well-known and widely used. Our English word is ultimately derived from the Hebrew *ḳinnāmôn*. **aromatic cane:** there were several species of cane used as a spice, and it is impossible to determine which is intended here.

24. cassia: two Hebrew words are thus rendered. *ḳiddāh*, used here, may be the bark of a tree closely related to the source of cinnamon.

shekel of the sanctuary: see above on verse 13, where it is estimated that this shekel weighed about ⅓ oz. (9.7 g.). Using that as a basis, we estimate that all of the spices named here weighed a total of about 32 lbs. avoirdupois.

of olive oil a hin: the *hin* was ⅙ of a *bath*, or 3.831 litres (slightly less than an imperial gallon).

26-29. Moses is instructed to anoint with this specially prepared oil the tent of meeting and all of its furniture, as they have been described in the preceding chapters. This anointing sets them apart for sacred use. There was an ancient tradition in Israel for the anointing of sacred objects—e.g., Jacob's anointing of the pillar at Bethel (Gen. 28:18; 31:13; 35:14).

whatever touches them will become holy: an equally possible rendering is, 'whoever touches them will become holy.' Holiness is here conceived as a quasi-physical quality that is contagious.

30. The anointing of Aaron has already been mentioned in 29:7, and of Aaron and his sons in 28:41. There are no clear pre-Exilic references to the anointing of priests. It appears that the earlier stratum of P speaks of the anointing of Aaron—i.e., the high priest (29:7; Lev. 8:12; cf. Lev. 4:3,5,16); and a later stratum speaks of the anointing of Aaron and his sons—i.e. the whole priesthood (28:41; 40:15; Lev. 7:36; 10:7; Num. 3:3).

32. This anointing oil is not to be used for secular purposes, and no other oil just like it is to be compounded. The use of oil and spices as perfume is indicated by Prov. 7:17; 27:9; Ca. 4:10 (cf. Isa. 3:20).

33. an outsider: a *zār* was anyone outside the priesthood, whether an Israelite or a foreigner.

shall be cut off from his people: shall be excommunicated from Israel.

THE HOLY INCENSE **30:34–38**

Moses is instructed how to make the holy incense which is to be burned before Yahweh, probably on the golden altar of incense. It is not to be used for any secular purpose.

34. stacte: *nāṭāp̱* is from a verbal root meaning to drip; it was probably made from droplets of gum from the storax tree or the *opobalsamum*.

onycha: a substance probably obtained from the closing-flaps of some mollusc; *šeḥēleṭ* may have the meaning 'flap'.

galbanum: *ḥelbᵉnāh* was a resinous gum from a plant such as *Ferula galbaniflua*. The yellow or brown gum looks like amber and is very fragrant.

pure frankincense: *lᵉḇōnāh* was the whitish exudation of certain trees that belong to the genus *Boswellia*, probably imported from S. Arabia. The name is derived from its white colour. It was widely used in OT times—e.g. added to the cereal offerings (Lev. 2:1ff.), placed on the table of the Presence-Bread (Lev. 24:7), and used as a perfume (Ca. 3:6).

35. seasoned with salt: the idea of seasoning is not necessarily implied in the verb used here; *mᵉmullāh* means literally 'salted'. The salt may have been added only to make the incense burn more quickly and with a white smoke; or, it may have had some kind of covenant connotation. Lev. 2:13 says that all cereal offerings must be seasoned with salt; 'you shall not let the salt of the covenant with your God be lacking from your cereal offering'. Both Num. 18:19 and 2 Chr. 13:5 speak of a 'covenant of salt'.

36. This probably means that the incense is to be burned on the golden altar of incense described in 30:1–10. That altar was set up within the holy place of the Tabernacle, in front of the veil, and behind the veil within the most holy place was the 'ark of the testimony' (see verse 6; 40:5,26f.). It is strange that it is not more clearly stated here where the incense was to be put. Some critics have thought it was to be placed in a hand-censer, but that is not likely.

37–38. Incense made according to this recipe is to be **holy to the LORD,** and is not to be used for any secular purpose; for example, **as perfume.** Cf. verses 32–33 above.

APPOINTMENT OF BEZALEL AND OHOLIAB **31:1–11**

Yahweh tells Moses that he has appointed Bezalel and Oholiab as special craftsmen for the making of the Tabernacle, and has given to all able men ability for the work. Then follows a summary of all the parts and furnishings of the Tabernacle. This section is most probably a secondary addition to P, because it shows acquaintance with the items described in chapter 30. 35:10–29 is a long account of how the Tabernacle was made by many able men (and women), and 35:30—36:1 tells of the work of Bezalel and Oholiab. In the latter, we read that Yahweh inspired them to teach (35:34). Their function must have been to instruct the other workers in the various arts and crafts needed in making the Tabernacle, and probably also to supervise their work.

2. Bezalel the son of Uri, son of Hur, of the tribe of Judah: 1 Chr. 2:19f. gives his name in this way, and describes him as a descendant of Caleb. The Calebites were absorbed into the tribe of Judah. Each of the individual names here occurs elsewhere, mostly in post-Exilic documents. Bezalel in Ezr. 10:30 is a Judahite. Uri in Ezr. 10:24 is one of the gatekeepers. Hur occurs in 1 Chr. 2:50; 4:1,4 (cf. Neh. 3:9). He is hardly the same as the Hur mentioned earlier at 17:10; 24:14.

3. I have filled him with the Spirit of God: in the *OT* the spirit of God is often regarded as the source of any exceptional human power or activity, as well as of supernatural gifts. Here the spirit is the source of that ability and knowledge which made Bezalel an outstanding craftsman and artist. (It is a mistake to capitalize spirit in the phrase 'spirit of God' in the *OT*, although it is often done in *RSV*. It is too likely to indicate that the 'Spirit of God' is an entity separate from God himself, whereas it is the outgoing power of God.)

6. Oholiab, the son of Ahisamach, of the tribe of Dan: these names do not occur elsewhere except in connection with the building of the Tabernacle. Oholiab means 'the (divine) father is my tent'. It may be compared with a Phoenician name meaning 'Baal is tent', or a Sabean name meaning 'El is tent', or with the

Edomitic name Oholibamah, the name of a wife of Esau and of
an Edomitic chieftain (Gen. 36:2,41), possibly meaning 'the high
place is my tent'. In each of these names the element 'tent'
expresses the idea of protection in a dwelling-place, usually by a
deity. By comparison, Bezalel means 'in the shadow of God (or
El)', expressing the idea of protection by the shadow of the deity.
Thus, Oholiab is a good Semitic name formation, although not
specifically found in the *OT*. It is possible that it is a name made
up to express this individual's devotion to his work in the *tent* of
meeting. Cf. the artificial names Oholah and Oholibah used in
Ezek. 23. Ahisamach does not occur elsewhere, but is a good name
formation meaning 'my (divine) brother supports'.

7–11. It is significant that this summary list of the Tabernacle
and its furnishings includes **the altar of incense** (verse 8), **the
laver and its base** (verse 9), and **the anointing oil and the
fragrant incense for the holy place** (verse 11), all of which
are described in chapter 30, which we have attributed to a
secondary hand of P.

COMMANDMENT TO OBSERVE THE SABBATH **31:12–17**

Moses is instructed to command the Israelites to keep his Sabbaths,
for they are a sign between himself and them. Anyone who
profanes the Sabbath is to be put to death. The latter part of the
section calls the Sabbath 'a perpetual covenant', and connects it
with Yahweh's resting after the six days of creation.

This whole section is verbose and repetitious. It is very likely
that Galling is correct in attributing verses 12–14 largely to P^A
and verses 15–17 to P^B. Verses 13–14 are close in their terminology
to Ezekiel and the Holiness Code (Lev. 17:26). P has not before
this time set down a commandment to observe the Sabbath,
although in 16:22–26 he has spoken of the observance of the
Sabbath in the story of the gathering of manna. Here he takes the
opportunity to lay down a strong commandment to observe the
Sabbath, purportedly issued to Moses on Sinai. It may come at
this particular juncture to emphasize the fact that even in the
building of the Tabernacle the Sabbaths are to be scrupulously
observed, but this is not specifically stated. On the origin of the
Sabbath, see discussion at the end of 16:22–30. Other references
to the Sabbath in Exodus are 20:8f.; 23:12; 34:21; and 35:1–3.

13. The wording of this verse is very close to that of Ezek. 20:12.
for this is a sign between me and you: cf. verse 17. *'ôṯ,* here

rendered **sign,** has a variety of meanings in the *OT*. Sometimes it is an omen of a future event (3:12; 1 Sam. 10:7); sometimes it is a miracle (4:8–9); sometimes it is a memorial, as of the stones taken from the Jordan (Jos. 4:6). P uses it frequently as here in the sense of a pledge of the covenant relationship. The rainbow is a sign of the covenant with Noah after the flood (Gen. 9:12ff.), and circumcision is a sign of the covenant with Abraham (Gen. 17:11). In Ezek. 20:12,20, as well as here, the Sabbath is a sign. Here it is specifically a pledge that Yahweh sanctifies Israel, setting it apart as a nation in covenant with himself.

that you may know that I, the LORD, sanctify you: this idea is found often in the Holiness Code: Lev. 20:8; 21:8,15,23; 22:9, 16,32.

14. Num. 15:32–36 (P) tells of the stoning to death 'by all the congregation' of a man who was picking up sticks on the Sabbath.

every one who profanes it: 'profane' is the opposite of 'sanctify'. The word is found often in Ezekiel and the Holiness Code, seldom in P.

shall be put to death: on the phrase *môt yûmāṭ* (also in verse 15) see 21:12–17 and comments there; it occurs frequently in Lev. 20.

16. The Sabbath is to be **a perpetual covenant:** this is a phrase and idea characteristic of P—Gen. 9:16 (the rainbow); 17:7,13,19 (circumcision); Lev. 24:8 (the table of the Presence-Bread); cf. Num. 18:19. The Sabbath is both a gift of God to Israel to mark them off as a separate people (verse 13), and an obligation which they undertake as one of the terms of the covenant.

17. It is a sign for ever: cf. verse 13. Here the emphasis is on its being a sign of God's activity in creation.

and was refreshed: this bold anthropomorphism is used only here of Yahweh. In 23:12 it is used of the refreshing of men and animals on the Sabbath, and in 2 Sam. 16:14 of David's refreshing himself after the trip to the Jordan valley.

CONCLUSION **31:18**

When he finishes speaking with Moses on Mount Sinai, Yahweh gives to him the two tables of stone.

The first part of this verse is P's conclusion to the section that began in 24:15.

the two tables of the testimony is characteristic of P, who regularly calls the decalogue 'the testimony' (see comment on 25:16).

tables of stone, written with the finger of God: probably from E, fulfilling the promise made in 24:12. Cf. Dt. 9:10. In Exodus, it is always God who is represented as writing on the tables of stone, except in 34:28 (see comment there).

THE GOLDEN CALF 32:1–35

1–6(E). *The people of Israel, impatient at the delay of Moses in coming down from Sinai, ask Aaron to make them a god who shall go before them. He takes their earrings from them, and makes a molten calf. Aaron also builds an altar and proclaims a feast to Yahweh. The people make sacrifices and engage in revelry.*

7–14(RD). *Yahweh tells Moses to go down from the mountain, because the people have corrupted themselves by turning aside from the way he had commanded them. He says they are a stiff-necked people, and he will consume them, but make of Moses a great nation. Moses intercedes for Israel, praying Yahweh not to destroy those whom he has brought out of Egypt. Yahweh repents of the evil which he considered doing to his people.*

15–20(E). *Moses descends from the mountain with the two tables of the testimony in his hand. When Joshua hears the noise of the people, he thinks it is the noise of war. Moses recognizes it as the sound of joyful singing. When Moses sees the calf and the dancing, he becomes very angry and throws the two tables down and breaks them. Then he takes the molten calf, burns it with fire, grinds it to powder, scatters it on the water, and makes the people drink it.*

21–24(Es). *Moses asks Aaron what the Israelites did to him that he has brought a great sin upon them. Aaron explains his action, ending by saying that he threw the gold (of the earrings) into the fire 'and there came out this calf.'*

25–29(Es). *When Moses sees that the people have broken loose, he cries out, 'Who is on the Lord's side? Come to me'. The sons of Levi respond. He tells them to arm themselves with swords, and go forth to slay their sinful brothers and neighbours. Three thousand men fall by the sword of the Levites. Moses then says, 'Today you have ordained yourselves for the service of the Lord'.*

30–34(Es). *Moses again intercedes with Yahweh for the people. He prays that Yahweh will forgive them, and if he will not, then blot him out of the book which Yahweh has written. Yahweh replies that whoever has sinned will be blotted out of the book. He promises that the time of the punishment will be in the future.*

35(E). *Yahweh sends a plague upon the people because they made the golden calf.*

The episode of the golden calf forms the transition from the making of the covenant (chapters 19–24) and the giving of instructions to Moses (chapters 25–31) on the one hand, and the renewal of the covenant on the other (chapter 34). By making the calf, the Israelites flagrantly break the second commandment (20:4–6); Moses' breaking of the two tables symbolizes their breaking of the covenant. Through the intercessions of Moses and the punishment of some of the people, the Israelites are given a new chance; the renewed covenant is described in chapter 34.

The present chapter is obviously not unified, but very complex. Moses learns of the people's apostasy in two different ways: in verses 7–8 Yahweh tells him of the making of the golden calf; in verses 17–19, he learns of the existence of the calf when he goes down from the mountain, and is deeply angered. There are two separate stories of Moses' intercession: verses 11–14 and verses 30–34. The second of these shows no awareness of the first. Then there are several different accounts of the way the people of Israel are treated as a result of their sin. Verse 14 says that Yahweh repented of the evil he thought to do them, implying that they were not punished. In verse 20, Moses makes them drink of the ground-up image mixed with water. In verse 29, three thousand are slain by the Levites. In verse 34, Yahweh promises to punish them in the future, at the time of his visitation. Finally, verse 35 says that Yahweh smote them with a plague. These can hardly be reconciled.

These discrepancies and duplications make the literary analysis difficult. Probably the basic narrative is from E, comprising verses 1–6, 15–20, and 35. Three different sections were then added by E Supplementers (Es) at different times—verses 21–24, 25–29, and 30–34. Some critics think that verses 25–29 may be of Judaean origin. Verses 7–14 are the product of the Deuteronomic Redactor (RD), who may have put much of the chapter into its present form. There is no P material, except the single phrase 'of the testimony' in verse 15.

We can outline the probable course of the history of the traditions which are recorded in this chapter as follows. The earliest narrative was an account of the founding of the bull-cult at Bethel, which was favourable to Aaron. It is recorded in Jg. 20:28 that a grandson of Aaron ministered before the Ark when it was at Bethel. This indicates that the priesthood of that sanctuary traditionally traced its origin to Aaron. Embedded in Exod.32:1–6

is the account which was given of the founding of the cult of the
bull at Bethel (and Dan?). It may even have been the 'cult legend'
of those sanctuaries. The founding of those cults was attributed to
Jeroboam (1 Kg. 12:28–33), but it is probable that the tradition
of an Aaronite priesthood is older than his time. Murray L.
Newman, jr., in *The People of the Covenant* (1962), has sought to
give a reconstructed form of this account as it originally appeared,
favourable to Aaron and to his making of the molten calf (pp.
182–83). The present narrative of the making of the calf has
doubtless been influenced by the account of Jeroboam's action,
for verse 4*b* is virtually identical with 1 Kg. 12:28*b*, and the
sentence which speaks of 'your gods, O Israel' is appropriate to the
time of Jeroboam, but not to that of Aaron, who made only one
calf. Like Jeroboam, Aaron is said to have built an altar and
proclaimed a feast (1 Kg. 12:32). In its present form the account
of the making of the golden calf is unfavourable to Aaron, and
must come from the time after prophets such as Hosea condemned
the worship of the bulls of Dan and Bethel as idolatry and apostasy from Yahweh (Hos. 8:5f.,11; 10:5f.; 13:2). The account
preserved by E here (1–6, 15–20, 35) represents the viewpoint of
those in the northern kingdom who considered the making of the
golden calf as a great sin, punished directly by Yahweh with a
plague.

The addition of verses 21–24 represents an attempt to rehabilitate
Aaron. In this section Aaron appears in a more favourable light:
Moses is made to ask Aaron what the people did to him to lead
him to such sin, and Aaron professes not to know that he was
making a golden calf—he only threw the golden earrings into the
fire and the calf came out! It is difficult to determine when this
attempt to restore some of the prestige of Aaron originated.
The sons of Aaron do not appear as the exclusive priests until the
time of P, in the early post-Exilic age (see 28:1—29:46). The
apology made for Aaron in the present section is rather weak;
perhaps we should date it relatively early—sometime well before
Deuteronomy.

The addition of verses 25–29 was made in order to account for
the ordination of the Levites as priests. Here the Levites are
depicted as loyal to Yahweh, not having taken part in the worship
of the golden calf, and thus they are given the task of slaughtering
many of the Israelites who had done so. This is described as their
ordination to the service of the Lord (29). This cannot be seriously

considered as the historical origin of the Levitical priesthood. This section is considered by some scholars as being of Judaean origin, because it is in Deuteronomy, the basis of Josiah's reforms of 621 B.C., that the Levites are designated as the priests of the central sanctuary. However, this section could just as well have originated among Levites of north Israel who were offended by the action of Jeroboam in appointing non-Levitical priests for the sanctuaries of Dan and Bethel (1 Kg. 12:31). The story may have originated before the fall of north Israel, but it could have been put in its present position at any time before Josiah's reform.

The record concerning Moses' second intercession shows no acquaintance with the first intercession in verses 11–14. Some critics have seen in verse 34 a reflection of the destruction of the northern kingdom in 721 B.C., as the time of Yahweh's visitation. The idea expressed in verse 33 is similar to Ezekiel's conception of individual responsibility (see below), but it need not be as late as the time of that prophet.

One of the latest portions of this chapter is verses 7–14, clearly of Deuteronomic origin, a product of RD (cf. Dt. 9:12–19,25–29). The purpose of this section is to show that Yahweh was well aware of what was taking place at the foot of the mountain, and to indicate his response to the intercession of Moses.

Finally, we may briefly raise the question: does the present chapter have any historical value as the record of something which actually occurred in the desert period at the foot of Mount Sinai? Our tracing of the history of tradition in the chapter shows that it represents developments which took place over several centuries. Aaron is so shadowy a figure in the early history of Israel that it is precarious to make any historical statements about him. He may not have appeared at all in the first form of the Judaean tradition (J); he appears more often in E, and becomes a person of great prestige in P. It would be fatuous to deny that the Israelites could have committed an apostasy—either the worship of some other deity, or the worship of Yahweh by means of an idol—in the desert period. The Pentateuchal narratives present them as frequently complaining against the leadership of Moses and longing for the fleshpots of Egypt. However, we may legitimately question whether they would have had either the materials or the skill for the making of a molten calf of gold at this time. Perhaps we should conjecture that they made a carved image of a bull of

stone or wood. The idea of a *golden* calf and of Aaron's partici-
pation in its manufacture originated with the cult legend of the
sanctuary of Bethel (and Dan?).

One of the strongest impressions of this chapter as a whole is its
portrayal of the noble character of Moses. He is here represented
as the prophet *par excellence*, standing vigorously for obedience to
the commands of Yahweh, condemning sinners, but presenting
himself in self-effacing intercession on behalf of the erring people
he had led out of Egypt. While the chapter as it now stands does
indicate that many of the Israelites were punished, it is the intercession of Moses which gives to them a second opportunity of
being the covenant people of Yahweh.

MAKING OF THE GOLDEN CALF **32:1–6**

1. See 24:13,18*b*. Moses had spent forty days and forty nights on
the mountain.

Up, make us gods, who shall go before us: it is better to
render, 'make us a god'. *²elôhîm* can be singular or plural; the use
of the plural verb is influenced by 4.

2. Take off the rings of gold: these were part of the 'jewelry
of silver and gold' which the Israelites had secured from the
Egyptians (11:2; 12:35f.). Gideon is represented as making
his ephod from the gold earrings the Israelites had taken as
spoil from the Ishmaelites (Jg. 8:24–27). See also 35:5ff. and
Gen. 35:4.

4. and fashioned it with a graving tool: better rendered,
'and cast it in a mould'; the renderings of *Am. Tr., NEB,* and *JB*
are similar; cf. Beer *ad loc.*, and Torrey, *JBL*, LV (1936), pp. 259f.
The use of a graving tool to fashion a molten image is not appropriate in this situation. The word *ḥéreṭ*, which is here rendered
'graving tool', occurs elsewhere only in Isa. 8:1, where it means
stylus. It should here be vocalized *ḥārîṭ*, rendered 'bag' in 2 Kg.
5:23; Isa. 3:22 (the basic meaning is 'container'). The verbal root
used here is *ṣûr;* the same form is translated 'cast' by *RSV* in
1 Kg. 7:15, the object being the two pillars of bronze before the
Temple of Solomon. This rendering of 32:4 is supported by the
statement of Aaron in verse 24 that he threw the gold into the fire.
The suggested translation 'he tied it up in a bag' (Noth,*VT*, IX
[1959], pp. 419–22) does not really fit the context.

a molten calf: better, 'a young bull'. An *²ēgel* might be three
years old (see Gen. 15:9, using the feminine form, *²eglāh*). Ps. 106:

20 calls Aaron's image an 'ox' (*šôr*). The word is not necessarily contemptuous here.

and they said: LXX (B text) may be correct in reading 'he said'. We expect the words to be said by Aaron rather than by the people.

The description of the making of the golden calf probably reflects the making of the two bull-images in the time of Jeroboam I, rather than the actual making of an image by someone in the desert period. If the bull-image was of fairly large size, as the record seems to require, since it was worshipped by a large group, we may conjecture that it was not cast of gold alone, but rather was cast of bronze and covered with gold. Gold is relatively soft and easy to mould, but would be very difficult to cast for a large object. Objects of gold (usually small) have been found in archaeological excavations in many parts of the Near East; it seems to have been particularly plentiful in Egypt, the ore being brought from Nubia. There are numerous examples of statues or statuettes from Syria and Palestine made of bronze and covered with gold or silver, or a combination of the two (*ANEP*, nos. 481, 483, 484, 497). A striking bronze statue of a bull representing the Egyptian god Apis has been found (*ANEP*, no. 570). For later times, gold-covered images are mentioned in Isa. 30:22; 40:19; Hab. 2:19. We have suggested above that the image actually made in the desert period may have been carved of wood or stone, since the Israelites are not likely to have had the skill and resources to cast one of metal. The oft-accepted conjecture that the Kenites were travelling smiths, and the presence of Egyptian copper mines at Serabit el-Khadem in the southern part of the peninsula of Sinai are not necessarily relevant to the situation of the Israelites.

These are your gods, O Israel, who brought you up out of the land of Egypt: virtually the same words are found in 1 Kg. 12:28, in the description of Jeroboam's making of the two calves of gold for Dan and Bethel. The present passage must be influenced by that account; the mention of 'calves' is inappropriate and awkward here. Some see in it a suggestion of the polytheism involved in the apostasy. It is clear from verse 5 that the bull was considered to be an image of Yahweh.

6. and rose up to play: this suggests a fertility ceremony, probably with obscene rites. In Gen. 26:8; 39:14,17 the verb *ṣāḥaḳ* (*piel*) has a sexual connotation. See comment on verse 18, and note that in 19, Moses sees 'the dancing'.

Many scholars maintain that the bull-images erected by Jeroboam (and any earlier image erected at Bethel, or in the desert period by the Israelites) were not really considered to be idols. Inasmuch as Near Eastern religions frequently represented a deity in human form standing upon a bull or other animal (see *ANEP*, nos. 474, 486, 500, 501, 522, 531, 534, 537), the bull is interpreted as being originally only a pedestal upon which the invisible Yahweh stood. Thus, the bull-image is considered as originally a northern counterpart of the Ark, which may have been conceived as a portable throne for the invisible Yahweh, or of the cherubim, which upheld the invisible Yahweh. This could be correct for the original image(s), but in the present account, offerings are sacrificed on an altar to the image; the same is said of the calves of Jeroboam (1 Kg. 12:32, 'sacrificing to the calves that he had made'). See also verse 8 below. Thus the records in their present form consider the images to be idolatrous objects.

MOSES' FIRST INTERCESSION FOR ISRAEL 32:7–14

This section is recognized by many critics as coming from a Deuteronomic Redactor (Rd). Much of the material, in similar terminology, is found in Dt. 9:12–19,25–29. The vocabulary and ideas are more closely related to Deuteronomy than to E. It is probable that Rd put much of the chapter into its present form, not attempting to reconcile the contradictions involved in some parts of it.

11. Moses is here represented as interceding on behalf of the Israelites. Intercession was one of the functions of the prophet in ancient Israel, and Moses is shown as the intercessor *par excellence*, along with Samuel, in Jer. 15:1. He is represented as interceding for Pharaoh and the Egyptians (8:8–13,28–31; 9:27–31; 10:16–19), for Aaron (Dt. 9:20), for Miriam (Num. 12:13), and frequently for the people of Israel (also 32:30–34; Num. 11:11–25; 14:11–25; 16:20–24; 21:7–9; Dt. 9:18–29). On the present occasion he urges upon Yahweh four reasons for him to refrain from destroying Israel: (i) Israel is Yahweh's people, not the people of Moses (as is implied in verse 7); (ii) their deliverance has required the exertion of great power; (iii) the Egyptians will mock Yahweh (cf. Num. 14:13–16; Dt. 9:28); (iv) Yahweh has sworn an oath to the forefathers to give them descendants and a land.

14. And the LORD repented of the evil which he thought to do to his people: The Hebrew rendered 'repent' is *nāḥam*, *nifal*, meaning 'change one's mind or purpose'. Not infrequently in the *OT* Yahweh is said to repent. See especially Jer. 18:5–11, where it is said that Yahweh may 'repent' either of intended evil or of intended good, in response to the action of the people. The bases of Yahweh's repenting are three: (i) intercession, as here and in Am. 7:1–6; (ii) repentance of the people (Jer. 18:3ff.; Jon. 3:9f.); and (iii) Yahweh's compassionate nature (Jg. 2:18; Dt. 32:36; 2 Sam. 24:16). The Hebrew belief that Yahweh could repent is of great significance for their conception of deity: Yahweh was not conceived by them as a static Being, but rather as a dynamic and living Person in a vital relationship with earthly persons, responding to their needs and to their attitudes and actions.

BREAKING OF THE TABLETS BY MOSES **32:15–20**

This is a continuation of the narrative in verses 1–6, which was interrupted by the insertion of verses 7–14 (Rᴅ). It is a part of the basic narrative of this chapter (some critics consider verses 16–19 in whole or part as secondary to the main narrative). Moses' surprise and anger at what he sees when he descends the mountain does not accord with the statement in verses 7–8 that he had been informed by Yahweh of their apostasy. In its present position this breaking of the tablets symbolizes the breaking of the covenant between Israel and Yahweh, which is renewed in chapter 34.

15. two tables of the testimony: 'testimony' (*'ēḏūṯ*) is characteristic of P, and the single word has been inserted here by a P glossator. P sometimes calls the two tables containing the decalogue simply 'testimony' (25:16,21; 40:20), and he speaks of the 'ark of the testimony', because the tables were put into the Ark, and of the 'tabernacle (or tent) of the testimony' (25:22; 38:21, Num. 9:15 etc.). This is the only passage which gives the information that the tables were written on both sides.

16 emphasizes the divine origin of what was written on the tables. 31:18 says that the tables were 'written with the finger of God', but in 34:28, Moses writes on the tables 'the words of the covenant, the ten commandments'.

17. Joshua had apparently ascended the mountain with Moses, according to 24:13. Since he had been present with Moses and

Hur at the battle with Amalek recorded in 17:8–13, it was natural for him to interpret the shouting of the people as **a noise of war in the camp.**

18 is poetic in form, consisting of three lines, with four stresses to each line (or 2:2).

the sound of singing that I hear: the translation of *'annôṯ* as 'singing' is not certain; it is taken to be the *piel* form of the same verb used in the two preceding clauses, rendered 'shouting' and 'cry'. But this is not certain and the Hebrew text may be corrupt. LXX has 'sound of shouting of wine', which suggests that a word may have dropped out of the Hebrew after *'annôṯ*. Beer thinks *'innûg* should be read instead of *'annôṯ*, 'sound of the joyous'. In any event a rendering such as 'the sound of revelry' would give the right connotation, whatever the Hebrew text may have been; cf. comment on verse 6.

20 has led to a variety of interpretations: (i) Moses threw the image into the fire to melt it down, then ground it, and proceeded as described. (ii) The image had a central core of wood or stone on a wooden pedestal, either of which would burn in fire; he then ground the gold covering, and so on. (iii) The verse results from two different traditions: one told of the destruction of a wooden image, and the other told of the treatment of a molten image. For the last interpretation see especially S. Lehming, 'Versuch zu Ex. XXXII,' *VT*, x (1960), pp. 16–50; he thinks the oldest tradition preserved here told of the making of a wooden image by the people, but connects it with the apostasy at Baal-Peor narrated in Num. 25:1–5. Wooden images are mentioned in Hab. 2:19; Isa. 40:20; 44:14–17; 45:20. In the light of our discussion of verse 4, we think the first of these is more probable, although the second is possible. We may compare the description in 2 Kg. 23:15 of the destruction by Josiah of the altar and high place at Bethel. The Hebrew text may be corrupt at that point (*RSV* follows LXX in part), but it says that he burned the high place and ground it to dust (the object is uncertain), and burned the Ashera (probably a wooden image of the goddess).

made the people of Israel drink it: this has superficial resemblances to the ordeal described in Num. 5:23–28, by which a woman suspected of marital infidelity was examined, but Moses' action here is not an ordeal. He must have assumed that all the people were guilty. The drinking of the powdered image in water was part of the punishment; perhaps it was thought of as leading to the plague with which Yahweh smote the people (verse 35).

REBUKE OF AARON AND HIS SELF-DEFENCE **32:21-24**
This section is from a Supplementer of E (Es). Its purpose is to offer an explanation and defence of Aaron's action in making the golden calf, and thus to rehabilitate him. It must have seemed strange to many Israelites that Aaron, who became in P the ancestor of all the priests (see chapters 28-29), could have been involved in this apostasy. But the excuse offered by Aaron in verse 24 is weak. The story originated in northern circles (at the sanctuary of Bethel?) well before the time of P.

21 excuses Aaron to some extent: it was the people who did something to him to lead him into so great an apostasy.

24. See comment on verse 4 above. C. A. Simpson, who thinks that the earliest material (E) in this chapter is an adaptation of the legend of the institution of the bull-cult at Bethel by Aaron, calls this verse 'a mocking satire on the cult saga of the origin of the golden bull, telling of the miraculous creation of the image' (*The Early Traditions of Israel*, p. 205). It appears to a modern reader to make Aaron ridiculous, and must have been so read by many an ancient reader.

In Deuteronomy's account of this episode, we are told that the Lord was so angry with Aaron that he was ready to destroy him, and Moses prayed for Aaron (9:20). That narrative then continues with the incident narrated in 32:20. Did the Exodus narrative at one time contain the information in Dt. 9:20?

ORDINATION OF THE LEVITES **32:25-29**
The purpose of this section, also from Es, was to show that the sons of Levi were loyal to Yahweh and did not participate in the apostasy of the golden calf. It also seeks to explain the origin of the ordination of the Levites to the 'service of the Lord'—that is, to the priesthood. There is nothing in the rest of this chapter to indicate that the Levites did not participate in the apostasy, and critics usually give little or no historical value to this episode. The history of the Levites and of the *OT* priesthood in general is very complex and much debated (see *IDB*, *s.v.* 'Priests and Levites'). We know that the Levites are designated as the priests in Deuteronomy, but in P (and the Chronicler) the sons of Aaron are priests while the Levites are minor cultic officials (Num. 1:50; 8:14-19 etc.).

Also in Ezekiel they have a minor role (44:10-14). It is generally assumed that, before the Deuteronomic reform, many of the Levites served as priests or ministers of the local sanctuaries away from Jerusalem in various parts of the country, N. and S. (Dt. 18:6), but not all priests were Levites.

28. Levi is represented in early traditions as unusually violent and cruel. In Gen. 34:25 Levi with Simeon kills all the males of the family of Hamor to avenge the violation of their sister. In Gen. 49:5-7, in the Blessing of Jacob, Simeon and Levi are cursed for their anger and cruelty. In Dt. 33:9, in the Blessing of Moses, Levi is said to have disowned members of his family. According to many scholars, the Levites were originally a secular tribe noted for their warlike nature, later becoming a priestly caste.

29. Today you have ordained yourselves for the service of the LORD: Hebrew here uses the imperative, and is literally, 'fill your hands today for Yahweh!' *RSV* follows LXX and Vulgate in vocalizing as a past tense. The idiom 'fill the hands' means 'institute to a priestly office', 'install', 'inaugurate', and the like. It occurs frequently in P, but also in earlier narratives (Jg. 17:5,12; 1 Kg. 13:33). It is always used in connection with the priests or priesthood, except in Ezek. 43:26, where it is used of the consecration or inauguration of an altar. The origin of the idiom is uncertain. It may have originated in a custom such as the one which is described in Exod. 29:22-24 and Lev. 8:22-29. There it is said that Moses placed in the hands of Aaron and his sons parts of a sacrifice, made the gesture of presentation with them, and then offered them on the altar. The 'ram of ordination' in those passages is literally, 'ram of filling (*millu'îm*)'. The texts describing this ceremony are late P texts. Some scholars think the idiom was derived from the custom of placing in the hands of the priest as he began to fill his office a first instalment of the fee due to him for his services; this view may find some support in Jg. 17:5-13, where the idiom is used in verses 5 and 12. The Hebrew idiom, may, however, be derived from—and it is in any event similar to—the Akkadian idiom (*ana*) *qāt X. mullū*, which came to mean 'appoint to an office', 'put in charge of something', and the like.

MOSES' SECOND INTERCESSION **32:30-34** (Es)
This intercession is independent of verses 7-14, and may be earlier than that one. Verse 34 may reflect the fall of the northern

kingdom of Israel in 721 B.C. In any event this intercession explains
why Israel was not immediately destroyed, by saying that the
punishment was put off until the time of some future visitation by
Yahweh.

30. And now I will go up to the LORD: go up to the top of
Sinai, where (according to E) Yahweh had his residence. Cf.
19:3; 24:12.

31. gods of gold: read, 'a god of gold'. The Hebrew can be
either singular or plural (cf. comment on verse 1).

32. But now, if thou wilt forgive their sin—: the apodosis
is missing in the Hebrew text; LXX, Samaritan text, and Targum
of Jonathan have the imperative, 'forgive!' This is to be understood,
even if it was not expressed.

thy book which thou hast written: the book in which the
names of the living were inscribed (Ps. 69:28; cf. Isa. 4:3; Mal.
3:16). The figure was probably borrowed from the practice of
keeping a register of the citizens (Ezek. 13:9). Thus, Moses asks
that, if Yahweh cannot forgive the Israelites, he must let Moses
die. In a similar situation later, Moses says, 'Kill me at once'
(Num. 11:15). Does he offer himself as a substitute for the people?
The *OT* 'book of the living' (Ps. 69:28) is different from the
'book of life' of the *NT* (Lk. 10:20; Phil. 4:3; Rev. 3:5; 13:8 etc.),
which was a book in which were inscribed the names of those
destined for eternal life.

33. my angel shall go before you: cf. 33:2-3, where the angel
seems to be conceived as separate from Yahweh himself.

**34. Whoever has sinned against me, him will I blot out of
my book:** cf. especially Ezek. 18:4, 'the soul that sins shall die'.
The present passage is not necessarily as late as Ezekiel, but it is
probably one of the latest additions to the chapter.

in the day when I visit, I will visit their sin upon them: at
the time of a future visitation of Yahweh he will punish them for
the worship of the golden calf. The sentence may reflect the fall of
the northern kingdom of Israel in 721 B.C., which was interpreted
as resulting from Israel's sins, including the worship of the golden
calves of Dan and Bethel erected by Jeroboam (2 Kg. 17:7-18,
especially verse 16).

THE PLAGUE SENT BY YAHWEH **32:35**

35 originally followed verse 20, as the conclusion to E's basic
narrative of the apostasy of Israel in worshipping the golden calf.

And the LORD sent a plague upon the people: literally, 'And the Lord smote the people'. Yahweh's smiting usually means sending a plague (cf. 12:23,27; Jos. 24:5; Isa. 19:22). The *RSV* rendering is a free interpretation, but probably is correct. The nature of the plague cannot be determined.

GOD'S PRESENCE WITH HIS PEOPLE AND MOSES 33:1-23

33:1-6(RD). *Yahweh promises to send an angel before the Israelites as they leave Sinai to go into the land of Canaan. Yahweh will not himself go with them, for they are a stiff-necked people. At the command of Moses, the Israelites strip themselves of their ornaments.*

7-11(E). *Account of the tent of meeting. When Moses goes into the tent, Yahweh meets him in the pillar of cloud, and speaks face to face with him.*

12-17(J). *Moses asks Yahweh to let him know whom he will send with him, and to show Moses his ways. Yahweh promises that his presence will go with him.*

18-23(J). *Moses asks Yahweh to show him his glory. Yahweh agrees to let his goodness pass before Moses, and to let him see his glory. Yet he will see only Yahweh's back, not his face.*

This chapter contains material that is quite varied, loosely connected by the common theme of the presence of Yahweh among his people and with Moses. The closing section, verses 18–23, is the promise of a theophany to Moses, continued by the account of the theophany in 34:5–7. There are also some dislocations and omissions that make full understanding impossible. It seems better to read verse 17 before verses 12–13, and to place verses 14–16 after 34:8–9; but such a re-arrangement does not settle all the difficulties involved here.

The literary analysis is difficult. Verses 7–11 are almost universally attributed by critics to E, and verses 12–23 usually to J. We follow this analysis, but observe that verses 12–23 are not well unified, and probably were not all part of the early J tradition. The connection of the latter part of the section, verses 18–23, with 34:5–7, suggests that this may be viewed as being in part J's parallel to the E theophany of chapter 3, in which the name Yahweh is revealed, for here there is a solemn proclamation of the name, and of Yahweh's nature. Verses 1–6 contain three inconsistencies: (i) in verses 1–3a Yahweh is speaking to Moses, but in verse 3b he is speaking to the people, who react in verse 4; (ii) in verses 3b and 5 Yahweh declares that he will not go up among the

people, but in verse 2 he promises to send an angel among them
(cf. 23:20ff., where the angel stands fully for Yahweh); and
(iii) verse 4 says that the people did not put on their ornaments
because of their mourning, but verse 6 declares that they stripped
themselves of their ornaments. We follow Noth in attributing
verses 1-6 in their present form to the Deuteronomic redactor,
but we think he has used J tradition in verses 1 and 3*a*, and
variant E traditions in verses 3*b*-4, 5-6. This section is somewhat
similar to two other RD sections, 23:20-33; 34:11-16. The analysis,
thus, is as follows: J—33:12-23; E—33:7-11; RD—33:1-6.

Chronologically this narrative, or at least the beginning of it,
belongs at the end of the promulgation of all the laws on Sinai,
and the time of the Israelites' departure from that mountain; thus
the natural place would be at Numbers 10.

THE DEPARTURE OF ISRAEL FROM SINAI **33:1-6**

  1. On this verse, cf. 3:8,17 (J); 32:13 (RD); 6:8 (P).
  2. And I will send an angel before you: cf. the angel of
23:20,23 (RD); 32:34 (E); and 'the angel of his presence' in Isa.
63:9. In 33:14 the promise is, 'My presence will go with you,
and I will give you rest'. The view of J, as well as of the Deuteronomic redactor, is that Israel gladly leaves Sinai, accompanied by Yahweh or his surrogate, to go to a land of milk and
honey.
  the Canaanites, the Amorites, etc.: see comment on 3:8.
  3. Go up to a land flowing with milk and honey: cf. 3:8,17
(J); 13:5 (RD).
  **but I will not go up among you, lest I consume you in the
way:** cf. verse 5. This is probably from an E tradition that emphasized the refusal of Yahweh to go with Israel; it is not consistent
with the promise in 32:34 of an angel to go before the people
(which is probably also E tradition), but it is consonant with the
somewhat abrupt promise of that verse, and the warning of
punishment at its end. It is noteworthy that Eissfeldt assigns
3*b*-4 to L, but 5-6 to E.
  4. The people mourn when they hear that Yahweh will not go
up among them, and as a sign of their mourning refuse to put on
their ornaments, which must have been associated with rejoicing
and gaiety.
  5. The refusal of Yahweh to go up with the people here, lest he
consume them, may be based upon the fact that they were wearing

ornaments associated with a foreign deity, though this is not
clearly stated; thus the removal of the ornaments would have
made it possible for him to accompany them. But the end of this
verse, **that I may know what to do with you**, is vague and
obscure. In Gen. 35:2–4, the renunciation of foreign gods is
accompanied by the disposal of earrings and the changing of
garments. **You are a stiff-necked people:** also in verse 3; 32:9
(RD); Dt. 9:6,13. The phrase is characteristic of D, but occurs
also in J (34:9).

**6. Therefore the people of Israel stripped themselves of
their ornaments:** see comment on 12:35f., and comment above
on verse 5.

Many scholars have assumed that between this verse and the
description in verses 7–11 of the tent of meeting there was originally
an account of the making of the tent of meeting and/or the Ark,
to the making of which the people contributed their ornaments.
According to those scholars, that account was suppressed when the
P account in chapters 35–39 was introduced. However, it is by no
means certain that the tent of meeting here described contained the
Ark. That is never stated. It is true that the sanctuary in Shiloh
contained the Ark (1 Sam. 3:3), and that the Ark was placed in
the tent-sanctuary of David (2 Sam. 6:17), but it is not likely that
either of these was the same tent of meeting used in the wilderness
period. The tent of meeting of Moses was very simple, not needing
ornaments for its making. Furthermore, it is not said here that the
people handed over their ornaments for making anything, but
simply that they 'stripped themselves of their ornaments'. It is
probable that the Deuteronomic redactor prefixed verses 1–6 to
the account of the tent of meeting in 7–11, and nothing has been
lost.

THE TENT OF MEETING **33:7–11**

This is an account of the tent of meeting from the E tradition.
It says nothing about the appearance of the tent, but describes its
function. It was primarily a place where Yahweh 'met' Moses in
the pillar of cloud, not a place of meeting or assembly for the
Israelite people. Moses went to the tent of meeting from time to
time to consult Yahweh, with whom he spoke 'face to face' (verse
11). Verse 7*b* indicates that other Israelites went out on occasion
to the tent when they 'sought the LORD', that is, when they wished
to consult the deity, probably through an oracle. But the primary

emphasis is on the meeting of Yahweh with Moses, who occupied a very special rôle in his relationship to the deity. The tent of meeting here is very different from the Tabernacle of P, described in chapters 25–27, 35–40. The tent of meeting was very simple in comparison with the Tabernacle. It was located outside the camp, whereas the Tabernacle was in the midst of the camp (25:8; Num. 2:1ff.). It had a fundamentally different purpose: the Tabernacle with its Ark was a place in which Yahweh permanently 'dwelled' with his people, whereas the tent of meeting was a place at which Yahweh would from time to time 'meet' with Moses, and perhaps others. See further the introductory comments on chapter 25. The present account has much more claim to represent the authentic tent of meeting of the wilderness period than the Tabernacle described by P. The existence of such a tent of meeting in the wilderness period is evidenced by the casual mention of it in Num. 11:24ff.; 12:4f.,10 (cf. 1 Sam. 2:22 and the late references in 1 Chr. 16:39; 21:29; 2 Chr. 1:3,13).

7. Moses used to take the tent and pitch it outside the camp: the Hebrew verbs in this section are imperfects, representing repeated and customary action in the past; they describe the custom during the wilderness period. Instead of 'the tent' LXX and Syriac read 'his tent'. It is not likely that the tent of meeting was Moses' own family tent, but it was a tent primarily under his control.

And every one who sought the LORD would go out to the tent of meeting: this indicates that the tent of meeting was a place to which ordinary Israelites went, apparently to consult an oracle which would give them the will of Yahweh for specific occasions. Perhaps Joshua, as the permanent attendant of the tent of meeting, ministered to such people. The tent may have contained some kind of oracle device, but we are not told that it contained the Ark (see comments above).

9. the pillar of cloud would descend: the pillar of cloud, symbolizing the presence of Yahweh, did not rest permanently on the tent, but descended only when Moses entered it. Contrast the P conception of the pillar of cloud in 40:34–38, and see comments on 13:21–22.

11. Moses had a very special relationship to Yahweh, who spoke with him directly in a manner different from others. Cf. the strong statements in Num. 12:6–8; Dt. 34:10–12.

Joshua the son of Nun was apparently a constant attendant of

the tent of meeting, serving under the direction of Moses. Cf. the
references to Joshua in 17:9-14; 24:13; 32:17.

PROMISE OF YAHWEH'S PRESENCE WITH MOSES **33:12-17**
This section presents Moses' plea that Yahweh will go, or send
someone, with him as he departs from Sinai, and Yahweh's reply.
This naturally follows after 32:34a, although loosely, and largely
ignores 33:1-11. This is J tradition which has become attached to
the E tradition of the tent of meeting; verses 1-6 were prefixed by
R_D, but somewhat awkwardly, since those verses in their present
form contain the promise of the accompanying angel.

James Muilenburg sees in 33:1a,12-17 an ancient liturgy, originally used in the early amphictyonic sanctuaries of Israel; see his
'The Intercession of the Covenant Mediator (Exod. 33:1a,12-17)',
in *Words and Meanings* (1968), pp. 159-81. Here Moses as the
covenant mediator makes a plea on behalf of the people, and
receives Yahweh's assurance in reply. Muilenburg thinks this is a
well-organized, unified liturgy in the form of a dialogue, and
notes especially that the word 'know' occurs six times (in the
Hebrew) in five verses, with a wealth of meanings. Israel here
receives assurance of the Presence of Yahweh with them in Canaan;
he is not confined to Sinai.

Because this section is not poetic in form, it is doubtful that it
was really a liturgy, but Muilenburg has called attention to
important themes in it.

12. I know you by name here means virtually to 'single out',
to 'choose', as the mediator of the covenant; cf. *RSV* rendering of
'have known' by 'have chosen' in Gen. 18:19. In 34:27 the covenant
is with Moses and Israel; see comment on that verse.

13. show me now thy ways, that I may know thee: it is in
knowing the ways of God (and also his demands) that Moses
knows God; in the *OT* the very being of God himself is hidden
from man; cf. verse 23.

14. My presence will go with you, and I will give you rest:
in E and in R_D the presence of Yahweh is in the angel who goes
before them (14:19a; 23:20; 32:34; 33:2), whereas in J it is in the
pillar of cloud by day and pillar of fire by night (13:21-22;
14:19b; Num. 14:14). In the land of Canaan, it is most probable
that the presence of Yahweh was conceived as symbolized by the
Ark of the covenant.

16. Is it not in thy going with us ... upon the face of the

earth: It is the presence of Yahweh with Israel and his leadership of them that indicates his favour upon them, and marks Israel off as a nation distinct from other nations. Only Israel has a covenant with Yahweh.

PROMISE OF A THEOPHANY TO MOSES **33:18–23**

The subject of this section is slightly different from the preceding. Here Yahweh promises that he will reveal himself to Moses, apparently as a proof that he will really go with Israel through the wilderness. The preceding section has been concerned with the promise of God's presence on the journey. The promise made in the present section is fulfilled in the theophany recorded in 34:5–7. Those verses may have originally formed the continuation of the present section (see below).

18. show me thy glory: 'glory' (*kāḇôḏ*) is characteristically used by P for the theophanies of the exodus period (16:7,10; 24:16,17; 40:34–35; Num. 14:10 etc.) and by Ezekiel (1:28; 3:12,13 etc.). See the comment on 24:16–17. The present verse is, however, earlier than P, and the word occurs in verse 22.

19. my goodness: this is the only occurrence of the phrase in a theophany. Elsewhere it means either (a) beauty, fairness in appearance, as in Hos. 10:11; Zech. 9:17; or (b) the goodness of Yahweh in bestowing good things upon his people (Neh. 9:25) or in saving them (Isa. 63:7; Ps. 25:7; 145:7). Some scholars take the former to be the meaning here, but in the present context it is more likely that the 'goodness' of Yahweh refers to his forgiveness of Israel and his willingness to save Israel by leading them out of Egypt; cf. 34:6–7.

I will be gracious to whom I will be gracious . . . : this is the Hebrew syntactical construction known as *idem per idem*, used when the author does not wish to be more specific, or cannot be more specific. For the construction, cf. 3:14; 4:13; 16:23; 1 Sam. 23:13; 2 Sam. 15:20; 2 Kg. 8:1. This is quoted in Rom. 9:15, but with a somewhat different emphasis from the present context (see Rom. 9:18).

20. This idea is expressed also in Gen. 32:30; Dt. 4:33; 5:24,26; Jg. 6:22f.; 13:22.

21–23 assume that Moses is standing on Mount Sinai (Horeb). The closest parallel to this theophany is to be found in the account of Elijah's experience on Horeb, 1 Kg. 19:9–13.

23. you shall see my back: *aḥōrîm* is used elsewhere of (i) the 'back' of the Tabernacle (26:12); (ii) the 'hinder parts' of the twelve bronze oxen which held up the molten sea in the Temple courtyard (1 Kg. 7:25); and (iii) the 'backs' of the men who worshipped in the Temple in the time of Ezekiel, their backs being to the Temple and their faces to the E. (Ezek. 8:16). In the present theophany Yahweh is presented in very anthropomorphic terms, with references to his face, his hand, and his back. The meaning is that, while man can know something of the ways of God with man in his world (verse 13), the ultimate mystery of God's nature is hidden from man's knowledge.

RENEWAL OF THE COVENANT 34:1–35

34:1–4(J). *Moses is instructed to cut two tables of stone like the first and ascend the mountain, and Yahweh will write the words that were on the first tables.*

5–9(J). *Yahweh reveals himself to Moses as a merciful and compassionate God. Moses bows down and prays that Yahweh will go in the midst of the people.*

10(J). *Yahweh announces that he will make a covenant and do great marvels.*

11–16(R_D). *Yahweh promises that he will drive out the foreign peoples before the Israelites, and he commands them to make no covenant with those peoples, but break down their cult objects, and worship him only.*

17–26(J,R_D). *Miscellaneous laws concerning feasts, sacrifices, and the like.*

27–28(J). *At the command of Yahweh, Moses writes on the tables the words in accordance with which Yahweh has made a covenant with Moses and Israel.*

29–32(P). *When Moses descends from Sinai, his face shines, and the people of Israel are afraid to come near him, but he gives them the commandments which Yahweh spoke to him on Sinai.*

33–35(P). *Whenever Moses would go in before Yahweh to speak with him, Moses would remove the veil with which he covered his face while speaking with the Israelites.*

In its present form, the first part of this chapter (verses 1–28) is an account of the renewal of the covenant which had been broken by the making of the golden calf. However, there is little indication that this is in fact a *renewal*, apart from the statement in verse 1*b*, and 'like the first' in verse 4. When they are removed, we appear to have a narrative which is basically the J account of the making

of the covenant, largely parallel to the E account in parts of
chapters 20–24. Thus its original place may have been immediately after chapter 19. This J account has been transformed into a
story of the renewal of the covenant and placed in its present
position by the redactor who put J and E together.

If we recognize that the basic narrative of verses 1–28 is J, and
that verses 29–35 are P, the literary analysis is not difficult. The
Deuteronomic redactor has interpolated verses 11–16 and 24, as
will be shown below. Thus the analysis is as follows: J—34:1–10,
17–23,25–28 (with some additions in verses 1 and 4); R_D—34:11–
16,24; P—34:29–35.

The major question in the interpretation of this chapter is the
question whether we have in verses 14–26 (or 17–26) a form of the
decalogue, a set of 'ten commandments' referred to at the end of
verse 28. As the chapter now stands, Moses is clearly told that he is
to cut two tables of stone on which Yahweh will write the words
that were on the first tables which he had broken. Yahweh promises to make a covenant (10) and at the end Moses is reported
to have written 'the words of the covenant, the ten commandments' (28), which are the terms upon which the promised covenant is based. It is natural to expect that in the interval between
verse 10 and verse 27 we have a series of 'words' (laws, commands,
or the like) which constituted the terms of the covenant.

In modern times, it was Goethe who in 1773 first proposed that
this chapter contains the ten commandments on which God made
a covenant with Israel, not the 'most universal truths' which are
contained in the classic ethical decalogue of Exodus 20. A century
later Julius Wellhausen, without initially knowing of Goethe's
theory, arrived at a similar conclusion. He found in Exodus 34 a
ritual decalogue which he believed to be more ancient than the
ethical decalogue, although his enumeration did not coincide
entirely with Goethe's. Many scholars after Wellhausen adopted
the view that the original decalogue, consisting primarily of cultic
instructions, is contained here. It is usually maintained that this
is a J decalogue in contrast to the E decalogue of chapter 20, and
that the ethical decalogue shows a great advance in religious
progress over the cultic laws of the present chapter. Elaborate rites
preceded high ethical standards, according to this view.

As the chapter now stands, there are twelve or more commandments, and various devices are used to reduce the number to ten.
H. H. Rowley holds that the primitive ritual decalogue of this

chapter originated with the Kenites, and that it was taken over by
the southern tribes when they adopted the worship of Yahweh
(*Men of God*, pp. 7–18). R. H. Pfeiffer offered a reconstruction of
what he believed to be an early Canaanite decalogue dating from
before 1200 B.C., from the present chapter and related verses in
the Covenant Code (*Introduction to the O.T.*, pp. 221–23).

Various methods are used to derive a decalogue from this
chapter; the following is a possible enumeration, adopted by some
scholars, using only a brief form for each command.

1. You shall worship no other god (14a).
2. You shall make for yourself no molten gods (17).
3. All that opens the womb is mine (19a).
4. None shall appear before me empty (20c).
5. Six days you shall work, but on the seventh day you
   shall rest (21a).
6. Three times in the year shall all your males appear
   before Yahweh, the God of Israel (at the Feasts of
   Unleavened Bread, Weeks, and Ingathering) (23).
7. You shall not offer the blood of my sacrifice with
   leaven (25a).
8. The sacrifice of the feast of the Passover shall not
   be left until the morning (25b).
9. The first of the first fruits of your ground you shall
   bring to the house of Yahweh, your God (26a).
10. You shall not boil a kid in its mother's milk (26b).

In this form the commandments have been adapted to Yahweh
worship, and are addressed to the individual Israelite. They are
concerned largely with the duties of the laymen in the cult, not
with priests.

The view that an original ritual decalogue is contained in
chapter 34 has been disputed by a number of scholars, especially in
recent times. They note that the commandments here are heterogeneous in both form and content, and that the arrangement is
very unsystematic. All attempts to extract a unified set of only ten
commandments must rest upon arbitrary judgement. Also, the
majority of the commandments reflect the cult of an agrarian
people who are settled in the land, not that of a nomadic or
semi-nomadic people. All attempts to rescue an original decalogue
from these regulations are complicated by the fact that most of the
instructions occur also in the Covenant Code, particularly in
Exod. 23:12–19. Finally, there is an inner contradiction in the

chapter, inasmuch as it is clearly stated at the beginning that Yahweh intends to write upon the two tables the same words that were on the first table, and the Exodus narrative in its present form presupposes that the classic ethical decalogue was written upon the first tables.

Many scholars have adopted the view that the phrase 'the ten commandments' is a gloss at the end of verse 28, and thus think it is idle to seek to find a decalogue from the preceding verses. Some think the gloss was made under the influence of Dt. 4:13; 10:4. The phrase does not occur elsewhere in Exodus.

The most natural and logical theory regarding a decalogue in this chapter is that which was proposed by W. Rudolph (*Der 'Elohist' von Exodus bis Josua*, p. 59), and adopted and expanded by W. Beyerlin (*Origins and History of the Oldest Sinaitic Traditions*, pp. 77–90). The phrase 'ten commandments' in 28*b* must be original, they think, because no one would have thought to add it to the verse in view of the heterogeneous and unsystematic nature of the preceding verses. This would not in any case have been a Deuteronomic gloss, for the Deuteronomists considered the ethical decalogue, which is reproduced in Dt. 5:6–21, as the original terms of the covenant (see Dt. 4:13; 10:4; 5:22). The most natural supposition, then, is that *the ethical decalogue itself (in an early form) originally stood in Exodus 34*, prior to verses 27–28, in the place of 17–26, or 10–26. In a later stage of the tradition the ethical decalogue was replaced by the material that is now in chapter 34, which never constituted a decalogue. The motive and the date of the substitution are difficult to determine. In the opinion of Beyerlin, the substitution was made, not simply to avoid a repetition of the ethical decalogue of chapter 20, but in order to promote the view that the maintaining of the Sinai covenant in the new situation in which Israel found itself after the settlement in Canaan required that these new, cultic laws be observed. Beyerlin thinks that the cultic laws of Exodus 34 were developed in one of the early Israelite shrines, perhaps at Shiloh, and were substituted in the J tradition in the pre-monarchial period or the time of David—that is, before the writing down of the J tradition by the Yahwist. The question of the date of the substitution is one which can be left open, but the fact and its motivation as suggested by Beyerlin may be correct. Such a view explains why it could be said that the second tables of the law contained the same words as the first. The time of the substitution

L

is more probably *after* the redactor who combined J and E, but before the Deuteronomic redactor. The assignment of verses 17–26 to J is then very questionable. On the origin of these verses see below, the comment on verses 18–26. We retain the assignment to J because verses 17–26 occur within a J context, and the redactor who placed them here was probably a Judaean.

REVELATION OF YAHWEH TO MOSES 34:1-9

Moses ascends the mountain with the two new tables of stone, and experiences a theophany. The appearance of Yahweh here is in fulfilment of the promise made in 33:19–23, although it may not correspond closely to what one might expect from that promise. Verses 5–8 may once have stood immediately after 33:19–23, but the intervening verses are a part of the J tradition, not the product of the Deuteronomic redactor. The corresponding account in Dt. 10:1–5 says that Moses made the Ark before he went up the mountain, and placed the tables in the Ark after he descended. It is possible that at one time the present account similarly recounted the making of the Ark, but after the account of the making of the Ark was added by the Priestly writer in chapter 37, all references to the Ark were deleted here.

1. like the first . . . which you broke: these words were added, probably by the redactor who joined J and E, when the present account was transformed from the record of the making of the covenant to an account of its renewal (see above).

4. like the first: these words were added at the same time as 1*b*.

5. And the LORD descended in the cloud: this type of theophany is characteristic of J; see 19:9,18.

and stood with him there, and proclaimed the name of the LORD: the *RSV* rendering makes it appear that Yahweh is the subject of the verbs. While this is possible, it is more likely that Moses should be considered the subject. That he **stood with him there** is a fulfilment of the command in 33:21. The more natural rendering of the last clause is: 'and he (i.e. Moses) called upon the name of the Lord'. Yahweh's proclamation of his own name comes in the next verse.

6–7. Yahweh proclaims himself as a God who is gracious and merciful, but one who visits the sins of the fathers upon the children and their descendants. This revelation appears in some respects to be the J parallel to E's account in 3:13–15, since Yahweh here proclaims his proper, personal name 'Yahweh' (see

comment on 3:14). The theophany is more directly related to the
promise made in 33:19-23 than to what follows (see especially the
promise that Yahweh will make his 'goodness' pass before Moses,
33:19). Yet, in emphasizing Yahweh's grace it contains the
implication that Yahweh can forgive those who have sinned by
making the golden calf, and renew the covenant with them. The
words in which the revelation is here made are repeated frequently
in other passages, sometimes with variation or abbreviation:
20:5-6 (=Dt. 5:9-10), Num. 14:18; Neh. 9:17; Jer. 32:18;
Nah. 1:3; Jl 2:13; Jon. 4:2; Ps. 86:15; 103:8; 145:8. Most of
these passages are relatively late, but this is probably an old cultic
formula preserved in the worship of Israel. It is not Deuteronomic
in origin (see Dt. 24:16).

steadfast love is the phrase usually employed in *RSV* to render
ḥéseḏ when it refers to God's continuing attitude toward Israel.
The Hebrew word is often used to represent the ideal relationship which should exist between parties who are in a covenant
union.

9 is not appropriate to its present context. It may have stood
originally before 33:14-16.

MAKING OF THE COVENANT **34:10-28**

As noted above, this account reads much more as if it were a
record of the original formation of the covenant, not its renewal,
as the present position requires it to be. There is nothing in the
language which suggests a covenant renewal. In the J narrative
here the emphasis is upon the fact that Yahweh made the covenant
with Moses (verses 10, 27). It is only indirectly a covenant
with Israel; Moses must serve as mediator of the covenant with
them. The present account tells nothing of a ceremony in which
the people accept the covenant and its terms, as one finds in
24:3,7. It is possible—but not certain—that 24:9-11 is J's account
of a ceremony in which representatives of Israel 'beheld God' and
partook of a communion meal to seal the covenant (see comments
on chapter 24). The present account emphasizes the initiative of
Yahweh in making the covenant on the basis of the words he
speaks to Moses.

10. Behold, I make a covenant: the Hebrew participle is
better rendered, 'I am about to make a covenant'. The **marvels**
which Yahweh will perform are not specified. They are not the
past marvels associated with the exodus from Egypt, but those

which lie ahead in the period of the wilderness and the settlement
in Canaan.

11–16 are from the Deuteronomic redactor. The themes are
characteristic of D: Yahweh will drive out the native inhabitants
of Canaan; Israel must not make a covenant with them, but
destroy their cult objects, lest they be tempted to worship other
gods. Other Rᴅ passages in 23:20–33 and 33:1–6 are similar; see
especially Dt. 7:1–5, but also 12:2–3,29–31; 31:16 etc. One reason
for the interpolation here is to contrast the covenant which
Yahweh makes with Moses and Israel with the forbidden covenant
between Israel and the inhabitants of Canaan.

11. the Amorites, the Canaanites, the Hittites . . . : see
comment on 3:8.

12. See comment on 23:32.

13. See comment on 23:24. This verse is almost verbally identical
with Dt. 12:3.

Asherim: plural of Asherah. This was sometimes the name of a
goddess (the Canaanite goddess of fertility), as in Jg. 3:7 (plural);
1 Kg. 15:13; 2 Kg. 21:7. Sometimes it was the name of a cult
object as in Jg. 6:25–30; Dt. 16:21; 7:5; 12:3, and in the present
passage. As a cult object it was something wooden which could
be **cut down.** It has been interpreted as a sacred tree or pole,
but is most likely to have been a wooden image of the goddess
Asherah.

14. you shall worship no other god: this is usually taken to
be the first commandment of the 'ritual decalogue' by those who
find such a decalogue in this chapter. It would thus be equivalent
to the first commandment of the ethical decalogue, 20:3. The
second half of the verse **for the LORD . . . a jealous God** may be a
part of the J tradition, but it could as well be a part of the Rᴅ
interpolation, for the idea is characteristic of D; see Dt. 4:24;
6:15; cf. Jos. 24:19 (possibly Rᴅ). It occurs in the expansion of the
second commandment in 20:4 (=Dt. 5:9).

15. one invites you, you eat of his sacrifice: the situation
presupposed is that in which an Israelite is invited by a pagan to a
meal and partakes of meat sacrificed to a pagan deity. The same
problem occurred in the early Christian community, and is
wrestled with by Paul in 1 Cor. 8.

17. Cf. 20:4, the commandment not to make a graven image.
It is not known why the reference here is to **molten gods** only;
we should not suppose that it implies permission to make graven

images. Cf. also 20:23, which forbids the making of 'gods of
silver' or 'gods of gold'.

18–26 are closely paralleled, often verbatim, by 13:12–13;
23:12,15–19. We should not suppose that this chapter is dependent on the earlier passages, or vice versa, but rather that both
depend upon a common source, which was primarily an old calendar of feasts with appended regulations concerning sacrifices,
borrowed from the Canaanites in the period after the settlement
of the Israelites in Canaan. The form preserved in 23:15–19 is
more systematically arranged and is probably closer in some
details to the original form than the present section (see comments
on 34:22,25). For a good treatment, see H. Kosmala, 'The So-
Called Ritual Decalogue', *Annual of the Swedish Theological
Institute*, 1 (1962), pp. 31–61. Since most of this section is parallel
to earlier verses, we shall comment below only on some of the
differences in the present section from the earlier verses, which
should be consulted for details.

18. See 23:15.

19–20. See 13:12–13. In that chapter the law of the firstlings
and first-born is associated with the slaying of the first-born in
Egypt and the subsequent exodus. See also 22:29b–30.

21. in plowing time and in harvest you shall rest: not in
23:12; here it is appended to emphasize the need to observe the
Sabbath even in the times when there would be strong temptation
not to do so.

22. feast of weeks: called 'the feast of harvest' in 23:16, but
'feast of weeks' in Dt. 16:10,16; 2 Chr. 8:13. The name in 23:16
is probably the oldest name. It celebrated the harvest of wheat in
the late spring. It came to be celebrated seven weeks after Passover,
and eventually was known as Pentecost (Tob. 2:1), being observed
fifty days after Passover.

24 is not paralleled in the earlier chapters, and is clearly an
interpolation by Rᴅ. Cf. 23:28–31; 33:2; 34:11. It presupposes
the centralization of the worship in Jerusalem when the adult
males would **go up** (a technical term) to the Temple in that city
to appear before the LORD, at the three annual feasts. Cf. Dt.
16:16.

neither shall any man desire your land: Yahweh will
protect the land of those who go up to Jerusalem, apparently in
the main from covetous neighbours rather than from foreign
encroachments.

25. neither shall the sacrifice of the feast of the passover be left until the morning: the corresponding passage in 23:18 has, 'or let the fat of my feast remain until the morning'. The original Canaanite calendar doubtless had nothing about the Passover, which was a nomadic, Israelite observance. 23:18 is very general in its application, referring to the fat of various festal sacrifices. The present verse refers only to the Passover, and has in view not simply the fat but the whole of the Passover lamb, which was to be entirely eaten on the Passover night, with none to be left over until the morning; see the regulation in 12:10. Passover is nowhere else called a *ḥag*, 'feast', properly, a pilgrimage festival.

27. I have made a covenant with you and with Israel: the covenant is directly with Moses (second person singular is used here), and indirectly with Israel. Since **with Israel** is added lamely at the end of the verse, it is considered secondary by many scholars. But it cannot be denied that the covenant was in fact with Israel, for Israel was expected to follow the terms of the covenant, and receive its benefits. Moses was the mediator of the covenant to Israel.

28. he wrote upon the tables the words of the covenant: in the present context Moses is clearly the subject, although elsewhere it is said that Yahweh wrote on the tables (24:12; 31:18; 32:16).

the ten commandments: not to be considered a gloss, but as part of the J tradition; see above, the introductory comments on this chapter.

TRANSFIGURATION OF MOSES **34:29–35**
When Moses comes down from the mountain he is transfigured so that his face shines and the people are afraid to come near him. But he calls them to him and gives them God's commandments. Moses has here a very high position as a representative of Yahweh, and the shining of his face verifies the divine origin of the commandments. The account is a precursor of the *NT* accounts of the transfiguration of Jesus (Mt. 17:1–8 and parallels). This section is from P, as shown by its terminology and the prominence of Aaron; it does, however, contain some old tradition, particularly in 34–35. In P it followed after 31:18.

29. the skin of his face shone: the Hebrew rendered 'shone' is *ḳāran*, which is related to the word for 'horn', *ḳeren*. It is apparently a denominative verb meaning something like 'put out horn-like rays'; the *hifil* of the verb in Ps. 69:31 means 'displaying horns' (of a bull). The meaning was misunderstood by the Vulgate, which rendered it *cornuta est*, 'was horned'. From this arose the representations in art of Moses as having horns on his head.

33. he put a veil on his face: the *masweh* may have been a face mask. The Hebrew word occurs only in this section, and means literally 'a covering'. In numerous primitive religions and in ancient Egypt, a priest sometimes wore a mask to indicate that he was a representative of the deity. When the priest put on the mask he assumed the 'face' of the deity and thus identified himself with that deity. This practice is not otherwise attested in the *OT*. Some scholars think the *terafim* may have been masks (e.g. in 1 Sam. 19:13,16; cf. Jg. 17:5; Hos. 3:4; 1 Sam. 15:23; 2Kg.23:24), but this is not certain and in any case the *terafim* were not legitimate Israelite cult articles. It is quite possible that pottery masks found at Hazor and Gezer from the Late Bronze Age were used by Canaanite priests (Yadin, *Hazor*, I, pl. 163; II, pl. 183; Macalister, *Gezer* II, fig. 383); cf. the possibly masked figures on the fresco of *Teleilat Ghassul*, I, ed. A. Mallon *et al.*, pp. 135-40. If this is the correct interpretation, the present passage represents a later stage in the tradition, in which a different significance is given to the mask. The priestly mask was worn in order to identify the priest with his deity both in the presence of the people and within the temple as he officiated before the deity. Here Moses is represented as wearing the mask in order to protect the people from the divine radiance as he speaks with them, but he takes it off when he enters the presence of the deity (verse 34). The present passage is used in 2 Cor. 3:7–18 with a still different meaning: Moses wore the veil over his face 'so that the Israelites might not see the end of the fading splendour' (verse 13), and the incident is allegorized.

34. whenever Moses went in before the LORD: most of the following verbs are imperfect, or perfect with '*waw*-consecutive', to indicate repeated, customary action. We could more accurately render them, 'he would take the veil off... and he would come out and tell the people . . . the people of Israel would see . . .' This section must, therefore, describe some repeated action on the part of Moses, not the single action that took place when he descended from the mountain. If it has historical value, it could apply to his customary practice in going in and out of the tent of meeting, described in 33:7–11. Since the practice of Israelite priests wearing a *masweh* is not elsewhere attested in the *OT*, it is quite possible that it is a very ancient tradition, going back to an early time in Israelite history.

EXECUTION OF THE P ORDINANCES FOR THE CULT 35:1—40:38

These chapters relate how the instructions given in chapters 25–31 were carried out by Moses and the Israelites. In many cases the wording of the former chapters is repeated verbatim, with the tense of the verbs simply changed from future to past. In some cases there are abridgements or minor omissions, and there are some expansions, especially at the beginning (35:4—36:6), and at the end, where chapter 40 relates the setting up of the Tabernacle and its equipment, and the descent of the glory of Yahweh upon it. Occasionally these chapters add some new information to the chapters 25–31, but taken as a whole they contribute little to our understanding of P's conception of the Tabernacle and its priesthood. In our discussion of chapters 25–31 we have occasionally made reference to passages in these chapters that give additional information or help to clarify the earlier chapters— but these are not many. The consecration of the priesthood (commanded in chapter 29) is not recorded here, but later in Lev. 8.

It is obvious that these chapters are from the hand of a P writer who knew chapters 25–31 in virtually the form in which we have them in the M.T. Thus they are to be attributed, for the most part at least, to a later stratum of P; Galling assigns them mostly to P^S. The author re-arranges the material to some extent, recording the making of the Tabernacle itself before the making of the furniture and furnishings, a procedure that may strike us as more logical than that of chapters 25–31.

An interesting feature of these chapters is that the LXX translation of them differs more markedly from the Hebrew text than does any other portion of the *OT* of similar length. The Greek translator often uses different Greek words for the same Hebrew words than those used in the Greek of chapters 25–31. He has some glaring omissions, such as the incense altar, the boards (or frames) of the Tabernacle, the goats' hair curtains, and the two sets of skin coverings. He describes the making of the various items in a different order—e.g., he describes the making of the priestly vestments in chapter 36, whereas in the Hebrew they are in chapter 39. Occasionally he adds some information not in the Hebrew (e.g. at 38:2, see below). Many scholars have sought to explain these phenomena by saying that the Greek translator of chapters 35–40 must have been a different person from the translator of chapters 25–31, and some have conjectured that he worked from a different Hebrew text. The subject has been studied in detail by D. W. Gooding, *The Account of the Tabernacle: Translation and Textual Problems of the Greek Exodus* (1959). Among his conclusions are: (i) these chapters were translated by the same person as chapters 25–31, with the exception of chapter 38 (LXX numbering; this equals approximately 37:1—38:8 of our text); (ii) the translator had a Hebrew text approximately the same as our M.T.; and (iii) originally the order of the LXX translation was the same as the Hebrew, but it was changed by a later Greek editor.

SABBATH OBSERVANCE **35:1–3**
Cf. 31:12–17. Repetition of this command and placing it first in these chapters emphasize the importance of the Sabbath to P.
   3. you shall kindle no fire in all your habitations on the sabbath day: this prohibition is not stated elsewhere, but is partially implied in 16:23. It may have been intended here to prohibit making a fire for the metalworking involved in constructing the Tabernacle and its furniture.

THE OFFERINGS AND WORK OF THE PEOPLE **35:4—36:7**
An expansion of 25:1–9 and 31:1–11. This is a long narrative about how the Israelite men and women contributed offerings of various kinds and their own work for making the Tabernacle. It adds in 35:22 the offering of personal jewelry (cf. 33:6), and in 35:25f. the spinning of cloth by the women. In 35:34 the statement that Bezalel and Oholiab were inspired to teach the other workers is a new element. 36:3–7 emphasizes the overwhelming response of the people to the point of their having to be restrained.

THE TABERNACLE **36:8–38**
Cf. 26:1–36. This section omits 26:9b,12–13, which probably were difficult for the ancient P writer to understand, as they are for the modern exegete.

THE ARK **37:1–9**
Cf. 25:10–22.

THE TABLE OF ACACIA WOOD **37:10–16**
Cf. 25:23–30. It is strange that no mention is made here of the
Bread of the Presence which was placed on the table, although it
is in the list in 39:36.

THE LAMPSTAND **37:17–24**
Cf. 25:31–38.

THE ALTAR OF INCENSE **37:25–28**
Cf. 30:1–10. For some unknown reason this is omitted in the
LXX, but the altar of incense is mentioned in the LXX of 40:5,26.

THE HOLY ANOINTING OIL AND INCENSE **37:29**
A drastic abridgement of 30:22–38.

THE ALTAR OF BURNT OFFERING **38:1–7**
Cf. 27:1–8. The LXX adds: 'He made the bronze altar out of
the bronze censers which belonged to the men who rebelled
with the company of Korah' (LXX 38:22). This is a midrashic
addition that is anachronistic, since the rebellion of Korah did
not take place until later (Num. 16). Cf. the Hebrew addition
to 38:8.

THE LAVER OF BRONZE **38:8**
Cf. 30:17–21. The earlier account does not contain the information
in the latter part of this verse. It is a midrashic touch, and anachronistic, since it assumes that the Tabernacle has already been
built and that the women are ministering at the door of the tent of
meeting. The only other *OT* verse referring to such women is
1 Sam. 2:22, where we read that the sons of Eli 'lay with the
women who served at the entrance to the tent of meeting'.
In both instances an unusual word is used for 'serve', *ṣābā'*, which
most often means 'wage war'. It is used in the sense of religious
service of the Levites in Num. 4:23; 8:24. If such women did exist
in the second Temple, we do not know what function they performed. Was it cleaning and repairing the Tabernacle? Or dancing
and singing? Or prostitution, as 1 Sam. 2:22 seems to imply, and
the mention of the mirrors may suggest? Mirrors made of bronze

have been found in Palestinian excavations, sometimes of solid
bronze, sometimes with handles of wood or ivory. Glass mirrors
were not made until the Roman period. Cf. note above on 38:1–7.

THE COURT OF THE TABERNACLE **38:9–20**
Cf. 27:9–19.

SUMMARY OF METALS CONTRIBUTED **38:21–31**
This section has no correspondent in chapters 25–31. It gives **the
sum of the things for the tabernacle**—specifically of the three
metals which were contributed and used in making the Tabernacle
and its furnishings. This section contains two anachronisms:
verse 21 presupposes the appointment of the Levites under the
direction of Ithamar for service in the Tabernacle, but their
appointment is not related until Num. 3–4 (see esp. 4:28,33);
and verse 26 presupposes the census, which is reported later in
Num. 1.

24–29. Reckoning the talent at approximately 64 lbs. avoirdupois (29 kg.), and the shekel of the sanctuary at about ⅓ oz. or
9.7 g. (R. B. Y. Scott, 'Weights, Measures, Money and Time',
Peake's Commentary on the Bible [1962], sect. 35*ab;* cf. comment on
30:13), we get the following approximate equivalents for the
weights given here: gold—1,900 lbs., silver—6,437 lbs., and
bronze—4,522 lbs. (Some scholars arrive at larger figures by
reckoning the talent at about 75.5 lbs. and the shekel somewhat
larger than the above, but Scott's conclusions seem to be based
upon sound archaeological and literary evidence.)

25. The total of the silver is 301,775 shekels (3,000 shekels to the
talent), which is exactly half of the number of the people given in
verse 26, which agrees with Num. 1:46. It does not include
Levites.

26. beka is also used in the Hebrew of Gen. 24:22, for half a
shekel.

27–28 Here the contributions of silver, a half shekel from
each person, are used in making the Tabernacle; in 30:11–16
the half shekel poll tax is intended 'for the service of the tent of
meeting'.

THE GARMENTS OF THE PRIESTHOOD **39:1–31**
Cf. 28:1–43. The only significant difference from the former
chapter is that in verses 8–21 the article is called only **the breast-**

piece, not 'the breastpiece of judgment', as in 28:15ff., and the
Urim and Thummim are not mentioned, as they are in 28:30.
Did the P writer of the present section live at a time when the
Urim and Thummim had ceased to be placed in the breastpiece
and it had ceased to be called the breastpiece *of judgment?* Or was
he simply aware of the fact that, though the Urim and Thummim
were in the breastpiece, they were not used for oracular purposes?
Cf. comment on 28:30.

COMPLETION AND PRESENTATION OF THE TABERNACLE **39:32-43**
The Tabernacle is finished and is brought to Moses. When Moses
sees all of the work, he blesses the people.

ERECTION OF THE TABERNACLE AND ITS EQUIPMENT **40:1-33**
This section has two parts: (i) Yahweh gives instructions to Moses
for erecting the Tabernacle and its equipment, and consecrating
the priests (verses 1-15); (ii) the Tabernacle is erected and
furnished with its various pieces of equipment, and the regular
offerings are begun, but nothing is reported concerning the
consecration of the priesthood (verses 16-33). The consecration of
the priests is in Lev. 8. According to Galling's analysis, only verse
17 is from P^B, the rest being from P^S.

15. Here all the priests are anointed; cf. comment on 29:7.

17. In the P chronology, the Tabernacle is erected a year after
the Israelites left Egypt (12:2-3), and nine months after their
arrival at Sinai (19:1).

THE GLORY OF THE LORD FILLS THE TABERNACLE **40:34-38**
When the Tabernacle has been finished and erected, and its
services initiated, then the glory of the Lord comes down and fills
the Tabernacle. This not only gives Yahweh's stamp of approval
upon the work accomplished, but indicates the presence of
Yahweh with his people (cf. 25:8; 29:43-46). On the conception
of **the glory of the LORD,** see the comment on 24:16.

35 conflicts with statements expressed elsewhere, such as 25:22;
33:9 (E); Lev. 9:23 (P). It is more in accord with statements such
as those found in 1 Kg. 8:10-11; 2 Chr. 5:13-14; 7:2, all of which
have to do with priests ministering in the Temple. It is not without
reason, then, that Galling assigns this verse to P^B, who thought
of the Temple in his description of the Tabernacle, and assigns
verse 34 to P^A, whose model was the nomadic tent of meeting.

36–38. Cf. Num. 9:15–23, where this information is given in expanded form. Cf. the conception of J in 13:21–22 that the Israelites were led by Yahweh in a pillar of cloud by day, and a pillar of fire by night. The book of Exodus closes with the fulfilment of the promise that Yahweh would dwell with his people and, looks forward to the leading of Yahweh as they go on their way through the wilderness to the land of promise.

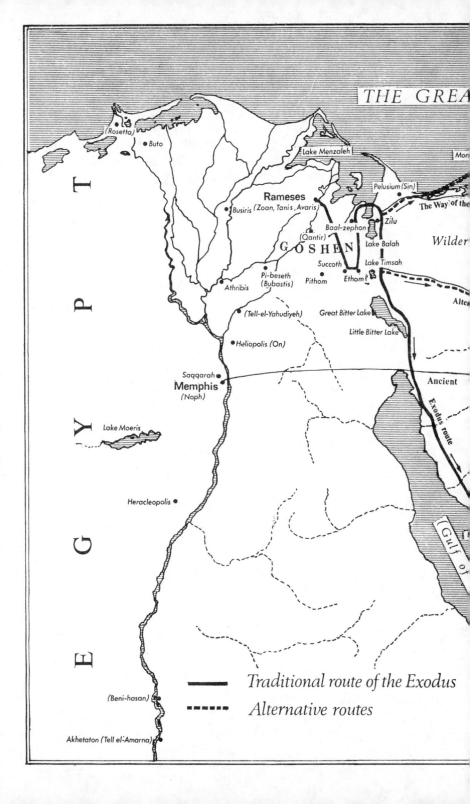

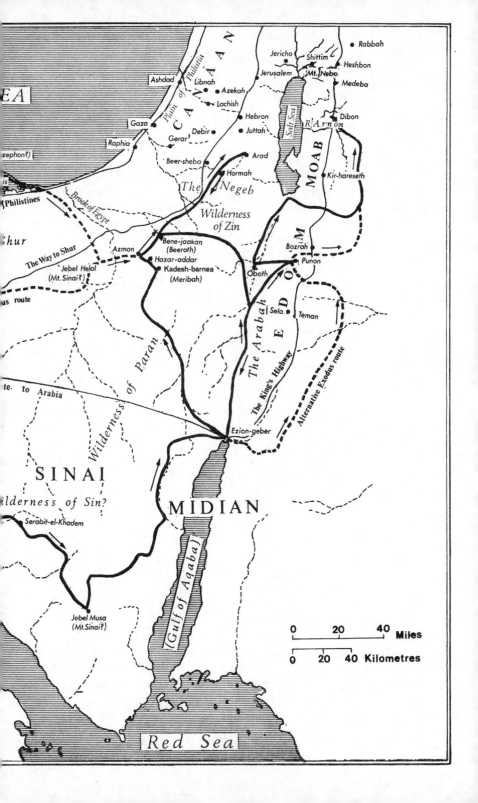

APPENDIX

THE 'NATURAL' EXPLANATION OF THE PLAGUES

The plagues of Egypt have often been explained as the heightening or the exaggeration of occurrences or phenomena which can be shown to be natural for the land of Egypt. Many scholars have attempted to demonstrate that the plagues could have occurred in that land over a period of not more than twelve months, drawing upon their knowledge of known phenomena of Egypt.

In order to understand these explanations one must have in mind the topography of Egypt and be aware especially of the great importance of the Nile river. Egypt has been often called 'the gift of the Nile' since the time of Herodotus, and that is almost literally true. Egypt lies in NE. Africa, to the east of the Sahara Desert, and if it were not for the Nile the land would support a very small population. Even with the Nile, the cultivable area in ancient times was 12,000 square miles, and the country is hot and dry most of the year. Cairo has a rainfall of one or two inches a year, and the rainfall south of Cairo is negligible.

The Nile has two principal sources in the region S. of Egypt in east central Africa. The western source, the White Nile, originates at Lake Victoria on the equator, where the daily rains of the tropics give the river a fairly constant flow. The Blue Nile rises in the highlands of Abyssinia. The rainfall of the late spring and the summer is greater than that of winter, and the snows on the mountains melt and run down at the same time. The Blue and White Niles come together at Khartum; a third source, the Atbara, joins them about 140 miles N. of Khartum. It also originates in Abyssinia, and has characteristics similar to the Blue Nile.

The variations in the flow of water in the Blue Nile and Atbara are responsible for the annual inundation of the Nile in Egypt. The Nile begins to rise in the latter part of June and reaches its maximum height in September, after which it begins to subside. The river is exceedingly important for the people of Egypt, both because it furnishes almost the only source of water, and because the inundation of the river in ancient times deposited organic matter that helped to fertilize the fields. Excessive rainfall in east central Africa at the headwaters of the river can cause unusually high flooding in Egypt, and deficiency in rainfall in that area can bring about distressing conditions in Egypt. It is not surprising that the ancient Egyptians worshipped the god Hapi, who symbolized the river.

Near Cairo the Nile branches off into the delta region, and in ancient times it flowed into the Mediterranean at seven points. The Hebrews are said to have lived in the land of Goshen, which must have been in the eastern part of the delta, in the Wadi Tumilat. This region was somewhat more favourable than the region to the south, having a little more rainfall and being a little cooler and more fertile. Along the Mediterranean coast in ancient times there were brackish lagoons.

Egypt thus presents an unusual situation. Its climate in general is that of arid tropical regions, and it is bounded on the east and west by deserts. Yet along the banks of the Nile there is fertile soil and a source of water supply that is reasonably dependable. As a country with a tropical climate it is subject to the insects, diseases, dust-storms and the like of such a climate, but it has the opportunities and problems associated with the annual inundation of the life-giving Nile. (This has been the situation through the centuries, but life in modern Egypt is being greatly influenced by the building of the Aswan dam.)

Most attempts to give a 'natural' explanation to the plagues are based upon the theory that they resulted in part from a departure of the Nile from its usual flow—that is, from an unusually low annual rise, or from an unusually high flood stage. As representatives of the various theories that have been offered, we shall summarize the views of two reputable scholars who have sought to account for the details of the ten plagues as reported in Exodus.

The theory of Ellsworth Huntington in his book, *The Pulse of Progress**, rests upon the view that the plagues resulted from an unusually low Nile at a time when it should have been in flood stage. At the time of the publication of this book, the author was Research Associate in Geography at Yale University, and had published numerous volumes on geography and climatology. He believed there was much evidence for the view that the 'thirteenth century before Christ saw the culmination of a pronounced period of climatic stress characterized by extremes of drought in

* New York and London, 1926, pp. 194-209. Huntington was also the author of *Palestine and Its Transformation* (Boston and New York, 1911). Many of his views, it must be said, have not survived the criticism of other geographers.

the dry regions around the Mediterranean' (p. 195). Part of the evidence consists of the indications that the Hebrews in their desert wandering experienced bad water, lack of food, and unusual dryness.

The first plague resulted from the phenomenally low level of the Nile, which became sluggish, dark and dirty, with a colour suggesting red. The fish in the river died, and the frogs left in search of a better habitat. Thus the second plague followed soon after the first.

The third plague was that of lice, which are always present in Egypt and would have thrived at a time when neither men nor animals were able to wash because of the low water. The decaying bodies of the frogs and the fetid river provided conditions for the reproduction of swarms of flies—the fourth plague. Huntington quotes the biblical description of this plague and remarks: 'All this is thoroughly scientific, even to the exception of the land of Goshen. That land was excepted because it did not lie near the river, it was not irrigated, and hence was not overwhelmed by the frogs to any great extent' (p. 197).

The flies afflicting the land included not only the ordinary housefly, but also horse-flies and others that spread disease. The livestock and the people were weakened by bad water and lack of food, and were easy prey for disease. Hence the next two plagues, disease among the livestock and the plague of boils on the people, accompanied by great clouds of dust.

The next plague, hail, is not out of place in a time of drought, for the low Nile was produced by lack of normal rainfall at the sources of the Nile, which lay in east central Africa. Hailstorms are characteristic of periods of extreme climatic stress. Huntington remarks at this point: 'Except for the fact that the words of Jehovah and the instrumentality of Moses are invoked at every turn, we seem to be dealing with a faithful record of the actual phenomena of nature' (p. 199). This is true likewise of the next plague, the locust invasion. Such swarms of locusts as the Bible describes are, he says, one of the best-known and most dreaded of evils that afflict dry regions, especially in times of scanty rain. The plague of darkness was caused by great clouds of dust in the land. In this connection the author cites his own experiences in dust storms in Chinese Turkestan. The Egyptian darkness-producing dust was borne in by a west wind from the desert.

The last and greatest of the plagues was a terrible scourge, perhaps famine-fever or typhus, diseases that are common when people have been weakened by hunger, boils, and other kinds of distress. Yet Huntington is compelled to say: 'Barring the fact that others as well as the first-born doubtless died, this seems to be merely a way of saying that the culmination of the afflictions of Egypt was pestilence' (p. 201). Yet the Israelites largely escaped all the plagues because 'as keepers of cattle and dwellers in tents on the borders of Egypt, they were not especially affected by the vagaries of the great river'.

Huntington's final remark on the Egyptian plagues is as follows: 'This remarkably full picture of the results of a climatic condition whose occurrence is suggested by other conditions at this period does much to give confidence in the general reliability of the biblical narratives' (p. 201). He writes as a scientist, not as a biblical literalist interested primarily in 'confirming' the Bible.

The second theory that we shall summarize is more detailed than Huntington's, and it gives closer attention to the biblical text, but it posits an unusually high flood stage of the Nile rather than a low stage. This is the theory advanced by Greta Hort in 'The Plagues of Egypt', in ZAW, LXIX (1957), pp. 84–103; LXX (1958), pp. 48–59. At the time of the publication of the second instalment of her article in 1958 the author was Professor in English Literature at Aarhus University in Denmark. In publishing the articles, the editors of the journal declared that they had been assured by reputable scientific authorities that the statements made in the areas of geology and microbiology were correct.

Dr. Hort attempts to show that the ten plagues occurred in the sequence as given in the Exodus account, within the space of eight to ten months. She distinguishes carefully between those plagues which affected all of Egypt and those which did not affect the Israelites; and also between those which ceased abruptly and those which did not. She thinks that her explanations adequately account for the differences.

The first plague, which began in July or August, resulted directly from the prevalence of unusually heavy rainfall and snow melting at the headwaters of the Blue Nile and Atbara. As they plunged through the steep gorges of Abyssinia, they picked up very large amounts of the red earth (*Roterde*) of those regions. This produced the reddish colour of the Nile in Egypt. But this was not adequate to account for the dying of the fish, the stench, and impotability of the Nile water. Those features resulted from the presence in the river of great numbers of the flagellates, *Euglena sanguinea* and *Haematococcus pluvialis*. Because of their presence the already red water became truly blood-red in colour. She explains the reason for the need to dig around about the Nile for water to drink (Exod. 7:24) as follows: the Egyptians who lived close to the river had no wells, and thus had to dig near the river to get the less polluted water which had filtered through the earth; whereas those who lived farther from the river had wells, but the flooding of the Nile had caused them to fall in and become useless. So the only drinkable water was that which could be found by digging near the river.

The frogs left the Nile soon after the first plague, perhaps in August. They had been infected by the *Bacillus anthracis* and soon died, in great masses, of internal anthrax. Because the frogs must have died at about the same time, this plague is reported to have ended abruptly when Moses prayed for it to end.

The third plague, which Dr. Hort interprets as one of mosquitoes, came in October or November. Mosquitoes multiply in time of high water. Goshen would not have been exempted, and the plague did not cease abruptly.

The fourth plague was one of flies, which the author identifies specifically as *Stomoxys calcitrans*, an insect which transmitted the skin anthrax of the sixth plague. This type of fly is liable to sudden mass multiplication under favourable conditions (provided by the rotting of vegetable debris when the Nile began to fall), and bites both people and animals, almost exclusively on the lower extremities. Goshen would have been exempted because the climate was more temperate there and conditions were not favourable for the multiplication of the flies. This plague occurred at the end of December or beginning of January.

The plague on livestock, the fifth of the series, was internal anthrax. Dr. Hort interprets the phrase 'your cattle which are in the field' (Exod. 9:3) very literally to mean the livestock that were in the pasture. She thinks that the livestock were under cover from May to December during the inundation, and by the beginning of January (when this plague occurred) some of them were brought out to pasture, while some were still left indoors. Thus the anthrax killed only those out on pasture, and those left in their stalls were affected by the next plague. In Goshen the livestock were not driven to pasture until later, for that region was water-logged longer than usual.

The sixth plague was skin anthrax on both livestock and men. This affliction can appear on any part of the body, but, being transmitted by the fly, *Stomoxys calcitrans*, of the fourth plague, it appeared mostly on the legs and feet, where that fly most often bites its victims. Dt. 28:27,35 is interpreted to mean that 'the boils of Egypt' attack mostly the lower extremities. At this time the magicians of Egypt 'could not stand before Moses because of the boils' which were on their legs and feet (Exod. 9:11). This plague did not affect the Israelites, for the fly did not penetrate into that region. The plague ended only gradually, as men and animals recovered from the boils. The time was probably January.

The plague of hail came in early February. The flax and barley were planted later than usual, because of the flooding waters, but by this time were sufficiently far along to be damaged, whereas the wheat and spelt were not. According to Dr. Hort, such a hailstorm would not have occurred in the Mediterranean climate zone, which includes Goshen, between November and March. The hailstorm vanished suddenly, as such storms are likely to do.

The plague of locusts is an ordinary phenomenon for Egypt. The locusts originated in the eastern Sudan, migrating to the region around Port Sudan and Jidda, where they multiplied in great masses. They were carried into Egypt by an east wind, and plagued the whole of Egypt, probably in March or April. At this juncture Dr. Hort finds it necessary to depart from the usual translation of Exod. 10:19, and to make an emendation of the Hebrew text. Hebrew *rûᵃh yām* is literally 'sea wind', and does not mean here 'west wind' as it would in Palestine, but a north wind off the Mediterranean. Such a wind would drive the locusts away toward the south. Then she is compelled to emend *yām sûp*, 'Red Sea', to *yāmîn*, 'south'. Thus the verse reads, 'And the Lord turned a very strong north wind, which lifted the locusts and drove them to the south . . .'

The ninth plague, that of darkness for three days, was caused by a *khamsîn*, a strong hot wind from the south, as most commentators agree. But this was no ordinary *khamsîn*; the red earth brought from the highlands of Abyssinia and deposited in Egypt had by now dried, and the reddish particles produced a darker atmosphere than was usual at such times. This was early in March, the first *khamsîn* of the year. The Israelites escaped, for they lived in their own dwellings in a limited area of Goshen, in the Wadi Tumilat.

The last plague causes the author difficulty, as it does to all who

seek to 'explain' the plagues. She notes that the account of it has
been worked and re-worked, and that it has become an aetiological
explanation of Passover. She thinks that the plague did not con-
sist originally in the slaying of the first-born (*bᵉḵôr*), but in the
destruction of the first-fruits (*bikkûrîm*), that is, of the wheat and
spelt harvest which escaped the locust plague. This was the
natural consequence of the ninth plague (a hot wind from the
south), and did not affect the Israelites in Goshen. Since the
Israelites had their normal quantity of grain, and the Egyptians
had none, there was all the more reason for the Israelites to leave
Egypt speedily, taking such bread or grain with them as they could
carry. The time would be the same as the ninth plague.

Dr. Hort ends her article by discussing briefly the reason for the
Israelites' wanting to go out into the desert, and for the scarcity of
straw in their brickmaking. They wanted to go out into the desert
to pray to their God because of the pending disaster of an unusually
high flood stage on the Nile; straw was scarce because of the flood,
and chapter 5 of Exodus is now out of place. One is led in the end
to wonder if the author has not weakened her case by trying to
prove too much!

There are other theories that seek to give a natural explanation
of the plagues in Egypt. Some are fantastic in the extreme.
These two, however, are typical and may provide the basis for our
discussion of the general problem.

One must at the outset recognize that most of the plagues can
be considered as being, at bottom, phenomena that are natural to
Egypt, and more or less common in that country. We have seen
above that Egypt has an unusual combination of topographical
and climatic features, combining the characteristics of a tropical
and arid climate with the presence of an annually flooding river.
Frogs, innumerable insects, diseases associated with the tropical
climate and the prevalence of dust at certain times of the year, and
the *khamsîn*—all of these are characteristic of Egypt. Hailstorms
are quite rare, and locust plagues are less common in Egypt than
in Palestine.

Nevertheless, we should not have too much confidence in our
ability to reconstruct with precision the historical core of the
plagues—assuming that they have developed from such a core—
for a number of reasons. We list below the more important reasons;
details of some of them will be found in the commentary at the
relevant verses or passages.

i. Source analysis has shown us that the accounts of the plagues went through a long period of development, during which important changes took place.

The most striking example of differences of representation in the three sources, J, E and P, can be seen in the account of the first plague. According to J, Yahweh struck the water, and the fish in the Nile river died; then the Nile water became foul and undrinkable. According to E, Moses struck the Nile water with his rod, and all the water in the Nile turned into blood. In the P narrative, Aaron stretched out his rod over the waters of Egypt, and all the water throughout the whole of Egypt turned into blood, including even the water 'in trees and stones' (7:19)! Yet, the magicians of Egypt were able to do the same by their secret arts. Here we have not only differences as to what actually happened, but a clear indication of increase in the miraculousness of the plague.

Also, source analysis has shown us that the third and fourth plagues, coming from two different sources (P and J), are very probably only duplicates of the same original event; the same may be true of the fifth and sixth plagues, but this is less probable. The plague of darkness could be a duplicate of—or in some manner confused with—the plague of locusts, since we are told in connection with the latter that the land of Egypt was darkened (10:15).

Because of the presence in the account of the ten plagues of narratives coming from different sources, and from different collections of plagues, we have inconsistencies. The most glaring, of course, is that which concerns the livestock of Egypt. In 9:6, all the cattle of the Egyptians die because of the plague on livestock; in 9:10, the livestock are stricken with boils; in 9:25, men and animals are struck down by hail; and in 12:29 the first-born of the livestock are smitten in the final plague. These inconsistencies are best explained on the basis of source analysis and the history of tradition, and not by the tortured explanations such as those of Dr. Hort.

ii. The explanations of the plagues do not recognize as fully as they should the purpose for which the plagues occurred, as the long narrative now stands, and do not take sufficient account of the representations of their nature made by the biblical writers.

For example, we should note that three of the plagues, as well as the introductory miracle of the rod turned into a serpent, are represented as transformation miracles—that is, as wonders in which one substance is changed into another. In the rod wonder the rod of Aaron becomes a serpent, and the rods of the magicians become serpents (7:10,12). In the first plague, E says that the water in the Nile is turned into blood (7:20), and P says the waters of Egypt become blood (7:19,21*b*). In the third plague, the dust becomes gnats (8:16–17); and in the sixth plague, the ashes from a kiln become dust, which becomes boils (9:9–10).

The purpose of the plagues, as they now stand and in the two sources (J, P) which are well preserved, was to show forth the power of Yahweh, and to produce belief in Yahweh on the part of the Pharaoh and the Egyptians. This is stated many times over, and very clearly in 9:14–16 and 10:1*b*–2. See the comment on these two passages, and also pp. 99, 102. With such a purpose we may rightly expect the narratives to be told in legendary form, with strong theological overtones, and not as factual chronicle.

iii. If we read the plague narratives in Hebrew, we must admit that some of them are told in such a manner that we cannot expect to recover with precision what happened. For example, we have seen that the meaning of the word *kinnîm* is not known; it has been thought to signify gnats, mosquitoes, lice, sand-fleas, and other insects. All we can be sure of is that it signifies a small insect, probably (but not certainly) of the flying variety. Likewise, *ʿārōḇ* is a perfectly general word meaning 'swarm(s)'; what kind of swarming insect it refers to is unknown. The word used for the plague on cattle, often thought to have been anthrax, is also a general word, *déḇer*, meaning plague, pestilence, or pest. We must add the additional fact that the diagnosis of diseases in ancient Egypt could not have been precise by modern standards. Thus we must remain in the dark as to the real nature of the disease(s) that struck the frogs, livestock and people in Egypt.

iv. The exemption of the Hebrews from some of the plagues because of their residence in the land of Goshen is a feature that can be too readily exaggerated. We do not know whether the narrators conceived of the Israelites as being spared only those plagues in which they specifically said they were spared. It is possible that some of the plague narratives in their earlier form spoke of the exemption of the Israelites.

In any event, though Goshen does have some distinctive features, it is not reasonable to suppose that it was so different or so far removed that it was spared even in the cases where this is specifically said. The purpose of such exemption was theologically motivated: Yahweh wished to make a clear-cut division between his own people and the people of Pharaoh.

We are led to the conclusion that the stories of the plagues have gone through a long process of transmission (some of them longer than others), and we cannot expect to be able to recover just what happened by reading them. We can, to be sure, recognize that something happened, and it happened in Egypt, a country with a strange combination of features. We can perhaps reduce the number of plagues to seven: the death of fish in the Nile, frogs, swarms of some kind of insect, hailstorm, locust invasion, a *khamsîn*, and diseases among livestock and men, striking even in the royal household. For the ancient Hebrew the significance of these plagues rested upon their severity, their coming together within a relatively short span of time, and—above all—his belief that they were the work of Yahweh on behalf of his people. To the Hebrew they were 'signs and wonders', showing forth the superiority of their God over the gods of Egypt (including Pharaoh), and being one of the means by which he delivered them from the bondage of Egyptian slavery.

INDEX

A

Aaron, 24ff., 82f., 88, 92, 95ff., 101ff.,
120, 123f., 153, 169, 279, 286ff.,
301ff., *et passim*
Abib, 131, 142, 248
Abihu, 254
Aistleitner, J., 274
Albrektson, B., 38, 77
Albright, W. F., 39, 43, 61, 67, 246
Alt, A., 29, 36, 79, 209, 215, 219, 221f.
Altar, 225f., 261f., 276f., 291, 330
Amalekites, 47, 183ff.
Amarna age, 41, 43
Amenhotep II, 39
Amenhotep IV (Akhenaton), 41f.
Amorites, 39, 73, 79, 324
Amram, 95
Andrew, M. E., 208, 211, 216
ᶜapiru, 39, 41f., 56f., 68, 228
Apodictic law, 36, 209, 221f., 241f.
Aqaba, 158f., 173, 203f., 252
Ark, 63, 179, 198, 251, 260ff., 265–8,
271, 275, 281, 292, 301, 315f., 322,
330
Arnold, W. R., 281
ᶜārōḇ, 111, 344
Augustine, 138

B

Baal-Zephon, 151f., 159f.
Balaḥ Lakes, 157
Beer, G., 22, 27, 122, 163, 168, 218,
261, 263, 304, 308
bᵉhēmāh, 116, 143
Bennett, W. H., 122
Bethel, 47, 301, 304f., 308f., 311
Beyerlin, W., 46, 198, 222f., 321
Bezalel, 297f.
Bitter herbs, 133
Bitter Lakes, 157, 159
Bodenheimer, F. S., 176f.

Book of the Covenant, 14, 19, 27f., 207,
217–52, 253ff.
Booths, Festival of, 195
Bottéro, J., 39
Bread of the Presence, 262, 268–70, 292
Brekelmans, C. H. W., 34f., 187

C

Camel, 114
Canaanites, 73, 142, 220, 229, 313, 324
Casuistic law, 36, 209, 219ff.
Cherubim, 267f.
Childs, B. S., 63f.
Coats, G. W., 138, 162, 171
Cody, A., 187, 189f.
Couroyer, B., 133
Covenant, 23, 47, 187ff., 195, 252–8,
318–20
Covenant Code, 195, 197, 207, 218ff.,
254, 320
Cross, F. M., jr., 80, 162ff., 167, 169, 263
Cubit, 266
Cult, 30ff., 146ff., 195f., 209f.

D

Davies, G. H., 263, 281
Decalogue, ethical, 14, 23, 28, 36, 47,
195, 197f., 207ff., 319
Decalogue, ritual, 207, 319ff.
déḇer, 118, 129, 344
Deuteronomic Redactor, 122, 137, 142,
171, 184, 197, 200–13, 218, 227,
250, 254f., 301, 306, 313, 324
De Vries, S., 171
Driver, S. R., 229, 246, 277, 282

E

E (Elohist), 19f., 24f., 33, 98, 124,
et passim

Edom, 166f.
Eissfeldt, O., 20, 70, 87
Elim, 173
Engnell, I., 30ff., 34
Ephod, 28off.
Eshnunna, Laws of, 224, 229, 235f., 240, 246
Etham, 149, 159
Ezion-geber, 173

F

Fensham, F. C., 187, 190, 229, 232, 243
Finger of God, 110, 116
First-born, 130, 138, 143f., 342
Firstlings, 128, 141–4, 146
Fohrer, G., 20, 34, 71, 87, 145, 162f.
Form Criticism, 29, 36f., 63, 101, 162, 171, 209, 219
Freedman, D. N., 162ff., 167, 169
Funk, R. W., 283

G

gāʾal, 94, 166
Galling, K., 22, 26, 225, 261, 263, 267, 272, 274, 280, 287, 291, 298, 328, 332
Garber, P. L., 283
Garments, priestly, 279–91, 331f.
gēr, 68, 140f.
Gershom, 68f., 188
Gilgal, 135, 179
Giveon, R., 79
Glueck, N., 40, 292
Golden Calf, 47, 300–12
Gooding, D. W., 329
Goshen, 42, 57, 111ff., 120, 138, 159, 338, 340ff., 344
Greenberg, M., 39

H

ḥabiru, 39, 41, 220, 228; see ʿapiru
ḥag, 90, 135, 142
ḥāmam, 154
ḥāmēṣ, 135
Hammurapi, Code of, 220, 222ff., 251
ḥartummîm, 104
Harvest, Feast of, 247f., 325
ḥāṭān, 68
Hebrew, 42

ḥēreṭ, 304
ḥésed, 191, 323
History of Exodus period, 37–47
Hittites, 73, 197f., 209f., 222, 224, 324
Hittite Laws, 224, 232ff., 236, 241, 244, 246
Hivites, 74
Hobab, 67f., 187
Holy war, 152, 155, 166
Horeb, 70f., 181, 187, 203, 317
Horites, 74
Horse, 114
Hort, G., 339ff.
Huffmon, H. B., 80
Huntington, E., 337ff.
Hur, 184, 258
Hyatt, J. P., 34, 80
Hyksos, 38, 41ff., 45
Hyssop, 136

I

Incense, 291–3, 296f., 330
Ingathering, Feast of, 248
Interest, 243f.

J

J (Yahwist), 19ff., 33, 97, 124, 148, et passim
Jebel Helal, 205
Jebel Musa, 72, 174, 180, 203, 206
Jebusites, 74
Jepsen, A., 219ff.
Jethro, 67, 71, 78, 85f., 186–94
Jochebed, 63, 80, 95
Jordan River, 161
Joseph, 41f., 58, 63, 235
Josephus, 38, 63ff., 132, 176, 227, 247, 268, 276, 280, 282, 286
Joshua, 183, 189, 258f., 307, 315

K

K (Kenite document), 21
kābôd, 26, 317
Kadesh-barnea, 46, 172f., 180, 183, 185, 187, 198, 205f.
kappōreṭ, 266f.
Kenites, 21, 67, 178, 187, 191f., 305, 320
Kennedy, A. R. S., 263, 272, 274

kᵉrāšîm, 274
kēsyāh, 185
khamsîn, 126, 160, 341f., 345
Kidnapping, 215, 231
kinnîm, 110, 344
Knierim, R., 193f.
Koch, K., 57, 263
Kosmala, H., 87, 325
Kramer, S. N., 107, 243
kussémeṭ, 121

L

L (Lay source), 20, 71, 87
Lehming, S., 308
Levites, 84, 95, 139, 143, 260, 303, 309f.
lex talionis, 221, 232, 234, 242
Lindblom, J., 77
Lipit-Ishtar, Code of, 224
Locusts, 121–5

M

maᶜat, 224
Manna, 174–9
Marah, 172, 205
mas, 58
mašḥîṭ, 134, 136
Mask, face, 327
Massah, 172, 179ff.
maṣṣôṭ, 134, 139
masweh, 327
McCarthy, D. J., 101, 197
Meek, T. J., 232
Mendelsohn, I., 229, 243
Menzaleh, Lake, 45, 155, 157, 159f.
Meribah, 172, 179, 180, 182, 205
Merneptah, 39, 43f.
Middle Assyrian Laws, 224, 233, 241, 244
Midian, 66, 78, 86
Midianites, 47, 66f., 71, 87, 187, 191ff.
Migdol, 150, 159f.
miḳneh, 114
Miriam, 96, 169
miškān, 262, 264, 271f.
mišpāṭ, 227, 275
Moab, 166f.
Monolatry, 211, 225
môpᵉṭîm, 85f.
Morgenstern, J., 21, 138
Moses, 18f., 23f., 26, 33, 89, 103, 116,
    119, 185, 193, 208, 304, 306, 315,
    et passim; origin of name, 64f.

Mowinckel, S., 33, 196
Muilenburg, J., 162ff., 316
Murmuring tradition, 152, 171, 175, 181

N

N (Nomadic source), 20, 71, 87
nābîʾ, 101
Nadab, 254
nāḥāš, 104
nāśîʾ, 218, 244
nāweh, 166
Newman, M. L., jr., 302
New Year, Festival of, 196
Nielsen, Eduard, 208
Nile River, 336ff.
Nims, C. F., 91
Noth, M., 27, 29, 32ff., 36, 42, 46, 57,
    63, 89, 98, 158, 168, 192, 244, 253,
    265, 267, 282

O

Oholiab, 297f.
ᶜōnāṭāh, 230
Oral tradition, 28

P

P (Priestly source), 20f., 25, 41, 93, 97,
    128, 148, 258ff., et passim; chrono-
    logy of P, 41f., 140, 175, 200, 332;
    subdivision of P, 21f., 263
pāḍāh, 166
Passover, 30, 44, 128f., 131–7, 140f.,
    161, 248, 325f., 342; origin of,
    144–6
Paul, S. M., 224, 230
Pedersen, J., 30, 32
Perizzites, 74
pésaḥ, 133f.
pésel, 211
péṭer, 142
Pfeiffer, R. H., 162, 320
Pharaoh, 58, 90, 98, 102, 105, 134; et
    passim
Philo, 63, 65f., 110f., 138
Philistines, 149, 167, 252
Phinehas, 95f.
pîᵃḥ, 116
Pi-ha-hiroth, 150, 152, 159
Pithom, 42, 59, 60

Plagues, 44, 96–149, 336–45
Puah, 60

R

Raamses (town), 42, 59f., 158
von Rad, G., 22, 25, 29, 32ff., 57, 195f.,
    209, 263
Rameses (town), 139
Rameses II, 39, 42f., 56, 58f., 69, 197f.
Rameses III, 57, 59
Rameses IV, 39, 42, 57
Rashi, 87
Redford, D. B., 60, 62
Red Sea, 158, 164, 252, 341; see yām sûp̄
Repentance of Yahweh, 307
Rephidim, 18, 180, 183, 200
Reuel, 67f.
Rost, L., 34f.
Rowley, H. H., 41, 43f., 78, 208, 319
Rudolph, W., 21, 63, 98, 255, 321
Rylaarsdam, J. C., 27, 122

S

Sabbath, 178, 212f., 247, 298, 329
Sabbatical year, 247
šaddai, 93f.
šāliš, 152
San el-Hajar, 60, 139
Sargon, 62
śārîm, 194
Schild, E., 77
segullāh, 200
seḥîn, 116
selāmîm, 256, 289
se'ōr, 135
šēpeṭ, 94
Serabit el-Khadem, 204, 305
van Seters, J., 39
Seti I, 42, 44, 56, 58, 69
Shechem, 195
Shekel, 294f., 331
Shiloh, 261, 321
Shiphrah, 60
Shur, Wilderness of, 171f.
Simpson, C. A., 20, 309
Sin, Wilderness of, 174

Sinai, Mt., 23, 25f., 32f., 36, 46f., 71, 78,
    150, 166f., 176, 181, 187, 195ff.;
    location of, 203–7
ṣir'āh, 252
Sirbonis, Lake, 151, 159f.
ṣîṣ, 284
Slavery, 228–31
Smend, R., 20
Snaith, N. H., 161
Song of Miriam, 28, 169
Song of the Sea, 28, 154, 162–9
Speiser, E. A., 232f.
Stamm, J. J., 208, 211, 216
Succoth, 59f., 139, 149, 159
Suez, 154ff., 159

T

Tabernacle, 175, 179, 258ff., 271–6,
    287, 315, 329ff.
Tanis, 60, 158
tannîn, 104
tēḇāh, 63
teḥāšîm, 264
Tell Defneh, 151, 159
Tell el-Maskhuta, 59f., 139, 149
Tell er-Retabeh, 59f.
Ten Commandments: see Decalogue,
    ethical
Tent of meeting, 47, 259ff., 314–16
tepillîn, 143f.
Thutmose III, 39
Timsaḥ, Lake, 157, 159
tôrāh, 193
Torrey, C. C., 304
tôšāḇ, 140
Tradition-history, 28ff.
Treaties, ancient Near Eastern, 35,
    197–9, 210, 251

U

Ugaritic, 39, 61, 165, 246, 274
Unleavened Bread, Feast of, 44, 128f.,
    131–7, 141–6, 247f.; origin of,
    144–6
Uppsala School, 30
Urim and Thummim, 281ff.
Ur-Nammu, Code of, 243

V

de Vaux, R., 145, 192
Vergote, J., 104
Vriezen, T. C., 77

W

Wadi Tumilat, 59, 111, 149, 341
Weeks, Feast of, 248, 325
Weiser, A., 21, 34, 35
Wellhausen, J., 208, 259
Winnett, F. V., 98

Wright, G. E., 149, 167

Y

Yahweh, 19, 24, 72, 75, 80, 187, 189, 219, 322f., *et passim*; origin of name, 78–81
Yahwist, The: see J
yām sûp, 45f., 63, 125, 158ff., 164, 341

Z

Zipporah, 68f., 87, 188